THE JUSTICE JUGGERNAUT

A VOLUME IN THE
CRIME, LAW, AND DEVIANCE
SERIES

THE JUSTICE JUGGERNAUT

FIGHTING STREET CRIME, CONTROLLING CITIZENS

•

DIANA R. GORDON

RUTGERS UNIVERSITY PRESS

NEW BRUNSWICK AND LONDON

First paperback printing, 1991

Library of Congress Cataloging-in-Publication Data

Gordon, Diana R.
  The justice juggernaut: fighting street crime, controlling
citizens / Diana R. Gordon
    p. cm. — (Crime, law, and deviance series)
    Bibliography: p.
    Includes index
    ISBN 0-8135-1477-0 (cloth) — ISBN 0-8135-1478-9 (pbk.)
    1. Crime prevention—United States. 2. Punishment—United States.
I. Title. II. Series.
HV7431.G67 1990
364.4´0973—dc20   89-34882
British Cataloging-in-Publication information available   CIP

TO

HALLETT D. AND MARY ELIZABETH SMITH

AND

MAE CHURCHILL

CONTENTS

PREFACE

THIS BOOK ORIGINATED, not in the curiosity of the scholar, but from the uneasiness of the administrator. As I stumbled through five years (1978–1983) of working in various executive capacities at the National Council on Crime and Delinquency, I became increasingly perplexed by what appeared to be paradoxes in the directions and sources of criminal justice policy. For one thing, members of the public who most strongly supported harsh penalties for the terrifying urban street crimes of the past quarter century were often not those who suffered most from them. And when reported crime dipped in the early 1980s, policies of capture and confinement became, if anything, more punitive. I also noticed that legislators and judges, while publicly sponsoring bills for mandatory minimum sentences and imposing longer prison terms, declared themselves in professional gatherings to be opposed to the rush to confinement and the narrowing of defendants' rights, and often worked behind the scenes to find other, less costly and restrictive approaches.

As I gave talks and attended meetings around the country I saw that the public and the professionals in criminal justice seemed to have very different notions of the seriousness of street crime and what could be done about it. To the public it was a scourge that government should be able to vanquish. To many who worked in or observed the justice system—academics as well as practitioners—street crime was a social problem whose very insolubility created opportunities for challenging and sometimes well-paid work. Both perspectives gave lip service to U.S. social and economic organization as sources of our extraordinarily high levels of assault on persons and property; yet both supported only individual, after-the-fact approaches to crime control that clearly were not working and were very costly in both economic and social terms.

I only began to put these paradoxes in perspective when I got some distance from them, safe in an academic setting. This book is the result. It paints a picture of a justice system as much engaged in observation of ordinary citizens as it is in "getting tough" with serious criminals, as responsive to its own organizational needs as to the suffering of crime victims. And it suggests that the public is confused and angry—not only about crime, but about other troubles of which crime becomes symbolic. What I have called structural discontents are as important in creating public demand for more coercive control by the state as the high incidence of street crime.

Many people helped me fill in the picture along the way. Particularly useful were the conversations I had with scholars and practitioners about the programs of observation which, though little understood by the public, are increasingly important in the expanded justice system of the late 1980s. Many thanks to Erio Alvarez, Todd Clear, Don Cochran, Andrea Cooper, Gary Cooper, Ron Corbett, Pat Dennard, Robert Gallati, Harvey Goldstein, Marc Johnson, Joan Petersilia, Lou Sakin, Joe Salyga, Gary Schreivogel, Diane Scott-Bey, Richard Talty, Lisa White, and Fred Wynbrandt. For reading and commenting on an early version of Chapter 4, on computerized criminal records systems, I am grateful to Kenneth Laudon, Gary Marx, William Preston, and Robert Heilbroner—and especially Jim Dempsey, who also patiently explained to me many times the intricacies of FBI recordkeeping. Todd Clear and David Greenberg reviewed Chapter 5, on intermediate punishments, at an early stage.

Elliott Currie, David Greenberg, and Sam Walker all read the entire manuscript and gave me detailed and invaluable suggestions. David Gordon did that more than once and, in addition, proved himself the very model of a modern academic husband by not only comforting and criticizing but referring me to works on economic policy and producing the final manuscript on his printer. Phyllis Schultze, who presides over the Rutgers University criminal justice collection, was the librarian every writer dreams of, leading me to sources I could not have discovered on my own.

Financial support for my research was provided by the Field Foundation and the Research Foundation of the City University of New York, to which I am grateful. Stanley Cohen, Murray Edelman, and Stuart Scheingold, though not personal acquaintances, provided basic intellectual sustenance through their work. Mae Churchill was the indispensable gadfly.

This book represents one stage in a mid-life transition from administrator to academic. For boosting me into my new career, I am deeply grateful to Joyce Gelb and Leonard Kriegel.

PART I

•

INTRODUCTION

1

•

CAPTURE, CONFINE, AND OBSERVE

The criminal sanction is the paradigm case of the controlled use of power within a society.
  ● Herbert L. Packer, *The Limits of the Criminal Sanction*

THE TWO TRACKS OF THE JUGGERNAUT

EVEN BEFORE THE Democratic and Republican conventions of 1988 each of the potential presidential candidates was portraying himself as a relentless crime fighter and his opponent as more sympathetic to criminals than to victims. Vice President George Bush attacked Massachusetts Governor Michael Dukakis for endorsing a state prison furlough program from which a convicted murderer named Willie Horton had escaped, raping a woman in Maryland and stabbing her fiancé. On his side, Dukakis assailed the Reagan Administration for "collaborating" with Central American drug lords and providing insufficient funds for the coast guard's efforts to fight drug trafficking in the Gulf of Mexico. Polls and interviews with voters suggested that the charge of being "soft on crime" could be a knockout blow. Dukakis was particularly vulnerable, since he also had to contend with his membership in the American Civil Liberties Union, seen by his opponent and other Republicans as tantamount to endorsement of deviance. After all, a former U.S. attorney general had once called the ACLU "the criminals' lobby."[1] Furthermore, because of the organization's frequent representation of dissidents of various stripes, the ACLU membership also suggested an association with that other bogeyman, the communist sympathizer.

At the same time, law and order politics was going beyond the symbolic battle of the presidential candidates to legislative action. On September 22, the House of Representatives overwhelmingly passed the Anti-Drug Abuse Act of 1988, which not only imposed severe new minimum sentences for drug offenses and permitted the death penalty for murders committed in the course of a drug transaction, but also added civil penalties—cancelling FHA mortgages, suspending drivers' licenses, and denying student loans and public housing—to criminal convictions for drug offenses, even minor possession charges. Liberal Democratic congressmen like William J. Hughes of New Jersey and Charles B. Rangel of New York had few kind words for the bill—during debate Rangel called it "absurd" and Hughes in a speech pronounced it of "doubtful constitutionality"—but they bowed to political realities and voted for it anyway.[2] (The bill as finally approved by both houses was somewhat less draconian, but it retained most of the "user accountability" provisions described here.[3])

These events expressed the "get-tough" sentiments that have, in one way or another, driven much of U.S. street crime policy in the last two decades. At another less visible level, however, they also reflected equally important policy developments moving in a quite different direction, less concerned with getting tough on people than with keeping tabs on them. The brouhaha over the Willie Horton incident, for instance, obscured the fact that in this same twenty-year period furloughs or other temporary release programs have become the norm for state prison systems; all fifty states had them in mid-1988, and "lifers" as well as lesser offenders were eligible in most states.[4] The posturing of legislators dickering over the death penalty for drug lords gave no hint of the extent to which low-level drug dealers and abusers are being placed on probation or given other nonprison punishments. The provision of funds for increased federal-local law enforcement cooperation did not reveal the extent to which most police work increasingly relies, not on costly, complex crime-fighting maneuvers, but on checking out the computerized records of suspects, arrestees, and law-abiding citizens.

Theoretically, there is a wide range of approaches a state society may take toward social disorder. It can try to alter the physical environment in which crime takes place or the social environment most likely to breed crime. It can redefine the categories of behavior that are to be designated as criminal, or, more drastically, it can change the social and political order and thereby restructure the definition of criminality as a whole. It can seek to influence the behavior of individuals through restraint, deterrence, or rehabilitation. Crime control policies in most developed societies focus primarily on the policies that deal with individual offenders.[5]

The politicization of street crime in the U. S. over the past twenty years has put great emphasis on a rather narrow slice of these alternative policy approaches. Since the early 1970s the coercive power of government over individuals has been augmented with a program that I will call the justice juggernaut. While this program has developed along two quite different tracks, its theoretical base is generally neoconservative, attributing street crime to general moral decline during the postwar period and to "the psychology of radical individualism and the philosophy of human rights."[6] It has paralleled the trend, in areas of economic policy, to back away from the mildly redistributive policies of the New Deal and the Great Society. Where a resource retrenchment prevails in social spending, tax policy, and protective regulation, a rights retrenchment is underway in policies of coercive control.

The most evident manifestations of the trend are get-tough measures that intensify the traditional activities of capture and confinement at all governmental levels and in each of the three principal institutions of criminal justice. Particularly striking is the change in corrections: longer prison sentences, mandatory terms for many offenses, and a shift in theory that embraces punishment for its own sake and for its ability to restrain offenders. Changes in criminal court practices like focusing on "career criminals," preventively detaining offenders before trial, and disallowing insanity pleas have helped to increase the likelihood that an arrest will result in a prison sentence. Perhaps police conduct has been least affected; while defendents' rights have been narrowed by the federal courts, their decisions do not yet appear, in practice, to have relaxed procedural restraints on officers significantly. The police presence in local communities, increased by a big jump in expenditures during the 1960s, ceased to expand (and in some places actually shrank) in the mid-1970s.[7]

This pattern of intensified control (sketched in more detail in the next chapter) is not completely uniform or consistent. While incarceration rates have increased, the growth in nonprison penalties is even greater. Despite the theoretical embrace of the "tougher" punishment rationales of retribution, deterrence, and incapacitation, rehabilitative ideals and practice live on in many programs. "Eclectic" is probably the best description of the theoretical underpinnnings of the penal system of the late

1980s; the criminal is variously conceived as a rational actor driven by self-interested calculation—the classical image—and as pawn of psychological or sociopathic forces—the positivist view. The narrowing of defendants' rights seems unlikely to return us to the standards that prevailed before the due process revolution.[8] Public and judicial support for some constitutional protections, like the right to representation, remains strong. The growth of investment in police may always have been more important as a part of the general expansion of local government than as a major contributor of social defense buildup.[9] Innovations in police since the 1960s have been primarily in areas of training and technology, rather than in more aggressive tactics for patrol or investigation.

These developments suggest the other track of the justice juggernaut. United States crime policy increasingly emphasizes another kind of state power that sometimes conflicts with the traditional measures of capture and confinement but usually complements and supplements them. Still shaped by what Durkheim called "repressive law," observation as a primary method of state coercion is a less blatant but more pervasive form of state coercion than the get-tough measures. It broadens the reach of criminal justice, where longer prison terms and more aggressive police practice deepen it.

Almost as soon as the conservative winds began to blow, policy implementers in criminal justice found themselves unable to cope with the fiscal and managerial (and occasionally the human) implications of law and order politics. Taking advantage of the availability of federal funds and ideas through the now defunct Law Enforcement Assistance Administration (LEAA), they instituted or expanded what have become widespread observation programs in police, courts, and corrections. These developments rely on information—replacing or augmenting force—as the instrument of power. They are characterized by integrative strategies like surveillance, rather than segregative ones like arrest and prison. They may be driven more by administrative convenience than by get-tough imperatives. They blur distinctions that facilitate judicial regulation of criminal justice activity; when does punishment begin if someone has been under pre-trial supervision for six months before guilt is determined? Bifurcations that have traditionally helped to define the boundaries of the criminal law—a suspect was either under investigation or not, a defendant was in custody or not—now often give way to indefinite, invisible tracking. In targeting new groups of subjects, as well as coming down harder on those already within the sphere of control, the observation programs increase state control over social space, making surveillance a key strategy of the justice juggernaut.

THE ARGUMENT

This book provides a critical analysis of both the get-tough trend and its partner, coercive control by observation. It begins by setting forth the dimensions of the juggernaut and then moves on to explore the sources of these two tracks—to capture and confine, and to observe. I then attempt some rather informal assessments of the impacts of the whole and, becoming still more speculative, examine what the future may hold. My conclusion suggests a few policy alternatives that might improve our record on crime but warns against undue optimism. The book's architecture is simple. Chapter 2 describes the get-tough measures, the sentencing policies and narrowed defendants' rights that seem to respond most directly to the public plea to "do something" about the scourge of mugging and murder we all abhor.

The following chapters concentrate on the much less visible observation track of the juggernaut that is both separable from and dependent on the get-tough track. Chapter 3 introduces the contours of observation programs that, in contrast to the conventional measures that intensify the impact of criminal justice, broaden its reach. Chapters 4 and 5 illustrate the broadening thrust of the juggernaut with case studies of two of the most robust of its policy developments, computerized criminal record systems and intermediate punishments. Policy studies of law enforcement rarely go beyond the assessment of different forms of patrol or the examination of how police use force and persuasion, ignoring another major resource, automated criminal records systems. What is becoming a vast, national network, fed by smaller local tributaries, is both fundamentally changing the nature of police investigation and making tens of millions of records—many of them inaccurate, stale, and trivial—available not only to law enforcement nationwide but to employers and others outside the criminal justice system. Similarly, the growth of intensive supervision outside prison seems likely to become a permanent expansion of the correctional landscape. Human and electronic surveillance outside prisons keeps some less serious offenders out of prison, intensifies probation for others, and subjects families, neighbors and friends of offenders to "benign" control as well.

It is very difficult to trace the policy origins of the complex byplay of get-tough and observation measures. Surely the suffering of street crime victims and their families and friends has contributed to deepening and broadening the exercise of state coercive power. It is hard to pinpoint, however, the modus operandi of an instrumental linkage between the public's plea for relief from street crime and the policy responses to it. To explain both get-tough and observation measures as outcomes solely— or even primarily—of the articulation of popular will would be as simplistic as to maintain that increases in reported crime and the public outcry that has accompanied them have played no part. Part III (Chapters 6, 7, and 8) examines the influence of victimization and public demand on the growth of the juggernaut as well as two other, less obvious but equally important sources.

The first involves symbolic politics. Politics channels the expression of fears and dreams. Politicians, even more than other leaders, sniff the wind of public opinion, alert for breezes that carry promise of the electorate's response to threat, reassurance, or exhortation.[10] The recourse to symbol by both citizens and their representatives is particularly tempting in the politics of street crime. Actual and imagined victimizations fed larger fears of disorder, social change, and domination that took root in the 1960s and became increasingly legitimate as they were endorsed by the political right. On that level, it hardly matters that the recourse to punishment has not been effective at solving the street crime problem; it is symbolically, if not substantively, logical. Messages of dread have been sent; messages of appeasement have been returned.

As symbolic politics nourished get-tough measures, so the organizational needs of criminal justice fueled observation policies. Directions like the proliferation of computerized criminal records systems and the growth of community punishments did not flow directly from the symbolic bargain that political leaders would crack down on street crime. Instead, they evolved from a quest to evade the programmatic, organizational, and fiscal implications of that bargain. Probation and police officers, state legislative staffs, researchers from universities and think tanks, federal agency officials, and professional associations in criminal justice constituted a policy subgovernment working together to find affordable alternatives to the vast new investments in labor and capital that would be required in order to deliver on the promises made at the representative levels of politics.[11] They found ways to adapt that would expand their terrain, reduce uncertainty, and enhance their professional status. Some of the most important extensions and expansions of criminal justice control have flowed from those adaptations.

Chapter 6 briefly introduces the logic and dynamics of these three principal determinants of recent trends in criminal justice policy—the instrumental response to concrete public demand, the symbolic nod to inchoate fears, and the imperatives of subsystem politics. Chapter 7 traces their interaction in driving the get-tough trend, with special emphasis on the role of symbolic politics. Chapter 8 examines a quite different mix of influences on observation policies, with an emphasis on organizational needs. The interactive and dialectical relationship between the two tracks of the juggernaut is discussed here, too. Far from being independent policy developments, the get-tough trend begat the observation programs as policy operatives scrambled to adapt to its fiscal and bureaucratic demands.

To what effect? The impacts of the juggernaut are several, but, as Chapter 9 argues, they do not include reduced street crime. The official National Crime Survey reported that in 1985, despite almost two decades of law and order politics and a get-tough program, 5 million households were burglarized at least once and members of 5 million households were victims of at least one violent crime—rape, robbery, or assault.[12] In 1987 the FBI reported more than 20,000 murders (including nonnegligent manslaughter), a rate 15 percent higher than in 1969 (and three times higher than that of Canada, if Interpol data for earlier years can be relied upon.)[13] While the available data sources appear to be in conflict about whether such crimes as robbery and burglary have increased since the early 1970s, no one suggests that there has been a substantial reduction. And few knowledgeable observers, noting the persistence of widespread illegal drug use and its attendant violence, expect much improvement in the near future.

The justice juggernaut has not provided significantly increased protections to crime victims, either, despite rhetorical recognition of the economic hardship and psychological trauma that many crime victims suffer and a few strong service programs.[14] What participation they have in the justice process is generally frustrating, and few victims receive financial compensation for the harm done to them.[15]

It might be said that we have gotten tough with criminals, not crime. Certainly the impact of the juggernaut is keenly felt by serious felony offenders, whose experience with the justice system—already essentially negative and perhaps counterproductive in terms of crime control—has worsened as increased demands on the justice system crowd prisons and clog courts. Lesser offenders may be punished either more or less severely than in the past; what is clear is that they are far more likely to be under some kind of surveillance. Law-abiding citizens, too, are more likely to be watched, either through the data surveillance of law enforcement or on the periphery of someone else's community supervision. Chapter 9 details these impacts, while Chapter 10 notes the likelihood that both the juggernaut and its effects will continue.

Many will undoubtedly argue that we have little reason to care about the repression of those who have already proved themselves to be bad apples infecting others in the barrel, that they have given up their civil liberties by their depradations. But a harsh, expansive criminal justice system tars many who are not the criminals we fear. Most of us, in this society, believe in "the maintenance of a decent distance between the individual and constituted authority," at least in the social realm.[16] This distance is being continually reduced by ever more pervasive intrusions and coercions of police, courts, and corrections. Legitimized as a substitute for the more benign controls of family and community (supposedly eroded beyond rescue), criminal justice has become a significant challenge to autonomy and dignity for millions of Americans, without protecting property and personal safety. Like American education, criminal justice labels and segments low-income and working-class people.[17] To the extent that the reach of this system becomes deeper and broader—particularly when its expansion exerts controls over new kinds of subjects—so does its capacity for stratification. The social relationships of a brutally unequal economic system are reproduced when the policies of police and corrections highlight divisions of class, race and culture. And if we are distracted by the need to assess and sanction individual guilt, we become less and less committed to working for larger social policies that can begin to close those divisions.

In drawing a picture of the juggernaut, I have chosen to pay attention solely to responses to street crime, defined as including the basic FBI Index crime categories (murder, rape, robbery, burglary, assault, larceny, auto theft) and drug offenses. By adopting this focus I am not suggesting that other kinds of crime are less harmful to either their victims or to society in general; I am persuaded, in fact, that white-collar crimes cause more loss of life and property than that group of offenses that make up what we think of as "the crime problem."[18] Nor do I think street crime policy reveals very much about what Americans really think should be done about crime as a whole.

This book examines policy directions on street crime because they have shifted so significantly in recent years and because these shifts influence and reflect other areas of social policy. For most Americans murder, mugging, and drug trafficking constitute "the crime problem," a major threat in many urban neighborhoods and an anticipated threat elsewhere. These perspectives—fed and exploited by the media and politicians—crowd out an appreciation of the seriousness of other social policy failures and their connection to high street crime rates. The public becomes incapable of analyzing crime in more complex, structural ways and demanding that their political leaders do so too.

PART II

•

CONTOURS

2

●

THE "GET-TOUGH" APPROACH

The relationship between the conservative movement and the Reagan Administration has not always been smooth, yet on matters of criminal justice and crime fighting, the Administration has kept its pre-election promises, and perhaps accomplished a bit more.

● Frank Carrington, *Crime and Justice:*
A Conservative Strategy

Courts and laws always interpret, articulate, and defend the social order of which they are part.

● Ernest van den Haag, *Punishing Criminals*

MOST AMERICANS get their information about shifts in crime policy from the popular press. We become aware of increased federal involvement in local law enforcement through news pictures of manacled mafia "drug lords" emerging from the court house with members of a joint drug task force—FBI and Drug Enforcement Administration (DEA) operatives and police. Or we note the trend to mandatory sentences by reading that prisons are now so crowded that cells built for one person now house three or that recreation rooms in prisons have been turned into dormitories.

These images do, of course, convey part of the picture. Many policies of the past twenty years, in a paradigm shift in criminal justice ideology from the "soft" approach of rehabilitation to the "hard" one of deterrence, retribution, and incapacitation, have raised the costs of crime at every point in the process. (This is not to assume either that the motive behind greater punitiveness is solely to change the calculation of those tempted by crime or that the calculation did, in fact, change.) The program is widespread and evident—in longer and mandatory prison terms, reduction in reliance on parole (probably temporary), prosecution resources targeted on "career criminals," narrowed defendants' rights, a greater likelihood that offenders will be convicted and given a prison term. To carry out the basic approach, investment in criminal justice rose sharply and legislative attention creating new crimes or making penalties harsher increased.[1]

This chapter will describe these policy trends of the 1970s and 1980s and sketch their differential impact on the groups they target. The following chapter will look at the other, related direction of the juggernaut—the trend toward greater reliance on observation, supplementing capture and confinement. Though less obvious and dramatic, these other contours of criminal justice policy leading up to the 1990s have at least as much significance in signaling the growing role of criminal justice in social policy.

THE RUSH TO CONFINEMENT

The get-tough program has not given equal emphasis to tightening the screws at all stages of the criminal justice process. Without question the hand is heaviest in the imposition of more and harsher penal sanctions. This is hardly surprising. As a practical matter, visible alteration in criminal justice practice is easier at the hind end of the system. At that point, the more problematic tasks of arrest and conviction are complete. The wrongdoers are now tangible targets for the exercise of the state's most definitive coercive power.

Most visible has been a dramatic and widespread increase in incarceration. At the end of June 1988, 604,824 state and federal prisoners were serving sentences of more than one year, a record number for the eighth year in a row.[2] Based on earlier data, it is fair to assume that another 300,000 inmates were in local jails, either awaiting sentencing or serving terms of less than one year.[3] These numbers represent gigantic increases in the incarceration rate—the number of sentenced prisoners (serving a term of more than one year) in state and federal institutions for every 100,000 U.S. residents. In the period from 1971 to 1987 that rate rose by more than 137 percent.[4] Between 1980 and 1987 the incarceration rate rose 64 percent, from 139—already a record—to 228.[5] Adult jail populations rose by 46 percent between 1978 and 1984.[6]

An examination of shifts in the incarceration rate around the country during the period from 1970–1987 reveals a good deal of variation from state to state. Some states increased only slightly; Minnesota, with a low prison rate to begin with (40 in 1971, in comparison with a national average of 96.4), kept it that way (60 in 1987, one quarter of the national average), and Colorado, an average state in the early 1970s, increased its rate so little that, at 145 in 1987, it is now well below the national mean. But at the other end of the scale was Delaware, which started out with one of the lowest rates (33 in 1971) and increased almost tenfold to 327 in 1987. Louisiana, well above the average in 1971 (113 per 100,000 population), was even more punitive in 1987 (346).[7] Southern states, as a group, have had extremely high incarceration rates throughout the period; however, in the 1980s the region has had the smallest increases and the western states the largest.[8]

There is also a considerable range among states in the jail rate and its change over time. Again, the southern states as a group have the highest rates: in 1983 Louisiana had 192 inmates per 100,000, with eight other southern states above the average rate of 98. But here the greatest increases (between 1978 and 1983, the only years for which state data are available) come from the northeast and north central states.[9] Rates are not the full story as a measure of the demographic significance of jails. They present the average daily census, a snapshot view rather than an account of activity during the year. Because jail stays are often short, one must look at admission figures, and here the numbers are vast. In 1987, 8.6 million people (including 97,000 juveniles) were admitted into U.S. jails; assuming that the 1983 pattern persisted, half of them were in the South.[10]

Despite a decline in the youth population, juvenile confinement is also on the rise, although the national increase for the entire period was not very great in comparison with the trends in adult incarceration. During the 1970s and early 1980s juvenile admissions to public correctional facilities nationwide actually decreased. The drop reflected a reduction in arrests and perhaps also the efforts of early 1970s reformers to keep kids out of adult jails and to limit the jurisdiction of the juvenile court. However, the one-day count of confined juveniles increased in both short-term detention centers and training schools.[11] Furthermore, in some states detention rates rose throughout the period, and there was a sharp increase overall in the 1980s. For example, after a dip in detention rates between 1974 and 1979, the states of Nevada, Washington and Delaware experienced huge increases just between 1979 and 1982 (115%, 51%, and 144%, respectively.)[12]

The Influence of Sentencing Policy

This picture of a gigantic and expanding jail and prison population might be explained by rising crime, or by greater criminal justice efficiency—more arrests and convictions—or by policy choices about criminal punishment. While the first two influences may come into play in individual situations or jurisdictions, they are far less important for the country as a whole than policies that have endorsed mandatory and longer prison sentences.

Reports of overflowing institutions and costly new prison construction suggest a corresponding rise in crime. The association is misleading. Nationwide, the incarceration rate increase far outstrips the crime rate increase. There are, of course, a few states—generally smaller ones—where incarceration and crime have risen in tandem since the early 1970s; Oregon, Rhode Island, and Wyoming are among those states. But in general the rush to confinement appears to have occurred independently of the rise in FBI Index crime rates. In statisticians' language, the jump in incarceration rates in the 1970s and 1980s is not positively and significantly correlated with national increases in reported crime.[13] The 64 percent prison rate increase of the 1980s occurred in a time when the reported rate for serious street crimes first dipped and then rose again; the FBI Crime Index rate in 1986 was actually 2 percent lower than in 1979.[14]

Criminal justice efficiency is only a slightly better indicator of incarceration increases. Clearance rates—the proportion of crimes reported to police which result in arrest—have not improved during the get-tough era. The share of offenses cleared by arrest (except for larceny) was slightly lower in 1987 than in 1969, before incarceration began to rise. In that year, for example, 56 percent of forcible rapes and 27 percent of robberies reported to the police led to arrest, whereas the comparable figures for 1987 were 52.9 percent and 26.5 percent.[15] The police are arresting relatively more people, but this may just reflect higher crime levels, not greater efficacy. The number of arrests per 100,000 population went up 24 percent between 1970 and 1987.[16] But the biggest increases were for larceny—not one of the crimes of greatest concern to Americans—and for rape, as the victims have become more willing to report the offense and law enforcement has become more responsive. Robbery arrests were up only 5 percent while burglary arrests did not rise at all.

No national data series on state court dispositions exists that would help us assess how changing conviction rates affect imprisonment. We do know, however, that the problems of getting a conviction are many and various. Witnesses do not cooperate or are not credible; evidence is scanty or can be interpreted in ways not favorable to the prosecution; police blunders may have tainted the case.[17] To arrest more people and therefore increase demands on criminal courts does not diminish these problems; in fact, it often creates new sources for delay and actually reduces the odds of a conviction, a problem that will be more fully discussed in Chapter 9. Career criminal programs in which police or prosecutors target those charged with serious offenses have only occasionally brought about substantial increases in convictions.[18] Surely the surge in prison inmates does not reflect a corresponding surge in convictions.

Eliminating these possibilities as major contributors to the immense growth in incarceration since the early 1970s lends support to the conclusion that the key determinant is widespread movement toward greater punitiveness in sentencing policy. It is significant that the odds of an arrest leading to a prison sentence went up 68 percent between 1970 and 1986.[19] Since an increase in convictions is not the likely principal explanation, the possibility remains that harsher judgments about the appropriateness of a prison term now influence sentencing decisions.[20] Giving weight to this hypothesis is the policy experience of states at either end of the spectrum of incarceration rates. Delaware, with its ten-fold incarceration rate increase between 1971 and 1987, increased the severity of its sentencing, while Minnesota, with a modest rate increase of 50 percent in the same time period, took positive steps not to intensify its sentencing policies.[21] In the last fifteen years a dominant theme in most states has been the trend toward mandatory and longer sentences, fueled by (or, alternatively, taking advantage of) changes in the dominant rationales for punishment.

Rehabilitating Retribution

The policy commitment behind the crowded prisons and the growing percentage of Americans who serve some time in them has several dimensions. Legislatures have lengthened sentences, and judges, often independent of legislative mandates, have been meting out stiffer penalties.[22] In California judges began choosing prison over probation for a larger share of convicted felons even before the legislature passed tougher sentencing laws.[23] The average sentence length for federal offenses increased 32 percent just in the seven years between 1979 and 1986.[24] In addition, legislatures have embraced new approaches to sentencing that have contributed to the rush to confinement. The major policy aims of both judicial and legislative activity have been to increase severity and to structure the broadly discretionary acts of sentencing and parole release; the principal operational devices for realizing these aims are narrowing the range of sentences for specified categories of crime, reducing the use of parole (although in the mid-1970s, prison crowding forced its increase again), and establishing mandatory prison terms.[25]

For the fifty years prior to the mid-1970s the indeterminate sentence dominated penal policy. It provided for prison terms of a very wide range—often from one year to life—for many offenses. The judge would set only the minimum sentence, and the parole board would determine when, after serving that minimum, a prisoner was "ready" to be released.

By the early 1970s, cracks were appearing in the modern consensus supporting the indeterminate sentence and the rehabilitation rationale behind it. (This development is discussed in some detail in Chapter 7.) Initially, policy recommendations for replacing the indeterminate sentenced stressed a system that would impose fixed criminal penalties justified by the ancient rationale of retribution, decorated with a new label, "just deserts." Prison terms would be no longer or shorter than was necessary to express society's disapproval of the proscribed act and would be based, not on some ephemeral estimation of the wrongdoer's rehabilitation, but on the seriousness of the offense and the seriousness of the offender's prior record.[26] Reality now looks quite different from that original prescription. The indeterminate sentence has lost its grip on penal policy, to be sure, though some states have retained it. But legislative politics, bureaucratic realities, and the desire to retain judicial flexibility in hard cases have led to substitutes less tidy and coherent than what was initially proposed.

In the 1970s and 1980s state legislatures have adopted many approaches to modify or replace the indeterminate sentence, embracing greater and lesser doses of determinacy. At one end of the spectrum, Maine requires a judge to specify a fixed term and has eliminated parole release and community supervision altogether.[27] California applies "presumptive" terms and retains a basic one-year parole supervision period (except for lifers, who are on parole for three years); the sentence can be modified for mitigating and aggravating circumstances and lengthened if the crime was heinous or involved the use of a weapon.[28] Arizona has adopted a hybrid system that gives the nod to determinacy by including presumptive sentencing and substantial increases for repeat offenders and heinous crimes, but clings to indeterminacy (and, by implication, some element of rehabilitative rationale) by retaining discretionary parole release and parole supervision that may last as long as 50 percent of the sentence period.[29]

In some states sentencing is not structured legislatively but through the use of sentence guidelines set by a commission theoretically independent of the immediate political pressures that motivate legislators. Minnesota, Pennsylvania, and Washington have adopted such a system. In general commission guidelines are more detailed and comprehensive than legislatively determined changes in sentencing structure.[30]

The overall effect of the adoption of greater determinacy on the size of the state prison population is not yet clear. Research has not yet been conducted on whether serious felony offenders sentenced under the new schemes actually served longer or shorter periods. As for sentence length, one survey has found that, for all offenses except murder, states using determinate sentencing imposed shorter terms than states using indeterminate sentencing.[31] But a report from North Carolina suggests that this effect may be temporary; that as judges learn to use the new sentencing schemes creatively, sentence lengths return to the levels set before the change.[32] And an analysis of sentencing ranges in Illinois, a determinate sentencing state, concludes that sentences have become longer for serious offenses and shorter for lesser ones.[33]

By itself determinacy does not bring more people into the prisons. But the other major trend in criminal punishment policy does. A state's reliance on mandatory prison terms for people who commit repeat felonies or crimes singled out as particularly atrocious like drug offenses, gun use, or murder more directly influences the numbers of people sent to prison than the retreat from indeterminate sentencing. Also a product of disillusionment with the rehabilitative approach to correctional control, mandatoriness has come to dominate the sentencing schemes of

many states. As of 1983 forty-three states had mandatory prison sentences for one or more violent crimes, and twenty-nine
states and the District of Columbia required imprisonment for
some narcotics offenses.[34]

However, the relationship between manditoriness and the
rush to confinement of the 1970s and 1980s is not simple. Adaptive behavior of prosecutors and judges—screening out or dis-
missing charges in case-by-case resistance to harsher laws—can
and has defeated the intent of some policies setting mandatory
penalties. In 1977 the Michigan Felony Firearm Statute went
into effect, mandating that any defendant using or possessing a
gun during a felony receive a two-year prison sentence on top of
the sentence for the primary felony. Such a definitive policy—
accompanied by a bumper-sticker campaign with the slogan
"One with a gun gets you two"—might be expected to yield
dramatic increases in the certainty and severity of criminal
punishments. But researchers evaluating the impact of this law
in Detroit, where the county prosecutor had also prohibited plea
bargaining on the gun law, found that this was not so. The law
brought about no statistically significant change in minimum
sentences for murders and armed robberies, though sentences
did increase for assaults when the defendant had a gun (but by
much less than two years).[35] The evaluators hypothesized that
the "going rate" for the more serious offenses penalties was
already substantial enough—an average of six year sentences
for armed robbers—that "the sentencing judge could simply
shave a couple of years off the murder or robbery sentence,
making the net sentence the same as it had always been."[36]
They also noted that for armed robberies and some assaults the
share of cases dismissed before the pretrial conference went up,
presumably reflecting in part the reluctance of prosecutors and
judges to incarcerate on some of those charges.[37]

What this research suggests is not that manditoriness has
had no effect on prison rates, but that our prisons would be even
more crowded if it were not for the tendencies of justice system
operatives to adapt to policy directives they find undesirable or
impossible to effect.[38] Even without full compliance, few doubt
that manditoriness has had a significant impact on both the
likelihood of incarceration and on sentence length.

The state of Delaware dramatically illustrates the effects of
manditoriness on the prison population. The huge increase in
the state's incarceration rate can apparently be attributed to a
new criminal code enacted in 1973 that decreed that all sen-

tences would be served consecutively and prescribed longer sentences with mandatory minimums, ensuring that the effect of legislating longer terms could not be undercut by early parole release. Both greater and lesser offenders were affected. Mandatory life sentences were provided for some violent offenses and life without parole for first degree murder and for "habitual offenders." By 1985 one out of every seven prisoners in Delaware was serving a life sentence; 90 percent of the lifers had been sentenced under the new code.[39]

Criminal justice officials are very aware that shifts in sentencing policy have driven up the prison population to levels that risk violent reaction and fiscal disaster. Many are concerned that legislators, motivated by political survival, pay insufficient attention to the institutional consequences of get-tough policies. In 1985 state statisticians in Delaware warned that the new mandatory penalties had added 6,000 prisoner-years to time served since the enactment of the new criminal code—in a state with a prison population of only 1,325 in 1978.[40] Both federal officials and scholars are concerned that the federal sentencing guidelines scheme implemented in November 1987 in accordance with the 1984 Comprehensive Crime Control Act will, as the American Bar Association put it, "help insure dramatic increases in the prison population well beyond existing capacities."[41] One congressman asserted in 1987 that they would more than double the federal prison population, then about 50 percent over capacity.[42]

THE RETURN OF THE DEATH PENALTY

The revival of the death penalty has been a very important feature of the get-tough program. Throughout the 1980s majority support for capital punishment for murder has remained firm at around 70 percent, and politicians from presidential candidates to New York's Mayor Ed Koch have capitalized on that sentiment.[43] State legislatures have continued to expand the situations in which death may be imposed; for example, in 1987 Colorado, Illinois, Maryland, and Montana all revised their death penalty statutes to include additional aggravating circumstances that may be considered in sentencing someone convicted of a capital crime.[44] Congress passed the Omnibus Anti-Drug Abuse Act of 1988 with a provision that allows the death penalty for homicides that occur in the course of a drug transaction.[45] In 1987, 299 prisoners (five of them women) were admitted to death row, and by early 1988 the total under sentence of death exceeded 2,000.[46]

It is by no means clear that widespread execution will follow from all this activity. For the years between 1976 and 1983 judicial review of state capital statutes and continuing appeals held the total number of executions to eleven.[47] Since 1983, when the Supreme Court decried lawyers' efforts at persistent appeals and approved a summary procedure for reviewing death penalty cases, the numbers have grown, but it is hard to know how to interpret that growth. On the one hand, twenty-five executions took place in 1987, more than a quarter of the total since the Supreme Court reaffirmed the constitutionality of the death penalty in 1976, more than had been executed in any year since 1962.[48] And the Supreme Court in recent years has shown itself to be indifferent to social science evidence that juries purged of opponents of the death penalty are biased and that the death penalty is applied disproportionately when the murder victim is white.[49] Some observers predict a rapid rise in the number of executions as legal appeals are exhausted.[50]

On the other hand, the apparent eagerness of many states to pull the switch—or empty the syringe, since lethal injection has become the preferred method—is belied by a backlog of death sentences growing at a rate of ten times the number of executions.[51] As of the end of 1988 there had not been a single execution since the restoration of the death penalty in any one of the states mentioned above that have recently added aggravating circumstances to their capital statutes, although they had 124 death row inmates between them. In 1987, 79 death row inmates had their sentences vacated or commuted, more than three times as many people as were executed that year.[52]

So far, modern U.S. execution is an overwhelmingly southern phenomenon. Of the ninety-three executions between January 1977 and December 1987 eighty-seven were in Southern states; the other six were two each in Utah, Nevada, and Indiana.[53] Seventy-five percent occurred in four states alone: Texas (26), Florida (17), Louisiana (15), and Georgia (12). The trend reflects a pattern prevalent (for executions authorized by states) since the 1930s and the general tendency toward severity that can be observed in the use of confinement.[54]

As with the move to determinate and mandatory sentencing, the country's embrace of the death penalty can be seen in part as a repudiation of judicial behavior. From the 1930s on, executions declined in the U.S., until in the first half of the 1960s there were only an average of thirty-six a year.[55] At that time the NAACP Legal Defense Fund devised a "moratorium strategy" to try to end the death penalty altogether. Over the next few years its lawyers represented every death row inmate who requested assistance and used every anti-capital-punishment argument in each case—the racially discriminatory application of the death penalty, its disproportionality in crimes less serious than murder, the denial of due process when a jury imposed the sentence without standards or guidelines, and the basic argument that it violated the constitutional prohibition against cruel and unusual punishment.[56] By the time the U.S. Supreme Court held, in 1972, that "the imposition and carrying out of the death penalty in these cases constituted cruel and unusual punishment in violation of the Eighth and Fourteenth Amendments," no one had been executed in the U.S. in five years.[57]

The public reaction to *Furman v. Georgia*, which invalidated thirty-five state statutes, was intense. Public opinion, already leaning toward support for the death penalty after a period of decline, became more firmly committed, to the point that in 1985, fewer than 20 percent of the respondents to a national poll opposed capital punishment for murder.[58] Within four years of the *Furman* decision thirty-five states had passed death penalty laws with new provisions to correct the randomness and discriminatory application that had made earlier statutes constitutionally vulnerable.[59] However, this legislative fervor has not been matched by the behavior of those with more operational responsibility for implementing the policy. Jurors recommend the death penalty in only about one out of every ten capital cases, and prosecutors have been known to resort to promises that the Supreme Court will review the sentence to get them to hand down a verdict of death.[60]

NARROWING DEFENDANTS' RIGHTS

In the realm of sentencing policy government can act with observable results that are unrelated to effects (or the lack of them) on the overall level of crime. Indubitably, more people are now serving longer terms than before the flowering of the get-tough movement. To effect policies that increase the share of offenders who are caught and convicted is more problematic.

To begin with, a huge percentage of crime is never reported to the police. The federal government's victimization surveys, based on interviews with a representative national sample of U.S. households, have found that only a little more than a third of victimizations (excluding murder) are reported to the police.[61] While serious crimes like rape and robbery are reported at higher rates (53% and 56% respectively, in 1987), the far more common minor crimes like larceny are reported only about one-quarter of the time. (Motor vehicle theft, however, is an exception. It is reported about three-quarters of the time, since insurance claims require reporting.) Increasing these percentages appears to be largely beyond the control of law enforcement. In 1984 interviewees in the victimization studies were far more likely to say they hadn't reported crime because their injury was not important enough or because they didn't have sufficient proof of the crime than because they believed the police to be indifferent or incompetent.[62]

Then there is the problem of how many reported crimes lead to arrest. Here, too, the percentage is very low. (If history gives us any guide, this condition is not amenable to major change in this country; clearance of crimes by arrest has been low since the colonial era.[63]) In 1985 46.3 percent of reports of violent crime resulted in arrest, with a high of 70.2 percent for homicide and a low of 24.7 percent for robbery. Arrests for property crimes, which occur almost four times as often as violent offenses, are rare; only 14 percent of reported burglaries led to an arrest.[64]

It appears to be impossible to improve these odds significantly. Adding police is popular with the public, but it is wildly expensive. Besides, the weight of scholarly evidence is that merely adding police personnel will not decrease street crime or increase arrests.[65] Even rapid response time isn't enough to catch most robbers, and police on patrol don't generally encounter crimes in progress.[66]

However, a significant number of recent policy developments in the pre-conviction operations of criminal justice do focus on increasing the proportion of defendants who, once apprehended, are convicted. Principally this has meant narrowing defendants' rights. Both courts and legislatures have acted to limit several of the procedural protections extended to those charged with crime. The most significant changes with respect to police practice—that is, expanding law enforcement leeway in collec-

ting evidence that will build the case for the prosecution—
have been modifications of the Miranda protections against
self-incrimination and relaxations of the prohibition against
courtroom use of illegally obtained evidence. Once in court, a
defendant's options have been limited, too. Restriction of the
insanity defense has expanded the realm of criminal responsibility, and preventive detention has been endorsed in some
jurisdictions. (The latter represents the formalization of a prior
practice and is, therefore, important less as a change in criminal
justice practice than for what it says about the growing legitimacy of narrower concepts of due process.) These developments
are briefly described below.

Weakening *Miranda*

Miranda v. Arizona is the landmark case, decided by the Supreme Court in 1966, which applies the Fifth Amendment priv-
ilege against self-incrimination to suspects being questioned in
custody.[67] Although it initially generated an uproar in law
enforcement—the charge that the Court has "handcuffed the
police" comes primarily from this case—police have gradually
accommodated to reciting to defendants their rights to remain
silent and to be represented by an attorney.[68] While a 1986 case
suggested unanimity on the Supreme Court with respect to the
core principle of *Miranda*, the conservative majority has been
taking chunks out of its doctrine nonetheless.[69]

Though incursions during the 1970s were minor, they laid the
groundwork for more fundamental threats in the mid-1980s.[70]
Particularly relevant for later developments was a 1974 Supreme Court case that found the testimony of a witness admissible even though his identity had been revealed by the suspect
during illegal interrogation; Justice William Rehnquist's opinion read narrowly *Miranda*'s protection against compulsory
self-incrimination and conceded very little authority to its
requirements.[71]

This approach showed up again in two important cases in the
1980s. *New York v. Quarles* created a "public safety" exception
to the *Miranda* requirement that a suspect's rights be recited
before any questioning takes place, applicable to a situation in
which the suspect's statements are not "compelled by police conduct" and in which police officers ask only "questions necessary
to secure their own safety or the safety of the public."[72] The

decision balanced the threat to public safety if police could not pose a question against the need for what Rehnquist, again writing the majority opinion, called the "prophylactic rule" protecting defendants against self-incrimination.[73] A year later, *Oregon v. Elstad* built on this foundation, suggesting in an opinion written by Justice Sandra Day O'Connor that *Miranda* protected only against blatantly offensive police methods, "deliberately coercive or improper tactics."[74] Such an analysis does indeed reduce *Miranda* warnings to the status of "prophylactic rule," rather than acknowledging them as constitutional rights, although the *Miranda* case itself assumed that interrogation while in custody is inherently coercive and therefore unconstitutional without the suspect's informed waiver of the right against self-incrimination. Some constitutional scholars think that, with an increasingly conservative Supreme Court, *Miranda* is ripe for overruling in the 1990s.[75]

Qualifying the Exclusionary Rule

Erosion of the exclusionary rule, which prohibits trial use of evidence seized in violation of the Fourth Amendment's protection against "unreasonable searches and seizures," has had a similar history. Applied to federal courts in 1914 and extended to state courts in 1949 (both by Supreme Court decision,) the rule has always drawn fire from conservative judges, prosecutors and journalists. When critics—including former Chief Justice Warren Burger—inveigh against "technicalities" that set criminals free, they most often mean the exclusionary rule.

Limited by the Supreme Court in minor ways during the 1970s, the exclusionary rule came under frontal attack when the Reagan Administration took office. The Attorney General's Task Force on Violent Crime recommended in 1981 that the rule not apply when the police reasonably believed that they had obtained evidence lawfully, and the following year the President's Task Force on Victims of Crime recommended outright abolition.[76]

Major change was spurred by the Supreme Court in 1984, when, in *United States v. Leon* and *United States v. Sheppard*, it upheld the courtroom use of illegally seized evidence because police had made a "reasonable mistake" in believing that the warrants they obtained for the searches were valid.[77] Thus endorsed by the Supreme Court, the "good faith exception" to the exclusionary rule is spreading fast. Within two years twelve states had by statute, constitutional provision, or case law, adopted it.[78]

What remains of the exclusionary rule is also under siege. As Attorney General, Edwin Meese made no secret of his hope that it would be abandoned altogether; he had earlier called it "judicial hostage-taking," maintaining that the law-abiding public is held hostage to an ineffective measure for enforcing legal police behavior.[79] In 1988 a provision that would have allowed admission of evidence seized in warrantless searches passed, 259 to 134, in the House of Representatives, but was eliminated in conference committee.[80] Indicative of the direction of much public and official sentiment was California voters' approval, in 1982, of Proposition 8, appending to that state's constitution a "victim's bill of rights." Among other things, Proposition 8 requires admission of all "relevant evidence" in a criminal trial without regard to how it was gathered.[81]

These changes reflect more than an impatience with the inability to use in a trial what may be determinative evidence of guilt. Lying just below the surface of the exclusionary rule debate is the judicial view that the substantive protections guaranteed by the Fourth Amendment have been construed too broadly and that the authority and good will of police is to be presumed. (As Wayne LaFave, the leading authority on search and seizure, has written, "It is almost as if a majority of the Court was hell-bent to seize any available opportunity to define more expansively the constitutional authority of law enforcment officials."[82]) Courts have been expanding the range of exceptions to the requirement that a warrant be issued to protect citizens against unreasonable search and seizure by government. It is fair to say that the Burger Court abandoned the notion that a search without a warrant is unreasonable per se; the Supreme Court applies an ever-more-permissive standard in evaluating government searches.[83]

Restricting the Insanity Defense

The defense of insanity as an excuse for committing a particular act has been a matter of dispute since the beginning of the nineteenth century. The defense evolved from the traditional understanding that the general condition of lunacy rendered a person incapable of crime.[84] There are a number of different tests of a defendant's capacity. Evidence of the lack of consensus on a proper legal standard for insanity is that the U.S. states use four different definitions.[85]

Both scholarly and popular literature suggest that the insanity defense is vulnerable to policy change in the wake of unpopular and well-publicized cases.[86] Uneasiness with the insanity defense brought about some changes during the 1970s; in a number of states it became easier to commit and hold people acquitted of crimes by reason of insanity, and in Montana in 1979 the defense was abolished altogether.[87] But the major changes came about after the 1982 acquittal of John Hinckley for the attempted assassination of President Reagan. Within three years sixteen states had increased requirements of proof of insanity and eight had narrowed the test for insanity. Eight had added to the insanity defense the option of finding that the defendant was guilty but mentally ill, a disposition that permits a criminal sentence but leaves open the possibility that it will be served in a mental institution.[88] Between 1978 and late 1985 thirty-four states, by statute or case law, limited or abolished the insanity defense or made it procedurally more difficult to sustain.[89]

Endorsing Preventive Detention

In symbolic terms, the growing legitimization of preventive detention is extremely important. Historically, the declared purpose of bail has been to ensure that a defendant will return to court, and the constitutional prohibition of "excessive bail" in the 8th Amendment has been interpreted to exclude other grounds for denying freedom to an accused person awaiting trial.[90] But standards for pre-trial release have been transformed in the past decade. Once criticized for discriminating against poor defendants and subjecting the accused to punishment before conviction, the bail system has been rehabilitated and given license to detain for a broader range of purposes, including the general protection of society.[91] It might be said that this change is merely one of making overt what had been previously covert—the practice of many judges to use bail selectively to detain before trial defendants whom they thought likely to threaten the public or considered politically dangerous. But explicit approval of the practice of preventive detention sends the message that the protective ideal has been abandoned and may alter the judicial behavior of those who have tried to live up to it.

Perhaps the most dramatic evidence of the change is the contrast between the federal Bail Reform Act of 1966 and the legislation that repealed it less than twenty years later, the Bail Reform Act of 1984.[92] The earlier law stipulated that ensuring the appearance of a defendant was the only proper purpose of bail, except in capital cases. The new law, in contrast, endorses a "public safety orientation;" federal judges may now detain defendants charged with serious or repeated offenses if there appear to be no conditions of release that will reasonably ensure the "safety of any other person and the community." The predicted danger to the community that invokes the detention need not be as narrow as physical violence; drug sales are apparently sufficient.[93] Over an angry dissent by Justice Thurgood Marshall, who called the new law "consistent with the uses of tyranny," the Supreme Court, in 1987, upheld the constitutionality of its pretrial detention provisions. Chief Justice Rehnquist, writing for the majority, labeled the Bail Reform Act "regulatory in nature" and ruled that it "does not constitute punishment before trial in violation of the Due Process Clause."[94] He found the state's interest in preventing pretrial crime greater than the interests of the defendants in not being detained, and therefore ruled that the law does not violate the defendants' Eighth Amendment right to bail.

The federal law reinforced what many states had already done. As early as 1970 the District of Columbia allowed judges to consider defendants' dangerousness in making a bail decision in a non-capital case.[95] Many other states followed suit until by 1985 there were fourteen jurisdictions that allowed pretrial detention in noncapital cases, based on an assessment, explicit or implicit, of the risk of danger from the defendant before trial.[96] With the Supreme Court endorsement of preventive detention, that number is expected to grow.

TARGETING CAREER CRIMINALS

Preventive detention is one manifestation of a general strategy that has dominated the get-tough era: the focus on "career criminals." In 1972 Marvin Wolfgang and his colleagues found that, among almost 10,000 males born in Philadelphia in 1945, a small group of chronic delinquents (6 percent) were arrested for more than half of the offenses of the cohort.[97] Subsequent criminological research confirmed this pattern for adults, with some "violent predators"—perhaps 10 percent of those who deal drugs and commit robberies and assaults—responsible for hundreds of crimes a year.[98] Criminologists warned that to use these findings to shape sentencing policy was premature—that predicting which offenders were, in fact, high-risk was problematic.[99] Not surprisingly, however, law enforcement officials have pounced on the promise of these findings. The lure of an approach that holds out the possibility of reducing crime significantly at moderate cost by incapacitating a few indisputable losers has proved irresistible.[100] Career criminals—those who persist in serious crime for an extended period—have become the preferred targets at all stages of the criminal justice process.

The programs that have received the most attention are those that concentrate prosecution resources on defendants with long records for serious crimes. In 1973 the Bronx District Attorney, with a Law Enforcement Assistance Administrationn (LEAA) grant, set up the Major Offense Bureau, a unit that its chief praised as "a system that would put our energies where they're needed most."[101] It reduced trial delays and aimed to increase convictions and incarceration for cases identified as involving particularly heinous crimes and suspects with long records.[102] By 1979 LEAA, which had designated the Bronx program an "exemplary project," had funded forty-five such projects, many on the Bronx model.[103] In these units procedures are expedited, plea bargaining is limited, and no effort is spared to build a case. To insure continuity the programs generally assign a single prosecutor to follow a case through to sentencing. In some jurisdictions a special section of the criminal court hears only career criminal cases; in Chicago the Rock Court (a nickname derived both from the grim building in which it was housed and from the acronym of its formal name, the Repeat Offender Court) quickly became a powerful symbol of Cook County's law and order stance.

Police practice in some jurisdictions has also been affected by the emphasis on career criminals. Special surveillance programs exist in several cities.[104] Juveniles as young as eleven who have never been convicted of a crime but who have been arrested several times can come under special police scrutiny in the SHO/DI (Serious and Habitual Offenders/Drug-Involved) programs funded by the federal Office of Juvenile Justice and Delinquency Prevention.[105] Prosecutors cooperate with these programs, handling SHO/DI youth "just like they were adult career criminals," according to one police official in Oxnard, California.[106]

The significance of this emphasis lies more in what it tells us about the mood of criminal justice policymakers and practitioners than about its impact on criminal justice practice. The career criminal programs do not appear to have convicted or incarcerated a much larger share of the toughest offenders than conventional approaches. The National Institute of Justice evaluated four of the federally-funded prosecution programs, in New Orleans, San Diego, Columbus, and Kalamazoo. Although the researchers found that in two jurisdictions the defendants in the programs were convicted of more serious charges than others, they also concluded that the program had not affected incarceration rates in any of the jurisdictions. Furthermore, the special processing efforts did not appear to have changed the justice process, except that delays were reduced in one jurisdiction; the evaluators concluded that "criminal defendants prosecuted by the career criminal programs in these four sites are no more likely to be convicted, to be tried or to have the charges dismissed than would be expected given the performance of the local criminal justice systems with similar cases during a baseline period and with other noncareer criminal cases."[107] As for sending the rotten apples away for longer periods, the evaluation found that only in San Diego did sentence lengths increase for career criminals, an effect that could be attributed to the likelihood that they were now being convicted of the most serious charge against them.[108] Since people who repeatedly commit serious crimes are relatively rare, the career criminal emphasis probably does not contribute very much to the huge increase in the overall incarceration rate.

HOW BROAD IS THE TREND?

Usually we evaluate the effectiveness of the criminal law and the institutions that implement it in terms of their effect on the individual behavior of wrongdoers or those who might be tempted by wrongdoing. Sometimes—less frequently as we doubt the strength of the relationship between crime policy and social progress—we measure the success of criminal justice by fluctuations in the crime rate. A third approach—often overlooked or, alternatively, discounted for exhibiting undue sympathy with dangerous predators—is to look at how the targets of criminal justice activity are affected by it. If the target group is large and the impact profound, crime policy can affect U.S. cultural and political life in ways at least as fundamental as its influence on patterns of lawbreaking.

Some of the trends previously discussed have very pervasive direct effects, and some reach relatively few people. One of the most striking things about trends in criminal justice in the 1970s and 1980s is the incongruous relationship between the public debate over a policy change and its material effect on substantial numbers of people. It is only a slight oversimplification to say that the more hotly debated the policy shift, the fewer people it directly affects. The death penalty is an example. Similarly, the narrowing of civil liberties protections, while symbolically very significant and crucial to defendants and suspects affected, only rarely determines the outcome of a criminal prosecution. The record levels of incarceration and other penalties in the 1970s and 1980s—which have met with little resistance on other than fiscal grounds—affect many more people than the limitations on defendants' rights and obviously profoundly disrupt the lives of those subject to them. The expansion of data surveillance by police (and probation, to a lesser extent) affects the greatest number of all—perhaps one-fourth of the adult population—though for most the intrusion is minor and often invisible. Intermediate punishments and probation have the potential for the greatest growth, if only because they are so much cheaper than prisons.

The Limited Impact of Narrower Defendants' Rights

Civil libertarians have watched with horror in the last ten years as the Supreme Court, Congress, and many state legislatures have chipped away at defendants' rights. They worry that due process and the "criminal procedure Amendments"—the Fourth, Fifth and Sixth—are being fundamentally eroded by conservative federal courts and state and federal legislative bodies. They are certainly right to resist threats to fundamental fairness for those accused of crime, not only for the sake of that particular principle and the particular defendants to whom it will immediately apply, but because the procedural protections of criminal law are emblematic of this society's commitment to limits in the state's authority over the citizen. Although due process generally becomes a subject of public debate when criminal cases arouse our passions, its fundamental significance lies in the protection provided to all of us, innocent or guilty, when our interests do not coincide with those of the majority. In that sense, the rights of defendants are also the rights of students, employees, tenants, and everyone else who is ever in a position to be coerced by the exercise of government power over individuals. As Supreme Court Justice Robert Jackson wrote in 1949, "Uncontrolled search and seizure is one of the first and most effective weapons in the arsenal of every arbitrary government."[109]

These are the constitutional arguments, weighty in political and symbolic impact. They often overshadow the material effects of narrowing defendants' rights (at least at this stage of judicial interpretation). In fact, most recent policy changes with respect to defendants' rights—the narrowing of the insanity defense and the exclusionary rule, for example—actually alter the outcomes of very few criminal cases. Insanity defense "reform" in Illinois is illustrative. In 1984, three years after the passage of the law that allowed a finding of "guilty but mentally ill," only 112 defendants, or 1.56 percent of the state's felony cases that year, were convicted in that category.[110] It had been used in only 27 of 102 counties. Furthermore, findings of not guilty by reason of insanity had not declined, but in fact had increased by 28 percent between 1982–1984. If the new disposition has not substituted for the insanity acquittal, it is probably being applied to defendants who would previously have been found guilty anyway. In that case it serves primarily as symbolic reinforcement of the conviction. Such an outcome may provide public relations benefits to prosecutors and judges, but it does not increase public safety or hold defendants accountable for their behavior.

Similarly, the immediate, material effects on defendants of Supreme Court decisions narrowing the exclusionary rule are likely to be minimal. To begin with, the rule itself has little effect on the outcome of all but drug cases. Police and prosecutors rarely throw out otherwise promising cases because of search-and-seizure problems, and courts rarely grant motions to suppress evidence based on illegal searches. A General Accounting Office (GAO) study of federal courts found that evidence was excluded as the result of a Fourth Amendment motion in only 1.3 percent of the 2,804 cases handled during the summer of 1978.[111] Even when the courts do grant motions to suppress, conviction does not usually turn on the excluded evidence. A National Institute of Justice (NIJ) study of 520,993 felony cases in California between 1976 and 1979 found that 86,033 were rejected for various reasons, and that of those, 4,130 were dismissed because of illegally obtained evidence, 4.8 percent of the cases rejected but only 0.8 percent of felony complaints referred for prosecution.[112] James Fyfe, assessing the NIJ study, pointed out that the impact of the exclusionary rule is "miniscule in comparison to the effects of problems with victims and witnesses or evidence sufficiency."[113]

If the exclusionary rule itself doesn't free many defendants, creating an exception to it convicts still fewer. And the good faith exception is still very narrow. It applies only to cases in which the police conducted a search with a defective warrant reasonably believing it to be valid, and when the fault for the defect lay with the magistrate who issued the warrant, not with the law enforcement agency that applied for it and served it. Most criminal investigations don't require warrants, and when they do, judges rarely issue constitutionally defective ones. As one study of the effect of the search warrant process noted, "Relatively few search warrants are ever challenged, only a tiny percentage of the challenges are successful, and only a fraction of the successful challenges result in the loss of a case."[114] Recent rulings have relaxed the warrant requirement, and appellate courts are expected to presume a warrant's legality, so the issue of good faith in a search is likely to be raised very seldom.[115] If the Supreme Court extends the good faith exception to warrantless searches, as some think it will, of course more defendants will be affected.

Narrowing the procedural rights of the accused is sometimes part of a larger crime control strategy. Detention of defendants judged dangerous and likely to commit crimes while awaiting trial curtails the defendant's right to bail and is also a cornerstone of the current emphasis on harsher treatment of career criminals. Preliminary evidence suggests that the effects of preventive detention, like other limitations of defendants' rights, are primarily symbolic, rather than material.

As yet we do not have data on the extent to which the endorsement of preventive detention by the states that have adopted it—Arizona, California, Colorado, Florida, Michigan, and others—has actually affected criminal justice practice and increased the number of defendants detained before trial. We do know that the preventive detention provision of the federal Bail Reform Act of 1984 has been widely applied. By mid-1987, 2,500 defendants had been detained under it.[116] A GAO study released late in the year found that in four federal districts (Northern Indiana, Arizona, Southern Florida, and Eastern New York) 249 defendants had been detained out of 1,041 who met the criteria that authorize detention for noncapital charges based on a prediction of dangerousness.[117] These results raise a question, however, that makes research in this area problematic: how many of those defendants would have been detained under the old bail law, by the indirect method of setting a high bail that the defendant could not pay? The GAO study did find a higher percentage of federal defendants detained under the new law than under the old, but the increase was less than one-fifth—from 26 percent to 31 percent.[118] The percentage of those detained because they did not pay bail dropped sharply when the new law became effective—from 26 percent to 16 percent—suggesting that the new provision functions primarily to remove the hypocrisy from what was already a common practice.

There is one area of criminal activity in which narrowing defendants' rights probably has the effect of reaching larger numbers of offenders. Several studies have found that the exclusionary rule has the greatest impact on drug cases; in the NIJ study they accounted for 71.5 percent of the cases rejected for prosecution because the evidence was illegally seized.[119] Material evidence is much more crucial to a drug conviction than to an assault, for example; the police know this and may consequently be more aggressive. Even in these cases, however, successful use of the rule is still fairly rare; in a study of 512 drug and gambling cases in Boston, Sheldon Krantz and his colleagues found that only eleven motions to dismiss were granted, affecting 2 percent of the cases.[120] Most federal defendants preventively detained under the new law also appear to be accused drug offenders—93 percent in the four districts studied by the GAO.[121]

Also, career criminal programs don't affect many offenders since by definition they are focused on only that relatively small group of hard core offenders that the research of Wolfgang, Greenwood, and others has identified as responsible for large amounts of crime. The major offense bureaus in twenty-four cities funded by LEAA in the 1970s typically process only about

10 percent of the serious offense cases handled.[122] Further-more, while these cases may be processed more expeditiously and the defendants sentenced to longer prison terms, they are not, by and large, cases with defendants who would otherwise have been let off with the probverbial "slap on the wrist." Most who are prosecuted in career criminal programs would be likely to be convicted and go to prison anyway.[123]

The Prevalence of Correctional Custody

The U.S. public has the impression that few criminals are ever caught, convicted, or confined. All of us who live in big cities can tell endless anecdotes of burglaries unsolved, mug-gers released, and shoplifters let off with a "slap on the wrist." The media reinforce this picture with terrifying stories about predators back on the street after committing heinous and re-peated offenses. And, as mentioned earlier in this chapter, aggregate statistics paint a picture of a large amount of unre-ported crime—perhaps 50 percent of all violent crimes and 75 percent of thefts—and a relatively low share of reported crimes leading to arrest—perhaps 20 percent. A number of arrests can-not be prosecuted because the evidence is weak or the witnesses and victims are unable or unwilling to testify. Of the adult cases that are prosecuted, the majority result in a guilty verdict and some form of punishment; but many cases that the ordinary citizen may think serious are considered minor by law enforce-ment and are therefore processed as misdemeanors or bar-gained down to charges that carry light sentences.[124]

The popular metaphor of the criminal justice system as a funnel, with most defendants dropping out along the way to the penitentiary, was created by the 1967 President's Commission on Law Enforcement and the Administration of Justice.[125] It is misleading on several counts and has led to widespread crit-icism of the criminal justice system for failing to punish more than a tiny percentage of offenders.[126] As others have pointed out, it is illogical to measure justice system performance by comparing the number of cases handled successfully (by what-ever measure) to the total number of crimes, when most of them go unreported.[127] In addition, the impression conveyed that defendants who are convicted but don't go to prison are not adversely affected by the justice process is wildly erroneous. Nonincarcerative punishments may be quite punitive, as the picture sketched in Chapter 5 of intermediate punishments will show. Furthermore, the experience of the criminal process, which requires that the defendant seek bail, obtain an attorney, and mount a litigation strategy, can be more onerous for minor offenses than the legislatively-authorized penalty eventually meted out by the court.[128]

The greatest deficiency of the funnel image is that it captures a snapshot of the criminal process at a single moment and cannot therefore convey the impact that justice system decisions have on people or neighborhoods over time. In many communities, that impact is substantial and, with the developments of the past twenty years, is becoming more so all the time.

Statistical information on the use of imprisonment is usually presented in terms of the number of people in prison on a given day, and changes in the use of the sanction are reported in terms of a contrast between that count and a count of another day in a subsequent year. A more dynamic way to look at the effect of prison on the life of an individual or community or demographic group is to look at the prevalence of imprisonment, on a given day and over a period of time, say, an individual's lifetime.[129] Of course, the proportion of the adult population that experiences prison over time is much larger than appears to be the case with a one-day count, and prevalence measures can deepen our understanding of who goes to prison.

On December 31, 1987, for example, there were 228 sentenced prisoners per 100,000 residents in state and federal institutions, a little more than one-fifth of one percent of the population.[130] This figure is very high in comparison with other industrialized western countries; the United States incarcerates robbers at a rate of more than four times that of Germany, for example, and almost ten times that of England.[131] But it may seem low enough to have little effect on the social or economic life of the country. The full meaning of our high incarceration rates becomes much clearer, however, as we look at the prevalence of imprisonment among various groups. Gender differences are striking, with adult males twenty-one times more likely to be in prison than females. [132]

More disturbing are racial breakdowns, which put the disproportionate share of blacks in prison in somewhat sharper focus. One in every forty-nine black male adults (2.044%) was in state prison on a single day in 1982, and in 1979 (the latest year for which age breakdowns are available) the figure was an estimated one in every thirty-three (3.027%) for black males aged twenty to twenty-nine, eight times as many as for whites in that category.[133] (While we do not have good data or much research on the incarceration of Hispanics, they are apparently not as disproportionately represented in prison. About 10 percent of the state and federal prison population in 1985 was hispanic, as compared with 7.5 percent of the general population. Blacks, however, made up 45 percent of prisoners and 12.2 percent of the general population.[134])

It is important also to consider the prevalence of nonprison sanctions, since they too are at record levels and often have significant effects on families and communities. Over 2.6 million people were on probation or parole at the end of 1987.[135] In the 1980s probation has been about twice as common as imprisonment, parole about one-third as common. Furthermore, the increase in probation between 1983 and 1987 was greater than for prison and jail—more than 40 percent as opposed to about 33 percent.[136] Together, the rates for the different kinds of correctional custody in 1985 amounted to an overall custody prevalence of one adult in sixty-three (1.6 %) in 1985.[137] At the end of 1985 about one out of every thirty-three adult males in this country was under some form of correctional custody. For black males prevalence was much greater, of course—one out of every nine adults—and if we were able to break that down to black males under thirty, the ratio would be still lower, perhaps one in every six or seven.[138] The prevalence of custody of all kinds varies widely among states. In North Dakota and West Virginia only about one person in 200 was under custody of some kind in 1985, whereas in states like Texas and Georgia the figure was about one person in thirty-two.[139]

That the experience of prison, actual and anticipated, corrodes family and community life in many black neighborhoods becomes even clearer when lifetime prevalence—the likelihood that a person will do time at some point in his life—is considered. Statisticians from the U.S. Department of Justice have estimated that, at 1979 imprisonment levels, an American male born in 1985 had between one chance in thirty or forty-eight (depending on which prison census was used) of serving a sentence in a state prison during his lifetime. A black male, however, had between one chance in five or nine of doing time, almost six times the likelihood for a white male.[140] If we had the data to add the lifetime prevalence of incarceration in juvenile or federal institutions, jail stays that did not lead to prison, military imprisonment, and probation, we would surely conclude that correctional custody was a much more common experience than is generally perceived and that prevalence for black males is particularly high. I would not be surprised to find that in poor, black central city neighborhoods, half of the male residents would at some point in their lives be in prison or jail or under the supervision of correctional authorities. While my estimate is not scientific, more rigorous analysts have come to conclusions that would appear to be consistent with mine. Alfred Blumstein and Elizabeth Graddy have estimated that the lifetime probability of arrest for a serious personal or property crime is 51 percent for black males in cities over 250,000 population.[141] While not all such arrests lead to conviction and punishment, many people will have a number of arrests, multiplying the odds that they will receive a sanction at some point. Furthermore, arrests for quite trivial offenses as well as for serious ones may occasionally lead to jail stays or probation.

We have seen that the effects of intensifying crime control vary according to the group and the stage of the justice process that is affected. Many variables will determine future patterns. If sentencing policy continues in the directions of the recent past, the prevalence of incarceration will continue to increase; that is, unless financial constraints slow the prison building boom and ways are found to get around harsher sentences with nonprison penalties. If the federal government continues to become more and more involved in fighting drugs, perhaps more resources will be devoted to confinement of drug offenders; on the other hand, federal activity may replace local drug enforcement efforts on major trafficking cases so that lesser offenders are usually given short and nonprison sentences in state courts. If a more conservative Supreme Court abandons the exclusionary rule, drug convictions will increase, but we cannot know by how much.

Perhaps the only short-term certainty about the get-tough aspect of the juggernaut is that there is currently virtually no overt resistance to it. Civil liberties groups are no match for dominant conservative forces, locked into a contest over "rights" in which guilty defendants are bound to be losers when pitted against innocent victims. No countervailing symbols to the myth of crime and punishment have been found, no effective language of opposition to the individual perspective on remedies for crime. The values of tolerance, social protection, and brotherly love are currently no match for the justifiable fear and outrage over street crime and the law and order politics that exploits them.

3

•

THE "CHECK 'EM OUT" APPROACH

We can surely accept the general proposition that, in our societies, the systems of punishment are to be situated in a certain 'political economy' of the body: even if they do not make use of violent or bloody punishment, even when they use 'lenient' methods involving confinement or correction, it is always the body that is at issue—the body and its forces, their utility and their docility, their distribution and their submission.

    ● Michel Foucault, *Discipline and Punish*

INCREASING OBSERVATION

THE OVERTLY PUNITIVE policies detailed in the preceding chapter are not the whole story of the justice juggernaut. Equally important for the expansion of coercive state control is the growth, in the last twenty years, of observation policies: techniques of investigation and custody to keep close tabs on people who are (or perhaps are not) suspected of criminal activity or who are being punished outside of prison. Here the aim is not severity but comprehensiveness, a control that relies as much on the *potential* of state coercion as on the coercion itself. Surveillance can reach many more potential and actual offenders than can the marginal reduction of due process rights and imposition of longer prison terms. It can also be launched with fewer financial and political costs, initiated by justice system professionals themselves in less visible and conflictual policy arenas.

The programs described in detail in the next two chapters are by no means the only observation measures undertaken as part of the deepening and broadening of criminal justice control during the last two decades. At many stages of the process, a relatively clear jurisdictional divide has given way to boundaryless terrain that is difficult to assess empirically and regulate legally. The judge's decision whether or not to detain an indicted defendant, for example, is no longer an in/out decision, but may call into play various forms of semi-custody, pretrial release programs that supervise defendants in the community while they await their trial dates. Neighborhood Watch programs where citizens organize to report suspicious activity to police effectively broaden the patrol jurisdiction of law enforcement and obscure the boundaries of public and private space. The two areas that I have chosen illustrate many of the issues that arise more generally with respect to the spread of observation programs. They are also areas with vast potential for expansion.

Computerized Criminal Records Systems

By now most Americans have bowed to the inevitability of banking transactions, credit purchases and phone calls noted and saved by gigantic computer networks. Few are aware, however, of how justice system records, where the consequences of inspection and exchange are so much weightier, are collected and used. The proliferation of automated criminal records at all levels of government now includes not only files of outstanding warrants but detailed histories of all of an individual's contacts with criminal justice and, in many jurisdictions, information on people under investigation or merely "of interest" to law enforcement. Expanding the dissemination and linkages of these records—a process well underway for some systems, unlikely to develop in others—is turning the existing networks into a gigantic national data base of files on individuals, some who are serious offenders and many who are not. In most states criminal histories—more informally called "rap sheets"—are available outside the criminal justice system, generally for employment purposes. Federal agencies like the Department of Defense, the CIA, and the Immigration and Naturalization Service have access to these records, overriding whatever state privacy laws may exist.[1] While some states prohibit or restrict the dissemination of nonconviction data—decisions not to prosecute, acquittals or dismissals—the trend is toward increasing access to records outside the criminal justice system, even where an arrest did not result in prosecution or conviction.[2] In a few states, like Michigan and New Jersey, no statewide policy regulates noncriminal justice access; in Florida and Wisconsin, anyone can obtain criminal records for any purpose.[3]

One of the most enduring legacies of LEAA will surely turn out to be the centralized state repositories for criminal justice data created as part of the statewide organizations designated

to administer federal funds for law enforcement. Even where
LEAA's state planning agencies expired along with their parent
agency, data-gathering at the state level continued. Forty-four
states responding to a 1985 survey reported holding an estimated 35 million criminal history records.[4] Most of those states,
including all ten of the most populous, have at least partly automated their records system. Many have, in addition, local
systems that contain millions more records, some of them duplicated at the state and federal levels. As of late 1988, California
had sixty different criminal justice data bases with a total of
about forty million records (including many duplicates) in
them.[5]

Two arms of the FBI link state records to each other and to
federal law enforcement. The older is the Identification Division. For fifty years a storehouse of fingerprints and "rap
sheets," it now holds the print cards of 25 million people in its
criminal file.[6] As of March 1986 it had automated 9 million of its
records, but it continues to distribute most information by
mail.[7] It also now maintains and manages the Triple-I, formally
known as the Interstate Identification Index, a sort of electronic
directory to the criminal histories of 12 million people in twenty
states.[8] Until very recently, Triple-I was part of the FBI's other
record repository, the National Crime Information Center
(NCIC), a computerized criminal justice information clearinghouse. Available by computer to over 60,000 criminal justice
agencies around the country, NCIC contains about 8 million
records (as of November 1988) on people or objects sought by law
enforcement.

Criminal histories provide identifying information and chronological accounts of their subject's encounters with police,
courts, and corrections agencies. Also held by both the FBI and
the state repositories are what are called "hot files"—
outstanding warrants for arrest or current identifying information on stolen items like vehicles or securities. In addition to
these records of public information, many local and state law
enforcement agencies maintain investigative files with data on
people suspected of crime—identifiers, the names and habits of
friends or colleagues, license plate numbers, and so on. Some
now track probationers and parolees with automated files. With
the exception of the Secret Service Protective File, which contains leads on twenty-five people (as of May 1989) thought to be
a threat to the President and others whom the Secret Service is
assigned to protect, the NCIC does not contain on-line investigative files, although they have been recommended.

Intermediate Punishments

During the mid-1970s it became increasingly apparent that across-the-board imprisonment for property offenses and crimes of interpersonal violence was a very costly crime control strategy. Faced with criminal justice expenditures that were rising faster than other budget categories, taxpayer resistance to the costs of prison construction, and penal institutions so crowded that federal courts declared them unconstitutional, state and local officials began looking to "intermediate punishments," "those sanctions that exist somewhere between incarceration and probation on the continuum of criminal penalties."[9] Most popular are intensive supervision in probation (ISP), home confinement, and electronic surveillance—imposed separately or in combination.

By late 1987 forty states were implementing ISP programs in at least one county—thirteen of them statewide.[10] The model for many of these is Georgia's intensive probation supervision program, started in 1982 as a response to prison crowding. Program participants are mostly offenders who would otherwise have gone to prison, people convicted of a wide range of crimes, though few have committed serious violent offenses. Probationers are assigned to two supervisors, a probation officer and a surveillance officer, who meet with them three to five times a week at home or on the job. They must hold down a job or attend school full-time, observe a curfew, perform community service, and submit to random drug and alcohol testing.[11]

While some ISP programs are described as experiments, the general trend has caught on with a rapidity that may preclude extensive testing. As a group of scholars put it in 1987, "The chorus of approval for intensive probation is so strong and seemingly uniform that we are tempted to call it 'the new panacea of corrections.'"[12] Joan Petersilia, who has evaluated many aspects of probation, warns that the program trend may be shortlived if practitioners' "incautious enthusiasm" leads to adoption of "model" programs without consideration of local offender populations and political environments.[13] The approach is no longer intended solely to substitute for prison sentences but often to put teeth into regular probation.

House arrest, both with and without electronic surveillance, is another intermediate punishment that is catching on fast. Florida's program is the largest so far, with 20,000 participants since 1983, and it is the model for many other jursdictions.[14] Offenders are sentenced to serve terms of up to two years at home, sometimes twenty-four hours a day, usually during the hours when they are not at work. "Community control officers" conduct surveillance of the offenders, checking their whereabouts by phone and personal contacts. Telephone robots are also used in southern Florida to call offenders and ask them to verify their presence at home. Offenders must pay a supervision fee, make restitution payments to their victims, support their families, and do 150 to 200 hours of community service. Program participants are usually property offenders, drug offenders, and drunk drivers.

Twenty-four-hour surveillance is problematic even with the most vigilant programs, so house arrest is increasingly supplemented by electronic monitoring. There are several technological possibilities, most of which entail the wearing of a bracelet or anklet that identifies the offender electronically when a computer calls to ascertain his presence.[15] While only 2,277 offenders were being supervised electronically at the time of a 1988 survey, that number was almost three times the number of a year earlier.[16] The appeal of house arrest programs as a fairly reliable way to keep offenders off the streets assures that they are likely to continue to expand rapidly.[17]

HOW BROAD IS THE EFFECT?

The previous chapter described policy developments of the get-tough track of the juggernaut. They are visible and dramatic, corresponding to the citizen's sense of state coercion as overt and decisive demonstration of power. The observation programs described in the next two chapters are discreet rather than ostentatious, relying on "a subtle, calculated technology of subjection."[18] The key to their power, then, is not in the extent to which they declare and execute the state's monopoly on force. Sometimes, in fact, they are instituted, at least in part, to *counter* the harshness of get-tough policies. However, in their capacity to propel and merge with disciplinary measures in the larger society beyond the criminal justice system, they may have more impact in making us a more regimented society.

In the most obvious sense this capacity is not yet fully utilized. The greatest significance of both observation trends reported here is still in their potential. Not all of the many millions of criminal records are yet on line, links between data bases are often informal—by telephone conversation rather than tele-communications network—and access to records outside the justice system remains significantly limited. Intermediate punishments are in a still earlier stage of development. Only an estimated 50,000 people have been through intensive supervision programs thus far, and it will take some time to convert a sizable portion of ordinary probation programs into the new improved model.

But the greatest growth in criminal justice is in the programs of observation. Determining how many people are likely to be affected, and who they are, is more complex than counting prison inmates or calculating the number of times illegally obtained evidence taints a criminal prosecution. Aggregate data similar to prison counts do not exist for intermediate punishments and would be meaningless for the collection and dissemination of criminal records. One must look at more elusive measures of influence. There are many different ways of being touched by the dissemination of a criminal record or the thrice-weekly visits of a surveillance officer. And how is the universe of people affected by both policies to be circumscribed? Does a record subject "count" as affected by data surveillance if he or she remains unaware of inclusion within the system or if, in fact, that record is never called up or disseminated? Can we say that the families and neighbors of participants in intermediate punishment programs are under surveillance in a way that ordinary citizens are not? In what circumstances? The next two chapters will try to convey the programs' actual and potential reach without the security of many numbers.

A few comments on dimensions are in order. In 1979 a U.S. Labor Department study estimated that 36 to 40 million living Americans had arrest records for something other than a traffic offense.[19] The criminal records systems of states, localities, and the federal government have the potential for covering all of them, plus people who don't have records but are "of interest"— wanted for questioning, suspected of first-time offenses, and so on. Of course the number might be smaller because old and minor records are less likely to be automated than those of more recent vintage. On the other hand, new information needs and circumstances that trigger record creation occur every day— creating local gang files is currently popular—and swell both the ranks of record subjects (some of whom haven't been charged with a crime) and the number of inquiries on them. NCIC transactions increased from 95.4 million in 1977 to 207 million in 1987; in New York requests for record checks for noncriminal justice purposes jumped from about 100,000 in 1979 to an estimated 209,000 in 1984.[20]

Relative to many other justice programs, intermediate punishments currently affect only a handful of people. At the end of 1985, out of a total of 94,461 probationers in Georgia, 1,569 convicted offenders were on IPS.[21] New Jersey had an approximate caseload of 350, of 48,466 probationers.[22] But the potential for broad impact is there. IPS doesn't require expensive construction; electronic monitors are cheap and efficient, if the technological bugs can be worked out. Most important, the approaches taken by these new programs can be transferred to regular probation, the status of almost two-thirds of the correctional caseload of the country. Intermediate punishments can become cheap alternatives to putting failed probationers in prison, or be adopted as simply an intensification of the standard probation program. Every probation official interviewed for this book thought this latter prospect likely. Furthermore, the popularity of intensive probation and electronic monitoring rests at least as much on their promise of greater control over minor offenders as on their low cost—and far more than on a reform orientation that sees such programs as more humane than prison.

I have noted that observation programs, by their nature, are discreet rather than blatant in operation. They are also usually undertaken discreetly, with a good deal of subgovernmental initiative and a minumum of public attention given to their development. Observation is often begun as an experiment or a narrowly focused effort but becomes routine without examination of its impacts. In the process—not generally an open one— observation expands to take in many who do not share the characteristics of the original targets. At the extreme is the FBI's counterintelligence program (COINTELPRO), which started with the Communist party in 1956, added many dissident groups during the 1960s, and ended by destabilizing hundreds of organizations exercising their legal rights to protest racial segregation and U.S. foreign policy.[23] Less dramatic examples also confirm the pattern of surveillance that expands boundaries defined by officials not generally held to public account. This tendency seems likely to drive the growth of both criminal recordkeeping and intermediate punishments.

I assume that at least some readers will be sympathetic to the idea that the get-tough program—greater severity of punishment and narrowed rights for defendants—does not reduce crime, threatens cherished liberties, and further marginalizes the poor. Many of those—and presumably all who do not share my conclusions about the more punitive policies—will nonetheless be skeptical of my concern about the broadening of coercive control, the emphasis on observation that permeates all aspects of the justice process. They will argue that it's a good thing if people are made to behave as though someone is watching at all times, that tracking people through computerized records or community sanctions is a relatively benign way of reinforcing moral behavior. But state surveillance at the end of the twentieth century has little in common with the social control of the nosy neighbor that contributed to public order at its start. The next two chapters will illustrate some of the important differences.

4

•

THE ELECTRONIC PANOPTICON

The mighty, irresistible current of world-wide, cosmic forces, have [sic] created the necessity and impetus for the inception and growth of an organization which will serve to centralize and crystallize the efforts of those who would meet the exigencies of our changing times by a pooling of all the wisdom and power of the guardians of civilization, the protectors of Society.

● J. Edgar Hoover, 1925

As we are forced more and more each day to leave documentary fingerprints and footprints behind us, and as these are increasingly put into storage systems capable of computer retrieval, government may be able to acquire a power-through-data position that armies of government investigators could not create in past eras.

● Alan Westin, *Privacy and Freedom*, 1967

We used to have a lot of people that maybe were having some trouble outside and had come up here to get away from it all. We didn't know who we were dealing with a lot of times, because we didn't have the communications available. But when we received new communications technology, it pretty much opened us up to current information on everybody.

● Art English, commissioner, Alaska Department
of Public Safety, 1988

DURING THE SPRING OF 1984 Anthony Alvarado, chancellor of the New York City public school system, resigned his post as the result of an investigation into "financial improprieties."[1] Several months later day care center workers in the Bronx were arrested for sexually abusing children in their charge.[2] Late in the year a Boston school bus driver was arrested for possession of marijuana and heroin.[3] These incidents had much in common. In each case the principals had been entrusted, directly or indirectly, with the care of children. Charges against them attracted considerable public and media attention. And in each instance the official in charge—president of the Board of Education, mayor of New York City, Boston school superintendent—

called immediately for checks of the criminal histories of all employees performing functions like those of the identified wrongdoers, regardless of whether they were suspected of any misconduct.

Background checks are, of course, routine for job-seekers and people seeking licenses of various kinds. Especially for jobs involving the public trust or necessitating the handling of confidential materials, we accept the intrusion into privacy that results from close scrutiny of past and present activities, including, in some circumstances, the review of criminal records. In recent years, however, the range of positions that require a check of criminal histories has expanded enormously. In addition, the circumstances that trigger record reviews for both job applicants and current employees have become more numerous. A single, dreadful crime, highlighted by the media and accompanied by political and public outrage, sweeps innocent and guilty alike into an investigation that in turn leads to permanent policies and procedures imposed to prevent a repetition of the dreadful incident. Technically this dynamic is facilitated by computer technology that efficiently collects and maintains data and disseminates them almost instantly. Politically, it is legitimated by universal concerns like the safety of children and by a growing willingness to rely on law enforcement surveillance as substitute for more informal social controls.

Criminal histories are not the only sort of records that have become primary instruments for maintaining social order. Police making a spur-of-the-moment arrest are, in fact, more likely to have recourse to computerized warrant files—records of outstanding warrants for arrest for anything from murder to failure to pay a fine for a dog off the leash. A quick search of state (and sometimes federal) "hot files" on stolen cars, traffic violations, and wanted persons is a routine part of the traffic stop in the 1980s. As with the use of criminal histories, record checks often go beyond those actually suspected of wrongdoing; the license plates of every car parked near a restaurant frequented by the mafia, for instance, may be checked as officers cruise by.[4] Computerized recordkeeping has enabled a strange inversion of usual investigative practice; instead of starting with an event and a suspect and hunting for clues, the officer often starts with a fragment of information—a license plate number, or a name and date of birth—to which he or she hopes to attach an event or suspect. It doesn't have the intrigue of the whodunit, but it gives law enforcement a lot of business.

Indeed, the collection, combination and dissemination of computerized criminal justice records at all levels of government is a major growth activity of criminal justice. The past twenty years have seen the creation, through electronic storage and linkage of local and state records with each other and with the FBI's National Crime Information Center, of a gigantic national database of hot files and criminal histories. (I use the latter term with reservation because it refers to records of no more than an arrest as well as to those that include convictions. It is, however, the standard nomenclature for the rap sheets that contain identifying information and chronological accounts of a person's contacts with police, courts, and corrections.) While these files are stored in literally thousands of separate record systems, it is not inaccurate to think of them also as parts of a single national system, since electronic message-switching makes linkage so easy.

In addition to the hot files and criminal histories that make up the emerging national system, there are other kinds of criminal records: investigative and intelligence files. While both contain the leads and hunches a law enforcement investigator must develop in crimefighting, their purposes are different.

Investigative data are compiled for the relatively narrow purpose of identifying the person who committed a particular crime or otherwise solving the crime. Intelligence information, by contrast, is compiled for the rather broad purpose of identifying a particular individual, or, more often, a group of individuals thought likely to commit crimes in the future.[5]

These files necessarily include personal information on individuals that is sensitive, may be inaccurate, and, if publicly known, would be at least stigmatizing. For these reasons—and because of revelations in the early 1970s about using criminal intelligence operations as a cover for surveillance of political dissidence—investigative and intelligence records have not generally been shared electronically. Few insurmountable legal barriers exist, however, and tolerance for relatively unfettered intelligence-gathering was high in the law-and-order 1980s.[6] Computerized dissemination of investigative information is on the rise and can be expected to become, in a limited way, part of the national criminal records system.

This chapter outlines these developments as a little-noted aspect of the expansion of criminal justice control in the era of the justice juggernaut. It argues that, while modern computer technology could be brought to bear on the crime problems that most concern us, it is instead being used on a sweeping scale that includes intrusive forms of data surveillance for trivial matters. While automated records systems have certainly put a few dangerous criminals out of commission, the principal outcomes of building a gigantic national criminal records system have little to do with crime control in general. Millions of people who are not the criminals we fear are subjected to the unregulated use of damaging—and often inaccurate—personal information. In addition, efforts to decentralize computerized criminal histories and warrants, and thereby avoid the concentration of police power that threatens democracy, have failed. These failures attest to both the power of organizational imperatives in law enforcement and the ease with which computer networking can be put in their service.

The problems detailed in this chapter have serious implications for the privacy and due process rights of individuals. But the effects of the national criminal records system may go even farther. The second critical danger is that in the breadth of its reach it becomes a tool of discipline more generalized than the democratic ideal of targeted, publicly accountable administration of justice. Michel Foucault's use of Jeremy Bentham's model prison as image of the "machinery of power" is apt here.[7] Bentham's Panopticon was a circular prison with individual cells around a central tower so that a single warden could observe the movements of all inmates at all times. With the national computerized system the entire function of crime control, not just the prison, becomes a "panoptic schema," with the record a surrogate for the inmate and all of law enforcement as warden. Such an image has no boundaries; the warden becomes boss and landlord and banker. And then our fundamental autonomy is compromised; we are all enclosed in an electronic panopticon.

A BRIEF HISTORY OF COMPUTERIZED RECORDKEEPING

Early police records could not have been effective crimefighting tools. Through the nineteenth century they were anecdotal narratives, as likely to glorify the exploits of the pursuing officer as to chronicle a subject's criminal background and present conduct. Daguerreotypes, sometimes posted in rogues' galleries, were not very reliable identifiers. Records were maintained at the neighborhood level and shared only informally from department to department.[8]

From the late nineteenth century on, advances in recordkeeping have been part of the developing "professionalism" of police work. At first the impetus was external; Progressive Era reformers like Theodore Roosevelt, who was president of the New York City Board of Police Commissioners from 1895–1897, were concerned with inefficiency and corruption among urban police.[9] But soon the law enforcement community generated its own police training and datakeeping reforms. In 1896 the newly-formed International Association of Chiefs of Police and organizations of state police chiefs created a private criminal identification bureau with individual files which it then turned over, in 1921, to the new Bureau of Investigation established by the young J. Edgar Hoover. At about the same time many of the larger states set up identification bureaus to aid the interstate exchange of information on criminals.[10]

What began as a movement for administrative efficiency was soon used to ensure employee loyalty and political security. In the 1930s the Veterans' Administration and the Civilian Conservation Corps fingerprinted everyone who participated in their programs. When World War II began, the FBI checked fingerprints for industrial employers with defense contracts as well as for the War Department and the armed forces. In the latter months of 1942 alone, 12 million prints were analyzed. This practice, originally incidental to the FBI's expanded wartime jurisdiction, carried over to the Cold War years and was, in fact, expanded; in 1947 President Truman required criminal record checks for every person employed in the federal government.[11]

The surge of government and business activity after World War II sowed the seeds of both the crime wave of the 1960s and the instruments, electronic and bureaucratic, applied to its control. Inequality of earnings rose steadily from 1948 to the mid-1960s, and the segmentation of the labor market into primary and secondary jobs—the former well-paid and firmly fixed on a career ladder, the latter unskilled and leading nowhere—increased.[12] Particularly hard hit were black workers, whose migration north coincided with substantial movement of manufacturing jobs to the Sunbelt. Within that group young males, who commit a disproportionate amount of street crime, lost the most ground. Unemployment rates for black teenagers, which were only slightly higher than those for whites in the early

1950s, shot up toward the end of the decade and after 1965 became double those of whites. Most of the jobs available to these workers were low-wage, unstable and unrewarding.[13] While a direct correspondence between unemployment and crime cannot be presumed, sociologist Elliott Currie is surely right to conclude that "whether work can avert crime, in short, depends on whether it is part of a larger process through which the young are gradually integrated into a productive and valued role in a larger community."[14] The opportunities for inclusion in such a process were deteriorating decisively for many already disadvantaged people.

At the same time the computer revolution was brewing. Automated data processing, which had been used primarily in the military, could now be efficiently employed in business and in hardware-oriented government activities like the space program. By the early 1960s the focus expanded still farther. Why couldn't computers be used to deliver health care, manage public education, fight crime? There was little soul-searching about the policy implications of making information on individuals infinitely preservable and portable.[15] A new breed of liberals in the federal government was eager, as President Kennedy put it in his Yale commencement speech of 1962, "to face technical problems without ideological preconceptions."[16] For them the crime problem was not only a threat to domestic tranquility; it was a growth opportunity.

As the federal planners saw it, the challenge of modern criminality could be met only with a flexing of national muscle. Over and over, reports of the President's Commission on Law Enforcement and Criminal Justice formed in 1965 emphasized the need for supplementing traditional state and local crime control activities with federal research, federal experiments, and federal money. (This emphasis reflected more than concern with crime. It was also a response to national anxieties about demands for social change—the civil rights movement, urban riots, political dissent, the embrace of counterculture. These themes are dealt with in greater detail in Chapter 6.) Federal coordination could best be achieved by such Commission proposals as the creation of "a central computerized office into which each federal agency would feed all of its organized crime intelligence."[17] The Commission's Task Force on Science and Technology went farther, recommending "an integrated national information system" for courts and corrections, as well as police, a computerized network that would ultimately link law enforcement activities of all kinds at all levels of government.[18] Congress fell into line by passing the Omnibus Crime Control and Safe Streets Act of 1968, thereby creating the Law Enforcement Assistance Administration, which, before its demise in 1980, would dole out over $7 billion in federal grants.[19]

Nationalizing the war on crime ensured the growth and development of the electronic panopticon. LEAA's ambitions for a nationwide criminal history records system quickly became a principal theme of the agency's program. Although California and a few municipalities had begun to automate their criminal history data bases before the birth of LEAA, that agency's money financed the great leap forward. By mid-1975 over 500 state and local systems were being put online, most of them partially or wholly funded by LEAA.[20] To link up the state systems, LEAA also funded the National Law Enforcement Telecommunications System (NLETS), a sort of electronic switchboard that maintains no files but sends queries and responses. And starting in 1975, the agency began to support regional networks for interstate sharing of criminal intelligence, information developed on suspected organized crime groups, narcotics traffickers, and white-collar frauds.[21]

The particular balance of national and decentralized control over the records was determined by a fierce bureaucratic battle between LEAA and the FBI over the development of a national system of computerized criminal histories.[22] At stake were traditional assumptions about the primacy of local control in law enforcement, the dominance of the FBI in collecting crime statistics, and the status that goes with control over large amounts of federal grant money. Although LEAA won some of the battles, the FBI won the war.

In its first year of operation LEAA invested $600,000, its largest discretionary grant, in a six-state prototype of a computerized criminal history information system that would link records held in Arizona, California, Maryland, Michigan, Minnesota, and New York by means of a central, national index. But the plan became mired in technical and political problems almost from the start. It proved nearly impossible to bring together within a state disparate data on a person's contacts with the four main branches of criminal justice—police, prosecution, courts, and corrections—and then make of them a meaningful and comprehensive picture comparable to what was maintained in another state. And without fingerprints, which could not yet be transmitted by computer, rap sheets provided only tentative identification of an offender. (Again, the term "offender" is used advisedly, since records might include arrests only.) A year after the end of the first test of the prototype, an article in *Datamation* magazine concluded, "SEARCH [the federal contractor for the project] met its demonstration objectives from a conceptual point of view, but did not achieve much operational success, because of design compromises, lack of updating capability for the central index and failure to develop record formats acceptable to all users."[23]

The development of LEAA's model of a decentralized criminal history system was also impeded by resistance and competition from the FBI. In the late 1950s the FBI had automated its file of career criminals. Then in 1967 it created the National Crime Information Center, with its hot files on wanted persons, stolen vehicles and guns, missing persons, and securities. Now it too planned a national computerized criminal history system, but with the complete records—not just an index to state-held data—maintained in Washington. At first Hoover seems to have figured that LEAA would simply go away if ignored. The FBI refused to maintain the central index for the prototype system LEAA was funding. Its public position was that taking on the task would unduly increase the Bureau's workload, but what is more likely is that Hoover did not like the decentralized control contemplated and reasoned that no comprehenisive criminal history system (that would compete with what he had in mind) could be constructed without FBI help.

But LEAA had both money and zeal. As plans for its network developed, including proposed privacy and security regulations that were an anathema to the FBI, officials at the Bureau worried that LEAA was becoming a threat to its leadership in law enforcement. Backed by the politically influential International Association of Chiefs of Police and arguing that the LEAA plan would duplicate work the FBI had already done, Hoover went to work on John Mitchell, Nixon's Attorney General, to approve the FBI's alternative plan for a national automated criminal history system that would maintain complete files in NCIC. Ignoring an Office of Management and Budget (OMB) study that he himself had commissioned—a report that favored a system like that of the prototype and praised the LEAA/SEARCH plan as "an example of how the 'New Federalism' can work"— Mitchell decided in favor of the FBI. In December 1970 he awarded it the exclusive authority to develop a nationwide criminal history file—and $1.3 million of LEAA funds with which to get started. In 1971 the Bureau began to store automated rap sheets obtained from several states in the new computerized criminal history file of the NCIC.

This development aroused some civil liberties qualms. The FBI system which the Attorney General had endorsed looked to some like an instrument of the police state. Where the core concept of the LEAA/SEARCH project was interstate criminal history exchange, the NCIC computerized criminal history file was centralized management of a national data bank. Where the LEAA/SEARCH plan called for control of the system by an independent board of state participants, the FBI would control its own system by appointing an Advisory Policy Board whose members served at the pleasure of the FBI Director. LEAA/SEARCH had set up a committee to recommend policies to protect security and privacy in a national criminal history information system. Its draft report, which contained strong support for limiting data in the system to matters of public record, provided access only to criminal justice agencies, and recognized a citizen's right to inspect and challenge his or her own records was anathema to the FBI; one NCIC official wrote to a SEARCH committee member, "There are many objectionable statements, assumptions, and conclusions throughout the report. . . . 'Rights' to individual privacy should be considered always in the context of their reasonableness."[24]

Initial expressions of civil libertarian concern were heartfelt but ineffective. In 1971 U.S. District Court Judge Gerhard A. Gesell warned, in *Menard v. Mitchell*, that "Control of the data [supplied by states to the FBI] will be made more difficult and opportunities for improper use will increase with the development of centralized state information centers to be linked by computer to the Bureau," but then concluded that he could not prohibit the dissemination of criminal records held by the Bureau to employers.[25] A 1973 report of the National Lawyers' Commitee for Civil Rights Under Law complained, "Neither the FBI nor LEAA, the two agencies of the Justice Department with the resources or powers to impose regulatory controls, has developed adequate safeguards for the fast-growing computer files on criminal offenders."[26] The report was largely ignored.

Although logistical problems with data collection, turf conflicts between federal agencies, and civil libertarian quibbles slowed the progress of the central link of a national criminal history system, computerized criminal justice information systems were springing up at lower governmental levels all over the country. Large states like New York and Pennsylvania lined up eagerly at the LEAA spigot. By 1977 thirty-three states (including the District of Columbia and Puerto Rico) had received approximately $37.5 million from the agency's Comprehensive Data Systems program for their collection of computerized criminal histories, and many more millions had come from the block grants that LEAA made to the states.[27] Many, like the Police Information Network of Alameda County and the Kansas City Alert System, were local. Aided by LEAA, police departments like New York and Los Angeles computerized more than 1 million criminal history records each by the end of the decade. And 30,000 terminals around the country were linked to the FBI's NCIC, where 6.5 million records—both hot files and criminal histories—were stored.[28]

The contest between the FBI and LEAA was not over. The FBI's victory in the contest over who would control the national criminal history system proved shortlived and hollow. During the next two years members of Congress, law professors, and civil liberties groups constantly criticised the NCIC file of criminal histories for its perceived threats to privacy. Directors of state criminal justice planning agencies (not coincidentally funded by LEAA and advised by SEARCH on the conversion of records to NCIC standards) alleged that the centralized system would bypass state interests and privacy standards.[29] Many states turned out to be unwilling or unable to spend the money to get on line, and some were unwilling to join the system until privacy safeguards were improved. The General Accounting Office criticized the NCIC's file for permitting dissemination of arrest information without showing whether it resulted in a conviction and found that most requests for information from the file were not based on crime control needs.[30]

The FBI became increasingly sensitive to these attacks during the mid-1970s. Hoover had died in 1972, and the Bureau was under close scrutiny following disclosure of widespread political surveillance, from the COINTELPRO campaign of the 1950s and 1960s to the Stop Index of the early 1970s, which tracked thousands of individuals exercising their lawful right to dissent.[31] In addition, the Bureau was plagued by the states' reluctance to participate in its criminal history system—by 1977 there were only eleven states with 1 million records on line—and by the management headaches of building a fifty-state data bank.

The FBI scrapped its original plan. Instead of maintaining all those criminal histories, it was now willing to adopt a system that looked much like the earlier LEAA/SEARCH concept, with the FBI providing for all single-state offenders (70% of the total) a central index that would direct inquirers to criminal history records held in state repositories. This concept eventually prevailed, and at the end of the decade a "test" was begun of what has turned into the Triple-I. Beat officers and investigators in the 64,000 criminal justice agencies that are NCIC users can inquire of the Triple-I (often through a clerk) to find out whether an arrest record on someone exists in another state, what the charges have been, and which state holds the full records. If the inquirer wishes to know more, he or she can then use the electronic switchboard, NLETS, to obtain the full record. Although Triple-I is theoretically controlled by the participating states, with an NCIC Advisory Policy Board made up of state representatives of law enforcement, the FBI is very much at the nerve center of the national criminal history system.

The FBI lost on another count, too, at least in the short run. Unwilling to cede control of the day-to-day record exchanges between states, the FBI sought to monitor them. By getting access to NLETS, which sends messages from one state to another or between law enforcement agencies within a state, the Bureau could have the benefits of a national criminal history system without its burdens; every exchange of criminal history information would then automatically pass through the FBI computer (and could then be flagged and its content noted if of interest). The Bureau had squabbled with Congress and LEAA throughout the 1970s over "message switching," the term for the electronic process of receiving, storing and sending information between databases. LEAA, the agency that controlled NLETS funding, had opposed FBI message switching out of concern for "(a) the development of a 'Big Brother' system; (b) reduced state input and control over security, confidentiality and use of state-originated data; and (c) dangers resulting from using non-updated, and hence inaccurate, centrally maintained rap sheets."[32] Congressional critics had maintained that message switching should not be allowed until criminal justice privacy legislation could regulate it; it turned out to be an endless wait. Then, in 1977, members of the House Committee on the Judiciary once again refused to grant the FBI's request and ordered the federal Office of Technology Assessment to conduct what turned out to be a highly critical evaluation of NCIC.

Although rejection of the message-switching proposal was a bitter pill for the FBI, it was sweetened by the approval, a year later, of a "communications controller" to improve the efficiency and reliability of the NCIC computer—and to provide it with message-switching capability, just in case.

LEAA was not in a position to take advantage of the FBI's capitulation on the mode and method of providing criminal histories nationwide. Throughout the 1970s it too was the target of abundant criticism from journalists, politicians, and agency evaluators of various kinds. Even its own administrators attacked it; in 1970 its first director Charles Rogovin told a Congressional committee, shortly after resigning, that the agency was "a gigantic subsidy program making little contribution to the improvement of criminal justice administration."[33] In the ensuing years Congressional reports, Justice Department studies, and independent evaluation echoed Rogovin's view. Critics alleged that the agency's management was chaotic—it had ten chiefs in eleven years and was in a perpetual state of reorganization—and that priorities were unclear and strategies incoherent. Furthermore, crime rates were going up, and, unfair or not, LEAA had to answer for that. The directors of its state planning agency issued a report in 1976 that reluctantly concluded, "Wholesale and lasting crime reduction through limited planning efforts and financial assistance confined solely to the criminal justice system is an unrealistic expectation."[34] Finally, after a decade of LEAA as the goose that laid many golden eggs for local law enforcement, a General Accounting Office review concluded, "At this time it would not be possible for GAO—or any other group, for that matter—to determine whether the LEAA program, overall, has had any measurable impact upon preventing, controlling, and/or reducing crime and delinquency; or improving the performance of the criminal justice system."[35]

In an era of high inflation and budget crunch, an agency with such bad press was doomed. Congress dug in its heels and cut the LEAA budget from $905 million in 1975 to $647 million in 1978, after which the agency was restructured in 1979 and "zeroed out" in 1980.[36] But even as the major federal funding agency for criminal justice slipped into decline, its dual legacy was apparent. As the patron saint of the technological revolution in law enforcement, it had elevated the local police officer into Supercop by making state and national collections of hot files and criminal history records instantly available. And, while there were a few naysayers who doubted the crime control efficacy of criminal history networks or worried about their intrusions on privacy, the idea of a national criminal justice information system, fed by thousands of local and state databases, many of them linked to one another, had gained nearly universal acceptance in law enforcement.

DIMENSIONS OF THE PANOPTICON

Record Types and Volume

Computerized criminal justice recordkeeping has grown to immense proportions in the U.S. since the early 1970s. In 1971 the National Crime Information Center contained almost 2.5 million records; in late 1988 (before Triple-I was transferred to the Identification Division) it stored or indexed a little over 20 million, about 12 million in the Triple-I and most of the rest in hot files. For October 1988, NCIC handled a daily average of almost 800,000 transactions, 94 percent of them inquiries, 92 percent of those inquiries of the wanted persons and stolen vehicles files (for outstanding warrants).[37] The other FBI source of computerized criminal records, the Automated Identification System (AIS) in the Identification Division, launched in 1973, contained over 10 million criminal history records and, as of March 1986, was growing by 15,000 records per week.[38] It is not an on-line system; that is, it receives and sends records by mail (with an exception that will be discussed shortly).

Growth is even greater at the state level. In the last twenty years central repositories of criminal history record information in all fifty states "have been the focus of a data-gathering effort more massive and more coordinated than any other in criminal justice."[39] Forty-four states that responded to a 1985 survey reported holding an estimated 35 million records (manual and automated) in their central repositories. Thirty-five of the responding states had at least partially automated their records system, and three others had plans to do so.[40] These numbers do not include warrant files, which are used more frequently than criminal histories; every state has its own warrants system, as do many metropolitan areas or urban counties.

The majority of these records are used for criminal justice

purposes, such as arrests, bail-setting, and sentencing. But the fastest-growing area of use is employment and licensing.[41] In states like California and Pennsylvania, more than half of criminal history record requests are for noncriminal justice uses.[42] In some states criminal histories are more widely available, to landlords and financial institutions, for example, and in a few "open record states" like Florida and Wisconsin, anyone who goes to the courthouse and pays a modest fee can obtain a full record.[43]

Investigative records, which consist of information on suspects including identifiers (date of birth, physical characteristics, vehicle numbers), associates, and activities, are considered more sensitive than individual records of official acts like warrants and criminal histories. They are the raw material of an invesigator's work, necessarily based as much on conjecture as on fact. They represent what law enforcement is learning about a suspect *before* an officer can justify an arrest by the standard of probable cause that a crime has been committed.

Until recently these records have generally either not been automated or were not on line. There are exceptions, including the NCIC's Secret Service Protective File. Since 1972 Colorado has had an on-line Persons Index. In addition to information on those for whom a warrant has been issued, it includes suspects, victims, missing persons, probationers, parolees, and, to use the words of one official there, "anyone we want to talk to."[44] Several other states have a similar file that is not on line but is accessible to law enforcement representatives with a phone call. Often, as in New York, it is maintained by the state police. Some files that contain public information are organized in such a way as to be primarily useful for identifying suspects. Arizona law, for example, requires all those ever convicted of a sexual offense (indecent exposure, adultery and "crime against nature" as well as assault and sexual expoitation of a minor) to register with the local sheriff when they move into an Arizona county.[45] The Sex Offender Registration Tracking Database is an on-line file that contains information provided by this registration and presumably serves as a suspect file when sexual crimes are committed.

Some states are hoping to automate investigative information on suspects for serious violent crimes and drug trafficking and put those records (or indexes to them) on line, making them available—sometimes automatically, without a separate inquiry— to someone who calls up a warrant file or criminal history. (In

February 1989 FBI Director William Sessions rejected a similar proposal for NCIC after objection from a Congressional committee and civil liberties groups.[46] If requests for information in criminal history files flag investigative records or indexes, they too become part of the national system.

Intelligence records are closely related to investigative files, in that they contain information that is not the record of an official act of police, courts, or corrections. But they reach into a still more preliminary, and therefore ambiguous, stage of law enforcement activity, in which the information is "compiled in an effort to anticipate, prevent, or monitor possible criminal activity."[47] California defines the criminal intelligence file as "stored information on the activities and associations of individuals and groups known or suspected to be involved in criminal acts or in the threatening, planning, organizing, or financing of criminal acts." The file may also include information on groups that are "operated, controlled, financed, infiltrated or illegally used by crime figures."[48] Since the mid-1970s many states and some large cities have instituted specialized police units that maintain criminal intelligence files, some of them automated. While these files are generally not on-line, most are quickly available to law enforcement by phone and can provide suspect information. Illinois, for example, has no on-line suspect files, but its intelligence files on gangs, organized crime groups, activities or organizations that are of law enforcement interest but aren't under investigation for a specific crime that has already occurred can be used to retrieve suspects, as can the federal intelligence files on serial murders. Los Angeles has a gang file reputed to contain 30,000 names.[49] The seven federally-funded multistate regional intelligence projects collect and computerize information on suspected organized crime, white collar frauds, and drug trafficking; they make it available by phone to law enforcement investigators in their geographic areas, who often retrieve the information by suspect.

Users

As the reach of information collection broadens, so does authorization of access to records. Virtually everywhere, law enforcement agencies have access to records held in local, state, and national repositories without reservation. This does not mean that inquiry of the databases is made for the same reasons by all law enforcement users. The variations in use illustrate different kinds of informal criminal justice policymaking by officers and investigators (and sometimes by the clerks who process their communications with the data).[50]

There is a great variety of local and state systems available to even middle-sized police departments, files for stolen boats and firearms and victims as well as the most-used warrants and stolen vehicle files. In general, they are fragmented, individual systems created to service specific needs; only rarely are they fully cross-referenced, although there are some situations in which records are flagged so that the inquirer is encouraged to look further. In general, beat officers use few of these resources. They routinely make inquiries only to the local warrant system and state motor vehicle records, and the decision to make an inquiry is completely discretionary, most likely to be exercised if the officer observes "suspicious behavior" like nervousness of a car's occupants or a car stopped by the side of a dark road. Many officers don't even know how or why they might use criminal history files, either within the state or through Triple-I. State criminal histories may be checked (whether by terminal or, more often, through a dispatcher or clerk) only when the officer is trying to decide whether to give someone a citation or take that person in to be booked, or when the officer is going out to arrest someone for a serious offense. In the latter situation the criminal history check is often conducted out of a concern for officer safety, not to provide additional information on which to base the arrest. Officers use record checks for several different purposes. One purpose is the "fishing expedition," in which officers will, for example, hunt for an outstanding warrant for failure to pay parking tickets so they have a justification for bringing in someone they think is a drug dealer or has had one drink too many.

Investigators, usually detectives or sergeants, are most likely to inquire of the criminal histories, suspect files, and intelligence databases. In the most specialized units the user is not content with the index record held in the Triple-I, the rap sheet is carefully examined, and evidence is pieced together before an arrest is made. But in routine cases, the opposite may be true: the officer checks the state criminal history summarily and may go no farther than the NCIC index record and never ascertain the details of charges in other states or even that they resulted in conviction. Police use of records testifies to the working presumption of guilt that often prevails in police culture.

Non-criminal justice use of criminal histories, generally by employers and licensing agencies, is growing rapidly. Most striking in light of the traditional image of law enforcement federalism is that federal law may override state privacy standards to authorize the screening by federal agencies of state and local records for employment purposes. Recent federal legislation allows the Department of Defense, the CIA, the Office of Personnel Management, and the FBI access to local records for security clearances, which are now held by 4 million people.[51] Another federal statute denies some social service grant funds to states that do not permit access to criminal histories of child care workers.[52] This legislation also illustrates the growing tendency to require record checks for menial as well as skilled and high security occupations.

New York illustrates the trend toward increasingly open records. That state allows or requires government agencies, schools, day care programs, museums, hospitals, banks, and law enforcement agencies, among others, to screen criminal records for employment purposes. Those who seek licenses for such enterprises as games of chance, guns, check-cashing operations, securities firms, funeral homes, and insurance adjustors are screened. In all of these cases, nonconviction data may be disseminated; that is, information about arrests that are pending or charges that were dismissed or for which the defendant was acquitted. Requests for record checks for non-criminal justice purposes jumped from about 100,000 in 1979 to an estimated 209,000 in 1984.

California makes even greater use of record checks for employment and licensing. Screening is authorized for the following occupations, among others: auto mechanic, barber, cosmetologist, optometrist, liquor store owner, shorthand reporter, pest control employee, TV repair person, real estate broker, notary public. If a "compelling need" is demonstrated, records may also be released to out-of-state district attorneys; to the Inspectors General of most federal agencies with any regulatory powers; to the Postal Service and the Veterans Administration; to state hospital officers; to security officers for a number of state and local agencies; and to others. As of 1983, more than 3.7 million state records had been reviewed for employment purposes. Access has gone from public agencies to youth-serving organizations to banks; as Fred Wynbrandt, a California Department of Justice official and former head of the NCIC Advisory Policy Board, says, "It just crept and crept."

Linkages

The reach of the national and local records systems and the political problems they pose can be analyzed only if the variety of linkages among them is well understood. Consider, for instance, one way in which the FBI's two theoretically separate computerized criminal history files are combined. The FBI's Identification Division includes a partially automated criminal file (AIS), which holds fingerprint cards and criminal histories on 25 million people, sent to it from the states. And NCIC, the FBI's computerized criminal justice information clearinghouse, contains Triple-I, the locator for about 12 million criminal histories stored in twenty states. The Identification Division file is directly available to law enforcement agencies and authorized employers and licensing agencies only by mail, and the complete records indexed by Triple-I are supposed to be exchanged between states only through NLETS, in order to maintain local control. But NCIC now accesses AIS in order to respond electronically to NCIC users when they request criminal histories from the thirty states that do not participate in the Triple-I. So some of the information that state and local law enforcement could not get quickly from the Identification Division can now be accessed almost instantly through Triple-I. And the FBI is running state records through its computer, effectively message-switching, doing indirectly what it was prohibited from doing directly by Congress and the Attorney General in the mid-1970s.

Other connections of FBI and local files are being made. An inquirer to Triple-I is now notified not only about what state has a complete criminal history on the record subject but also about any outstanding warrant information the FBI may hold.[53] The developing technology of electronic fingerprint image comparison will soon enable California, New York, and the FBI to match a job applicant's fingerprint or a "cold print" found at the scene of a crime with computerized fingerprint files that come from all over the country and are held in the Identification Division.

SOME PROBLEMS OF THE SYSTEM

Defenders of the national criminal records system generally justify its vast reach—the range of its subjects, the variety of data included in it, the increasingly easy access to it—by maintaining that it provides significant benefits in the war against crime. But those benefits are slight and could probably be obtained by a much smaller, more tightly controlled system. They are outweighed by serious deficiencies caused by inadequate regulation—errors and omissions in records, possibilities for abuse, excessive availability to non-criminal justice users—and by apparently epidemic expansionism.

Ineffective as Crime Control

For the criminal records system to reflect a proper balance between the state's legitimate interest in criminal law enforcement and the individual rights of record subjects, it must be shown to improve the quality of information that decisionmakers need to control crime, and to improve it for a significant portion of the cases that law enforcement could not otherwise resolve. The availability of warrant information from other states is theoretically very useful for assisting an arrest decision or aiding a police investigation, but only for a very limited range of situations. Most arrests are of local people on local matters, the large majority spur-of-the-moment. The experienced beat officer usually knows immediately which suspects are local and therefore doesn't want to be bothered with the time it takes to check more than the local warrant file.

The officer or investigator may know, furthermore, that many of the warrants in the national system contain erroneous identifying information, reflecting local mistakes. They may have been discharged locally but not removed from NCIC. In 1988 a Michigan man won a summary judgment and a $55,000 settlement in a lawsuit against the Los Angeles Police Department for four mistaken arrests in two states over fourteen months. The arrests resulted from the Department's failure to remove the plaintiff's name from the NCIC wanted persons file after it was discovered that a man who was wanted for murder had been using his lost birth certificate as identification.[54] The lack of fingerprint identification for most warrants also results in cases of mistaken identity. Finally, the file is not comprehensive, since contribution of warrants to the NCIC wanted persons file is totally voluntary and NCIC charges a fee for each warrant entered into the system. As a result of these problems, police tend to use NCIC warrants only when they are investigating a very serious crime or need an excuse to pick up someone they suspect of current crime but have no evidence on which to base prosecution. The availability of the information neither improves the reliability of decisions that would be made anyway nor provides a sound basis for making new ones; instead it justifies the broadest possible discretion by police, an outcome that transforms the stated objectives of the system.

With criminal histories the problem is similar. With the exception of interstate investigations of very serious crimes, police do not need a suspect's prior record in another state to make a local collar. The Triple-I is rarely used in routine law enforcement. When it is used, it is primarily to give an arresting officer notice that he or she may be dealing with a dangerous offender and should be well protected. And records obtained through Triple-I may be meaningless for most common needs. A judge's determination of what to take into account in sentencing, for instance, only becomes more complicated when the record from another jurisdiction is considered. Police standards vary greatly from state to state, even from city to city. "In Oakland [California], for a black male to have five or six arrests is unremarkable," says Kenneth Laudon, author of *The Dossier Society*, a comprehensive examination of the use of computerized criminal history records. "Busting them is part of controlling the streets."[55] And police don't usually need another state's files to conduct routine investigations; most offenders commit crimes in only one state.

Law enforcement officials, justifying large system expenditures, publicly cite dramatic examples of the one that didn't get away because of the computers' fancy footwork.[56] (Recent achievements are often traceable to the new computers that compare fingerprint images found at the scene of a crime to prints on file.) But privately they most often justify computerized criminal history records in terms of internal office efficiency, not as investigative tools for police or management information for judges. Laudon has concluded that any assertion that the billion dollars invested in reporting systems thus far is cost-effective in crime control terms is based only on "a wing and a prayer." "The empirical relationships are unproven, maybe irrelevant," he says.

Crime prevention, not capture or containment, is the issue when employers or licensing agencies use criminal records. Recent experience induces skepticism as to the cost effectiveness of records searches for ferreting out dangerous criminals. The results of criminal records checks on New York City current or perspective child care workers may be indicative. As of late 1985, record checks had been run on 21,778 people. One hundred fifty-two (.7%) were found to have records for such offenses as assault, robbery, drug offenses, or possession of a weapon; fourteen (.06%) were for sexual offenses (rape, sodomy, sexual abuse) and four (.02%) were for endangering the welfare of a child. Almost half of those with records were custodial staff, rarely even in sight of the children; many of the records were very old.[57] The seven people in the Bronx day care centers who actually committed the crimes that led to the screening requirement would not have been found if the system had gone into effect before the incidents of abuse; none of the seven had a criminal record of any kind.

Unregulated and Inaccurate

The U.S. state structure of multiple centers of power has advantages and disadvantages. Local responsibility for some functions maximizes participation and accountability, but local interests may promote inequality or repress fundamental rights. National power can impose uniform standards for distributing rights or benefits but may prove unresponsive or tyrannical. The emergence of the computerized national criminal records system reflects, among other things, tensions between the political tradition of local control of law enforcement and the greater efficiency and equity that national regulation of recordkeeping could provide. Although other Western democracies (Sweden, Great Britain, Canada, Germany) have central agencies charged with oversight of computerized data systems, that seems unlikely in the United States. Setting aside the costs of significant regulation, law enforcement officials maintain that federalism precludes a larger national regulatory role.[58] Yet without uniform standards to see that the system is not inaccurate or overinclusive, it manifests many of the disadvantages of both local and national control while providing few of the advantages of either.

In the early 1970s civil libertarians were concerned with this possibility. Senators, scholars, journalists, and a few law enforcement officials worried about the consequences for due process and the right to privacy of an essentially unregulated computerized criminal records system that could reach into any police precinct and would be accessible to employers and the military as well as law enforcement officials. They pointed out that such a system would, in the words of U.S. District Court Judge Gerard A. Gesell, "inhibit freedom to speak, to work, and to move about in this land."[59] Robert Gallati, then director of the New York State Identification and Intelligence System, testified in 1971 at Senator Sam Ervin's hearings on federal data banks that "there is an absence in American law of institutional procedures to protect against improper collection of information, storage of inadequate or false data, and intragovernmental use of information for farreaching decisions about individuals outside or inside the organization."[60]

The protestations of the early 1970s now seem merely ritualistic. Nothing more resulted than a meaningless exhortation to keep criminal histories private and secure and to use them for "lawful purposes," a stopgap measure awaiting more comprehensive legislative attention.[61] But as the scope and intrusiveness of data surveillance in criminal justice mushroomed, resistance to it dwindled. The Privacy Act of 1974, which establishes standards for personal records maintained by federal agencies and some federal contractors, excluded specific provision for law enforcement files "until such time as more comprehensive criminal justice legislation is passed."[62]

That time never came. Although hearings were held on half a dozen criminal justice privacy bills, none ever passed.[63] Finally, in 1975, LEAA issued administrative regulations requiring state and local systems receiving federal funding to establish procedures to ensure the accuracy and completeness of records. Revised a year later to meet the objections of law enforcement officials, the regulations are virtually toothless. They acknowledge, for example, that to maintain complete criminal history records is "administratively impractical . . . at the local level."[64] They do not even suggest that dissemination of records might be limted to law enforcement personnel, and states are not prohibited from sharing their criminal justice computers with non-law enforcement agencies. It is no wonder that a consultant study in 1977 found little compliance with the few existing regulations.[65]

State policies as a whole are not much more protective. All states have established central record repositories, and most expressly require that arrest data (including fingerprint impressions) be reported to them. But what may happen to data on subsequent actions by criminal justice agencies is not specified in detail in many states. Fewer than half, for example, require the reporting of court dispositions—convictions, dismissals, acquittals—to the central state criminal record repositories where virtually all arrests for felonies or serious misdemeanors are reported. Only thirteen states require the central repository to conduct an annual random audit of state and local records submitted to the system, and only eleven require the repository to audit its own records annually.[66] So it is not surprising that criminal records are full of mistakes. While there are probably fewer errors in computerized records than there were in manual files, mistakes have more impact now because they travel farther, are seen by more people, are copied and recopied, and have more uses. The national system is only as accurate as the local and state law enforcement records that constitute it.

One common problem is the incomplete criminal history record. The meaning of a particular record is unclear unless it indicates that the arrest ended in an acquittal, dismissal, conviction, or was simply not prosecuted. Even in the get-tough era, most felony arrests do not lead to convictions. A 1988 report by the U.S. Bureau of Justice Statistics looked at data from nine states concerning arrests for serious crimes and found a variation from 50 percent resulting in conviction in Ohio to 79 percent in Utah.[67] (This was a sizable increase from the previous report five years earlier.) In 1984 in eleven states only 55 percent of felony arrests for violent offenses, 66 percent for property offenses, and 54 percent for drug offenses led to conviction.[68]

Both state and federal criminal history files (computerized and manual) contain many arrests without dispositions. An Office of Technology Assessment study found, for example that only about two-thirds of a state's criminal history records, on the average, contained timely accounts of how the case was disposed of. Eight states reported that less than a quarter of their records were complete.[69] Officials at the California Bureau of Identification acknowledged the truth of an allegation in a 1984 law suit that 100,000 dispositions received during the previous year had not been added to the automated records. They admitted that fiscal problems keep them from monitoring disposition reporting at the local level, where judges often feel they have more important things to do than fill out forms for state agencies. While law enforcement officials say that problem has improved in the decade since data for the OTA study were collected, police investigators who inquire of the files regularly report that it is still common.

Incomplete criminal history records have significant consequences for the way record subjects are treated by law enforcement and by employers and licensing agencies. A police officer
who sees a record of arrests without dispositions will often presume that they led to conviction and act accordingly. This is
most likely to be a problem for young, urban, minority males
who may get picked up and have charges dismissed frequently
on minor matters. Without dispositions (and purges of minor
offenses after an interval), the records of these defendants may
make a restless adolescent look like a career criminal.

Employers seeing an arrest without a disposition are unlikely to take the risk that the job applicant is among the group
not convicted. Not surprisingly, several studies have found
that an arrest record has a negative effect on employment opportunity. Even an arrest without conviction is an obstacle to
employment.[70]

No systematic review has been done of how many or what
kinds of people have lost or been denied jobs as a result of records that failed to report a dismissal or acquittal. Anecdotal
evidence suggests that the impact is felt by professionals and
workers in a wide range of occupations. Two California teachers
successfully sued the state for disseminating to the education
licensing agency records that failed to show that criminal
charges brought against them had been dismissed. Their injury
included not only many months' delay in granting their teachers' licenses but dismissal by their local school boards from the
temporary jobs they had held.[71] Presumably most people injured by incomplete records do not go to court; two students who
were denied jobs because of inaccurate traffic offense reports
told me they no longer applied for jobs for which record checks
were likely. People with records in rural areas are probably most
vulnerable; rural courts are said to be slowest to record their
dispositions. Blacks may be more vulnerable than whites. Some
research has found that blacks are more likely to be released
after arrest, so the probablility that an incomplete record con-
ceals a dismissal may be higher than for whites.[72]

Error is not limited to criminal histories; it extends to other
types of files. The Michigan case referred to earlier is by no
means the only lawsuit that has arisen out of mistaken identification of a warrant subject. Plaintiffs in Louisiana, California, New York, and Massachusetts, to name a few, have sued
police for wrongful detention of up to four months.[73] The victim
is typically black or Hispanic, has a relatively common name,

and is picked up in a traffic offense or border check on the warrant of someone charged with a serious offense. Sometimes the problem is the failure to remove a warrant that was in error in the first place; a Boston plaintiff was jailed because the police had not corrected the report of a stolen car that had, in fact, been borrowed by a relative. FBI audits in 1985 revealed that at least 12,000 inaccurate or invalid reports on wanted persons alone are sent each day by state and local law enforcement agencies to the NCIC.[74] The Bureau also acknowledged an estimated 7,000 errors daily in the transmission of reports on stolen cars and license plates. (In 1988 an FBI official reported a 13.5 percent improvement in record quality on the second round of audits.[75]) Law enforcement officials are the first to admit that once these errors are made they are hard to correct. When Shirley Jones, a New Orleans woman who was taken from her home and small children and held overnight on a "wrong warrant" for welfare fraud, was finally released, a sheriff's deputy told her to change her name or she would face a repeat of the incident.[76] As anyone who has tried to get a credit record corrected knows, the computer does not always obey orders.

And the errors can multiply. When a victim of mistaken identity has been arrested, his or her name goes into the FBI's Triple-I (assuming that the crime charged is a felony and that the arresting state participates in the program) and the arrest record goes into the state repository, from which it may be sent to requesting law enforcement agencies in other states even if the mistake in the original warrant file was corrected. A court order—and, therefore, the time and expense of consultation with a lawyer—is usually required to alter the record, and even that does not correct the mistake in the other locations to which it has traveled. If a criminal history is released to an employer or licensing agency, there is no guarantee that it won't get into other hands and become untraceable.

Sometimes accuracy in computerized criminal history systems is less a question of competent management than of confidence in the face of modern technology. The computer will never know whether the person named on an outstanding warrant is the two-time murderer the record says he is or an unfortunate motorist whose name is the same or whose identification has been appropriated. Ordinary men and women trusting more in their own human judgments than in the infallibility of the data on the screen must ultimately interpret what they see before them. Lucas Guttentag, a lawyer for twenty-six mistaken identity victims who were detained in Los Angeles for up to twenty-six days, points out that one of his clients, a black male, was arrested on a warrant for a white man. He explained, "The police just abdicated their judgment to the computer." And the sheriff of New Orleans, commenting on a spate of "wrong warrants" cases, acknowledged on national television that "the benefit of the doubt may be given to the computer" in that split second when a police officer must decide whether to hold someone.[77]

Data quality is not the only operational problem of the system; abuse of record dissemination is another. Sometimes the prevention of crime becomes the justification for an illegal use of the system, such as getting access to Triple-I or state records for unauthorized employment checks. In Lousiana, for example, despite state legislation calling for "the privacy and security of information" contained in the state repository, it became common practice in New Orleans for employers needing an unauthorized record check to obtain it through personal contacts with people who had access to records in a law enforcement agency.[78]

Abuse may also stem from efforts to track possible political dissent. Revelations of law enforcement spying, though less common than in the 1970s, have surfaced in recent years, in local police units like the Public Disorder Intelligence Division in Los Angeles and in the FBI.[79] Personal financial gain is sometimes the motive for abuse of the files; criminal history system officials in California and New York recount anecdotes of information sold by police to political campaigns, disgruntled spouses, and landlords.

Centralized and Expansionist

Even if the system was more tightly regulated, it would contribute to the Foucaultian "machinery of power." Its basic character is all-encompassing and centralizing—brought about at least as much by the ease with which dispersed databases are turned into networks as by the direct exercise of authority. The dynamic operates at three levels: In an age in which information is power and more is almost always better, the overarching imperative for system expansion is very powerful. Our current predisposition for using state power to regulate personal behavior drives particular policy measures that spread the reach of the national computerized records system. As the number and type of computerized records mushrooms, along with the amount of data contained in them and ways of using those data, judgments about the persons and behaviors that are appropriate subjects for surveillance become less and less discriminating.[80] And as crime control becomes an increasingly tenuous justification for added increments of power, larger political priorities play more of a role.

The FBI's setbacks in trying to control criminal history records nationwide have proved to be only momentary, an illustration of the system's dynamic tendencies. In 1984 alone the Bureau made at least six significant proposals for either expanded access to or additional information for its NCIC files.[81] It also instituted a procedure whereby a criminal history search in Triple-I would trigger a notice to the inquirer of a record held in the wanted persons file, effectively combining records. The FBI has learned how to get information not only from the records but from traffic in the records. Any inquiry of an NCIC file that involves a federal employee is now flagged; the presumption is that the employing agency should know when anyone on its staff is arrested. And the FBI follows up on inquiries on federal informants, undercover officers, or participants in the federal witness protection program. As law enforcement watches citizens, the FBI watches those who are watching.

Recent proposals for new files to be added to NCIC illustrate the system's expansionary tendency. In 1983 the NCIC's Advisory Policy Board considered setting up several new files of investigative data, including a file on people not wanted for or suspected of a specific crime but thought by NCIC users to be involved with terrorism, organized crime or narcotics.[82] That file was not intended to include matters of public record like arrests or convictions but rather investigative information on people "known to be, believed to be, likely or may be" associated with a drug dealer, whether or not they were suspected of participating in or knowing of the dealer's illegal activities.[83] Although the FBI tabled that idea in response to Congressional concern and press attention, in 1988 the NCIC's Advisory Policy Board proposed a new way to do a very similar thing. NCIC would add a file for suspected drug traffickers that would enable a local investigator to trace any inquiry made of the NCIC around the country on a name in the file. Record subjects would not be people for whom the investigator had probable cause for an arrest—otherwise a warrant could be issued and they could be put in the wanted persons file and be arrested by any officer who picked them up—and the file might well contain innocent people (including undercover officers posing as drug dealers). In March 1989 FBI Director William Sessions rejected the proposed file.

The Bureau is very skilled at adapting to the doubts of those responsible for Congressional oversight of FBI files. In 1985 it postponed the testing of an inclusive new investigative file, the Economic Crime Index (ECI). Originally intended to become part of NCIC, it would have eventually made available to its 64,000 law enforcement user agencies the name, physical description, address, phone numbers, social security and license plate numbers, bank account numbers, and names of associates of people suspected of white collar crimes.[84] The FBI did not say what crimes it would be investigating, nor did they define the term "associates" or indicate what standard they would use for index entries. Presumably anyone who worked with a suspect could be included in the Index, and surely all family members and close friends. The House Subcommittee on Civil and Constitutional Rights balked at this, and the "test" of the file was delayed. In 1988, however, the file was approved by the new FBI Director, with some changes. It would not be part of NCIC (though NCIC users could enter information into it indirectly), and it would not include associates.[85]

The ECI proposal is related to another innovation in federal law enforcement that illustrates the proposition that centralized, federal control may supplement the law enforcement justification for the system with more general political imperatives. In April 1984 the four federal bank regulatory agencies and the Justice Department entered into an agreement to record suspicions of bank fraud in an FBI computer (not part of NCIC) to enable, among other things, the earliest possible Justice Department "assessment and evaluation."[86] This expansion of authority for bank fraud investigations gives federal law enforcement access to bank records before the depositors are even reasonably suspected of a crime. No evidentiary standard need be applied by the regulatory agencies when they make a referral, and the new system applies equally to suspicions of individual teller theft and massive frauds that may lead to a bank's collapse.[87] (In fact, the overwhelming majority of suspected frauds reported to the Justice Department in a test of its referral form were for what the Attorney General's Working Group considered the "smaller" crimes of suspected losses not involving bank insiders and worth less than $10,000.)

Fishing expeditions that involve the screening of child care workers and bank depositors will yield a catch of some sort. But record checks are surely less effective at reducing crime than careful noncriminal background assessments on job applicants and training that alerts day care administrators to spot abusive tendencies in employees. And greater regulatory vigilance in financial institutions would probably prevent more crime than giving the FBI access to bank records on the basis of the examiner's first hunch. After studying four major bank failures caused by insider fraud, the House Subcommittee on Commerce, Consumer, and Monetary Affairs concluded in 1984 that "in each of these failures, the appropriate Federal bank regulatory agency had ample advance warning of unsafe and unsound banking practices, particularly insider misconduct, prior to insolvency, but failed to take prompt and effective remedial action."[88]

EXPLAINING THE PANOPTICON

Several analytic perspectives are necessary to explore the expansionist dynamic and the failure to regulate, on the one side, and the lack of effective resistance to those tendencies, on the other. Pluralist political influence expressed through public concern about street crime provided a general license for developing more efficient law enforcement measures, but it does not explain the development of uncontrolled national data surveillance. Similarly, bureaucratic imperatives such as the "vigor to expand," interagency competition, and the availability of the LEAA goose's golden eggs, contributed to the expansion of the system, but did not determine its lack of regulation.

Neither of these perspectives tells us much about how government actors have used public concern and bureaucratic imperatives to bring us the electronic panopticon. For an understanding of policy strategy in the development of the criminal records system we must look to symbolic politics. Criminal justice entrepreneurs have been able to manipulate traditional law enforcement symbols of public protection, modern visions of the unmitigated good of unlimited information, and broader images of the U.S. political system to support a virtually unregulated, centralized crime information system. By contrast, system opponents—generally civil libertarians—have been able to rely only on largely indeterminate legal rules and symbols that could often be invoked with equal effect by proponents of the system. In what follows I suggest that the competition of symbols has played a critical role in policy development in this area.

Forces for Expansion and Centralization

Viewed from a long historical perspective, a records system with centrally controlled expansion and political direction (at both federal and state levels) is perhaps to be expected, given the forces for standardization and comprehensiveness in modern states. But in the short run it is quite surprising, given the vogue of the New Federalism among conservatives and the traditional bias toward local control of law enforcement. What influences have prevailed over the latter imperatives to shape such a vast, centralized criminal records system?

Mainstream, instrumental policy models would be most likely to find explanations in policymakers' rational, causal response to serious crime.[89] Corollary propositions would be that centralization improves the efficiency of criminal justice recordkeeping and responds to public doubts about law enforcement efficiency and effectiveness.

There is some support for the "crime problem" hypothesis in the initial creation of computerized files at federal and state levels. NCIC came into being in 1967 when serious property and personal crime as reported by the FBI had been increasing for several years and had become an issue in local and national political campaigns.[90] Laudon confirms the empirical hypothesis that high crime rates (along with population and incarceration rates) are statistically associated with the early adoption of computerized criminal history systems at the state level.[91] But the continuing development of the dynamic central core of the system cannot be explained by rising crime. System development at state and federal levels continued throughout the 1970s and into the 1980s despite the drop in reported crime at the turn of the decade. In fact, the big push to automate name and fingerprint searching in the FBI's Identification Division occurred as rates of reported crime declined in the early 1980s.

To find public support for quickly available records on currently wanted persons does not imply a direct link between the general concern over crime and the development of the kind of sweeping national criminal records system that now exists. None of the criminal justice officials interviewed in three years of research for this book has ever attempted to maintain that there was a traceable, articulated link between public fear of crime and proposals for a national information system; a few did mention pressures from interest groups that either represent criminal justice or monitor it for "good data" on "career criminals."

What V. O. Key called "permissive consensus" certainly exists for taking strong measures to reduce crimes like murder, rape, and robbery.[92] National polls taken during the 1970s and 1980s consistently show that most Americans think too little is spent on crime control, and a majority of respondents has consistently thought that courts are too easy on offenders.[93] But these views do not necessarily indicate support for either the inclusiveness of a national system or the control and widespread dissemination of information by state and federal authorities.[94] Furthermore, the traditional American antagonism to concentrations of power appears to have intensified since the late 1960s, with polls consistently showing a loss of faith in major U.S. institutions, including government.[95] Revelations in the 1970s and 1980s of FBI spying have surely contributed to this crisis of authority.

A more useful perspective on the pressures for central control of the system can be found in the interacting forces of federalization and elite influence in the administration of justice. While criminal justice is still primarily a local function, national involvement has grown steadily. In the first decade of the twentieth century the FBI (then called the Identification Bureau) was created and the U.S. Children's Bureau developed the first juvenile justice standards; a national campaign against prostitution soon followed, and in the 1920s drugs and organized crime first appeared as national threats. Starting with the "Lindbergh law" against kidnapping, federal jurisdiction over criminal activity has continually expanded.[96] (The most recent major nationalization of crime was the Comprehensive Crime Control Act of 1984. Blurring distinctions between local and national criminal threats, new federal offenses included the burglary of a drug store, as well as contract murder and assault carried out as part of a racketeering scheme.[97]) Elite influence has shaped crime control policy through developments such as Supreme Court definition of the rights of defendants, Progressive reform of police practices, and, most recently, the adoption of intermediate punishments discussed in the next chapter.[98]

The two tendencies have often overlapped. Of particular significance is the President's Commission on Law Enforcement and Administration of Justice. Chaired by a former U.S. attorney general and including the president of Yale and a future U.S. supreme court justice, among others, the group's 1967 report provided the initial push for a national criminal history system and lent authority to the legislative proposal that created LEAA.[99] That agency set up state repositories, funded the electronic pathways between local law enforcement and the FBI, and, as we have seen, challenged J. Edgar Hoover's fifty-year dream of a comprehensive national crime information system.

The continuing development of the criminal records system no longer commands the attention of blue-ribbon commissions or Senators. But elite influence continues in the federal courts' endorsement of wide dissemination of rap sheets held by the FBI. And it can be seen in the aura of the system's technology and its application in organizational settings. The recent literature analyzing the social and political implications of computer use in government is helpful in understanding this dynamic. The initial view of computers as apolitical tools for rationally improving services to people has been supplemented by the conclusion that computer applications in government constitute a kind of "reinforcement politics" that serves the values and status of those in charge.[100] The development of the criminal records system bears out this perspective. Early endorsements of central control of recordkeeping are reinforced by the technological superiority of the FBI (and some of the larger states; California is far ahead of the FBI in its use of computer technology to analyze fingerprints), the new class of information managers in the FBI and the state record repositories, and the increased capacity of criminal justice officials to provide technical support to other government agencies and to mayors and governors. This patina of technical expertise exercises a persistent, relatively persuasive pressure for central expansion of and innovation in the system. In 1986 a $4.3 million contract for modernizing the NCIC, a project called NCIC 2000 to properly dignify its significance for the future, was awarded to the MITRE Corporation, an elite research organization spawned at the Massachusetts Institute of Technology.

An offshoot of the nationalizing influence on this aspect of law enforcement is the creation, thanks to LEAA, of a policy subgovernment to ensure that any federal largesse to be distributed to local and state law enforcement includes a chunk for the development of criminal justice information systems. Initial funding by LEAA of NCIC and state repositories nourished this arm of the network of law enforcement officials. Although the immediate material benefits of close association are now much reduced, law enforcement conferences and the NCIC Advisory Policy Board meetings keep it alive. In addition to managers of records systems, those in attendance include vendors and contractors (like the SEARCH Group, which still consults with NCIC) who supply technical expertise and, not incidentally, stand to profit from the occasional morsels that can be scraped off the bottom of the pork barrel. They keep up the pressure on law and order members of Congress, but federal distribution has been meager in the 1980s. (An exception is funding for the regional intelligence systems, that reached $10 million in 1987.[101]) The policy network is important nonetheless, as a way of spreading information and as legitimation of system expansion and innovation.

Forces Opposing Regulation

The mainstream rationalist perspective helps to explain the lack of regulation at state and federal levels of file size, data quality, and access to the system. It is a monumental administrative and fiscal burden to monitor data collection and dissemination in many thousands of jurisdictions. Imposing a comprehensive federal regulatory scheme also challenges legislative initiatives already taken in most states and therefore raises political issues. From the criminal justice official's point of view the costs of regulation weigh heavily against the benefits of protecting the privacy and social justice interests of criminal defendants. The costs are concrete and predictable, the benefits intangible and to be realized by an indeterminate number of record subjects. Furthermore, many of those who would be directly benefited are poor and powerless and are therefore unlikely to use the political process to assert their interests and raise the costs of not protecting their privacy.

Predictable bureaucratic imperatives have also determined the lack of regulation. The pressure for continuous and impersonal rationalization of program activities and the Weberian "vigor to expand" help explain the seemingly limitless discovery of new uses for the criminal records system—for finding missing children, for controlling ghetto youth who may or may not be drug dealers, for tracking informants—and the unwillingness to set limits on that process. Agency competition is relevant, too; LEAA abandoned its early support for comprehensive regulation of the criminal history system as soon as the battle with the FBI heated up. As for state passivity about regulating its systems, the "budgetary feast" of LEAA grants for criminal justice information systems development simply overwhelmed most initiatives for developing a regulatory scheme.[102]

Perhaps most important in this context is the relative power of the symbols manipulated by proponents and opponents of regulation in both their organizational relationships and their representations to Congress and to the public. Political scientist Murray Edelman's analysis of politics as a symbolic form is useful here.[103] He asserts that most controversial or important political acts serve as "condensation symbols," that is, evoking through an act or position memories and emotions that will affect the observer more than the objective consequences of what has just occurred. The Constitution is therefore seen as important more for its condensation of human dreams and fears than for the rational appeal of its provisions.[104] Administrative agencies commonly rely on symbolic politics to rally support for their programs, sometimes creating or inflating an intangible political threat to legitimize their own aggrandizement; Edelman cites the FBI's traditional posture on the communist "conspiracy" in the United States.

The conflict of system managers who opposed regulation and civil libertarians who sought it may thus be seen as a competition of symbols. Unable to demonstrate the crime control effectiveness of an inclusive criminal records system controlled by the FBI, criminal justice officials now rely on various images of the police role to protect their autonomy. Police serve as mediators between the community and the law, empowered with broad discretion for the protection of the community in emergency.[105] To monitor information for police use is to challenge that protective discretion that is the essence of the law enforcement role. To impose management checks is just as threatening. When legislation was proposed that would have shared policy control of the system at the federal level with private citizens and officials outside the Department of Justice, former FBI Director Clarence Kelley responded by defending the autonomy and professionalism of law enforcement, rather than by addressing the objective consequences of the proposal.[106]

One of the most powerful symbols law enforcement has at its

command is that of federalism, the sharing of political power between national and local governments. Defying the evolution since World War II of centralized federalism, under which most domestic policy problems have been seen as calling for national remedies, criminal law enforcement has continued to be largely a local function (except in situations in which federal crimes are at issue) guided by state law. The imposition of detailed, comprehensive privacy and security regulations would surely be a complex administrative task and would alter local political culture to some degree in every state. But law enforcement officials at both state and federal levels cast the issue in constitutional terms, describing the prospect of audits, logs, and expungements as violations of state sovereignty and the Tenth Amendment. (That federalism is not seen as a barrier to the central control of the system is a contradiction that reflects the relative power of those who bear the costs of the system. Regulation would burden law enforcement personnel, while the deleterious effects of central control affect only individual record subjects, many of whom are criminals.)

Law enforcement officials also have recourse to the ideal of comprehensiveness in crime control. Here, as in the push for central control, "computer madness" plays a part. Criminal justice is perpetually under the gun for its inability to capture and contain all wrongdoers. While reality inevitably falls far short of the desired end of nabbing every wrongdoer, stakes are also high in pursuing the ideal, since the alternative is crime without punishment and regulation without sanction. The computer's ability to store nearly infinite amounts of information and transfer it instantly symbolizes the quest for perfect efficiency. For the criminal justice official, regulating the collection and dissemination of data means depleting the raw material of a level of law enforcement effectiveness which has previously been only theoretical. The analogy of the "panoptic schema," which oppresses its subjects with the potential for surveillance as well as its actuality, is relevant here. The managers of the modern panopticon have at least the option of using every bit of available information. Going beyond the symbolic to the operational level, however, that option is often not exercised. Laudon found that two-fifths of the states don't often use their criminal history systems, suggesting that for many communities computerization may not be perceived to be a practical way to fight everyday crime.[107] My own, less systematic research tends to bear that out.

Those who fought for regulation—civil libertarians in Congress, scholars, ACLU lawyers—also did so with symbolic weapons. At first glance their arsenal might appear to be even more compelling than that of system supporters, resting as it does on prevailing legal ideology in general and legal rules derived from widely accepted constitutional ideals in particular. But these concepts have limited value when competing with the symbols of security, efficiency, and state sovereignty that can be invoked to support government coercion of individuals in the 1980s. Furthermore, proponents of the system can also have recourse to compelling legal symbols.

Consider the constitutional ideal of equal protection. Although it has been a powerful force for the preservation of human dignity in the face of arbitrary state action, its application to the administration of justice has been limited to outlawing overt discrimination—making it difficult for prosecutors to exclude black jurors in trials of blacks, for instance—or developing the right to participate in the criminal justice process—like ensuring adequate appellate review and the right to counsel. Equal protection has not gone very far in compensating for inequalities of condition among those who run afoul of the criminal law; for example, the Supreme Court has held that it does not require equal access to bail or consideration of a defendant's financial circumstances in sentencing.[108] Even though it is clear that an overinclusive, inaccurate criminal records system is most likely to entrap low-income citizens, the constitutional concept of equal protection is unlikely to mitigate its effects.

Due process is not a very useful concept for the system's critics either. Lurking within it, in fact, is the primary justification for very broad access to criminal records. Fundamental procedural fairness requires that the State's power of compulsion be exercised within certain limits to protect people against governmental arbitrariness and excess. One limitation on official sanctions, which finds constitutional expression most directly in the right to trial guaranteed by the Sixth Amendment, is that they be imposed and recorded publicly.[109] With respect to warrants and criminal histories, this presumed requirement of publicity serves as powerful justification for unbridled data collection and for dissemination to employers and landlords, as well as to law enforcement agencies. Middle-level administrators in the state record repositories of California and New York being interviewed on the application of state crime information policies repeatedly cited the public nature of the original records as justification for their collection and combination, even while they acknowledged that the totality of the picture of a subject's contacts with police, courts, and corrections has qualitatively different impact from that of a contemporaneous record of arrest, charge, or conviction. Both a federal agency head and a Harvard professor stated in conversation with me that they didn't really see what the fuss was about since the data on individuals were all matters of public record.

Judicial interpretations of the right to privacy are generally consistent with this perspective.[110] While a few state and federal cases have prohibited the dissemination of incomplete records beyond criminal justice agencies, *Paul v. Davis*, one of only two Supreme Court cases dealing with the use of arrest records, summarily rejected the record subject's allegations of a right to privacy. After holding that a person's reputation is not a "liberty" or "property" interest sufficient to invoke the due process protections of the Fourteenth Amendment, then Associate Justice William Rehnquist, writing for the majority, found that "none of our substantive privacy decisions" support the "claim that the State may not publicize a record of an official act such as an arrest." [111]

A more recent case takes a somewhat more protective stance. The Supreme Court ruled, in March 1989, that the Freedom of Information Act does not authorize the Department of Justice (nor, by implication, the FBI) to release criminal histories to a third party, even though the information contained in the records was once publicly available.[112] For the first time the Court found that a record subject has a substantial privacy interest in a rap sheet, but it came to that conclusion in the context of a federal statute, not on the basis of a constitutional privacy right. The implication of this ruling for state and local records at their source is unclear.[113]

One legal justification for the inclusiveness of the criminal record system is not a legal rule but a concept inherent in the nature of a legal order. Central to the ideal of the rule of law is the principle of generality, the notion that legal rules should regulate categories of behaviors and individuals rather than specific actions or individuals. Taken together with the principle of universality, the idea that legal rules are applied to king and commoner alike, this principle "establishes the formal equality of the citizens and thereby shields them from the arbitrary tutelage of government."[114] Implicit within the principle of generality is an ideal of comprehensiveness, the notion that legal rules should apply to all situations falling within the designated categories.

Application of the ideal is more symbolic than real, of course, perhaps particularly with respect to the criminal law where the State is often too large and diffusely focused to realize its part in the legal relationship. The computer is understandably seen as a force that narrows the distance between symbolism and reality. In collecting data centrally and conveying it widely, it can ignore boundaries of time, distance, and information source. Computer technology put to use in collecting and disseminating crime information becomes a methodology for the realization of generality in criminal law.

To see the relevance of the principle of generality to the development of the electronic panopticon requires making some assumptions about the principle's implications. Although the records system is not justified by its creators explicitly in terms of the nature of legality, reference is sometimes made to the fifty-year-old legislation authorizing the U.S. Attorney General to collect and disseminate criminal records.[115] While finding that the statute did not permit the FBI to disseminate criminal records without convictions to employers outside the Federal government, one Federal case was willing to allow criminal justice agencies to receive those records for law enforcement purposes on the basis of the "compelling necessity" of data exchange in police work and because administrative rulings authorize FBI collection and exchange of identification records.[116] (The restriction on dissemination was later nullified by federal legislation.) With this case, as with the national criminal records system in general, a strong cultural value with respect to information (more is better) came together with a legal premise in part derived from the principle of generality (the guilty must pay) to override the fundamental fairness concern that supplies the content of formal protections of individual rights. The FBI record would not be expunged, although it reflected a burglary charge that had been dropped as "unable to connect with any felony or misdemeanor." [117] And it would continue to be available to law enforcement agencies nationwide and to Federal employers.[118]

The arguments that provide legal justification for an inclusive, open records system—that it merely records public information and that it advances comprehensiveness in uncovering criminal conduct—have answers, of course. As Justice Brennan said in his dissent in *Paul v. Davis*, it is basic constitutional doctrine that the government not "single an individual out for punishment outside the judicial process;" yet the criminal records system does just that.[119] The requirement of publicity for criminal records and the principle of generality have both been stood on their heads to justify the panopticon. Intended as defenses against state power, both are invoked to endorse its encroachment. The contradiction should tell us something.

It is not inherently impossible to have computerized criminal records systems that would be efficient, effective, and broadly accountable. Such systems might include a national data base, linked to state and local law enforcement agencies, containing complete and accurate criminal history records on a relatively small number (probably about a million) of serious, multistate offenders—as proposed, for example, by Kenneth Laudon.[120] This file would be subject to continuous public oversight, either through unremitting Congressional vigilance or by an independent body including citizen representatives. It would be accessible only to criminal justice agencies, for crime control uses and for limited high-security job checks, and would be subject to strict dissemination regulation by the states. Supplementing the national criminal history system would be separate, unlinked state systems covering a wider range of offenders and tightly regulated as to file content, data quality, and access to records. State and federal warrant systems would regularly be audited for timeliness and accuracy, and national dissemination of warrant information would be limited to serious felonies. Online investigative records or indexes would be prohibited on both state and federal levels, and penalties for violating system regulatory standards would be enforced.

Such a system is unlikely to develop. The contest of legal symbols that currently proscribes meaningful regulation provides a clue to the system's most fundamental significance, its place in a retreat from many welfare state initiatives of the past fifty years. Regardless of whether there is a way to reconcile electronic recordkeeping with systematic protection of personal rights, there appears to be no will to discover it in the current political climate.

THE BIGGER PICTURE

Because the long-term effects of the electronic panopticon are as yet either potential or unmeasured in a systematic way, some may dismiss it as a minor civil liberties issue unrelated to the fundamental directions of U.S. society. But the continuing extension of record checks goes beyond the right to be let alone or the right to procedural fairness when subject to state coercion. Those who have records in the system—disproportionately poor and dark-skinned—run the risk of more or less permanent unemployability. As more employers, landlords, and insurers gain access to the system on a national basis, and as more investigative files are included within it, criminal records, however minor or outdated, become a secret stratifier of social and economic power, channeling millions of Americans away from jobs and services because they have been arrested at some time for something other than a traffic offense. It is not fanciful to worry about the emergence of a sophisticated computer quarantine that has profound implications for social structure.

Part of the cleverness of Bentham's idea of the panopticon was that the warden did not have to be continually watching the prisoners. That they knew that omniscience was *possible* was as important in the exercise of power as the watching itself. This feature has two important implications for the national computerized record system. One is simply that a person need not know for a certainty that he or she has a record in the system in order to refrain from applying for a job, participating in a demonstration, walking past a corner where police patrol regularly, having a meal in a rumored mafia hangout. Fundamental life choices and trivial daily activities alike, legal and harmless, can be constrained by the mere possibility of surveillance, whether or not it actually takes place. Choices of those other than records subjects are affected, too—employers, for instance, who won't even consider job applicants who they think might have a record.

The potentiality for surveillance has another significance, similar to a dimension of power that parents have over children. A parent can on occasion instill values and determine conduct merely by letting it be known that he or she will be alert to adherence and compliance. The ideology of socialization is as important as good behavior. Similarly with data surveillance, those in authority convey latent but powerful aims beyond the reduction of crime. The power of watching people lies partly in its ability to discipline them to "traditional values," which translate to mean conservative social and economic policies.

Let us return to the screening of records for public day care workers. Federal legislation now requires that states receiving funds for day care training conduct national criminal records checks (and checks of child abuse registries) on current and prospective employees. Some states are reaching beyond the regulation of the relationship between children and their caretakers to screen not only employees but their family members, vendors that supply juice and cookies to the centers, and volunteers. Day care agency directors report that the screening requirements have added to the low wages of day care employment to make it very difficult to hire workers. "People look at the screening requirements—the many forms that have to be completed and the three to six month wait for approval of a job application—and they say 'Forget it,'" reports Dr. Anthony Ward, executive director of Child Care, Inc., a New York City child care resource and referral agency. Quality of care is affected, too. "Workers have become very skittish," says a union official. "They no longer know what constitutes abuse. They are afraid that if they touch the children at all, they'll be liable. What about changing, toileting the children? It's almost to the point where workers can't touch a child." Confusing messages sent by government create terrible problems for program administrators. If a day care agency director hires someone with a minor criminal record, and abuse occurs, the parents may sue or the state may revoke the center's license; on the other hand, if the center dismisses the employee, it may be liable for having violated state and Federal law forbidding denial of employment because of a prior record unless the offense for which the employee was convicted bears a "direct relationship" to the job in question. The quality of program administration suffers. City agencies that fund youth programs are spending money on staff units to interpret the workers' records, but they maintain they can't afford to perform careful noncriminal background assessments on job applicants or train center administrators to spot abusive tendencies in their employees.

Government seems more interested in requiring a submission from workers than in discovering child abusers. In New York most workers found to have records, and half of those with crimes for which dismissal is presumed under the guidelines, have nonetheless been retained. The employees with records have gone through a painful ordeal and are now watched carefully by their supervisors; those who were "clean" are nonetheless subject to the supervison of the computer. There is no evidence that the state has made day care safer for children. It has, however, reinforced the ideology of the nuclear family, warning us all about seeking the nurturance of children outside the home. Mayor Koch underscored this disciplinary aspect of the policy when, lacking proof of effective crime control, he called for extending the screening program to foster parents and non-day care youth workers, including volunteers.[121]

In both the dragnet of child care workers and the expansion of Federal law enforcement authority over financial institutions it does not seem to matter that law enforcement may be driving out good program management. There is a tradeoff here that, given the generally conservative political climate, the state finds easy to make. The social cost of subjecting millions of bank depositors and their friends to the perpetual risk of criminal investigation is a small price to pay in order to convey the message that surveillance and punishment are government activities preferable to business regulation. Learning to live with the panopticon means learning to live with the ideologies of those who control it.

5

•

COMMUNITY AS PRISON

This program helped me develop self-control. I've been sober two years on May 3. I'm buying a house now. I would never have been able to do this without the program.

● New Jersey offender, on "graduation" from the
state Intensive Supervision Program

The promise is the drastic reduction of incarceration; the strength lies in realism about the punitive nature of the experience of surveillance.

● John Conrad, "The Intensive Revolution"

Some kid got five years in prison for going down to the corner and getting his aunt a chicken dinner.

● Jack Nichols, probation administrator,
Dade County, Florida

BEYOND PRISON WALLS

CONFINEMENT HAS NEVER BEEN the sole punishment for U.S. wrongdoers. The liberal use of the death penalty in England carried over to the colonies, where it was applied to horse thieves as well as murderers, and prescribed for recidivists of all kinds.[1] In the eighteenth century the most popular penalties were the fine and the whip.[2] More imaginative were the various forms of public shame, including the stocks for drunks and debtors and branding for loose women. The noninstitutional punishments of that period often reflected the enforcement of social roles; a gossip might be punished by "a cleft stick pinched on the tongue."[3]

Contemporary Americans tend to believe modern judges are "soft" as never before, a charge that cannot be sustained. From the seventeenth century lenient judges released defendants who could find friends as sureties for them in Massachusetts and elsewhere.[4] And suspended sentences were common in many states from the early 19th century.[5] In those early cases, furthermore, no supervision by the state was presumed or promised. Almost since the creation of the American penitentiary in the 1820s there have been advocates for dealing with wrongdoers outside its walls. In 1841, at a time of nearly universal belief in the reformative possibility of incarceration, the Boston shoemaker John Augustus saw it differently. He began bailing out public drunkards and petty thieves, taking them home or finding shelter for them, believing that "they could more effectually be reformed by kindness, than in the House of Correction."[6] Often called the "father of probation," he linked service and surveillance for petty offenders, a social control legacy that continues to expand. Although probation did not become common until early twentieth-century Progressives championed state responsibility for individualized treatment of criminal offenders, the idea caught on then with great rapidity. Between 1900 and 1915, thirty-three states adopted it.[7] By the time data began to be kept on a national basis in the 1970s, the 1.3 million adults on probation made it the most common form of official punishment.[8]

Until the 1970s, the declared justification for a nonprison sentence was rehabilitation, the possibility of reducing recidivism by exhorting and assisting nonviolent offenders to mend their ways. The probation officer's visits were certainly intended, in part, to detect and repress criminal conduct, and there was often too little time and money to include the provision of concrete services in the officer's role. But reality doesn't necessarily modify rhetoric. Until very recently probation's professed principal aim was to stimulate the client's internal reformation, not to control or deter criminal acts through punishment. Roscoe Pound called the development of probation "putting the criminal law definitely in the humanitarian path."[9] (It should be noted, however, that pragmatism always supplemented principle. Even the saintly John Augustus—sometimes nicknamed by the contemporary press "the Good Samaritan"—partially justified his "humble instrumentality" in keeping people out of the houses of correction by pointing out the costs of prison and loss of support for families and the state if wage-earners were incarcerated.[10])

Since the early 1970s, however, other rationales for community penalties have surfaced. The ancient theory of retribution has attained new respectability as "just deserts," punishment as the expression of society's moral repugnance at the lawbreaker's acts.[11] This perspective allocates penalties according

to principles of proportionality, commensurate to the seriousness of the offense and the prior crimes of the offender. A just
deserts system (also often called a "justice model") can therefore
include alternatives to incarceration like fines and community
service as lower rungs on its ladder of penalties. Even probation,
originally touted as inherently rehabilitationist, has been rationalized in accordance with the new model.[12] (One scholar
describes this process as "adding just deserts as a third layer to
the probation cake built with control and assistance layers."[13])

Incapacitation, the theory that punishment reduces crime by
rendering people incapable of committing it for the time they
are restrained, has also come into favor as a rationale, also often
bearing the new label of "community protection." Much criminological debate revolves around its application to serious repeat offenders whose proper identification and confinement is
thought to result in substantial crime reduction.[14] But proponents of nonprison penalties argue that, if controlling enough,
they can keep lesser offenders on the straight and narrow, promoting "the safety of citizens."[15] This approach has given rise to
scholarly efforts to assess the risk that a given offender will
commit new crime while on the community sentence.[16]

Finally, a concern with limiting the coercive power of the
state over individuals has led legal, religious, and social service
organizations to call for "community-based programs" in lieu of
prison wherever possible.[17] Their arguments have often joined
the theoretical and empirical. Some stress the concern that in a
democratic society the criminal law should be used as sparingly
as is consistent with public safety and solely for purposes of physical restraint.[18] Others emphasize the views of criminologists
that the utilitarian case for prison sentences as effective crime
control (by whichever punishment rationale) is still unproven.[19]

ENTER INTERMEDIATE PUNISHMENTS

Penal policy in the last twenty years has given birth to literally dozens of types of custody imposed partly or wholly beyond
the prison walls. Some programs—often called "community
corrections"—have been attempts by the penal system to refine
the dominant program of prison, to let inmates leave the prison
for limited times in controlled circumstances but to retain the
basic elements of state residential control of offenders. Included

in this approach were federally-funded community treatment centers, halfway houses run by corrections agencies, and work and study release intended to shorten time served and ease inmates back into nonprison life.[20] Other programs reflected the "alternatives" approach of 1970s liberals to divert offenders from confinement (and direct supervision by the state) altogether. During that decade a number of private, nonresidential service programs emphasizing reconciliation, restitution, and reformation (sometimes paid for by the very state whose coercive powers the reformers opposed) were established by criminal justice reform organizations and religious groups.[21] Finally, there were corrections system attempts to expand the range of punishments beyond the dominant prison program and traditional probation but incorporate many of the features of both—the "intermediate punishments" that were tentative experiments in the 1960s and 1970s and have become in the 1980s what both administrators and academics describe as "the new panacea of corrections."[22] Some of these latter programs were (and are) intended as substitutes for incarceration, while some were meant to be an option, "tougher" than probation, not as "tough" as prison, on the increasingly refined continuum of penal sanctions.

Neither "community corrections" nor the "alternative" programs of the 1970s have grown as their proponents would have wished. State and federal inmates on work release have remained less than ten percent of the total population throughout the 1980s; the number in community treatment centers and halfway houses actually decreased, from 13,848 on January 1, 1982, to 13,223 on the same date in 1987.[23] Officials and reformers, in rare agreement with one another, had reasoned that small, decentralized facilities in urban centers would be less impersonal and isolating than traditional prisons. But to potential neighbors this argument for community corrections was a threat—to their safety, to their property values, to their confidence that they lived in a "good neighborhood." What came to be known as the NIMBY ("not in my back yard") resistance added a major political cost to the community corrections movement and slowed it to a crawl.[24]

For different reasons most of the nonresidential programs run by private groups and oriented toward diversion from official punishment have withered. Many did not survive when the federal Law Enforcement Assistance Administration went out of business in 1980. In some cases, as the political climate became more conservative, government or foundation support became contingent on program modifications that effectively coopted the antistate spirit of the originals. People who had operated the programs either abandoned their radical ideals and became annexed to the official control system or turned to other enterprises where they would feel less compromised.

The intermediate punishments, however, are thriving. According to a 1987 RAND Corporation study intensive probation supervision, cheaper than community residential centers and more controlling than the private programs, is underway and expanding in at least forty states.[25] Some programs aim to enhance regular probation, supervising "high-risk" probationers more strictly to lower the possibility that they will commit crimes or violate program conditions, while the "new generation" programs apply a community sanction to offenders who would otherwise have gone to prison.

This distinction blurs in important ways. Some of the programs that bill themselves as "alternatives to incarceration" seem to be going the way of former "diversion" programs and scooping up primarily "shallow end" offenders who would have received regular probation if the intensive program had not existed. On the other hand Massachusetts has one of the enhancement programs, described by its administrators as "risk management strategy." In that state the type of supervision an offender is to receive depends on officials' assessment, after a sentence to probation, of the risk of committing a crime or violating probation conditions and the offender's needs for education, employment, counseling, and so on.[26] While theoretically this approach is unrelated to the drive to reduce prison crowding or the view that more serious offenders can be managed in the community, in actuality some of these programs probably do keep people out of institutions; if the strict surveillance did not exist, judges might put only very minor and first offenders on probation.[27]

For all but the truly violent offenses, local culture contributes as much to the determination of who is prison-bound as the social harm brought about by the crime. Massachusetts, in fact, has offenders under intensive supervision who have been convicted of more serious crimes than many prison inmates in Georgia, the state with the largest of the surveillance programs intended to substitute for incarceration. Furthermore, the elegibility standard of offenders who would go to prison these days if there were no intensive supervision program shifts over time.

As mandatory and longer penalties have been imposed in the 1970s and 1980s, a larger pool of potential inmates is created, some of whom would never have gone to prison in the bad old days of the 1960s. For these offenders, diversion is a chimera. They will now be "diverted" from a sanction that would only have been applied during a very narrow slice of time.

Although the clarity of the distinction between the aims of "enhancement" and "alternative" programs can be misleading, I have observed it in choosing to examine at length in this chapter two of the latter kind: the state programs of New Jersey and Florida. In purporting to supervise offenders who would have been imprisoned had the programs not existed, these programs represent the bellwether of the transformation to a penal system that places as much emphasis on observation as on capture and confinement.

Usually operating at the front end of the corrections process, the most fully developed of the "new generation" intermediate punishments theoretically substitute community custody for a prison term. (Some programs, however, while purporting to divert offenders from incarceration during most of their term, include a brief preliminary period of imprisonment, intended to "shock" the offender into gratitude and good behavior when he or she is released.) They are at once departures from the generally permissive institutions of probation and parole and a return to them from the more open-ended possibilities of privately-run alternatives to prison.

Intermediate punishments have varying names and emphases, and the policy mechanisms establishing and maintaining them are different. Georgia's model, widely replicated, is called "intensive probation supervision" (IPS), Florida's label is "community control," Texas calls its program "surveillance probation." Some programs stress victim restitution, some the provision of community service; many require the offender to pay the victim's losses and sweep out the local YMCA, besides. Electronic enforcement of curfews is spreading fast, but it is by no means universal. Some programs encourage mutual support among participants (along the Alcoholics Anonymous model), and some prohibit offenders from any contact with one another. There are at least two basic organizational models for these programs. Georgia's IPS program, the first large statewide effort to keep offenders out of prison, is a sentence option that the judge hands down and the state Department of Corrections administers; New Jersey's Intensive Supervision Program (ISP) is a program to which sentenced inmates apply and are resentenced, administered in the judicial branch of government by the Administrative Office of the Courts (AOC).

The administrative differences in intermediate punishment programs reflect variations in bureaucratic style and criminal justice politics rather than independent conceptions of program. Shaped by various mixes of punishment rationales—the "justice model" and incapacitation dictated by legislators and administrators, usually with a dash of rehabilitation thrown in by service-minded probation officers—most programs feature the same basic repertoire of conditions. The offender must work (or occasionally study) full-time and abide by a strict curfew that can be lifted only when attending church or clinic or counseling sessions required by the supervising officer. Participants pay for their crime quite literally in these programs; they usually pay court costs and fees for their own supervision, as well as restitution to the crime victim or the victim's family. Community service, required in most programs, represents repayment to society. These conditions are enforced by almost daily surveillance, sometimes electronic as well as human, and by frequent and unannounced drug and alcohol testing. Of course the ultimate enforcement tool is the prospect of confinement.

BARGAIN BASEMENT PUNISHMENT

The techniques that are spreading now (with the exception of electronic monitoring) are not conceptually new. As long ago as 1967 the President's Crime Commission on Law Enforcement and the Administration of Justice called for intensive supervision programs in the community for juvenile and petty offenders.[28] Since that year the Court Employment Project in New York City (an offshoot of the Vera Institute of Justice, a private organization that has sponsored many criminal innovations) has been tracking offenders closely while providing school and employment opportunities. And a number of states have classified their probationers by offense seriousness and previous record and then differentiated the closeness of supervision accordingly. What is new is the cautious but growing consensus among judges, scholars, and state legislators around the country that the intensive supervision approach can broaden the range of sentencing options for felons and can also be sold to the public as an approach that is tough on crime.[29]

This consensus flows neither from the new eclecticism of punishment rationales nor from substantive policy directions suggested by the public debate over crime and punishment. The primary catalyst for the development of intensive probation supervision, house arrest, and electronic monitoring programs in the 1980s flowed from the interaction of contradictory tendencies in the rightward trend in social policy. On the one hand was a continuous push to "get tough" across the board; on the other, the costs of more intensive and widespread control (and sometimes professional concern about its toll on the lives of its subjects) forced a search for new forms of control.

Spurred by the get-tough policies described in Chapter 2, the nation's prison population doubled in ten years, from 196,092 state and federal prisoners at the end of 1972 to 395,516 at the end of 1982.[30] Prison crowding had become a serious problem in the mid-1970s, apparently contributing to prison riots in New Mexico, Michigan, and Indiana in 1980 and 1981.[31] By that time the federal courts were consistently intervening in penal management; at the end of 1982 thirty-one states were under court orders to limit prison populations, and another nine were in litigation over the crowding issue.[32]

In response to prison crowding, a number of states and cities established emergency release programs (sometimes by statute), usually providing that when population exceeded capacity, inmates who had served most of their minimum sentence would be given early parole review.[33] (Michigan, one of the first to act, released nearly 700 prisoners in 1982 alone.[34]) But this was too little and too late to solve the problem; California, admittedly the fastest-growing prison system, was adding 100 people a week to its inmate population. Even if early release had been adopted earlier and on a broader scale, it would have been politically risky.

The states were in a bind, caught between political demands and economic realities. The general public, the law enforcement community, and the media continued to call for tougher punishment of criminals, even as incarceration rates were soaring. But many states were still recovering from the fiscal crisis of the late 1970s and bearing large debt service costs from the unprecedented wave of prison construction that began in the late 1970s; state corrections costs (adjusted for inflation) rose by almost 45 percent between 1979 and 1983, the largest jump of any category of state spending.[35] The South was particularly hard hit by this combination of pressures. Billie Erwin, a researcher in the Georgia Department of Corrections, recalls, "All three governors during [the 1970s] (Lester Maddox, Jimmy Carter, and George Busbee) described the chronic prison crises as the worst problem of their administrations, one that sapped their energy and soaked up money desperately needed for other worthy projects."[36]

Ideological contradictions further complicated the states' policy choices. The country's rightward political trend presented legislators with the conflicting imperatives of cultural and fiscal conservatism. Law and order confronted smaller government, and some accommodation had to be found. Mark Corrigan, Director of the National Institute for Sentencing Alternatives, described what the states were looking for: "It's got to be safe, it's got to be tough—or punitive—and it's got to be inexpensive."[37]

The need for a new punishment form did not dictate its content. Scholars have noted that interest group politics in criminal justice is dominated by elites—often lawyers organized in bar groups—and by those who operate the system.[38] The policy development of intermediate punishments fits this pattern. Probation officials, bidding for institutional survival, played a major role in both the formulation and the legitimation politics of intermediate punishments.

In 1930 Sheldon and Eleanor Glueck could, without likelihood of contradiction, call probation "the most promising contribution to penology during the last half-century."[39] If that promise was the reduction of recidivism, it has not been realized. Beginning with a 1924 Massachusetts study that found only 51.8 percent of an early group of probationers had no local court record after eight years, research on probation's effect on recidivism has been discouraging.[40] A rash of studies done in the 1960s and 1970s found that probation usually provides only minimal services and supervision and that, even when it does, correctional outcomes are no better than for similar offenders who go to prison or, for that matter, those whose cases are dismissed.[41] In 1976 the federal General Accounting Office captured the general view when it entitled its report on state and local probation programs, "Systems in Crisis."[42]

Notwithstanding its loss of luster, probation has grown. The 1965 President's Commission on Law Enforcement and Administration of Justice found that 61 percent of adults under correctional custody (excluding jails) were on probation or parole; twenty years later the figure was 74 percent.[43] By the end of 1985 there were 1.9 million people on state or federal probation, almost four times as many as were in prison.[44] Despite funding cuts in many jurisdictions, thirty-nine states and the federal government reported in a survey that as of January 1, 1987, they employed 26,574 people in probation and parole services.[45]

Not surprisingly, the managers of this substantial and widespread program constitute a constituency for its expansion. Despite probation's fall from grace its mission is perceived by other corrections professionals as an honorable one and, in many states, it has attracted able and astute practitioners. They have formed the American Probation and Parole Association, a national group of about 2,000 members and twenty-seven affiliate organizations that meets yearly to exchange ideas on management and program issues in probation.[46] (An early professional group formed in 1907 for officers and administrators broadened its focus and became what is now the National Council on Crime and Delinquency, a leading criminal justice research and reform organization.) With training in sociology, psychology, or social work, and experience in public management, probation administrators are often both sensitive observers of the criminal justice world and intelligent bureaucrats. Viewing the fallout from the crowding crisis as a programmatic and institutional opportunity, they rushed to fill the political vacuum.

It would be a mistake to see the crowding and fiscal crises as a "window of opportunity" for the earlier movement supporting alternatives to incarceration, a victory for the reformers or criminologogists doubtful of the validity of the harsher punishment theories. It was finally punishment-oriented conservatives in state legislatures, squeezed by ideology on one side and practical politics on the other, who fashioned the new program of penal control that would keep criminals out of prison. The window let in managerial innovation by the state to relieve budgetary pressure and prison crowding, rather than the reduction of state coercion for which the reformers had hoped. Intermediate punishments as a new arrow in the quiver of corrections is a supplement to the get-tough imperative rather than an ideological retreat from it.

Citing cost considerations and, to a lesser extent, the just deserts and community protection philosophies, probation administrators have made a strong case for a new penal policy that will breathe new life into their faltering program and be, in the words of one scholar, "an attractive centerpiece for a new 'get tough' probation image."[47] Vince Fallin, Deputy Commissioner of the Department of Corrections in Georgia, the first state to have a sizeable intensive probation supervision program, is candid about his stake in the new sentencing option. "To compete for resources for community corrections, we had to get smarter with our marketing strategies," he says. "If I had stuck to the old attitudes [a rehabilitation perspective applied to less serious offenders] I would be stuck without resources. You have to be part of change or be left behind. Maybe later we can emphasize the treatment side more. We're doing what we need to survive."[48] And, despite overwhelming evidence that modern probation has been, at least in recent times, a largely ineffective and discredited progam, legislators and judges in many states turned to the probation agencies when there was no room in the prisons.

INTERMEDIATE PUNISHMENTS OBSERVED— NEW JERSEY AND FLORIDA

During the winter of 1987–1988 I tried to learn as much as possible about the new intermediate punishments—their origins and goals, their application and enforcement, and their likely future significance in the continuum of criminal penalties. I read program literature and preliminary evaluations, interviewed a dozen program administrators from eight states, and met informally with several judges. Because there is often such a gap between policymakers' conceptions of a program and what it actually does, I was briefly an observer in two states, Florida and New Jersey. I made the rounds with ten probation officers and spoke with (or sometimes just listened to) about forty "outmates," as one program participant called himself and his colleagues. What follows is a discussion of the application of intermediate punishments based on observations of the programs in those two states, the Intensive Supervision Program (ISP) in New Jersey and its counterpart in Florida, "Community Control." My field work took place in Mercer and Essex Counties, New Jersey, and in Tampa, Florida. While my view of these programs is hardly comprehensive, other scholars who are starting to assess intermediate punishments have suggested that what I saw was characteristic.[49]

I observed these programs with a continual sense of dissonance between my macro-level perceptions of their purposes and effects and my empirical observations of the conduct of practitioners and participants. At the most general level, my doubts were substantial. I was uneasy about the role of such a pervasive exercise of penal power in commmunities already debilitated by inequality and exploitation. By and large the penal surrounding for community control was characterized by a wide range of social and economic problems and by the frequent inequities and inefficiencies of governmental efforts to respond to them. I was skeptical about the ability of intermediate punishments, however applied, to reduce the problems of either the offenders or their neighborhoods. Furthermore, the contribution of these programs to a larger agenda for the establishment of a more regimented society seemed more fundamental, and more potentially effective, than their role in preventing and correcting predatory behavior. And yet alongside my doubts were perceptions that at the individual level justice was dispensed with fairness and supervision conducted with sense and sensitivity. I observed many acts of kindness by officers and pledges of trust by offenders. Furthermore, despite the punitive emphasis of judges, administrators, and officers, it was evident that control was combined with concrete services, particularly in the New Jersey program.

Off the Drawing Boards and Into the Community

Both New Jersey and Florida had serious prison crowding problems in the early 1980s. Florida's was the more dramatic; prison admissions in that state grew 196 percent between 1970 and 1983, compared to 9 percent in New Jersey; and the prisoner population increased by 187 percent, almost three times New Jersey's 61 percent rise.[50] This phenomenon should be understood in the context of the Florida population boom of the 1970s; the number of state residents grew by 43.5 percent during the decade, more than any other state.[51] Along with population growth came an influx of immigrants and resulting ethnic conflicts and a booming illegal drug industry. These developments produced both higher crime rates and increased incarceration. During this period New Jersey's population remained stable.

Under the gun of a consent agreement that set bed capacity for the prison system as a whole and for individual institutions within it, Florida began to build. In 1981 it opened two new prisons and the next year added almost a thousand beds by renovating old ones.[52] Although New Jersey was one of only a

few states not under a court order in 1982, the inmate population had increased 30 percent during the previous year alone,
and the state was desperately seeking cells. It was filling old
cells that had been intended for demolition because they were
small, poorly lit, and had no privacy and inadequate plumbing.
It was holding more than 1,500 state prisoners in local jails,
housing prisoners at the Fort Dix army base, and putting trail-
ers in prison yards.[53]

Part of the increase in sentenced prisoners can probably be
explained by increases in reported crime. During the 1970s the
FBI crime index for each state rose 133 percent.[54] But that is not
a sufficient explanation for the increased use of prisons; in both
states major policy shifts played a significant role as well. Florida instituted mandatory prison terms for drug law violations,
both states for violent offenses and gun crimes.[55] Parole release
dropped in both states.[56]

In both states responses to the crowding crisis included programs of community supervision. Much of the initiative came
from probation officials. That they had the authority to command political attention at the state level is a sign of the increasing centralization of criminal justice policy, a traditionally
local matter in most respects, and of the growth of the interest
group strength of probation. When the Florida legislature realized it had to act on the crowding problem, Leonard Flynn, the
state director of Probation and Parole Services, had easy access
to legislative and executive leaders. He took the intensive supervision program he had "had under wraps for some time" as a
way to enhance existing probation and repackaged it so that it
would "fit in with the overcrowding problem" as community
control for offenders who would otherwise go to prison.[57] The
Correctional Reform Act sailed through the legislature in the
spring of 1983, providing for "intensive supervised custody in
the community, including surveillance on weekends and holi-
days, administered by officers with restricted caseloads."[58]
When asked whether the legislature had weighed either the
effectiveness of strict surveillance or the opportunity to provide
services to participants, Erio Alvarez, probation and parole director of for the Tampa area, seemed surprised by the question.
As far as he knew, there had been no significant programmatic
concerns; "it was the pragmatic issues of cost and crowding."
The first community controllees were admitted to the program
in November 1983.

Although in New Jersey probation is a county rather than a

state function, with twenty-one autonomous departments, the adoption of a state ISP program was almost as easy. There, the Committee on Standards for Placement of Persons on Probation of the state judicial conference recommended intensive supervision as an alternative that would be appropriate for some offenders and obviate the need for constructing an additional prison. This position was strongly influenced by the probation representative from the state Administrative Office of the Courts, who had been part of a small group of probation administrators around the country that had been exchanging ideas about innovations that would strengthen the control function of probation. The governor pushed through a $1 million appropriation for the AOC to design and implement the program. It is the first probation program run from the state capital, and its creation was probably an important tactical advance in the bureaucratic struggle for state takeover of probation. One sign of the dominance as a policy influence of the prison crowding crisis was that the target number of 375–500 ISP participants was set not because the program designers determined that to be the number of potentially eligible inmates, but because that was the number of bed spaces in a typical prison. Described by AOC Assistant Director Harvey Goldstein as "a three-branch cooperative effort," ISP started in June 1983, with three field offices around the state.

The primary policymakers' clarity and consistency of intent is not duplicated at the level of street-corner bureaucracy. Although the officers I interviewed in both states knew that cost and crowding were dominant rationales for legislative and executive approval of the program, their own perspectives were often very different and in flux. As one officer put it to me, they were "adapting" to what the system wanted them to do, not playing out a conscious ideology.

In Florida I interviewed six officers: one young white female, one young white male, one young black female, one middle-aged white female, one middle-aged white male, and one middle-aged black male. The younger officers explained the program in terms of several different punishment theories and seemed comfortable with applying a program rationale to fit the course of action being taken. The two older officers, however, although no more principled in their embrace of a particular purpose for the program, said they missed the sense of mission to rehabilitate that once characterized probation. Unstated at the policy level but very explicit with the applicants and participants in

both states was the goal of "changing lives," whether by rehabilitation or merely control, so that people in the program
would become responsible and productive, as well as law-
abiding. Officers subscribe to the rehabilitative goal in differ-
ing degrees; while surveillance is the linchpin of the program,
rehabilitation is still significant.

Although the professional literature describes a number of
different models of intermediate punishment programs, the
basic elements of most are quite similar. The community control program's evaluators call Florida "the only state, to date, to
require 'house arrest' (home confinement) during 'non-working'
hours."[59] But, in fact, house arrest by any other name may be
just as confining. In Florida, program participants must be
home immediately after work, while in New Jersey most "outmates" must be in by 8 P.M. Florida controllees do have to remain at home during the day on weekends, but again this may
be more distinction than difference, because, with the approval
of their officers, they may be absent for religious services, weekly marketing and laundry, drug or alcohol counseling, community service assignments, and so on—exceptions to the curfew
requirements also allowed by New Jersey ISP. Both programs
last, for the average offender, about a year and a half. By using
the term "house arrest," however, the Florida program sounds
tougher to the uninformed.

In fact in some respects the New Jersey program is tougher.
While officers in both programs make frequent personal and
telephone contacts, several times a week, often unannounced,
the Tampa officers I spoke with don't generally monitor their
charges after 10 or 11 P.M., while the New Jersey officers occasionally check up after midnight. Community service of sixteen
hours a month is required and enforced in the New Jersey program, while Florida is more laissez-faire; a 1986 evaluation of
the Florida program found that 65 percent of controllees were
not being assigned to community service, and for those who were
assigned, the number of hours was considerably shorter than in
New Jersey.[60] In New Jersey urine samples are taken regularly
and at random for virtually all participants, but in Florida samples are taken only when the officer suspects drug use.

The Florida program also appears at first glance to be quite
different from New Jersey in its use of electronic monitoring.
Electronic devices for offender surveillance can be either passive, like the computerized, random telephone dialer that occasionally calls the offender's home, or active, like the transmit-

ters that attach to the offender to provide an almost continuous record of the controllee's presence at home. Florida's program is now regularly making use of the latter technology for offenders convicted of more serious crimes or for community control participants who have violated the conditions of house arrest.

Community Control II is simply the "house arrest" program supplemented by active electronic surveillance. The controllee wears a plastic anklet with a transmitter that sends a signal every ninety seconds to a monitor hooked up to the offender's phone line. If the offender leaves home when the computer in the probation department is programmed to expect him there or has not left home when the computer expects him to have left for work, the deviation is recorded, and the officer calls to verify the message. If there is no departure from the required routine, the electronic monitor calls in to the computer every eight hours with a report on the offender's presence.

Florida's use of electronic monitoring actually began in 1984 at the county level in Palm Beach as an attempt to reduce the jail population.[61] That program's publicity and lower cost as an alternative to jailing has led to widespread adoption. The state program began in April 1987 and included about 100 offenders in Tampa during the first year. Sixty devices were then added to the initial forty, and further expansion seemed likely. Elsewhere in Florida electronic monitoring is also flourishing; as of early 1988, 667 offenders were being monitored by some sort of device, more than in any other state.[62] The state paid for 266 anklets (at a cost of about $70,000 for a computer and 30 anklets), and the Governor had recommended that the legislature appropriate an additional $1 million for anklets, wristlets, and other monitoring equipment.

Although New Jersey does not highlight electronic monitoring as an important feature of ISP, its use is spreading there too. The state program also includes the use of a few wristlets and video monitors that take a still photograph of offenders when they answer the phone. The ISP state director notes that because these devices are being promoted by hotly competitive small manufacturers, he can get a good price and expects to expand their use, though not, he says, as a substitute for officer contact with program participants.

The most significant difference between the Florida and New Jersey programs lies not in their name or program conditions but in their procedure for admission. In Florida a judge may sentence an offender directly to community control, or may order the offender transferred to the program after someone has violated the conditions of ordinary probation. The offender plays no part in the decision and sometimes appears not to understand the requirements of community control. In New Jersey, however, the offender is initially sentenced to a prison term, applies for the program, and is resentenced after being incarcerated for at least sixty days (often much more).[63] Entrance into the program is a long and complex process. Inmates are usually informed about ISP before they are even sentenced, often by local jail personnel. They fill out an application that triggers an extensive background investigation leading to an "assessment report." These are reviewed by a three-member screening board composed of a corrections official, citizens appointed by the Chief Justice of New Jersey, and an ISP representative. The board then interviews an applicant "to gauge his/her motivation and sincerity for the program."[64] The panel's recommendation is forwarded to the resentencing panel of three judges, which makes decisions about entrance to and termination from the program, conducts 90-day reviews of participants' behavior, and rules on charges that participants have violated program rules. Applicants appear at admission hearings with their families and community sponsors, friends who provide support and services particularly in the first few months. Judges question offenders closely about their reasons for wanting to be put on the program and their knowledge of what it entails.

Program admission by resentencing in New Jersey is intended to ensure that ISP is not used simply as a stricter sanction for those that would otherwise have been put on probation. But it has other functions besides ensuring that participants will be selected from among the prison-bound. The period of incarceration is an idea taken in part from the notion of "shock probation;" probation combined with a dose of prison to convey to the program participants how lucky they are to be getting out and how bleak their future will be if they don't succeed "on the street." The period between application and resentencing hearing also helps the judges and probation officials to test the waters of public opinion with respect to a particular applicant; it allows for protest by the prosecutor, public, or victim.[65] With this procedure the state supports the notion of the program's toughness in the way the "house arrest" label supports it in Florida.

The states rely on other devices to ensure that the programs are acceptably tough to the public and to other criminal justice functionaries. In both Florida and New Jersey probation officials sold the programs to police and judges on the basis of their capacity to punish and control. The programs limit risk by excluding offenders they think unlikely to "make it," particularly in New Jersey where the prison crowding pressure is less intense. In that state, about 60 percent of the applicants are excluded because of the seriousness of their crime or their prior record, and another 15 percent withdraw their applications before the process is complete because they think the restrictions are too severe or the time to be served is too long compared to the time remaining on their sentence.[66]

The recent criminal histories of program participants in the two states are quite similar. For the majority the crime for which they were in custody was either a drug offense (18 percent in Florida, 40 percent in New Jersey) or a burglary (24 percent in Florida, 23 percent in New Jersey) or other property offense (27 percent in Florida, 18 percent in New Jersey).[67] Although both programs claim to take only nonviolent offenders, New Jersey abides by that restriction more rigorously, excluding from the program those who are convicted of first- or second-degree felonies, have long prior records, or have been given a mandatory minimum sentence. Twenty-six percent of Florida community controllees have been convicted of a violent offense, but that category includes a wide variety of conduct, some of which may not be very threatening to the general public.[68] I met or heard about Florida controllees who had committed manslaughter while driving drunk and a first offender who had beaten the woman he lived with when he was high on cocaine; but I encountered no repeat violent offenders or controllees who had committed deliberate stranger-to-stranger assaults.

A striking feature of both programs is the extent to which they reflect both the incidence of and the state response to illicit drug use and alcohol abuse. Although violations of drug laws constitute only one-fifth of the participants' offenses in Florida and two-fifths in New Jersey, drugs were a contributing factor in many more. Most of the violent offenses I heard about that qualified their perpetrators for an intermediate punishment were committed when the offender was drunk. It appears that most program participants have drug or alcohol problems; ISP Director Richard Talty estimates that 75 percent of the crimes of New Jersey participants are drug-related, and 78 percent of the Florida community controllees in 1983–1984 admitted to some form of drug or alcohol use.[69] The consensus among program administrators on the prevalence and seriousness of drug-taking among the offenders they see is so strong that they blur distinctions between use and abuse, although evidence is strong that the majority who take illicit drugs are only occasional users.[70] To acknowledge this fact would, of course, challenge the logic of treating most offenders as though their principal problem was drug abuse.

Conditions in the two programs are very similar, and officers seem to be equally committed to rigorous enforcement. In both states officers have a good deal of discretion, although the difference in program characterization rests more authority in the judges in Florida. New Jersey officers monitor compliance with ISP requirements very rigorously, and base that compliance on a clearly articulated administrative system of different stages of control, with participants moving to less frequent monitoring "as they prove themselves reliable."[71] When a participant breaks a rule of the program (short of absconding or committing a new crime) officers will devise punishments less drastic than returning the offender to court to be revoked from the program. For those I watched at work, it is crucial to the program's integrity to apply a sanction for every infraction: a weekend in jail for a second curfew violation, an extra Narcotics Anonymous meeting for a "dirty urine," added community service hours for failing to show up at a previous assignment.

Tampa enforcement is not as highly structured within the probation department as in New Jersey. As in New Jersey officers make unannounced, frequent visits to controllees; but when a rule violation occurs—generally absence from home when under house arrest—the judge, not the officer, is expected to make dispositions as to its seriousness. Officers usually wait for two or three violations of house arrest before they request a warrant to bring the controllee into court. At that time the judge may send the offender to prison or impose sanctions short of revocation, as the officer does administratively in New Jersey.

Failure to complete the program is common in both states. Forty-six percent of those terminated from the ISP program between June 1983–January 1987 were sent back to prison, most for curfew violation and drug use.[72] This figure is misleading, since it is not based on an assessment of outcomes for every single participant who entered the program before the research cutoff date of December 31, 1985. Some of the later entrants into the program were still participating in 1987 when the outcome measurement was made; the prison return rate for all those who entered the program before 1986 is not yet known. Most people who return to prison do so within the first six months, so the overall failure rate will surely be lower than the rate as recorded now. The evaluator believes an estimate of 40 percent to be reasonable.[73]

The picture is similar in Florida. About half of the sample studied in an evaluation of that program violated its conditions and were sent to prison, the bulk of them for periods of up to five years. More were revoked for technical violations than for new crimes (80, as opposed to 53); a few simply took off and were not apprehended.[74]

The "Outmates"

There is, of course, no perfectly typical "outmate" when the program includes participation of a wide range of offender types and considering the range of ethnic and class backgrounds to be found in urban and suburban New Jersey and Hillsborough County, Florida. But patterns of experience and expectation emerge in interviews with participants, particularly among those who have survived in the program for many months and seem likely to complete it without major violations. These patterns are reflected in an ISP participant I'll call Doug, a black male in his early thirties interviewed outside the hearing of his officer in Trenton, New Jersey. Convicted of drug trafficking stemming from a long-term heroin and cocaine habit. Doug works in construction and does community service in a women's shelter. He feels the program "keeps you honest," "helps with organizing your life," and is vastly preferable to prison. "I can get a lot more done out here with him [officer] visiting me than I can in prison." He also thinks it is harder to do time in the community than in prison; "in jail you just do as you're told; out here you have to take responsibility for your life." For him family relationships represent both supports and responsibilities central to his life; his community team includes several family members, including his fiance, and a priest. One senses the investment he has made in succeeding on the program. "I've been drug-free for two years," he says; "it would be a big setback to go back to prison."

There are strong demographic similarities between participants in the two programs. In both states blacks are overrepresented, though not as much as in the prison population. (In 1980
14 percent of the general population of Florida and 13 percent of
the population of New Jersey was black; the respective prison
populations in 1985 were 49 percent and 66 percent.[75]) Studies
of representative groups in the programs for 1985–1986 in New
Jersey and 1983 in Florida found that in both states the population was 32 percent black. In New Jersey 90 percent were male;
in Florida, 88 percent were male.[76] In New Jersey 9 percent
were hispanic; data on Hispanic controllees in Florida were not
provided, but my experience would suggest that the proportion
is higher in that state. Of the groups I saw, about half were
white, the other half black and Hispanic with a slightly higher
proportion of the latter in Florida and the former in New Jersey.
Most appear to be poor, but not all; of the New Jersey offenders I
saw, one was a professional man and another was a graduate
student in one of the sciences, both drug offenders. Most offenders were in their twenties, a few were in their thirties, and only
occasionally was there anyone over forty. Four of the six women
I saw were drug offenders.

Not all participants are as positive as Doug about the programs. A few rolled their eyes to the ceiling when I asked them
how they feel about it, an indication they did not wish to speak
freely even though in some cases the officer was not present.
One of the former participants I interviewed from the jail to
which he returned after violating his curfew and having dirty
urines said the program provided "good support" until he started to "mess up," and then "my officer didn't want to help me
anymore." A few participants said they thought the program
was irrelevant, that they would go straight without it. The
white middle class graduate student commented, "I was rehabilitated from the moment I was arrested."

Passive acceptance is a very common attitude toward the programs' requirements. By and large those being punished with
intensive surveillance expressed no resistance to the regulation
of their lives which, in fact, resembles the regimentation of
prison more than the haphazard supervision of routine probation. Perhaps most notable is the extent of the consensus that
the officer has a right to inquire into anything the offenders do
or say. In answer to my question, "Do you think some of the
questions Joe asks are none of his business?" one young drug
dealer said matter-of-factly, "*Everything* is his business."

The offenders' resignation is complex and must be understood on several levels. It represents rational calculation, acknowledgment of domination, and legitimacy.[77] When asked generally what they think of their program, most say, "It's better than being locked up." Furthermore, many believe as the officers do, that following the program requirements will increase the likelihood that they stay out of trouble in the long run. This faith is not necessarily shaken by failure. One program violator back in jail said to me, "I tell the guys who are thinking of applying for the program that if you abide by the rules and want to change your life, you can make it." (By and large these are not alienated career criminals just biding their time to move on to bigger and better ripoffs. They generally subscribe to the conventional morality with respect to property, interpersonal relations, and even drug use, despite their apparent inability to live by it consistently.) They also know that, in a situation in which the officer so clearly holds the reins, resistance would be counterproductive. And they usually view both the officer and the program as exercising a valid, even necessary, part in social control. Program requirements are rules of a game that to them is familiar and legitimate. "It's like riding a bike," a participant said, "difficult at first, then automatic."

This latter kind of acceptance of the program may vary by class. Many poorer offenders seemed to expect some kind of coercive control by the state over their lives, whether or not its source was a program of correctional custody. Some were simultaneously on probation or parole for another offense. Some had family members who were on public assistance (or, occasionally, were on welfare themselves) and lived lives constantly attuned to the eligibility and benefit rules of those programs. A few were in continual negotiation with the state over repayment of parking tickets, and two were dickering with disability agencies over benefits that had been repeatedly conveyed and withdrawn. The strictures of ISP or community control were just more of the same, tiresome but legitimate. Even the Florida offenders in Community Control II regarded their electronic anklets as merely another nuisance the state was forcing them to put up with. Far more restless with constraints imposed by the program were the few middle class offenders. Where most participants stressed the differences between the experiences of the program and prison, the graduate student was acutely aware of the similarities. For him the regulation of both kinds of custody was in sharp contrast to his ordinary life.

The Officers

The 1913 annual report of the New York State Probation Commission described probation officers as "persons of good character and education, exceptional intelligence, sympathetic temperament, tact, good judgment, and strong personality."[78] Such paragons may be difficult to find in ordinary probation in the 1980s (or, indeed, in other kinds of work), but I can attest that they do exist in the intensive supervision programs of New Jersey and Hillsborough County, Florida. They must work long hours; in the New Jersey program they are on call twenty-four hours a day. They become very involved with offenders, often going well beyond the parole contacts that one study found to be "typically amiable, superficial, and brief."[79] They must make far more complex judgments on the job than ordinary probation officers, sometimes setting standards for offender behavior that are not specified in any manual. Like other street-level bureaucrats they may yield to the imperatives of individual and organizational self-interest, reducing the burdens of their jobs with shortcuts that restore the dominance of routine over innovation; but these deviations appear to be only occasional and minor. Often perceived by program administrators as "the cream of the crop," the officers who impose the intermediate punishments I studied are generally open and sympathetic, but also canny and firm.

Political scientists have challenged the classical model of administration, based on Weber's ideal bureaucracy in which a small group of decisionmakers adopt policy that is carried out by underlings in a smooth, top-to-bottom process. They have noted that implementers often adapt policy conceptions to fit professional or institutional needs.[80] The gap between policymakers (legislators and corrections administrators) and policy implementers (probation officers) is nowhere more evident than in their attitudes toward the role of rehabilitation in intensive supervision. For policymakers, "rehabilitation" has become a four-letter word, connoting a service orientation that coopts the corrections worker and "doesn't work" in keeping offenders crime-free. Although they genuinely endorse the currently popular punishment rationales of just deserts and incapacitation many officers in the new programs also have a firm, if veiled, commitment to activities that provide limited material help and the guidance of friendly suggeston. Some go as far as to say that the rehabilitative aspects of their job are the most rewarding.

They feel no contradiction between surveillance and service, a frequent debate among probation and parole professionals.

Michael Lipsky notes that street-level bureaucrats are often idealists gone sour.[81] The officers who administer intermediate punishments may have lost their faith in regular probation, where they usually began their careers, but many retain a basic belief in the rehabilitative ideal. Some also embrace a rather crude form of behavioral psychology. They think that if only the proper arrangement of rewards and sanctions can be found to insure compliance with program rules, offenders can clean up their lives; and they often feel responsible for discovering the magic formula. The two perspectives coexist as complementary methods of control, one aimed at the mind, the other at the body.

But there are doubts, too, that, along with the long hours and constant pressure, may eventually corrupt the idealism that now inspires many officers. Some of the officers I interviewed seemed to cling to the possibility of the programs' rehabilitative effects because their professional and personal self-image required a service orientation, rather than because they were convinced that features of the program could induce participants to tread the straight and narrow. Several commented uneasily on the many influences in their clients' lives that worked against permanent effects of the program. They noted individual dysfunctions—longstanding drug habits, disrupted family lives, minimal skills—as well as structural dilemmas—work without a future, social circles in which everyone had a criminal record, the hopelessness that follows from rigidities of class. One Florida officer, planning to go to graduate school and pursue another profession, told me, "I've got to get out of here before I get so hardened that I blame all their problems on them [offenders.]" Although not very clearly articulated, the officers' awareness of structural sources of their clients' lawbreaking may eventually contribute to the debasement of the rehabilitative spirit that is noted by other analysts.[82]

Officer perceptions vary on some questions of job quality. Virtually all find their jobs more rewarding overall than those they previously held in traditional probation or parole.[83] They like the smaller caseloads and greater authority they have, and in New Jersey they appreciate the higher pay. The two officers in New Jersey with whom I spent the most time felt their jobs to be more pressured than regular probation jobs, while the Tampa officers thought they were less so. In New Jersey officers felt the pressure resulted from the fact that they are "on call" 24 hours a day; in Tampa officers don't carry beepers and don't have program participants calling them at home. The two New Jersey officers mentioned above illustrate the backgrounds and attitudes of this new breed of corrections professional.

Diane is in her thirties, black, a sociology graduate of a local college, married to a Newark police detective, and has an 11–year-old daughter who refers to Diane's ISP charges as "my nineteen brothers." She has lived in Essex County all her life and is a staunch defender of Newark in the face of what she regards as exaggerated reports of its dangers and depressions. She is relaxed and friendly with her clients, equally comfortable in reminding a participant that he must catch up with restitution payments and organizing an outing for her group to a boxing match in which one of the offenders is a contestant. She seems to have no trouble balancing service and surveillance; she runs a weekly discussion session for her "clients," but she does not hesitate to punish a recalcitrant curfew violator with a weekend in the local jail.

Joe is also in his thirties and is a local college graduate, white, married with two small children. With more of a no-nonsense demeanor than Diane, he expresses astonishment that participants sometimes try to manipulate him into being their "buddy," and stresses that his job is first and foremost surveillance; he disdains "the savior-type thing." Yet he also finds ways to provide service, and he does it with good will and imagination. When a client asks him for permission to organize the group into a softball team, Joe immediately suggests that the ISP program could sponsor it and provide shirts and that they could work out a game with a team of officers. Joe is a strong believer in individual self-reliance; "it's up to them to 'make it' or not." He likes the higher pay, lower caseload, and greater independence of his ISP job, but finds his responsibility an incursion on family life.

The Culture of Enforcement

The administration of intermediate punishments is oriented as much toward toward "social adjustment" as toward crime control.[84] Over and over one perceives a dual emphasis on reducing crime and making responsible citizens. Says Richard Talty, ISP Director, "People who find their way into prison have been unwilling to live within a structure. We need to give these people a sense of responsibility." Requiring a minimum of sixteen hours of community service each month (until "senior stage" just before release from the program, when the hours decrease) and a daily diary is intended to shape the participant's attitudes and habits, to establish the contours of the planned, orderly life.

Some requirements of ISP and community control are obviously and directly related to minimizing the participant's opportunity to commit crime. The prohibitions against illegal drug use and consorting with former partners in crime are clearly associated with the participant's criminal background. Other rules are still related, if less directly, including the requirement that a participant be working or going to school fulltime. These activities presumably substitute for the work the devil finds for idle hands to do. At least where property offenders are concerned, the program administrators are probably right in saying, "Participants must be economically self-sufficient in order to maintain a law-abiding life style." [85]

However, there are many other program performance requirements in which the relationship between following the rule and remaining crime-free is murky, and the program's aim of giving "structure" to participants' lives is clear. The program participant's diary, which must be submitted to officer or judge on demand, is justified as verification that he wasn't out committing a crime (though the diary could surely also be used by the offender to cover tracks) and by its function as the participant's record of daily accomplishments in the "straight" world. The weekly budget is important for ascertaining that a participant is not spending money on drugs, but also for developing the sense that he or she is taking care of his financial obligations to family and community.

These kinds of requirements are seen as both punitive and reformative. "By design, most of the community service work is physical labor (such as sweeping or mopping), and this contributes to the goal of providing a level of punishment that is intermediate between probation and imprisonment."[86] The theory is that structure imparts self-discipline. The officers know that, by itself, requiring the "outmates" to turn over their weekly budgets and tax returns for inspection will not keep participants crime-free. But they hope that the offender, under close supervision, will become so habituated to living by the clock, paying bills, and holding down a job that he or she will no longer be susceptible to the chaotic allure of drugs and instant gain when they are no longer being watched. Living sober is living well; program participants will internalize this connection and maintain it beyond the period of the program.

The metaphor for the desired character change is education, reinforced and evidenced by vocabulary and tangible symbol. Those who succeed in the New Jersey program are called "graduates," and on completion of their sentence they receive a certificate that looks as much as possible like the diplomas that have eluded most of them at school. The officers occasionally try to get offenders to use a community's cultural resources, taking them to a play or concert. Diane arranged a deep-sea fishing trip and helped participants plan a picnic that included the ISP Olympics, with thumb wrestling, rope pulling, and other events. The middle-class mania for self-improvement in the 1980s is reflected in the individualized conditions of the program; officers occasionally assign participants to go to Weight Watchers meetings and parenting workshops.

Many participants are grateful for the program, for the "structuring" as well as the crime control effects they presume it has. Officers report that they mainly express resentment over the rules only in the first six months and then begin to internalize them. Community service becomes popular with some offenders, particularly with those who don't have family or friends with whom to spend weekend and evening hours; it is not uncommon participants to put in more hours than are required by the program. Diane makes the point that when they get out of the program, some graduates choose to do community service, although they usually choose a job more rewarding than the menial labor of the program—for example, some graduates give talks at schools about drug abuse.

That the outmates accept the program as legitimate should not obscure its coerciveness. Every rule violation carries with it a sanction, and the constant prospect of being sent to prison if they "screw up" has a far greater than in traditional probation or parole programs. The nature of the coercion is also qualitatively different. The usual negative restrictions, "thou-shall-nots," are supplemented with affirmative coercions—to attend the Narcotics Anonymous meeting, to make the loan payment by August 1—that may cover broad areas of your life. Even some forms of self-expression are positively coerced. At a New Jersey meeting at which program participants counseled one another (under supervision, with attendance mandatory), the outmates who brought their problems before the group were ordered to do so by their officers.

DOES IT "WORK"?

The goals of the intermediate punishments of the late 1980s are more modest than those of earlier corrections innovations. The programs do not aim to "point the way to a reconstitution of the social structure," as the early penitentiary movement did.[87] Although judges and supervising officers involved in the programs hope—and sometimes allow themselves to believe—that offenders will go straight after they have been punished (the principal declared aim of both prison and probation during most of this century), the reduction of post-program recidivism is not required to justify the programs' existence. Policy goals are cast in terms of correctional system performance and the behavior of offenders during the program, not tied to resocializing wrongdoers through coercion, an elusive goal probably since the days of the ancient Greeks.

Three goals dominate the programs of both states: to save scarce prison space and money that would otherwise be spent on incarceration; to keep offenders from committing crimes in the community during their time on the program; and to punish— less severely than prison, more severely than probation. An evaluation of the New Jersey program by Frank Pearson of the Institute for Criminological Research at Rutgers provides evidence of substantial achievement for all these objectives, as does a less ambitious evaluation of the Florida community control program, supplemented with some reasonable inferences.[88] Viewing the programs in a somewhat broader perspective, however, raises some questions about whether the movement as a whole saves state resources and controls crime.

Saving Prison Space and Money?

To be sure that the programs actually save prison space, one needs to be certain that those who participate in them are offenders who, if the program hadn't existed, would have been sent to prison. Then to know how many days are saved, it must also be clear that the number of days participants spend in the community is not offset by the number of days they serve in prison if they are revoked from the program. The ISP program supposedly obviates the first of these problems by its admissions process, in which offenders already serving time on a prison sentence are resentenced after they apply. Researchers and program administrators, however, suggest that the resentencing system may not be a foolproof way to reach only the prison-bound. They report that occasionally the original judge will offer with his prison sentence for a minor offender an opinion that ISP would be an appropriate treatment in the present case, in effect pointing the way for the probation service and resentencing panel.

Even with a few such deviations, however, the program surely saves prison space under current sentencing policies. The 1987 evaluation of the experience of 554 ISP participants who entered the program on or before December 31, 1985, concludes that the program saved, on the average, at least 199 prison days per participant. It took into account the offsetting factor of days spent in prison by participants who were revoked from the program, and compared the ISP group with a similar group of offenders (a nonequivalent control group, pretest-posttest design) sent to prison and released on parole.

Florida participants, too, are probably most often prison-bound felons, though we do not have such rigorous research to support the conclusion. The 1986 study of the implementation of Community Control determined that 72 percent of 294 controllees placed in the program between October 1 and December 31, 1983, were "true diversion" cases, based on matching the state's sentencing guidelines to the offenders' record. It does not, however, calculate how many prison days are saved by the program.

As long as intensive community supervision is cheaper than prison, we can assume that saved prison days mean money savings. Because we know more about the space saved in New Jersey, we also know more about the cost effectiveness of that program. The New Jersey evaluator found that ISP saved an average of $8,367 per participant in operating costs over the amount that would have been spent for a similar group sent to state prison and released on parole. This compares favorably with the cost savings of $6,775 per offender found in a study of the Georgia program, the largest in the country.[89] We can get only the most general idea of the dimension of savings for the Florida program, since the number of days saved is not known, and there was no control group of prisoners to compare with controllees. Florida evaluators found that community control without electronic monitoring cost the state Department of Corrections $2.86 per day per offender in 1985–1986, as compared with $27.54 for incarceration, saving almost $25 for every day an offender who would otherwise be in prison remains on the street. (Electronic monitoring adds about $4 a day in the second year for operation of the equipment, which lasts three years or longer). Based on a yearly census of 4,600 regular community control cases and an estimate that 72 percent of these offenders would otherwise have gone to prison, the net savings of community control was projected at $27 million annually in operating costs and $300 million in prison construction costs. Other cost savings for both programs include the fees and restitution paid, as well as wages earned that generate taxes and reductions in welfare and other social service costs.

To sum up, it would seem that the money-saving claims for at least some intermediate punishments are well-founded. Where the programs are truly substitutes for imprisonment, the costs of custody are lower and likely to remain so. Periods of intensive supervision may become longer than prison terms for comparable offenders, but not so much so as to offset the savings of nonprison programs. And if the widespread use of elaborate electronic monitoring devices to supplement personal supervision reduces the fiscal benefits of surveillance, it will surely not eliminate them altogether.

But the cost arguments are undercut by institutional growth tendencies that cannot be measured by New Jersey and Florida evaluators. Techniques that make intermediate punishments apparently efficient for one purpose may be costly for another. If intensive supervision evolves primarily not as an alternative to incarceration but as an "add-on" to regular probation, the additional cost of that institution could be substantial. The taxpayer faced with rising custody costs will be no less distressed because their source is probation, rather than prison.

Probation now accounts for more than two-thirds of the sentenced adults in this country, or 2.2 million people as reported by state and federal agencies on December 31, 1987.[90] If the general trend toward increasingly refined type classification of offenders were to lead, say, to designating one-quarter of that number as "high-risk" and putting them on intensive supervision, the increased contacts and lower caseloads for officers would constitute a sizable bill for the country's taxpayers. For the hypothetical magnitude of the cost increase, look at the experience of Georgia. In that state between 1982 and 1985 supervising offenders intensively cost about six times as much as supervising regular probationers, and that was without electronic monitoring.[91] If that proportion were applied to the national average annual cost of a single probationer, $833, the added bill for intensive supervision of our 500,000 "high-risk" probationers would be more than $2 billion.[92] Adding devices like anklets and the transmitters and computers that support them would raise it still further.

The cost comparison between prison and surveillance may ultimately be a false one. It rests on two questionable assumptions. One is that sentencing and prison release policies will not be affected by the prison population crunch and its fiscal implications. The other is that, without these programs, prison space would be found for each (or at least most) of the offenders, no matter what kind of crowding problem the correctional system already had. Federal court orders setting limits on prison populations in more than half the states make clear the physical and legal constraints on fitting more inmates into existing structures. Fiscal constraints are harder to assess. No one can precisely predict public tolerance for continually expanding prison budgets, but it is surely limited. Voters in New York, Virginia, and Oregon have rejected prison bond issues, and Michigan voters rejected a tax increase intended to pay for new prisons.[93] Elected officials clearly believe the voters will balk at new taxes to pay for prisons, or budgets that shortchange schools and hospitals in favor of investment in penal institutions. The very existence of intermediate punishments is testimony to that. So it may well be that even the programs that most rigorously choose offenders who appear to be prison-bound are substituting in part for less restrictive community programs that the beleaguered corrections bureaucracies of a get-tough era would have had to develop had they not had recourse to intensive supervision.

Crime Prevention?

When policymakers justify intermediate punishments with any utilitarian rationale, it is the ideology of incapacitation. While intensive supervision cannot repress some kinds of behavior with the totality of prison, community surveillance is the theory of incapacitation made operational outside the prison. The incapacitation perspective dictates that the ultimate test of programs like ISP and Community Control is whether their curfews, anklets, urine checks, and unannounced officer visits curb the offender's mobility, block access to crime, and erect barriers between tempted predator and potential victim during the period of supervision. There is no answer to this question at this time.

Evaluations in both states found few convictions, less for serious crimes, among offenders while they were on ISP and Community Control. In New Jersey only 12.3 percent of the ISP participants were convicted of a new crime within two years of their entrance onto the program, and only 7.5 percent of a felony. In Florida the figure is somewhat higher, as is to be expected in a program that does not screen out all offenders with a conviction for a violent crime. Nineteen percent were "revoked for committing a new crime," 5.5 percent for unspecified "violent offenses."

Of course the program's control is not total, and crimes may simply have gone undetected, committed at unsupervised moments. The Florida evaluation found that, in a sample of seventy-five cases, 27 percent had at least one unexcused absence from home and that, of 2,113 telephone calls made at night by a computerized telephone dialer, 20 percent went unanswered. Even electronic surveillance cannot ensure lawful behavior. The officer cannot know whether the program participant is dealing drugs or running a fencing operation from his home unless he or she happens to visit when the crime is being committed.

Continuous monitoring with electronic surveillance of an offender's presence at home increases control, as long as there are no technical problems and the offender does not abscond or figure out how to disable the device. In Florida several offenders have taken off with the transmitters, and two figured out how to remove them. Also, lightning scrambles monitors during summer storms. However, an early comparison of fifty-four offenders on electronic anklets in Florida with forty-two regular community control cases over a five-month period concluded that electronic monitoring effectively increased surveillance over offenders, making electronic contact between the controllee and the probation office every ninety seconds, with few false signals.[94]

It is difficult to know how much electronic surveillance reduces the likelihood that an offender will violate the conditions of house arrest or commit a new crime while under community control. The assessment of Community Control found twenty-six unexcused absences from home for the regular group and twenty-eight for the monitored group, but the comparison is not very meaningful. The control group was not comparable to the experimental group, which was primarily composed of people who were more likely to have been convicted of serious personal crimes and who had failed on regular community control and were therefore considered higher risk. In addition, the officers do not check up on the offenders on regular community control after about eleven at night, while the electronic monitor operates twenty-four hours a day. It is probable that the control group had unexcused absences from home that would have been sufficient to get them removed from the program had they been detected.

The low reoffense rates found by evaluations are not necessarily attributable to the programs' influences; offenders selected for the programs may have been those less likely to recidivate to begin with. And the programs' effects cannot be discerned without a comparison between the behavior of program participants and their counterparts who were treated differently. We do not have fully experimental studies from which we can draw definitive conclusions. But the New Jersey evaluation suggests that the program may be having a modest crime control impact. A comparison of ISP participants with a random sample of offenders who did time in prison and on parole before ISP came into existence found that 23.12 percent of that latter group were convicted of new crimes during the two-year period, 14.3 percent of felonies, almost twice as high a percentage as for the ISP group. This finding may be somewhat undercut by differences between the ISP group and the control group, which had an offense history with fewer drug crimes but more burglaries and more prior felony convictions—a mean of 5.1, as opposed to 2.2 for the ISP participants. The ISP group was also twice as likely to be fully employed when they committed the offense for which they were sentenced to the program.[95] An Ohio study provides even more ambiguous findings going the other way. Regular probationers in Lucas County had lower recidivism rates than participants in an intensive supervision program.[96] The two groups were not truly comparable, however. Of those under intensive supervision 94 percent had been classified as "high risk" because of their employment histories and previous criminal records, as compared with only 27 percent of the regular group.

While evidence from other sources doesn't show that intensive probation has a strong crime control effect, it does point to higher recidivism among offenders who have *not* been under surveillance. A 1984 survey of fourteen states found that about

25 percent of people released from prison (whether on parole or otherwise) returned within two years, a significantly higher recidivism rate than for offenders sentenced to ISP or Community Control.[97] This figure should be interpreted with caution, however, because many people return to prison for technical violations of parole, which may or may not involve new crimes. On the other hand, some releasees later convicted of minor crimes are not sent to prison. A better indicator of recidivism might be found in a RAND Corporation study of California felons on regular probation. More than one-half of 1,672 male probationers originally convicted of such crimes as burglary, robbery, assault, and drug sale or possession were convicted of new crimes—some of them serious—within forty months, most of those within two years of being put on probation.[98]

The argument has been made that the political survival of intermediate punishments does not require that they justify themselves in terms of reduced recidivism, that evidence that intensive supervision does not *increase* criminality (relative to offenders when went to prison) will be sufficient to garner the support of the legislators who fund the programs and the criminal justice officials who run them. If the programs are initially justified by their low cost and apparent relief of crowding, the argument goes, isn't it beside the point to require a crime reduction effect? After all, prisons have never been required to reduce recidivism, or we would have abandoned them long ago.

This is a perfectly sound argument for those who assume that our present social, political, and economic arrangements preclude a significant reduction of street crime in the foreseeable future. And this is, of course, the supposition under which most system professionals and informed observers operate. The general public, too, has doubts that street crime can be reduced, but it is unprepared to accept that conclusion. Ordinary citizens continue to believe, against the evidence, that they can turn to government's regulatory power for relief from the threats of theft and mayhem. They continue to support longer sentences and the death penalty, despite their clear inability to stem violence, burglary, or drug offenses.[99] All but the most vigilant anticrime interest groups are unlikely to oppose intermediate punishments actively as long as they appear to be punitive—satisfying symbolic as well as instrumental demands—and to reduce a potential tax burden. But the perception that intermediate penalties do not make citizens safer in the streets will further solidify support for the get-tough track of the juggernaut.

Effecting Punishment?

While policymakers certainly care about the crime control effect of intermediate punishments, they are at least as concerned with reassuring citizens that, at their instigation, justice is being done. The currently popular "justice model," which supplies the non-utilitarian rationale for intensive supervision programs, is an effort to reconcile the ancient urge for retribution with a modern sensibility that equates fairness with the formal rationalism of the law.[100] Politicians' representative function in fashioning criminal penalties, therefore, consists in supporting measures sufficiently punishing to express the outrage felt by their consituents, but also proportional to the harm done (or perceived to be done) by the offense and to other penalties. To assess the question of whether ISP and Community Control meet these requirements, one must compare the restrictions on participants' lives to both probation and prison, since the intent is explicitly to provide a penalty intermediate between the two.

Intermediate punishments are clearly harsher punishment than ordinary probation, which, in urban areas at least, generally consists of minimal reporting by the probationer and the remote possibility of an occasional home visit. First, the deprivation of liberty in the programs is substantial. Confinement extends well beyond curfew restrictions during evening (and weekend, in Florida) hours. Privacy is nonexistent. The limitation on personal autonomy is more than physical. The regulation of expenditures, with the assessment of fees and restitution payments and the requirement in New Jersey of an itemized budget, leaves an offender with little control over his money. By virtue of their felony conviction, "outmates" have lost the right to vote, "the core symbol of democratic political systems."[101] They may not exercise much job choice, and their right to protest working conditions or to challenge an exploitive employer is sharply constrained by the requirement that they be employed to remain in the program. In short, the program's punishments include sharp limits on freedom of choice, economic and personal.

Even though these requirements are very constraining, most would argue that intensive supervision is less punishing than state prison. The human and physical environments are less brutal, and the opportunity to continue one's work and intimate relationships makes the punishment less wrenching. But prison is not always much less confining. Some work release programs run from prison are very open for prisoners who are considered trustworthy, and offenders who qualify for intermediate punishments might well be those who would be selected for those programs.

There is an argument to be made that, for many offenders, ISP and Community Control are really more punishing than prison. Though the confinement of intermediate punishments is less oppressive than prison, the overall period of correctional supervision (either the custody of prison or community surveillance) may last longer, at least in New Jersey. Because program participants tend to be minor offenders with relatively short sentences, many have done most of their minimum term by the time they can be resentenced to ISP, and choosing the program subjects them to eighteen months of intensive supervision, where otherwise they might have been released from prison in three or four months with only the minimal supervision of parole.

For those who do not "make it" on community supervision, a group that includes up to half of the participants in both programs, intermediate punishments are at least as harsh as prison in one important respect. Since some of those who failed on ISP and Community Control would probably have been troublemakers in prison or might have failed on parole, we cannot know precisely what term they would have served had they not entered the programs. But we can sensibly speculate that the time they spend on the program and then in prison when they falter will, in many cases, total a significantly longer period than if they had served a prison sentence. In both Florida and New Jersey the offender who violates the conditions of the program and is sent to prison gets no sentence credit for time spent in the community, and the fact that he or she violated the conditions of intensive supervision may well be taken into account at parole review, delaying the release date. Some officers are uneasy about the extension of custody that the programs impose on relatively minor offenders. "I worry that this is another kind of revolving door in the criminal justice system," said one candid officer in Florida. "They'll do a few months in prison, then eighteen months on community control before they screw up and get sent back to prison."

From the offender's point of view, the possibilities outlined above reduce the lure of an alternative to prison. In New Jersey, where the offender has some choice as to the program, about 15 percent of ISP applicants withdraw their applications before they are completed. Surely some do so because they do not want to face expected rejection, but others say the conditions are just too demanding and still others calculate the odds that they will return to prison and find the risk of doing more time in the future too daunting. The two New Jersey offenders I interviewed in jail after they had failed on the program (because of curfew violations and dirty urines) said that, while they generally approved of the program, they wouldn't apply if they had it to do over again. The simply believe the chances of ending up in custody for a longer period are too great. One said, "It's a great thing for the older guys who are, you know, settled, and are going to make it anyway."

That intensive supervision programs are objectively very punishing and that offenders concur does not, by itself, mean they will be found severe enough by policymakers, policy implementers, or citizens. Surveys of public opinion and legislator attitudes do not yet exist, but both Florida and New Jersey have assessed acceptance of their programs among criminal justice professionals. In Florida judges surveyed generally found community control to be more punitive than regular probation, but tended to wish that it were still more punitive and strongly supported the use of some form of electronic surveillance. More than half, however, supported the program with no major changes. Phone interviews with judges, prosecutors, and public defenders in New Jersey indicated a strong relationship between professional role and views of the program. Three-quarters of the prosecutors tended to think the screening of program applicants was too lenient, two-thirds of the public defenders who knew enough about the program to comment thought it was too strict, and the same fraction of judges thought the program screening was about right. The judges and public defenders tended to see ISP as halfway between probation and incarceration in terms of severity, while most prosecutors saw it as close to probation. About half of the prosecutors thought ISP should be discontinued, while only 6 percent of the judges and none of the public defenders would drop it.

Beyond the declared aims of both programs I studied is the covert hope (and sometimes the faith) that the program will address some of the participants' emotional, medical, and educational problems as prison cannot do. Since rehabilitation has become a dirty word, and these impulses—shared by officers, probation officials, and some judges and legislators I spoke with—look suspiciously like the service element of the rehabilitation ideology, program evaluations have not assessed the extent to which services are provided or what difference they make. What follows is therefore impressionistic evidence based on limited observations of the New Jersey and Florida programs.

Referral to jobs and placement in drug or alcohol treatment are services that are routinely provided because they are linked to program conditions. A universal requirement of intermediate punishment programs is that the participant be employed. Jobs of the sort most of these offenders get—construction worker, delivery person, machine operator—are relatively plentiful in the late 1980s in both Florida and New Jersey. While program participants generally find their own jobs, officers use the state employment services and their own contacts to help when they can. In the New Jersey program, in which participants have regular group meetings and may socialize with one another, they may help each other find work.

One of the most dearly held beliefs behind both programs is that keeping a job will both increase self-respect and provide the means to reduce the economic pressures that lead directly (burglary) and indirectly (through recourse to illicit drugs) to crime. There is certainly evidence that those accomplishments occur under some conditions; a number of outmates I interviewed spoke with pride about acquiring new skills on the job and being able to keep up with their expenses for the first time in their adult lives. But many of the jobs are low-skill, requiring education and skills below those of the outmate, and commitment to them is low. Participants often plan to leave these jobs when they "graduate."

The assumption that work will keep these offenders from crime may be naive. There is plenty of evidence that people with jobs commit crimes. White collar crime accounts for more property loss each year than street crime, and most of that is committed by people who are working and who have access to criminal opportunities through their jobs. Drug and property crimes, the types most frequently committed by participants in surveillance programs, are also committed by people who are working.[102] In fact, most of the ISP participants that I talked to or heard about who committed new crimes on the program were working when they erred.

Provision of services other than referring outmates to jobs and AA or NA programs is haphazard. With an ideology that explicitly rejects rehabilitation this is probably inevitable. Because the help that does exist is limited to informal brokerage or referral, it depends very much on the interest and energy of the individual officer and on the demands on his or her time. Some officers go to great lengths to help an offender find special medical services or vocational training and college programs. Others do very little, or even discourage program participants from seeking opportunities on their own. Activities outside the scope of usual routines may mean extra work for the officer. With offenders in educational programs, a visit to check attendance at a class, for instance, must be added to the on-the-job surveillance. Setting up a regular program of allergy treatments for an offender requires extra paperwork and an occasional phone call to confirm that the treatment is continuing.

So less of this kind of help is provided than in a program that frankly acknowledges the fact that services and contacts are an important part of a decent life, whether or not they reduce criminality. Nonetheless, I encountered touching examples of special assistance provided in both states, like the Florida officer's efforts to get a slow-witted, alcoholic offender into what the controllee called "temper school" and Diane's organization of her charges to give food and clothing to the family of one of their number whose apartment had burned.

THE TIP OF THE ICEBERG

Intermediate punishments today reach only a tiny fraction of the population under correctional supervision. Joan Petersilia, an expert on probation and author of the 1987 RAND study "Expanding Options for Criminal Sentencing," estimated in May 1988 that 50,000 people to date had been placed in intensive supervision programs.[103] (The number of adults in penal custody—prison, probation, parole and jail—on a single day in 1986 alone was 3.2 million.)[104] On June 30, 1987 there were 6,777 participants in the Florida community control program, compared to 65,758 on regular felony probation.[105] The number in New Jersey's state program (there are also programs at the county level) is still miniscule; 386 participants as of May 20, 1988, contrasted with 53,000 regular adult felony probationers.[106]

Surveillance as a Growth Industry

But these figures disguise the bandwagon quality of the intermediate punishments movement. All over the country expansions and spillovers, new sites, and devices for community surveillance are planned. Programs are admitting larger numbers of offenders and broadening eligibility standards to create new candidates. Related activities such as parole, regular probation, and pretrial programs, are taking on the surveillance thrust that intermediate punishments have legitimized. As fast as objections to expansion are raised, the political and technical means for overcoming them are discovered. The outer limit is not yet in view.

As of early 1988 New Jersey's plans are illustrative of the range and magnitude of growth for these programs. Under consideration was an appropriation (strongly supported by all three branches of government, I was told) that would increase ISP participants by one-quarter and expedite the processing of applications, a procedure that now takes more than three months, on average. Both the Governor and the state budget office favored even greater expansion. The Administrative Office of the Courts was also seeking funding for three half-way houses—for ISP applicants who would otherwise be qualified but are essentially homeless, high-risk cases who could be more closely surveilled than if they were at home, and participants being punished for infractions too minor to warrant reincarceration in state prison. The ISP Director hoped to start a small program for juveniles, a developing trend in other states. Union County (Elizabeth) was readying its program for operation in the fall, supplementing local programs in Essex (Newark) and Middlesex (New Brunswick, Perth Amboy) counties. A small intensive supervision program for state parolees had begun. Finally, program administrators hoped in the longer term to get the legislature to allow the resentencing panel to review some nonviolent offenders serving mandatory minimum terms. Inclusion of this group, now ineligible for ISP, could ultimately multiply the size of the program many times over.

Pressures for expansion come from a variety of sources—the financial and managerial constraints of the penal system, the political dynamics of demand and reassurance for tougher punishments of all kinds, and imperatives of professional self-interest within the justice system. To the extent that sur-

veillance programs are a substitute for incarceration, they will
be popular as long as they appear to be cheaper than prison and
prison crowding continues to be an issue. This could be a very
long time. As more people come into the prisons, fewer are leav-
ing, either because terms are longer or parole is rarer. As of
mid-1988 New Jersey was still adding state inmates at a rate of
120 per month, and its county jails were 173 percent over capacity.[107] In 1987 Florida projected a 63 percent increase in its inmate population by 1990, as compared with an increase for the
preceding three years of 24 percent.[108] Furthermore, crowding
in Florida is exacerbated by sentencing guidelines that have
greatly reduced the use of parole, from 2,139 releases in 1984–
1985 to 749 in 1986–1987.

With the currently popular emphasis on just deserts and incapacitation rationales for punishment, surveillance programs
that substitute for prison are hard to sell on get-tough grounds.
But the same is not true where intensive supervision is meant to
supplement traditional community penalties like probation and
parole. Probation departments beleaguered by deep budget cuts
during the state and local fiscal crises of the mid-1970s are now
recipients of new funding on the strength of their emphasis on
increased surveillance, often for the same kinds of offenders
they supervised in the past. While resources are concentrated
on the high-risk probationers and therefore do not insure
harsher punishment for all, the programs convey the message
that supervision of minor offenders is now more stringent, in-
suring incapacitation, and better able to force "offender accountability," thus promising just deserts.

Professional self-interest plays a part, too, in the growth of
intermediate punishments. "Social control entrepreneurship"
flourishes as much in the expansion as in the creation of intensive supervision programs.[109] If the program is an add-on to
probation, judges can demonstrate that they are not soft on
crime; if it substitutes for prison, they can share with the probation officers the burden of that label. Probation officials have
the most to gain from expansion. Their refinements of what the
programs should be providing—halfway houses and electronic
anklets and job readiness classes—and for whom they will provide it usually necessitate larger staffs and budgets.

Professional interests also impose substantial limits on expansion. Larger, more inclusive programs pose greater risks of
isolated but celebrated incidents that cast a shadow over the
whole enterprise and of studies that conclude that there is too

little control purchased for scarce public dollars. Rapid expansion, as many probation officials recognize, may not, in the longer run, enhance status or increase job opportunities for the professionals who run them. There is a particular tension in those programs that aim to divert offenders from prison. On the one hand, the probation officers urge caution in accepting offenders who are "bound to fail" and, thus, make the program appear ineffective; on the other hand, too much caution invites the charge that the program is admitting only the light cases and, therefore, merely widening the net of social control, rather than saving prison beds or dollars. The ambivalence tends to breed an understandable duplicity; at the same time that the administrators of the New Jersey program were lobbying for expansions of many kinds, they told me that growth would be only incremental.

Program evaluators can be ambivalent on the net-widening question, too. While a major measurement of the success of programs like those in Florida and New Jersey is whether their participants would otherwise have been prison-bound, the Florida evaluators of community control noted with disapproval that they had "observed many instances of controllees destined to fail: homeless offenders or offenders with unstable residence histories; unemployable offenders; offenders whose employment required travel outside of the county or state; offenders whose sentencing guideline scores called for the second (or higher) level of incarceration; and offenders whose scores were inaccurately calculated by the State Attorney's office."[110] They recommended steps that might reduce the failure rate on the program but would surely also simply increase surveillance of minor offenders who would previously have received the lesser sentence of regular probation.

The intensive programs were not originally intended to affect regular probation supervision directly, but my interviews suggest that excitement over the new surveillance programs is having a ripple effect. The eventual tightening of probation surveillance for many offenders not considered "high-risk" is a likely offshoot of intensive supervision in the states that can afford this bow to stricter punishment. Officers assigned to the new programs frequently say, "This is what probation was supposed to be," as though the new surveillance represented a standard to which probation was returning after a long absence. While it is true that the original concept of probation presumed far more frequent contacts between officer and offender, they were intended to be more like service calls than tracking.[111]

Rehabilitation, rather than incapacitation and punishment, was the declared ideology that drove the development of the institution of probation.

The use of electronic surveillance brings with it a number of problems: maintaining the equipment sometimes takes more time than is saved by not having to make a personal visit to the offender, the initial investment is substantial, and there are technical glitches. Occasionally a program participant will figure out how to fool the machine; in Florida an offender pilfered from a local jail the special screwdriver that worked in the fasteners for his anklet.

Nonetheless, use of these devices will surely spread, though I would not go as far as criminologist Georgette Bennett, who predicted in 1987 that "electronic monitoring will be the dominant means of probation and parole supervision" within the next generation.[112] The anklets and video phones strongly support the restraint ideology of intermediate punishments, by definition increasing physical control over the offender. They need not supplant the personal supervision of probation officers; in the programs I observed, electronic monitoring supplemented professional surveillance. They are relatively cheap once the start-up costs have been incurred (undeniably cheaper than prison custody) and will, if the usual trend in electronic gadgets applies, become cheaper still as the technology develops.

The Irrelevance of Rights

No one denies that intermediate punishments intrude significantly on the privacy of offenders and their families. They have to, the argument goes, or they wouldn't be more confining than ordinary probation. Yet the programs rely on frequent, unannounced home visits, although "physical entry of the home [by a respresentative of the State] is the chief evil against which the wording of the Fourth Amendment is directed."[113] Civil libertarians believe that the probation officer's license to search a home without a warrant on the basis of a hunch that the probationer is involved in crime—a principal weapon in the armament of control measures—violates the constitutional prohibition against "unreasonable search and seizure." Especially where electronic monitoring is concerned, it has been argued that intermediate punishments turn a man's castle into his prison, destroying the notion that in a democratic society the home is one's ultimate sanctuary and refuge against state authority.[114]

This concern seems unlikely to impede the spread of intermediate punishments. Adoption in the near future of privacy protections for persons controlled in the community would run counter to the general legislative and judicial trend away from development of the rights of criminal defendants and offenders. Current policy directions include expanded concepts of legal responsibility, restrictions on due process, and narrowed definitions of privacy.

To some extent the present trend mirrors shifts in punishment ideologies as well as more generally conservative political trends like increased deference to executive authority. Disillusionment with the rehabilitative ideal, for example, is reflected in legislative modifications of the insanity defense.[115] The revival of retribution as a respectable punishment rationale is certainly one factor in the decision in many states to try juveniles accused of violent crimes in adult court.[116] Deference to administrative convenience shapes many judicial decisions, like the Supreme Court's determination that practices like body cavity searches and housing more than one pre-trial detainee in a jail cell do not deprive them of their right to due process.[117]

Incapacitative aims of punishment have recently been reinforced by the Supreme Court in a 1987 decision that also underscores the lack of privacy rights for people under correctional custody.[118] *Griffin v. Wisconsin* affirmed a lower court's refusal to suppress as evidence in a firearms trial the gun found in the defendant probationer's apartment, even though it was seized in a search based on an unverified police tip and conducted without a warrant.[119] The majority held that exceptions to the usual warrant requirement could be made when "special needs" could be demonstrated, and that "supervision is a 'special need' of the State permitting a degree of impingement upon privacy that would not be constitutional if applied to the public at large."[120] Deferring to the probation officer's mandate to restrain probationers, the court found that he did not need "probable cause" for suspecting a crime in order to search. "Reasonable grounds," as interpreted by Wisconsin courts, was a sufficient basis—an apparently all-encompassing standard if it could cover, as it did in *Griffin*, mere speculation reported in a phone call that was never even proved to have come from a police officer.

That probationers are constitutionally entitled only to "reduced expectations of privacy" is rationalized in two ways. One is the notion that the offender has consented, as the price of staying out of prison, to the visits and searches of the officer, and to electronic monitoring, if it is part of the program. To many observers this is a hollow justification. In the first place, programs are often not offered as alternatives to prison and therefore can in no way be perceived by offenders as voluntary.[121] Even if they are substitutes for prison, the consent of participants to intermediate punishments seems more coerced than voluntary, given the unappealing prospect of the only alternative choice. One also wonders about how informed consent can be when some offenders are confused and unknowing at the time of sentencing and when, as my research revealed, there are so many situations in which the duration of correctional custody is unknown and unknowable. These arguments are unlikely, however, to make the programs vulnerable to constitutional challenge. The Supreme Court has explicitly denied the need for basing a police search on the "knowing and intelligent" waiver of Fourth Amendment rights, and police searches are subject to more constitutional limitations than are those of probation officers, who are dealing with convicted offenders rather than mere suspects or arrestees.[122]

The greater license of probation officers points to the other justification for the probationer's reduced expectation of privacy—his criminal status. One who has been convicted of a crime is presumed to give up many rights by his commission of it, including "the right to be left alone."[123] Even in cases in which the offender retains some constitutionally protected interests, as the Supreme Court has said probationers do, they must be balanced against those of the penal system in maintaining institutional order.[124] In the 1980s this balance usually comes down in favor of correctional authority. While court decisions have not been explicitly directed at intermediate punishments, *Griffin* suggests that the present Supreme Court would balance most rights conflicts as it does with prisoners.

Electronic surveillance raises a further issue not relevant for programs without it. There is no doubt that a probation officer's inspection of a program participant's closets and drawers constitutes a search within the meaning of the Fourth Amendment. But what of the continuous monitoring of the offender's whereabouts by an electronic device? The Supreme Court has ruled that police use of electronic surveillance does not constitute a search when the device does not monitor the contents of communication or, when it collects only information that could have been obtained by visual surveillance.[125] Under these standards, the electronic monitoring feature of intermediate punishments would not constitute a search. Even if it did, the diminished privacy rights of offenders would be likely to render presently anticipated uses of electronic devices immune to serious constitutional challenge on privacy grounds. "If the conditions of probation are reasonable, the use of technology to enhance the probation officer's efficiency in enforcing them would not be unconstitutional. All the technology accomplishes is increased surveillance proficiency."[126]

Most other constitutional questions raised by intermediate punishments are the same as for ordinary probation and seem likely to be resolved similarly. A probationer may be required to answer the officer's questions or otherwise provide information, for example, through polygraph tests, but does not lose the right against self-incrimination in a subsequent trial.[127] Curfew and travel restrictions have been held to be permissible limitations on the probationer's rights of association and speech as long as they appear to serve rehabilitative aims.[128]

Intermediate punishments raise a special issue when program conditions include the payment of money. The Supreme Court has ruled that it is a violation of the Equal Protection clause of the Fourteenth Amendment to revoke probation status when the probationer is unable, through no fault of his own, to pay a fine or restitution.[129] Many intermediate punishments (and some regular probation programs) require participants to pay a share of the costs of their own supervision; a New Jersey official told me that probation supervision fees (including ISP) for FY 1988–1989 would bring in more than $8 million of state revenue. A constitutional problem arises when the determination of an offender's eligibility for programs like ISP or Community Control is based partly on the presence of a phone in the home, at present a necessity for both passive and active electronic monitoring. A judge in New York City told me recently that he thought intensive probation supervision as an alternative to prison had only a very limited future there because of the large percentage of criminal defendants who were homeless. An offender who is rendered ineligible for an intermediate punishment by virtue of homelessness might successfully challenge the eligibility decision on equal protection grounds.

Surviving "Failure"

Research suggests that probationers under intensive supervision are no less likely to commit crime than regular probationers.[130] This finding does not necessarily negate the effectiveness of surveillance as a crime control technnique. It may be simply that more crime by probationers is detected when the officer is paying closer attention. What of the possibilities of reducing recidivism among those who would formerly have gone to prison rather than being put on probation? Virtually the only evidence available that intensive probation may have this effect comes from the New Jersey evaluation. It suggests a modest reduction of recidivism but does not track a large number of offenders for a substantial period of time. New Jersey may also be a special case. It prides itself on having "the toughest program in the country," a degree of control that is unlikely to be widely followed, at least in the near future.

If crime control policy were driven solely or principally by the rational, instrumental demand for social defense, the spread of intensive supervision programs would be seriously threatened by evidence that they are ineffective at preventing the street crime people fear. Criminologists occasionally warn that the whole movement could collapse either because the occasional heinous crime that gets a lot of public attention makes it politically untenable, or because program outcomes seem to suggest more of the same: high violation rates, high recidivism of offenders who complete the program, and little difference between the later records of these offenders and similar ones who did time inside.[131]

This concern is probably misplaced. To begin with, there are likely to be very few heinous crimes committed by program participants, not because the programs' surveillance is so effective but because relatively few offenders chosen for it have backgrounds of violence. In addition, the criminologists' worry overlooks both the politics of policy development in this area and the expressive functions of the programs that remain even when their crime control effects are slight. While the case of Willie Horton, the furloughed murderer whose attack on a Maryland couple did such damage to the presidential hopes of Massachusetts Governor Michael Dukakis, prompted reassessment of some programs elsewhere, it is unlikely that long-term damage will be done to the concept of prison furloughs overall. "Most corrections officials consider furloughs a sound part of effective corrections," said Hardy Rauch, director of standards and accreditation for the American Correctional Association, less than a month after the end of the Presidential campaign in which furloughs became a major issue.[132]

The programs under discussion are well protected politically.

The get-tough era has brought greater legislative involvement in penal policy and with it a stake in the protection of that arena. No longer can legislatures make political hay by attacking the leniency of judges or corrections officials because they have probably helped to structure it. Policymakers and implementers are likely to work in tandem to defend intensive supervision programs against citizen attack because they resolve, at least momentarily, the principal contradiction of the get-tough policy thrust, its burden on already-reluctant taxpayers.

Florida probation officers tell of a primitive version of intensive supervision that was tried and abandoned in Florida in the early 1970s. Initiated by the corrections bureaucracy, it met with officer resistance and did not have the clout to survive a finding that more violations resulted from that program than from regular probation (a likely outcome if the program is structured to watch offenders more closely).[133] No one worries much about a similar fate for the current Florida program, and they are probably right. This time the community correction program has been presented in the context of Florida's terrible crowding problem and the large share of tax money going for crime control, and it has already weathered a couple of incidents involving controllees in serious violence. (As of spring 1988, the New Jersey program had not been tested.) Legislatures, now balancing the competing interests of keeping taxes down and reassuring a fearful public, get their political leverage out of minor modification of programs that seem threatening or inadequate. If a murderer on prison furlough commits a rape, they press for narrowing program eligibilty; if an embezzler on ISP steals again, they require participants to tell their employers of their criminal record within a few weeks of starting work.

More ordinary program failures can be handled routinely or even ignored. A 1982 evaluation of the impact of New York State's ISP (at that time a case management program, rather than an intended alternative to incarceration) was "inconclusive" and found that the program "does not appear to reduce the overall failure level of 'high-risk' probationers."[134] The program continued nonetheless. In fact, four years later the legislature vastly expanded it and added the even more difficult mission of successfully diverting prison-bound offenders.

The survivial of the programs also seems assured because their limitations as crime control do not negate other, symbolic uses. Intensive supervision is punitive enough to satisfy the social functions of punishment noted by Durkheim. Outcomes that satisfy the instrumental need for safer streets are not essential to program survival if the process of the punishment can still be defended as inflicting a deprivation that observers believe underscores its subjects' misdeeds. The ritual of punishment attests to moral boundaries and reinforces social solidarity among those of us on the righteous side of them.[135] The programs need not prove themselves with high completion rates or crime-free "graduates" as long as they appear to the public to be more than a "slap on the wrist," a set of restrictions that sets offenders apart from the law-abiding citizen.

One Florida supervisor summed up perfectly the sources of legitimacy for intensive supervision programs. He noted that, while "most" people on community control violated its conditions, those failures don't threaten the program's survival because the program is measured by fiscal and symbolic standards. In part it is perceived as successful to the extent that it keeps violators out of prison—and thereby saves the taxpayers money—even for short periods. "We win by the day," he said, "not by the old success rate measures." And features of the program still conjure up the separation of the guilty and the innocent. "House arrest still sounds good even if it isn't really what the public thinks it is," he said.

Of course the media can increase the vulnerability of these programs. A celebrated crime makes good copy for the nightly news, even better if committed by someone whom the criminal justice system could have restrained. Releasing a serious offender on parole to go out and kill again becomes an additional crime to be tried on television, with officials as defendants. But many of the new intensive supervision programs have taken steps to build loyalty among the press to blunt possible attacks. "We've had 90 percent favorable media attention," says Harvey Goldstein, assistant director of the New Jersey Administrative Office of the Courts, perhaps because they have invited the press to go into the field to see how restrictive the program is and to what lengths law enforcement goes to pick up an absconder. Programs like Massachusetts's "risk management" approach have adopted a different strategy. They release research results but do not invite media attention out of concern that the risks of the program will be publicized before its punitive aspects are well understood.

BREEDING CONTROL

Innovations in punishment are usually viewed in terms of their cost-effectiveness as crime control or their sufficiency in expressing the moral outrage of the lawabiding members of society. Sometimes their fairness and the extent to which they help their subjects or the community is taken into account. By these standards, intermediate punishments can be cautiously endorsed. As they are imposed at the end of the 1980s they appear to be cheaper and, in most respects, less oppressive than prison. Even a substantial expansion seems unlikely to increase the kind of predatory street crime that terrifies and outrages most citizens. The programs I observed are without question punishing enough to constitute retribution for the offenses committed by participants. Threats to civil liberties can, in some cases, be addressed with program revisions: to honor equal protection ideals, for example, economic eligibility qualifications could be removed. And finally, intermediate punishments may include real services to people who need them; outmates may get concrete help and moral support, victims may receive restitution, and nonprofit organizations often benefit from the participants' community service assignments.

But such an assessment does not go far enough. Many of the arguments for intermediate punishments are powerful when the programs are viewed on their own terms but weak as social and political contexts become clearer. "Society is not the mere sum of individuals, but the system formed by their association represents a specific reality that has its own characteristics."[136] To determine that intermediate punishments are a promising direction for crime control policy, we must move from micro-level questions of whether they benefit their subjects without increasing the risk of victimization to a macro-level concern with their contribution to more general social policy.

The ideal criminal justice system protects life, limb, and property without increasing conflict, inequality, or deprivation. By that standard, intermediate punishments become part of the problem, not the solution. They add to the machinery of a crime control system that is minimally effective in utilitarian terms but that thrives on symbolic politics and the organizational needs of its component parts. As the scope of correctional control expands to include intermediate punishments, it can also serve to widen the social divisions among us by repressing behavior and people that pose little threat to moral order and who are already finding it difficult to swim in the mainstream.

Building the Machine

Some commentators have thought that "the potential for the intensive revolution may be enough to level some old prisons and depopulate some of the new joints."[137] This strikes me as naive. The hard-core cases will still go to prison, and no one predicts a significant drop in the foreseeable future in the volume of murder, rape and robbery. Although the trend of mandatory sentencing laws seems to be slowing, and ways of evading some of its impacts are being found, people serving mandatory minimum terms will continue to fill up the prisons. This phenomenon is a good illustration of what Samuel Walker calls the "trickle-up effect" of get-tough policies.[138] Many, if not most, of these offenders are not dangerous predators but, rather, drunk drivers, small-time thieves, or drug dealers with more than one offense who would not have received prison terms in more lenient times.[139]

Prison populations will also be fed by the intermediate punishment programs. They will include the "failures" from those programs that are intended to be alternatives to prison—perhaps as many as half of the participants, if the current programs of Florida and New Jersey are typical. Intermediate punishments will also contribute to the prison population with those who fail on the programs not intended as substitutes for prison but as add-ons to regular probation. This group will be in the paradoxical position of being new recruits to prison who, without the advent of this non-prison program, would previously have stayed in the community.[140]

Penal control outside prison is likely to become more extensive as well as more *intensive*. The probation population increased 71 percent between the end of 1981 and the end of 1986.[141] Intermediate punishments have probably contributed indirectly to that trend, in that the availability of intensive supervision in many jurisdictions has made probation seem more appealing to judges, as an alternative either to a prison term or simply to sending the offender home. (I have heard judges express their opinion that "Now that probation may mean something, I'll use it.")

Intermediate punishments are an integral part of the

"toughen up" role of probation, perfectly illustrated by a National Institute of Justice "Crime File Study Guide," a state-of-the-art report on probation in the U.S. in the late 1980s. It notes that "probation officers are now directed to be less concerned with the provision of services for offenders (e.g., counseling, employment assistance) and more concerned with drug testing, curfew violations, employment verifications, arrest checks, surveillance, and revocation procedures."[142] It concludes that "probation is slowly and necessarily changing," and embraces the infusion of personal and electronic surveillance into probation with a section of the report entitled, "Restructuring Probation as an Intermediate Sanction."

The picture of penal control is thus one of expansion in every program, with intermediate punishments feeding the prisons, contributing to the "trickle-up effect," and legitimating the spread of observation and control for the majority of convicted offenders outside prison. In fact, the spread is affecting some of those not yet convicted of crime; in New Jersey and other states the surveillance techniques of intermediate punishments are being used for pretrial release programs, too. With the federal government at the reins, the juvenile system is also getting on the bandwagon. In 1987 the federal Office of Juvenile Justice and Delinquency Prevention funded two programs to identify and promote intensive supervision programs, one for juveniles after they have finished doing time in an institution.

Even those who can accept the expansion of an already vast formal system of penal control may be troubled by the kind of control that programs like ISP and Community Control exert. In prison the fundamental control of the person is through the deprivation of physical liberty, to which all else is incidental. All that is demanded in prison is that the inmate eat, sleep, and refrain from predatory behavior. Intermediate punishments have more ambitious aims; as the Florida statute puts it, community control is "designed to encourage noncriminal functional behavior. . . ."[143] The encouraging techniques regulate both mind and body through coerced therapy and parenting workshops as well as curfews and urine checks.

This is not to say that offenders are always cowed into mindless submission by being told what child-rearing techniques they must use or where to purchase inexpensive shoes (directives I observed.) It is easier to defy the regulations of mind than those of body, and many do. The litany of good intentions and self-awareness recited by outmates is so ubiquitous that I suspect it has become the shield that they know will deflect their officers from further invasions of what they regard as private space. But it is a very limited defense. The disincentive to protest openly is even greater than it was in the 1960s for the midnight raids of welfare workers looking for violations of the "man in the house" rules of public assistance.

The successful completion of an intermediate punishment program requires the participant to yield a great deal of fundamental dignity. The primary institutions of society—work, family, neighborhood—become sites of penal control, annexed to the justice system in a way that recalls Foucault's image of the "carceral archipelago."[144] Participants must notify employers that they are in the program, exposing themselves to exploitation by bosses who know that they cannot quit without risking revocation. In New Jersey some officers prohibit offenders from quitting a bad job and from "talking back" to an oppressive employer. Pressure in both states is strong to maintain conventional family arrangements, to stay with a wife and support her, to marry a girlfriend or move out. "Normal" community life becomes a domain of custody extending beyond overt behavior to habit and will.[145]

Control also extends to those around the offender. The probation officer, perhaps accompanied by police, may have to go to a wife's job site to discuss the participant's whereabouts with her if they think he has absconded, or to a child's school if there is some possibility that the offender might try to contact the child there. If the officer sees bruises on a family member, he or she will question the injured person out of the hearing of the participant. These actions have protective possibilities, of course, as wives of formerly abusive outmates are the first to note. But it is protection incidental to state coercion, not the organic support of community.

Control for What?

Many participants in intermediate punishment programs are people on the bottom, living in neighborhoods beset with the structural economic changes of the post-World War II period and suffering the social isolation and disorganization that has resulted from them.[146] Penal control cannot, of course, address this level of social dysfunction, but the officers and administrators who are committing so much of themselves to these programs often cannot face that. Lacking the tools and the authority to resolve structural dilemmas in their participants' lives, they seek to discipline their charges to their own definitions of "the responsible life." While some aspects of that life embrace growth and strength—the mutual support among participants that some programs foster, for example—others do not.

Acceptance of authority is a dominant theme. Since the officer's (and judge's) primary task is to prevent participants from violating the law and the rules of the program, it is understandable that the message would be generalized. It can, however, become a license for the exercise of power for its own sake or for purely disciplinary ends. The New Jersey program illustrates this point; it requires everyone (with an occasional exception) to attend weekly drug and alcohol counseling sessions, whether or not they are substance abusers. The emphasis on authority can also amount to enforcing a meaningless conformism; for example, I observed a New Jersey officer order a new and nervous participant to never again wear his "Official Beach Bum" T-shirt. Or it can convey the notion that defending one's rights is not part of being a responsible adult, as when an officer will not allow an outmate to quit a job or protest working conditions on the ground that his boss's harassment tests the offender's self-control.

The old-fashioned values of thrift and self-denial constitute another theme of the life into which participants are indoctrinated. Two immediate problems are apparent. These virtues are probably not avenues to the tangible successes to which participants aspire; no amount of frugality will reward a minimum-wage worker with a Mercedes. Furthermore, the primary vehicle for living by these values is the program requirement that the outmate pay fines, restitution, court costs and supervision fees. The offender is as likely to conclude that money saved is money appropriated as that thrift can build a future. Kant's matter-of-fact observation that criminals being punished were "slaves of the State" is perhaps more literally true for offenders who pay for their supervision in the community than for prisoners.

It is hard to escape the conclusion that intermediate punishments include social and economic disciplinary functions that strongly reinforce the inequalities of U.S. society. Requiring that participants have a job means that they often take lesser jobs than they would get if they could make real job choices. They generally work in secondary labor market jobs in small businesses like tire retread services, small roofing companies, nursing homes, or on non-union construction crews. Once hired, they are expected to be compliant workers, to give up a large share of their earnings to the state, and not to display independent thought. If U.S. cities were peopled with successful graduates of the more vigilant of these intermediate punishment programs, and if they continued to live by program precepts, we would have little risk of crime, but also little possibility of popularly-instigated social change.

The Next Round

In the previous chapter I sketched the outlines of national and state computerized criminal records systems that could make criminal justice more efficient without expanding its reach. Here, too, I feel a responsibility to note that intermediate punishments could have a place on a spectrum of criminal penalties that reflects larger social priorities of substantive justice and procedural fairness. In such a system they would be true alternatives to prison and would be limited in time to the duration of a prison term imposed for an equivalent offense. While they would impose frequent reporting requirements, supervision would not extend to control over matters of choice like working conditions and personal associations (with the exception of prohibiting friendship with a crime partner). Job placement services and drug or alcohol counseling would be available on a voluntary basis. Support for the programs would not depend on evidence that they produced substantial reductions in crime or recidivism, an unrealistic aim for any penal measure in a democracy.

The odds that intermediate punishments will, in the short run, reflect a more generous and rights-oriented atmosphere than now exists are very small. There are also influences on their development that mitigate against the kind of restraint that I recommend.

Public opinion is surely one of those influences but not necessarily a dominant one. The social crisis of street crime has produced either ambiguous or symbolic demands from the general public. Recent surveys show support both for longer sentences for all felons and for alternatives to prison for nonviolent offenders.[147] Support for the death penalty and longer prison terms for serious offenders is based on general political and social beliefs as well as on concern about crime.[148] The public position on punishment overall can perhaps best be understood as a desperate generalized appeal to "do something!" combining the instrumental and the symbolic. If that appeal were more differentiated and better informed—an unreasonable expectation, given the quality of the information about crime purveyed by the media and political leaders—it might include the justice model's emphasis on punishment for its own sake and therefore be quite hard on the truly predatory crimes. But it would also surely include lighter penalties for lighter cases and would endorse approaches to crime that supplemented punishment with services.

Criminal justice professionals, on the other hand, have an immediate, material stake in the expansion of the punishment machinery at all levels. They also have continuing relationships with political decisionmakers, who themselves are rewarded by investments in punishment. The nonprison penalties present particularly appealing professional opportunities. Two characteristics enhance their potential for expansion: they are guided in part by the incapacitation rationale, which means that theoretically more control is always better; and they don't require buildings that cost millions of dollars and take years to construct. In addition, the general political climate legitimates the job of penal surveillance outside the prison. Tracking offenders in the community fits right in with "workfare" programs, drug testing in the military, and polygraphs in the workplace.

PART III

•

SOURCES AND IMPACTS

6

•

CONTEXTS OF THE JUGGERNAUT

Any topic of interest in the social sciences has a peculiarly amorphous quality. It looks distinct, tangible, separate—empirically or conceptually—but the closer you examine it, the more it merges into its surrounding space. So it is with crime control. A matter of restricted scope, the subject of the parochial discipline of criminology, starts dissolving into much wider issues: political ideologies, the crisis in welfare liberalism, the nature of professional power, conceptions of human nature.

● Stanley Cohen, *Visions of Social Control*

INTRODUCTION

THERE IS NO DENYING that street crime is a very pervasive and destructive fact of life in the U.S. at the cusp of the 1990s. The best available data on its dimensions estimate that almost 30 million crimes of theft and violence (excluding murder) were committed against people age twelve and over in 1986.[1] While this figure includes many minor property crimes—almost 9 million were larcenies of property worth less than $50—it does not include more than 4 million attempts, which can sometimes be as traumatic the completed crime. Sixteen percent of the victimizations reported in the National Crime Survey for that year were for rape, personal robbery, and assault. Young people, males, and blacks were more likely to be victims of violent crimes than older people, women, and whites.[2] Urban residents are particularly afflicted. For all crimes taken together, the likelihood of being victimized was more than 50 percent greater for those in central cities than for others; for rape and robbery it was at least twice as great.[3]

It is easy to assume that because this terrible social problem generates so much concern in all quarters, the policies instituted in its name constitute a rational response to the focused demands of a representative electorate. But "popular" demand, in fact, issues from a highly selective sample of attentive citizens, skewed toward the powerful and the noisy. And that demand is both instrumental and expressive. Voices are raised in supplication to government to express general anger and aspiration as well as to secure particular benefits and rights.[4] Politics cultivates policies that are mixtures of motive and accident and may or may not have been guided by conceptions of the public good.

Becoming more sophisticated about the complexities of the nature and process of policymaking does not, however, fully protect against myopia. When policy touches on what is perceived to be fundamental security, a dangerous innocence with respect to its sources may prevail. Political trends of the 1980s demonstrate that, as a nation, we still reduce foreign policy to a Manichean contest between the Free World and the Evil Empire. And we assume that it is the near-universal condemnation of predatory behavior that gives us our criminal justice policy.

Such oversimplification overlooks the fact that crime is not an event of nature, but a legal and social construct. It is merely behavior on which the state has conferred the status of nastiness. (Most citizens may think of the labeled behavior as nasty, too, but their disapproval does not make it a crime.) The social and economic arrangements chosen by a society—or, more often, by its various elites—determine what and whose behavior is considered nasty enough to proscribe and punish. From this general process crime and justice are created.

A few simple examples are enough to illustrate the cultural relativity of many definitions of crime and to suggest some forces that shape them. Killing a cat was criminal in ancient Egypt, but in Paris during the sixteenth century a favorite Midsummer Day ceremony was burning a dozen live cats on a pyre.[5] Tudor laws made it a crime to profit from the sale of grain, because feeding the people was such a fundamental moral duty. But when improved agricultural techniques were adopted to satisfy the demands of the new world market and produced yields that exceeded local demand, grain became no more than a commodity. By 1769 the death penalty was prescribed for participation in food riots over grain shortages caused by fluctuations in the world market.[6] A contemporary example of the cultural relativity of crime is when an explosion in a coal mine cited for over 1,000 safety violations, in which many miners are killed, is considered an accident resulting in civil liability at most, while a sniper's spree during which six people are killed is considered a "mass murder."[7]

The long-range trend in Western Europe (and, to a lesser extent, in the U.S.) is toward reduced criminal violence and less harsh punishments.[8] But it is too simple to assume that these two tendencies are consistently and causally connected. That they are not can be seen in the increase of capital penalties in England from the late seventeenth century to the early nineteenth century when the "revolution in manners" was beginning and violence was actually on the decline.[9] Public punishment as a spectacle disappeared in France in the early nineteenth century, though the statistics and contemporary accounts record huge increases in "nightly assaults, hold-ups, daring robberies."[10]

Viewing crime as a political and social construct makes it easier to see criminal justice policy as shaped by forces more fundamental than crime rates or victimization—or even the intense political contest that exploits the fear of crime. The larger sources of crime policy may also be more visible when viewed with the advantage of historical distance, divorced from the emotions of rage, scorn, and shame that color any contemporary view of crime. This chapter provides some of the tools for exploring this broader and deeper view.

The first main section of the chapter steps back from recent policy trends, providing examples of the interaction between historical development and ideological responses in the formation and reconstitution of criminal justice policy. It reviews historical episodes in which social responses to crime reflected a particularly evident combination of "rational" and historically contingent influences. From these examples, we can begin to see how reductionist it would be to assume that each generation of policymakers applies the same rule in adjusting the intensity and severity of punishment to the intensity and severity of crime.

The second principal section of the chapter moves beyond the familiar idea that social policy in general, and criminal justice policy in particular, represent a rational, instrumental response to a manifest public desire to vanquish crime. It discusses two alternative analytic perspectives that are necessary to begin to understand the related trends of the contemporary justice juggernaut: the get-tough program and a growing emphasis on observation. These approaches supplement the pluralist, instrumental perspective by focusing on relatively independent influences of symbolic politics and the growth of policy subgovernments that provide criminal justice professionals with avenues for satisfying organizational needs.

THE SOCIAL DETERMINATION OF CRIME POLICY

The Emergence of Crime Control

Particularly compelling in shaping crime control policy is the state's need for authority and stability. The very emergence of criminal justice, in fact, was intimately tied to state formation. Initially, the centralizing force of feudalism necessitated at least partial control over private disputes. The evolution of feudal hierarchy in the twelfth century gave the princes of Angevin England and the south of France the monopoly of authority that could gradually supplant private vengeance and reconciliation as the legitimate means of resolving conflicts. "Criminal justice arose out of changing relationships of freedom and dependence in the secular world."[11] The early people's courts of Anglo-Saxon England were no longer voluntary forums where freemen judged themselves, but became part of a hierarchical system of feudal legal institutions, in which the king took a special interest in criminal cases.[12]

The development of centralized authority turned what was essentially folklaw into a formal justice system but did not create a function benefiting the populace as a whole. Quite the contrary. Class justice was the norm, although the English tradition of communal courts gave some protection to the poor not found elsewhere.[13] Administered by nobles and later by the patrician class of the growing towns, local courts increasingly substituted punishment for reconciliation as part of the stratification of the new urban society of the fifteenth century.[14]

The public view of official punishment during the feudal and early modern periods is not a reliable indicator of either the level of concern about crime or a developed perspective on the role of the state in controlling it. Crime, madness, and poverty, and the violence that accompanied them, were simply part of life, a sign of fate or God's will. Though there might be objections to the way punishment was imposed, or to its targets, the state's exercise of violence was taken for granted.

Physical punishment was simply introduced into a world which was accustomed to the infliction of physical injury and suffering. In that sense it was not an alien element. The authorities took over the practice of vengeance from private individuals. As private retaliation had often been violent, so was the penal system adopted by the authorities.[15]

We cannot know precisely the incidence of common crimes in medieval and early modern Europe. Studies of court records in individual jurisdictions in England and elsewhere starting in the fourteenth century suggest that theft and assault were very common.[16] Those who set the social standards in Western societies through the fifteenth century were, after all, warriors whose feuds and jousts, as well as chronic and ubiquitous wars, framed the social relations of burghers and peasants. "It is well known how violent manners were in the fifteenth century, with what brutality passions were assuaged, despite the fear of hell, despite the restraints of class distinctions and the chivalrous sentiment of honor, despite the bonhomie and gaiety of social relations."[17]

Though direct comparisons with later times and locations are almost impossible, Barbara Hanawalt has made an effort, comparing rural and market towns in twentieth-century Indiana with those of comparable size in fourteenth-century England. She concludes that homicide, rape, and torture were more common in medieval England, and property crime more common in modern Indiana.[18] She also estimates that fourteenth-century London had 3.6 to 5.2 homicides per 10,000 population (depending on the year and the population figures used), rates that are a good deal higher than the rate of 2.2 per 10,000 population in New York City in 1986.[19] Furthermore Ted Robert Gurr, reviewing a number of studies, concludes that "rates of violent crime were far higher in medieval and early modern England than in the twentieth century—probably ten and possibly twenty or more times higher."[20]

The rise and fall of public execution is a somewhat more specific example of an important long-term trend in penal policy that reflects state formation and changes in the social and economic order. In the early preindustrial period, when states were still relatively weak, public punishment demonstrated and reinforced state authority and dramatized its assumption of vengeance that had only recently been carried out by victims or their representatives.[21] Visible, drastic punishments (mutilation, burning, and whipping, as well as death) were common.

As states became more stable the severity of punishment fluctuated. One historian attributes the rise of harsh penalties in Amsterdam between 1650 and 1750 to the increasing stratification of society, "the process of aristocratization," in which the increasing social distance between law-breakers and judges legitimated more intense repression.[22] Another attributes the

high execution rate in Tudor England (as high as twenty per
100,000 people annually, more than 46,000 people a year if applied to the U.S. in the late 1980s) largely to the runaway inflation of the late 16th century. Theft of property worth more than
1 shilling was considered a capital crime, making even petty
thieves subject to the death penalty.[23] Rising violence is an im-
plausible explanation for increased severity, as several historians agree that homicide rates were declining by the sixteenth
century.[24]

Between 1630 and 1750, executions in England dropped dramatically, perhaps as much as 90 percent. To some extent this
decline can be attributed to the gradual reduction of violence at
all levels, what Norbert Elias called "the civilizing process." But
the late sixteenth and early seventeenth centuries were also a
turbulent period, with social disorder attributed to high inflation and war. Furthermore, convictions for capital crimes escalated after 1650.[25] The key to the shift away from execution
during those years probably lies in the labor needs of colonial
expansion. Transportation to America or the Caribbean became
an increasingly popular sentencing disposition, and by the late
seventeenth century it was perhaps more widely used than execution.[26] Public punishments of all kinds declined in Britain
and on the European continent after the mid-eighteenth century. With the greater stability of modern regimes, the sensitivity of the aristocracy and the bourgeoisie to official violence
increased.

From the seventeenth through the early nineteenth century
the long process of capitalist development was also an important influence on the development of justice policy.[27] During the
eighteenth century a flood of legislation resulted in more than
200 capital crimes in England, most of them property offenses
and many of them minor.[28] (This was, after all, the country in
which John Locke was revered for having written, "Government
has no other end but the preservation of property."[29]) As in
modern times, capital statutes were honored more in their
breach than in their observance; as their number increased,
actual executions declined, the result of pardons and procedurally defective trials. Nonetheless, the criminal law served
as a vital legitimizer, "constantly recreating the structure of
authority which arose from property and in turn protected its
interests."[30]

The place of labor in the emergence of industrial capitalism
probably helped the nineteenth-century development of the

penitentiary. Dario Melossi and Massimo Pavarini argue that the introduction of prison work—the manufacture of items for state use, the contract system in which private manufacturers ran workshops in the prisons—was intended to lower production costs and suppress wage scales in some industries.[31] Even if they overstate the case, the industrialized prison altered both the aims and the consequences of the prison sentence. The prison now produced "propertyless proletarians" for whom submissive and diligent working behavior was as important as penitence for demonstrating good conduct in prison.[32]

The Role of Punishment Rationales

Directions in crime policy often appear to be shaped by prevailing punishment rationales. A decline in the portion of persons arrested that actually go to prison is attributed to the prevalence of a rehabilition ideology; or revived support for the death penalty is explained by the new embrace of retribution. It is surely correct that sentencing philosophies influence, at least in the short run, the shape of justice policy; they legitimize the state's repressive function. But those philosophies themselves have their roots in larger ideologies and the material forces that shape them.

It is not coincidence that the birth of modern criminology dates from the eighteenth century, that era of reform, rationality, and the supremacy of market relations.[33] The dynamics of emerging capitalism were explained by contemporary analysts and pamphleteers as reflections of human nature—its self-interest and tendency to make rational calculations based on the prospect of material gain. A model for the economy based on human motivation could easily be transported to the realm of social life to become "a part of the secular ideology that replaced traditional social assumptions in England by the end of the [seventeenth] century."[34]

Cesare Beccaria, the Italian nobleman generally credited as the father of criminology, shared with Adam Smith, the illustrious economic philosopher who was his English contemporary, a belief in the individual will as the spur to human behavior. Criminals were no longer "puppets of the supernatural," but calculators of the relative advantages and risks of crime being contemplated. As the self-interest of economic man is regulated by market competition, so is the hedonism of the social being restrained by punishment that will "exceed the good expected from the crime."[35] While deterrence had been a function of punishment for many centuries—the public element of medieval executions was important because the hanging was intended to set an example for its observers—it was only fully articulated by classical criminology.[36] The much later shift in penological fashion from deterrence and retribution to rehabilitation also reflects currents in the broader stream of society. A century after the publication of Beccaria's great work, *Essay On Crimes and Punishments*, the intellectual and ideological landscape had changed, and criminology changed with it.

Two themes are crucially important. One is the influence of science, the view that human beings, like other animals, are products of nature and nurture, with behavior conditioned by their biological, psychological and social characteristics rather than freely willed or impelled by supernatural forces. The other is the Romantic confidence in human progress in general and the potential of the individual in particular. Tying the two themes together was the theory of evolution, the endorsement of "a process of development in time as the fundamental fact in human experience."[37]

The positive school in criminology set out to apply the scientific method to the study of criminal behavior to better understand what makes some people commit crimes while others remain law-abiding. They argued that scientific expertise should determine the fate of criminals. In the U.S. the spirit of science and the faith in human nature joined with a new perspective on the role of the state to support rehabilitation as the proper rationale for criminal punishment. Although the theory was only selectively applied, and it dominated penal ideology only among progressive prison administrators, it was the enlightened view for almost a century and it crowded out other justifications for punishment.[38]

These themes become apparent in the economic and social movements that followed the Civil War. Reactions to industrialization and urbanization included defiance of classical economics through the development of a new social gospel. The most important sociologist of his generation, Lester Frank Ward, attacked the laissez-faire doctrine as a reflection of "this tyrant of nature—the law of competition" and maintained, in 1893, that, "all human institutions—religion, government, law, marriage, custom—together with innumerable other modes of regulating social, industrial, and commercial life are, broadly, viewed, only

so many ways of meeting and checkmating the principle of competition as it manifests itself in society."[39] Proponents of the
social gospel—dissenting protestant ministers of the last three
decades of the nineteenth century—put Christian ethics of the
Golden Rule and the general welfare ahead of the pursuit of
wealth, and saw the prevailing economic system as their
nemesis. Josiah Strong wrote in 1889, "[The] existing competitive system is thoroughly selfish, and therefore thoroughly un-
christian."[40] The social gospelers called on employers to pay just
wages and institute profit sharing and on the church to provide
recreation and hospitals for the poor.

Richard T. Ely, the man to whom Strong wrote his indictment
of laissez-faire, perhaps best illustrates the linking of the two
movements into support for government regulation of business
and assistance to the poor. (Woodrow Wilson did it too, arguing
as a young political scientist that government should perform
"ministrant functions" including the management of railroads
and the operation of public utilities.[41]) A Johns Hopkins economist and lay advocate of the social gospel, Ely wrote into the
founding document of the American Economic Association
the core commitment of affirmative government: "We regard
the state as an agency whose positive assistance is one of the
indispensable conditions of human progress."[42]

The positivist theme and the reformist perspective are evident in the "Statement of Twenty-two Principles" set forth in
1870 at the founding of what is now the American Correctional
Association. Since the criminal's behavior was largely beyond
his control, "reformation, not vindictive suffering, should be
the purpose of penal treatment of prisoners."[43] The amount of
time it would take to reshape the characteristics that led an
offender into crime would obviously vary from individual to
individual, so "indeterminate sentences should be substituted
for fixed sentences," an objective realized in most states by the
mid-1920s. (Most states had instituted the supposedly thera-
peutic programs of parole and probation, besides.[44]) A belief in
individual self-determination, a holdover from eigtheenth century rationalism, shown through in the admonishment that
"the prisoner should be made to realize that his destiny is in his
own hands." The new American liberalism that aimed to secure
opportunity for individual development surfaces in the statement, "The aim of the prison should be to make industrious free
men rather than orderly and obedient prisoners."[45]

Of course this last imperative also speaks to the contemporary (and nineteenth-century) American belief in salvation through work. As the deterrence rationale of the classical school reflected faith in the preindustrial economic model of choice in the free market, so the rehabilitation ideal of positivism underscored the need for the "dangerous classes" to embrace (not merely to be regulated by) bourgeois industriousness. Mainstream morality included the work ethic, that virtue necessary to socialize a worker who cannot find within himself any other justification for the unrewarding and poorly paid labor of the factory or foundry. The paternalism of Progressivism and the later faith in technical solutions to social problems maintained the association between morality and industry for many decades. It was only with the tumult of the 1960s that the work ethic was broadly challenged—and with it, the assumptions of the rehabilitation model of criminal punishment.

SYMBOLIC AND SUBSYSTEM POLITICS

Many forces have been at work in the last twenty years in deepening and broadening the exercise of state coercive power in this country. It would be absurd to maintain that increases in reported crime and the public outcry that has accompanied them have played no part. But policymakers respond to other motivations, too. An analysis that tries to bring recognition of the part played by the other forces that are shaping crime policy in no way denigrates the suffering of crime victims and their friends and families.

Like war, street crime is classically vulnerable to symbolic politics. Its sources are complex and murky, hidden in the dark corners of the human soul and in the social conflicts that pass for accomodations people have made to share an uncertain world. For those most exposed, the stakes in reducing the problem are large. It is easy to assume that everyone is at risk; "vicarious victimization" through media reports or the anecdotes of acquaintances may be as important a source of fear of crime as the experiences of actual victims.[46] However, the ancient, mythic association of crime with punishment provides an easy recourse that does not yield long-term benefits and crowds out other ways to approach crime.

The political scientist Stuart Scheingold has developed a model of the politicization of crime that stresses the effect of cultural forces on transforming victimization and vicarious victimization into fear of crime and then into punitive responses and policy initiatives.[47] He argues that the mythic relationship of crime and punishment has deep roots in the U.S. vigilante tradition and in our commitment to the ideal of individual responsibility. Contemporary society sustains the myth in several ways. The media depict crime as the product of predatory strangers who are not only evil, but also black or young, and therefore to many doubly menacing. These presentations allow us to evade the reality that violence and larceny take place in our midst, often perpetrated by those close to us. They heighten our tendencies to project the insecurities of modern life into the policy arena, making punishment seem the only sensible recourse. So does our need to maintain social solidarity by defining some people and behaviors as beyond the community pale; as Durkheim put it, the main function of punishment is "to maintain social cohesion intact, while maintaining all its vitality in the common conscience."[48]

The symbolic appeal of a get-tough approach also extends beyond perceptions and fears of street crime. Scholars conclude that while the anxiety expressed by the public in opinion polls is considerable, it does not amount to the "runaway fear" that might be expected to justify the crackdown of the last two decades.[49] And the fear of crime is apparently not correlated with either punitiveness or the likelihood of victimization; for example, women, who are, as a group, less frequently victimized than men, are, nonetheless, more fearful but less punitive than the rest of the white population.[50]

Quite independent of fear and anger over crime is another sort of social stress, what might be called structural discontents, which contributes to punitive reactions to crime. People whose material well-being is deteriorating, or who equate social change with the disruption of cherished values, or who feel their voices are not heard in important public debates, may displace their anger and frustration on to the "undeserving," however defined. Added to the cultural forces identified by Scheingold are some others that mediate structural discontents; for example, the U.S. tendency to attribute social problems to individual defects and address them with short-term, individually-based remedies.[51]

Scheingold makes the point that law and order politics develops out of "a search for salable issues," not a popular call to action or, as some Marxists would argue, a concerted effort of economic elites to distract us from the failures of capitalism.[52] This observation makes sense of the great gulf between the symbolic exchanges of law and order politics and actual policy outcomes. Both the democratic and the Marxist theory of how crime is politicized are instrumental; if they were valid, one would expect to see activity of the state consistently reflecting the values of policy entrepreneurs, either the polity or the holders of capital. But there is no such straight, continuous thoroughfare linking law and order politics to the juggernaut. Instead, the route is curved and rutted, and when it enters a new jurisdiction with greater resources and alternate traffic patterns, it breaks off entirely and resumes, newly paved, in a different (though not opposite) direction.

A theory that acknowledges expressive influences better explains the policy direction. It views the get-tough measures—harsher punishment and diminished defendants' rights, for example—as products of a process of politicization of crime in which politicians turn misfortune into campaign fodder, the media turn personal disaster into mass entertainment, and we, the general public, "willingly, even eagerly, participate in our own seduction."[53] The observation programs, on the other hand, are creatures of subsystem politics. Bureaucrats, legislators, and criminal justice interest groups promote their organizational needs through routine policymaking at all governmental levels.[54] I have traced these dynamics in some detail as they operate in the development of computerized criminal records systems and intermediate punishments.

Law operates at both formal and informal levels. I am not speaking here of the possibility of abuse or incompetence by those who implement legal regulation, but rather of policy as a layered entity, conveying a license to adapt as well as an order to obey. Law may confer a duty on a judge and simultaneously give him or her the power to act in a quite different manner.[55] Thus "the law can have it both ways, instructing its enforcers to do one thing, while allowing them to do something else."[56] What appears to be a command may be administered as a game instead, with the enforcer and the subject colluding in a pattern of selective enforcement.[57] This duality pertains also to larger policy movements, in which the symbolic message is carried by the general trend, but mirroring it is the subtrend that moves in a different direction. So it is with the juggernaut: stiffer sentences, narrowed rights, and bigger corrections budgets are decreed; but new probation programs, continuing defendant protections, and data surveillance by police are also allowed. In this case the adaptations of the game may be transforming the overall program of criminal justice.

THE POLICY SPIRAL

As an academic discipline criminology has made a good deal of progress since the days when social psychology determined a very narrow view of the causes of criminal behavior. Modern research is almost as likely to focus on the interplay of large political and economic forces that underly criminality (and our perceptions of it) as on traditional psychoanalytic or cultural transmission theories focused primarily on lower-class criminality.[58] Furthermore, the "new criminologists" and the historians who have recently become interested in the role of crime and law enforcement in the context of state power are coming to know the dancer from the dance.[59] They have undertaken to examine the determinants of a society's choice of what behavior to criminalize, challenging the assumption of political neutrality as the starting point for the development of criminal law.[60] The aridity of the old discipline that concentrated on the understanding of individual sociopathology is being transformed into the richness of a broader and more diverse pursuit, with room for inquiry into both the political determinants of the state's actions in defining and repressing crime and the many causes of crime.

What remains to be done is to look more closely at the consequences of choices made about defining and controlling crime. The principal U.S. approach to this area of inquiry is to maintain varying degrees of vigilance over the tension between crime control imperatives and the protection of individual rights, perhaps best embodied in the constitutional notion of due process.[61] The importance of this attention is not to be underestimated in a rights-oriented society like this one. But it ought not to be the only perspective; only a very limited liberal ideology excludes notions of the desirable distribution of power and resources from a vision of the good society. Crime policy must be measured in terms of its effect on well-being and social relations as well as for its impacts on crime incidence and individual freedom. We need to be looking at the macrosocial effects of such measures as massive drug enforcement programs, the increasing federalization of crime control, and the continuing relative disregard of corporate and political crime.

In political campaigns the pledge of toughness is a totem that—along with baby-kissing and flag saluting—identifies the candidate as a member of the clan of virtue, loyalty, and patriotism. To keep the pledge with a hard-line policy proposal is virtually costless, since although experienced observers know it will, at best, have a minimal crime control effect, the name of the game is still the politics of promise.[62] From that point the bureaucrats who devise and manage the concrete programs that emerge from the policy system take over, and they are almost invisible to the public—which, in any case, is not well equipped to distinguish between feckless drift and purposeful change.

It would be an error to assume that we have moved from a model of crime control that emphasizes due process for defendants to an alternative model that pursues the repression of criminal conduct as its primary goal.[63] Rather, a kind of policy spiral may have taken us beyond that duality to a new characterization. What might be called the umbrella model does not abandon the value systems of either individual liberties or efficiency. Instead, it subsumes them in an overarching concern with involving the largest number of possible miscreants, however defined, in the justice process. Comprehensive coverage, whether achieved by the clearcut contacts of arrest, indictment, or conviction or through the shadow of the criminal record or curfew, is the aim, not structuring a relationship between state and citizen or wrapping up a successful prosecution.

The policy spiral works somewhat as follows: The national mood—whether a generally anxious one, one more focused on crime, or perhaps a combination of the two—provides what one political scientist calls the "fertile soil" for law and order politics.[64] Public demand (manufactured or spontaneous) and political manipulation of symbols puts punitive policies on the governmental agenda, as I have described briefly in the early pages of this chapter and will develop further in Chapter 7. The choice of policy alternatives contains such contradictions—principally the incapacity of the traditional program of capture and confinement to be protective in any comprehensive way—that new programs with very different ends emerge from subsystem politics. Public frustration with the instrumental failures of crime control policy combines with the availability of techniques and perspectives from the spreading observation programs to make more fertile soil, this time for policy proposals that impose control outside the traditional boundaries of the criminal sanction.

The policy spiral is likely to lead ultimately to a far more regimented society than we have now, one in which workers are routinely screened for alcohol and drug use and pilferage, and social services are conditioned on the willingness of recipients to work at dead-end jobs. Justified by deepening moral distinctions between the respectable and the "undeserving," the new regimentation would most affect those who already have the least access to the education and skills necessary to live productive, comfortable lives in the post-industrial economy. Perhaps a healthy economy could mitigate this trend as labor demand rose and the structural discontents that support law-and-order politics fell. But we have seen in the 1980s that economic growth does not necessarily bring with it significant public and private investment in the labor force. In addition, the more regimented society would legitimate stigma so that even in a prosperous time subsistence survival might be deemed acceptable for many Americans.

7

·

UNDERSTANDING THE PUSH TO
CAPTURE AND CONFINE

The critical thing to understand is not where the seed comes from but what makes the soil fertile.

● John Kingdon, *Agendas, Alternatives, and Public Policies*

THE SOURCES OF CONTEMPORARY
STREet CRIME POLICY

ONE OF THE POLITICAL mysteries of the last twenty years is the growing defection of what was previously considered part of the "natural" constituency of the Democratic party: blue-collar and service workers of the lower-middle class. An examination of this phenomenon may help us understand the development of harsher criminal justice policies, from the political turmoil of the 1960s through the late 1980s.

In recent years a number of books by perceptive political journalists have begun to explain this apparent conversion to conservative principle and Republican party allegiance. They find their sources in the social and economic circumstances of working people in the late 1960s and early 1970s, and the alienation and defiance triggered in that period. Thomas Byrne Edsall discusses the repudiation by large segments of the middle class of the commitment to domestic spending that has characterized the Democratic party since the New Deal.[1] Godfrey Hodgson considers the growing cultural conservatism of voters during the 1960s and Nixon years.[2] And Robert Kuttner examines the sources of tax revolt in California and elsewhere.[3] A detour into the pattern of conditions and reactions that these writers suggest can shed some light on the law and order campaigns of the 1960s and their subsequent translation into get-tough criminal justice measures. For many areas of domestic policy, the 1960s was a kind of watershed, dividing the innocence and arrogance of the developing U.S. welfare state from the cynicism that has fueled much subsequent social policy. Taken together, Edsall, Hodgson and Kuttner analyze workers' disaffection and its policy consequences in three clusters of events that might be called the *erosion* phase, the *restatement* phase, and the *exploitation* phase.[4]

The erosion phase begins the process of workers' disaffection. Working people experience real economic and social distress: rising taxes, distributed regressively; income stagnation; challenges from heretofore powerless groups such as blacks, youth, and women; and neighborhood deterioration and disorder. Political representatives of the middle class largely disregard these concerns.

The restatement phase includes interpretation by politicians, the press, and the political parties of public grievances. This interpretation tends to generalize them, highlighting anti-government sentiments and surface rhetoric at the cost of discovering structural sources for the specific complaint. As these reformulations seem to ratify public sentiment, some voters desert their traditional political allegiances (generally Democratic, though some Republicans voted for George Wallace in the 1968 presidential primaries and general election), aided by Republican legerdemain and Democratic default.

In the exploitation phase, Republicans and Democrats, building on the reformulated grievance—tax inequities have become revolt against big government, anger at rioters and black protesters has become rejection of the welfare state—have outdone each other in promoting their conservative credentials.[5] The other major outcome of the process, with a long-term effect that may last into the twenty-first century, is the translation of the generalized protest into specific policy measures favorable to some powerful group other than the initially restive citizens. The tax relief obtained from California's Proposition 13 primarily benefited corporate and wealthy property owners; cuts in domestic spending and "supply-side economics" have lowered overall tax rates only for households in the top 6 percent of the income distribution.[6]

The parallel with the development of the get-tough program is evident but imperfect. The erosion phase consisted of psychic anguish, rather than economic or social, in that law and order emerged as an issue in response to the largely nonmaterial threats of 1960s rebellions.[7] Most U.S. workers had lived by what had been nearly universal standards for respectability—

they were clean, industrious, and patriotic. Then students, blacks and peaceniks began saying, in one way or another, that it was all for naught, and acting out their challenge in full view in the streets or on television. Furthermore, it seemed that parents, professors, and liberal politicians tolerated this slur on values that most of America held dear.

The restatement phase interpreted the anxiety over these challenges as a general cry for a more punitive and regimented approach to individual behavior. Politicians who reaped the benefits of the law and order appeal were guided by intellectuals of the left and right who urged a shift in punishment rationales. Together they guided the public away from the fuzzy hopefulness of the rehabilitative ideal to the moral logic of just deserts and the cynical authoritarianism of incapacitation.

As with the trends discussed by Edsall, Hodgson, and Kuttner, the get-tough program most clearly benefits groups other than those that made the initial political demand. Political candidates have found that the hard line on crime, building on the myth of the relationship between crime and punishment and the structural discontents of voters, is as much a winner as anticommunism used to be. Harsher penalties and expanded observation policies have created new and refined criminal justice career opportunities; job growth for guards (private as well as public) outstripped all but seven other occupational categories in 1987.[8] Subsystem politics is the name of the game. Clusters of legislators, administrators, and interest groups—local groups of justice system officials or, on the national level, the International Association of Chiefs of Police and the American Correctional Association—plan and execute far-reaching policy developments. Rewards to the citizens who pled for relief from street crime have been meager. In fact, observation policies may be doubling back on the law and order voter, extending the reach of criminal justice over many people who are neither the rebels that Americans reacted against nor the predators that pose a genuine threat to the safety of person and property.

But this is leaping ahead. The remainder of this chapter traces the interplay of material forces, cultural symbols, and political manipulation from the age of anxieties (the latter half of the 1960s) up to the program's realization in the crowded prisons and expanding surveillance of the late 1980s. It organizes the historical material in rough correspondence with the policy development phases traced by Edsall, Hodgson, and Kuttner.

The Erosion Phase

The upheavals of the 1960s created fault lines that have structured the social policy of the 1980s. The rearranged landscape now includes the demand—legitimate and insistent, though not fully satisfied—of blacks and women for legal and economic equality. Just as pervasive a legacy of that turbulent period (and perhaps more fundamental) is a nearly ubiquitous cultural conservatism, coached and congratulated by opportunistic politicians and business elites. Although the ideology now reaches beyond middle America into ghettoes gilded and otherwise, it started there. Voters were, in the words of Richard M. Scammon and Ben J. Wattenberg's widely-read 1970 book *The Real Majority*, "unyoung, unpoor, unblack and uncollege," and they began, in the mid-1960s, to fight back against the perceived excesses—in both words and deeds—of efforts to bring about social change.[9] In embracing drugs and rock music and open sexuality, the free speech movement and the new youth culture elicited as much reaction as the more overt threats posed by political dissidents committed to the civil rights and peace movements.

Law and Order Appeals.   The revolt found its voice in an appeal for "law and order" that simmered through the middle of the decade and erupted in 1968, the tumultuous year of assassinations and violent confrontations between police and demonstrators over the Vietman War. By then respondents to Gallup polls were starting to record "crime and lawlessness" as one of their principal concerns; the presidential election was, in part, a contest of pledges to end disorder.[10] During President Richard Nixon's first term support was strong for legislation to lengthen prison sentences, authorize preventive detention, and limit Supreme Court jurisdiction over criminal appeals. The tide was so powerful that Senator Sam Ervin (the North Carolina Democrat who was later to distinguish himself as Chairman of the Senate Judiciary Committee conducting the Watergate hearings) said, during a floor fight on the 1970 bill that enacted various get-tough measures for the District of Columbia:

The siren voice of that old devil, political expediency, has been whispering in my ear, "You had better vote for the District of Columbia crime bill because it is a law and order bill, and it is not politically sagacious or politically profitable for Senators to vote against a law and order bill such as the District of Columbia crime conference report, even to preserve the individual liberties of our people."[11]

It was apparent to some contemporary observers that more than street crime was at issue in the public outcry over law and order; but just what was often unclear. As President Johnson's former U.S. Attorney General Nicholas Katzenbach wrote:

There are many ingredients to the confusing calls for "law and order," and while these do not have to be mixed up together, they have become so. In this respect, liberals and conservatives, intellectuals and rednecks, racists and civil libertarians, adults and juveniles are all contributors to confusion.[12]

Those calls became "a cry, as things begin to break up, for stability, for stopping history in mid-dissolution."[13] Rioters and muggers and those who would set the terms of their restraint—permissive judges and an unaccountable Supreme Court—substituted for the Evil Empire which had dominated public demonology in the 1950s as the prime target for many people now threatened less by challenges foreign than domestic.

To say that the embrace of law and order had symbolic sources is not to deny that street crime was also a serious and growing problem, contributing to the public demand for protection. There has been widespread criticism of official crime statistics that show huge increases in both violent (104%) and property (123%) crime rates between 1960 and 1969 alone.[14] Some of that increase can be attributed to technological and cultural changes that made the reporting of crimes more likely and professionalization of police that increased the likelihood that citizen reports of crime would be recorded. Some offense increases reflect changes in local reporting systems that resulted in overstatement of crime increases.[15] Even acknowledging these limitations on the reliability of the data, thoughtful criminologists conclude that it is "difficult to argue that no real increase in crime has taken place in the United States in the last few decades."[16]

Whatever the dimensions of the increase, perceptions of it were probably colored by an unusually peaceful period immediately preceding it. Both personal and property crimes had dropped during the generation before 1960—perhaps reflecting the absence of young males during World War II and the demand for their labor in the years immediately following.[17] As crime rates fell, so did tolerance of violence and theft in both low-income and affluent neighborhoods. Expectations of police efficacy rose, too, with generally greater reliance on social protection from government stemming from the New Deal. Scholars encouraged the naive idea that police were now a public bureaucracy with primarily technical problems to solve in bringing about a peaceful society.[18] Perhaps the improved standard of living of the post-War period contributed also to an unprecedented expectation of domestic tranquility as a right promised by the Constitution to all respectable people.

When the crime threat intensified in the 1960s it took new and frightening directions. While good trend data on the prevalence of drug offenses and the crimes spawned by the drug business do not exist, public and professional consensus in the mid-1960s held that "drug traffic and abuse were growing and critical national concerns."[19] Lending a particular edge to those concerns was the prevalence of illicit drug use in the cities and among the young. The citizenry was increasingly urban; metropolitan populations rose by 43 percent between 1950 and 1970.[20] It saw "the drug problem" as intimately connected with recorded increases in urban offenses that enraged and terrified citizens. During the decade, reports of street robbery rose by 186 percent and residential burglary by 286 percent.[21] (It may be argued that these data overstate actual increases, but they are unlikely to be mere reporting artifacts.) The association of drugs with organized crime heightened the worry.

Another major source of concern was that juveniles were increasingly involved in serious offenses. In 1967 the President's Commission on Law Enforcement and the Administration of Justice found that young people accounted for a majority of arrests for major property crimes and that arrests of adolescents for serious crimes had jumped more than 50 percent during the first half of the decade.[22] This pattern can be partly explained by increased investment in law enforcement and heightened attention to the behavior of at least some youth. Real per capita expenditures for police protection rose 22 percent (adjusted for inflation) between 1962 and 1967; and much of that increase was in cities with large proportions of poor and minority youth perceived by police to be prone to crime.[23] Furthermore, some increase in the volume of youth crime was a predictable result of the baby-boom bulge in the proportion of the population under eighteen. But justice system performance and demographics do not fully explain the jump in arrests. The increased attention of the justice system to juveniles in the early 1960s was as likely to be diversionary and rehabilitative as repressive, and the surge of juvenile arrests was twice as great as the surge of juveniles.[24]

To deny a real increase in street crime committed by the young is to overlook what Stanley Cohen has called "the social context of aspiration" for low-income youth who compose the bulk of youth arrestees.[25] As powerless outsiders to all meaningful modern adult activities except consumption, often unconstrained by family bonds of support and control, postwar American youth were highly vulnerable to the drift into delinquency.[26] Unemployment rates for males age 16–19 began to rise in the early 1950s, slowly for whites, sharply for blacks, so that by 1964 25 percent of black males in that age group were out of work and seeking employment, almost twice as high as the percentage of whites.[27] It is not hard to understand how black youth, trapped in segregated neighborhoods and irrelevant social roles, were lured by the "hustle." The arrest of almost twice as many blacks as whites under the age of eighteen for urban robberies in 1964 surely reflects not only differential justice system treatment but differential behavior.[28]

The Fusion of Symbols and Substance. The public demand for harsher penalties and more aggressive police activity, starting in the latter half of the 1960s, does not reflect a measured assessment of either rising criminality or the performance of law enforcement. Its origins lie more in expressive than in instrumental needs. Two broad population groups were key: working people who had only recently acquired a toehold in the middle class, and prosperous conservatives whose values dominate the elite consensus.

The political scientist Murray Edelman illuminates the drama of symbolic politics. He points out that generally political action shapes our knowledge of the world, not the other way around. We respond to political words and deeds that cast our experiences in reassuring or threatening light, and that interpretation then shapes our immediate political demands.[29] The emergence of the get-tough program reveals this process at work. Political messages began to transform the raw material of the chaotic events of the 1960s into potent symbols of rebellion against self-reliance, conformity, and hard work—the value structure of most Americans. Those who, for whatever reasons, were most engaged with this value structure tried to secure it by supporting crime control measures that they hoped would suppress what was perceived as out-and-out rebellion by disaffected black, young, and antiwar groups. Two phenomema legitimized the process: the actual rise in street crimes and the inclusion of crimes like theft and assault in collective upheavals like urban riots, sit-ins, and peace demonstrations.

The transformation had many ingredients. One of the most politically significant was the conversion of demands for racial equality into hooliganism. While local southern officials made this connection in the wake of the 1963 demonstrations that turned violent in cities like Cambridge, Maryland, and Birmingham, Alabama, it was Senator Barry Goldwater who endorsed it on a national scale. In his acceptance speech for the 1964 Republican Presidential nomination, he decried "the growing menace in our country tonight, to personal safety, to life, to limb and property, in homes, in churches, on the playgrounds and places of business, particularly in our great cities." He went on to warn that "nothing prepares the way for tyranny more than the failure of public officials to keep the street safe from bullies and marauders" and then honed in on black demands: "Equality, rightly understood as our founding fathers understood it, leads to liberty and to the emancipation of creative differences; wrongly understood, as it has been so tragically in our time, it leads first to conformity and then to despotism."[30] It is important to note that this speech was given before major urban riots blurred the distinction between riot and the "direct action" of protest. The very day Goldwater spoke, an off-duty policeman killed a young black male in Harlem. Two days later, in the aftermath of this event, the ghetto exploded, inaugurating the "long hot summers" of 1964–1968.[31]

Politicians often reacted to the urban riots by repudiating the idea that they stemmed from, or expressed, racial protest. After eruptions in several New Jersey cities in August of 1964, Governor Richard Hughes called for "firm resistance" by police, urged stiff sentences for rioters, and denied that racial tensions motivated the riots.[32] Two weeks later the mayor of Philadephia echoed Hughes' sentiments, saying the riot in his city was unrelated to black grievances.[33] As the decade progressed, the association of blackness and crime no longer depended on the context of civil rights demands, partly because the looting and assaults of urban riots legitimized more blatant references.

Alabama Governor George Wallace frequently denied that his allusions to law and order were racist, but at a 1967 press conference, he said, "Politicians are always trying to explain why some people don't obey the law—because they didn't have any watermelon when they were small children."[34] The following year his staunchly anti-civil rights constituency turned law and order into a Presidential campaign issue that rivaled Vietnam in importance. Louise Day Hicks, the Boston School Committee Chairwoman who attracted a great local following with her opposition to busing and support for "neighborhood schools," alluded in her 1967 campaign for Mayor to "special privileges for the black man and the criminal" and made great political capital out of protestations that, as a white woman, she could not walk safely on the streets of Boston.[35] (An interesting sideline on the political careers of both Wallace and Hicks is that neither one began as a diehard segregationist; both seem to have moved into more blatantly racist postures as they developed their constituencies.[36]) The fusion in the public mind of damage done in demonstrations and riots with individual acts of predatory robbery and assault became a vision of criminality in which blacks figured very prominently. Vice President Spiro T. Agnew summed it up in his definition of "troublemakers": "muggers and criminals in the streets, assassins of political leaders, draft evaders and flag burners, campus militants, hecklers and demonstrators against candidates for public office and looters and burners of cities."[37]

He might as well have included the Supreme Court, since it was the focus of as much antagonism as any individual activists or muggers. The Court became the primary institutional scapegoat for crime, another manifestation of the conversion of racial hostility into calls for "law and order." Senator John L. McLellan, an Arkansas Democrat, playing on the South's resentment of the Court's civil rights decisions, embodied the disdain expressed by Wallace and other prominent politicians. Once described as "a stern and obdurate man with the mien of a Puritan patriarch who has just led his band ashore and now must get down to the real task of saving them from themselves," McLellan sponsored a 1967 bill that attempted to overturn the Court's recent decisions on criminal confessions. He continually maintained that "the reason the police cannot stop crime is the Supreme Court."[38] Nixon went almost as far. In his acceptance speech for the Rebublican nomination he warned that "some of our courts have gone too far in weakening the peace forces, as against the criminal forces, in this country."[39] Senator Euguene McCarthy was the only presidential candidate that year who would not get into the law and order debate, maintaining that the phrase had become code for the suppression of blacks.[40]

The law and order presidential campaign of 1968 was an expression of U.S. political life as "an arena of uncommonly angry minds."[41] At issue was the legacy of several years of disruption and unease, with protests, occasionally violent, by students and opponents of the Vietnam War as well as by blacks. The law and order issue was also the product of immediate events, including the assassinations of that spring, the riots that followed the death of Martin Luther King, and the "Battle of Chicago" at the Democratic convention in late August. The majority of Americans approved of the way the Chicago police handled antiwar protesters outside the Democratic convention; a Harris poll taken shortly after the fact found that 66 percent of respondents agreed with the statement, "Mayor Daley was right the way he used police against demonstrators," while only 20 percent disagreed and 14 percent were not sure.[42] The issue had ripened in 1968; the presidential election became a test of its harvest.

The transformation of tangled and multidimensional forces into symbolic expression of fear and discontent is essentially a process of simplification. A recapitulation of the elements of such a transformation can be seen in the 1960s creation of the longer-term get-tough policy trend, as follows:

1.   Misfortune is interpreted primarily as incipient criminality. (Willard Wirtz, secretary of labor in 1964, expressed his concern about 350,000 unemployed youths—many of them poor and black—by warning that they could constitute an "outlaw pack."[43])

2.   Dissent becomes deviance. Remember that Agnew lumped campus radicals and demonstrators of all kinds together as "troublemakers" with muggers, assassins, and looters.

3.   Collective expressions of rage are equated with individual acts of violence. The looting and assaults that arose out of the urban riots of the 1960s became as blameworthy as the random, predatory acts whose upward trajectory was reported in FBI stastics.

4.   Countercultural rebellion constitutes revolution. The theme of "tune in, turn on, drop out," embraced by a very small segment of an electorally marginal group—young people are less likely to vote than older people—was often perceived as a threat to the value system that undergirds basic public order.

5.   Demands for equality are seen as insurrection. The civil rights movement, particularly in the South and particularly as it moved from aims of integration to black nationalism and from legal rights to black power, was regarded by many as an effort to overthrow the government, subvert the capitalist system, and alter the balance of power in favor of ignorant, stupid, and evil Negroes (and, later on, weak but tyrannical women). In Wallace's basic campaign speech of 1964 he said, "If victory for freedom is impossible, then surrender to communism is inevitable and we can begin fitting the yokes of slavery to the necks of our children even now as the riots and mobs lap at the streets of these United States."[44]

Supporters of the New Perspective.   To understand why these complex forces were conflated into ephemeral but imminent threats, one must know something about those who fed the process. In 1967, as the law and order issue assumed national proportions, Louis Harris and Associates was asked by the Joint Commission on Correctional Manpower and Training to survey the U.S. public on its attitudes toward corrections and criminal offenders. One of the principal conclusions of its report was that "the desire for the most severe penalties and the greatest degree of uneasiness about contact with ex-criminals are found among the lower-income and less-educated groups."[45] For example, while respondents with a college education were as likely as those with only high school or eighth grade educations to think that a convicted robber or a drug pusher who sells to minors should receive a long prison sentence, the less educated groups were far more likely to support heavy penalties for looters or prostitution. They were also much more likely to support severe punishment for juveniles, whatever the offense.[46] Those with family incomes of $10,000 or less were twice as likely as respondents with higher incomes to be uneasy at the prospect of working with a convicted car thief, forger, or shoplifter.[47]

But the conclusion that it is "lower-income and less-educated groups" who supported the hard line on crime in 1967 is too simple and probably misleading. Those who expressed punitive attitudes in the Harris survey were not atypical Americans. In the year that followed 77 percent of the electorate had no college education and 65 percent had family incomes of less than $10,000 a year.[48] The more punitive and cautious positions, therefore, represented a view held by people in the educational and economic mainstream.

A more focused understanding of attitudes toward crime and disorder in the late 1960s comes from examining Wallace voters as one segment of the law-and-order constituency. Although the issue was important to all three major candidates in the 1968 Presidential election, Wallace built his campaign around it. Couching his appeal in the vague context of "the domestic plight of this nation," he raised the specter of riotous cities, anarchic schools, and hobbled police ("the Supreme Court of our country has made it almost impossible to convict a criminal").[49] He tied his opposition to civil rights legislation to the need for law and order by maintaining that it encouraged lawlessness; he railed at "powerful central government" as a kind of violence to individual rights, deploring "this beatnik mob in Washington."[50]

Not surprisingly, Wallace supporters were more law and order oriented than Nixon or Humphrey supporters, at least as measured by their views on political protest and civil rights activity.

Jody Carlson's research on Wallace voters, based on the Michigan Survey Research Center's 1968 American National Election Study (ANE), is instructive.[51] Those who backed Humphrey, for example, were more than four times as likely to approve of taking part in authorized protest marches than were Wallace supporters. Of Wallace supporters 71.2 percent disapproved. Furthermore, 90.5 percent of Wallace supporters agreed that most actions "taken by blacks to get things they want" were violent, compared with 62.3 percent of Humphrey supporters who felt this way. This was a startlingly one-sided perspective, since almost all fatalities during the urban riots were at the hands of police or the National Guard. Half of the Wallace voters thought the Chicago police had used "not enough force" with demonstrators at the Democratic national convention, as opposed to a quarter of the Humphrey voters. Perhaps most revealing is their general perspective on dealing with urban unrest: on a seven-point scale presenting solutions to the problem, a majority of Wallace voters supported the use of "all available force" at the "hard" end of the scale, while almost half of the Humphrey supporters chose the option at the "soft" end, to deal with problems of poverty and unemployment. Carlson concludes, "On such measures Wallace voters' responses differ markedly from those of other voters. They repeatedly state that the government should 'get tough' in solving problems, and are unquestionably more authoritarian-minded than other candidates."[52]

Of course, fifty percent of Wallace voters in 1968 came from the South, but another quarter came from the midwest, and almost half came from or then lived in rural areas. While a larger majority of Wallace supporters identified with or grew up in the working class than did either Humphrey or Nixon supporters, their discontents cannot be explained in terms of class status. In fact, Wallaceites were more likely to be middle or upper class than Humphrey voters.[53] They were also in the middle with respect to class mobility, more likely to be upwardly mobile than Humphrey voters and less than Nixon voters. Carlson's analysis is most interesting when she suggests that Wallace voters differed most from others in their sense of political anomie and powerlessness. Wallace voters were more likely than others to feel that they had no say in what government did, that members of Congress didn't care about their views, and that parties didn't represent their interests. They felt most powerless when confronted with forced school integration by the federal government.

To some commentators this set of attitudes all boiled down to the message, "Keep your tainted federal dollars if it means putting my kid in school with the colored."[54] But others saw what Garry Wills has called an "interaction of resentments," a complex composite of threats that made Wallace voters, and others, vulnerable to a social conservatism with law and order at its core. To some it was apparent even early in the decade. In late 1963, as Lyndon Johnson and his aides were preparing to launch a major national anti-poverty effort, a Presidential speechwriter warned, "America's real majority is suffering a minority complex of neglect. They have become the real foes of Negro rights, foreign aid, etc., because, as much as anything, they feel forgotten, at the second table behind the tightly organized, smaller groups at either end of the U.S. spectrum."[55] At the end of the decade Wills looked back and noted:

We have now a vast middle range of the comfortable discontented. They are not, as Nixon knows, the kind who march or riot. They just lock their doors. And they vote. They do not, most of them, go to Wallace rallies; but those who do go speak for them in growing measure. This is the vague unlocalized resentment that had such effect in the 1968 campaign, tainting all the air around talk of law and order.[56]

The "comfortable discontented" that supported law and order was, as Wills noted, a much broader group than Wallaceites. Of Nixon voters surveyed in the American National Election Study, 30.1 percent also thought the Chicago police had used "not enough force" with demonstrators at the 1968 Democratic convention. To understand their perspective it is necessary to look to structural influences.

The sociologist Elliott Currie, in an important book about criminal violence and U.S. approaches to it, has made the point that U.S. economic development in recent decades has taken directions that rend community bonds and accentuate economic divisions, looking more like the patterns of "disruptive development" characteristic of third world countries than like the growth of other advanced industrial societies.[57] He notes that the great migration of rural southern blacks to the urban north, a product of the decline and mechanization of agriculture, occurred just as the flight of capital reduced the number of manufacturing jobs in northern cities available to low-skilled workers. His analysis is intended as a partial explanation of crime patterns among the minority poor. But the phenomenon of disruptive development has consequences for those who castigate crime as well as those who commit it.

The 1960s were not easy years for working people. The record economic prosperity was often won at the cost of uprooting old ties. Though it was often made possible only by low-cost housing loans available to veterans, the middle-class exodus from the cities to the suburbs symbolized greater affluence; but it also meant abandoning families and customs that were precious and reliable.[58] The migration of almost 9 million people to the sunbelt states of Florida, Texas, New Mexico, Arizona, and California between 1950 and 1970 brought new opportunities but also new travails.[59] Public services rarely substituted for the supports of home and family; per capita welfare expenditures for sunbelt cities were only about one-seventh as generous, on the average, as for frostbelt cities of equivalent size.[60]

Despite the predictions of intellectuals who thought the "end of ideology" had arrived, prosperity had not brought a distribution of wealth and income that ironed out class differences. The percentage share of aggregate income received by the families and individuals who occupied the three middle fifths of the income distribution remained remarkably stable between 1960 and 1970, from 53.6 percent at the beginning of the decade to 54 percent at its end.[61] The postwar confidence that vast national abundance would render the question of equal distribution irrelevant had revealed itself as an illusion, as black demands for equality escalated.[62] While a majority of whites expressed sympathy with the civil rights movement in the early years of the decade, many also felt economically and socially threatened by the prospect of black competition for jobs and housing as well as the possibility of "racial mixing."[63] After 1965, wages began to stagnate; growth in after-tax pay slowed to 1 percent a year and, to make up for the slow-down, workers increased the average number of hours they worked annually.[64] It appeared to many that hard times were ahead, and they looked to political leaders and programs for reassurance.[65]

The role of Richard Nixon should not be overlooked in giving voice to the anxieties of middle America and fashioning those anxieties into a "get-tough" program. In his basic campaign speech of 1968 he drew in his audience by referring to the "forgotten American" (a concept lifted from the Goldwater campaign four years earlier), and then blended his concern about the Vietnam war with his disdain for crime in the streets: "I am proud that I served in an Administration in which we had peace in the United States, in which we did not have this problem of violence and fear which pervades this nation and its cities today."[66] He nudged the voters with racial appeals hardly more veiled than those of Wallace, casting a shadow even over school desegregation: "I don't think there is any court in this country . . . including the Supreme Court of the U.S.—that is qualified to be a local school district and to make the decision as your local school board."[67] Once in office, he sponsored anticrime legislation that gave as much attention to the forms of deviance (drugs, pornography, and vice) that threatened the "traditional values" of his constituency as to the predatory acts that threatened their persons and pocketbooks. His Administration exploited the inchoate fears of middle-class parents that their children would be lost to them through exposure to heroin. As Godfrey Hodgson puts it:

By the early 1970s . . . heroin had become the convenient outward symbol for deep, irrational fears: for the white man's fear of the black man, for the fear (never far below the surface in a society of immigrants) of losing beloved children to an alien culture, for the Puritan's Manichean fear of the lurking powers of darkness. In a way, heroin had taken the place of communism.[68]

These appeals to the deepest fears of many Americans went a long way toward legitimating the long sentences, narrower due process rights, and more aggressive police practices that would have been unthinkable in the more innocent and generous early 1960s.

The Restatement Phase

By the early 1970s the restatement phase had begun, and appeals like those of Nixon and Wallace had become the rule rather than the fear-mongering exception. The era of protest and social chaos had ended, but other anxieties kept the soil fertile for law and order politics. The U.S. economy no longer surged forward. Decline replaced rebellion as the threat that could channel public wrath into social policy. In 1980 median family income before taxes was virtually identical to what it had been in 1970 ($27,974 as compared with $27,862, in real dollars), the result of wage stagnation, capital flight, and inflation that went from 5.5 percent (already up from 2.7 percent, the average of the 1960s) to 9 percent.[69] In addition, millions of Americans were suffering from "bracket creep;" that malady of progressive taxation heretofore reserved for the wealthy had infected the working and middle classes. Inflation had boosted incomes to levels with sharply escalating tax rates, so that at the end of the decade the marginal rate for all taxpayers was 25 percent higher than at the beginning.[70] Furthermore, the contribution rate for Social Security taxes paid by employees had increased by 28 percent, to 6.13 percent in 1980, taking another bite out of pretax income. The upshot of these economic onslaughts was that by 1981 average real after-tax hourly earnings were at the same level as they had been twenty years earlier.[71]

Channeling Structural Discontents.   Many working people during the 1970s understandably felt they were bearing the brunt of increases in public expenditures and wondered why the two-job family had now become necessary for basic economic comfort. Their anger and frustration often manifested itself in resentment toward the poor (and, by implication, blacks, who were disproportionately represented among the poor).[72] The poor were, after all, recipients of social programs that provided food stamps, Medicaid, and, most galling of all, Aid to Families with Dependent Children; workers were paying for these programs but did not benefit from them. The Democratic Party also came in for much of the blame. As Edsall summarizes it, "Throughout the 1970s, a growing block of once-solid working-class Democratic voters, their party allegiance eroded by inflation, wage and work-rule concessions, and the threat of unemployment, no longer saw programs directed towards the poor as an integral part of the broad Democratic commitment but as a source of personal, social, and economic depletion."[73]

The party of the worker became, for some, part of an alliance of elite liberals and blacks whose indifference to the traditional Democratic constituency had brought about the losses workers now suffered. Conservative commentator Kevin Phillips announced in 1969 that the political revolt of "the American masses" was against the "mandarins of Establishment liberalism," and the 1970s seemed to bear him out.[74] Godfrey Hodgson and others have suggested that the rage of so many Americans was not an intrinsically conservative revolt, not a rebellion against affirmative government, but was easily captured by conservatives who could mine the widespread sense of injury and betrayal.[75] Whatever the ideological source of the trend, it invited recourse to retribution.

During the 1960s numerous politicians had already made the associations between the liberal agenda and the disorder that all good conservatives deplored. As usual, Wallace had made the connection most baldly. In an interview in *U.S. News and World Report*, he said, "You can walk safely on the streets in Birmingham and in Montgomery (Alabama), our State's capital. You can walk anyplace at any time—either race can—without fear of molestation. But that's not true in the citadels of 'liberalism' in the nation's capital or New York City or places of that sort."[76] In the 1968 campaign Nixon had derided Humphrey as "a man who says and honestly believes that the answer to problems is a knee-jerk reaction of government program." He described the outcome of such an approach: "Over the past four years and the past eight years we have government jobs, government housing, government welfare, billions and billions of dollars poured into those programs. And the result? Failure and frustration and riot across the land."[77] In the 1970s the riots had ended, but the frustrations remained, with liberals as their targets.

It is unclear whether street crime had also continued to rise, providing substantive as well as symbolic fuel to demands for government action. The FBI statistics certainly supported the media picture of rising violence and property crime; they reported an increase of almost 30 percent in robbery and more than 75 percent in rape between 1971 and 1980.[78] But the Justice Department's new victimization studies, heralded by many as less subject to political manipulation and mistake than official data, recorded no change in violent crime between 1973 and 1982 and significant declines in personal thefts and burglary.[79] Nevertheless, crime continued to be a real threat in many urban neighborhoods, and perception of that threat supplied context for policymaking. A 1975 Harris poll found that 70 percent of adults surveyed believed that crime was on the rise in their area, and 55 percent said they felt more uneasy on the streets than they had a year before.[80]

Proponents and Resisters. It was, of course, officeholders and officeseekers, not the disgruntled populists among the citizenry, who politicized the yearning for security and the fear of crime, and criminal justice officials who translated inchoate demands for order into the particular measures of the get-tough trend. They were guided, in part, by criminologists and other scholars who, in retreat from the 100–year-old tradition of positivist criminology, advocated a paradigm shift in the justifications for criminal punishment. And some of them, in turn, were part of the emergence of an influential group of neoconservative intellectuals (many of them disenchanted liberals of the

1950s) like Nathan Glazer, Irving Kristol, Edward Banfield, and James Q. Wilson. Articulate and well-connected, they became legitimators of a new approach to social policy, driven by what they perceived as "a crisis . . . of values, morals, and manners."[81] In articles in *Newsweek* and *Reader's Digest* as well as in intellectual journals, they attacked what they saw as the excesses of the 1960s.[82] Some, like Edward Banfield of Harvard, had a particular interest in crime.

A word coined by socialist critic Michael Harrington, "neoconservative" suggests more than relatively unrestrained faith in the market economy and a foreign policy that boosts the "distinctive greatness" of the United States as a world power.[83] It also connotes, in James Q. Wilson's famous summation, "a sober view of man and his institutions that would permit reasonable things to be accomplished, foolish things abandoned, and utopian things forgotten."[84] As it applied to human beings, the "sober view" took account of challenges to respectability far short of serious street crime—the free speech movement and draft-dodging, for example. Its implications for institutions included the view that government was suffering from "overload," crippled by its inability to respond to the excessive demands made on it. Still worse, this view implied that authority figures encouraged criminality by forgiving hoodlums their transgressions because they were deprived.[85]

The message to those who made social policy was clear: in the face of weakening social controls and the threat of anarchy, repressive authority was legitimated as it had not been since before the Progressive era at the beginning of the century. Furthermore, it could now substitute for the "helping" interventions of government. The consequences for penal policy were very evident by 1976, when for the first time in thirty-five years the incarceration rate rose to 120 per 100,000 population.[86] That year Arizona Congressman Sam Steiger expressed the emergent majority view when he testified to a Congressional Committee on the evils of the indeterminate sentence and concluded, "I think that there is no alternative left to lawmakers but to turn to mandatory (or determinate) penalties."[87]

Why was there no significant opposition to this policy trend? Those with the greatest stake in limiting the reach of criminal justice were most likely to be members of the "dangerous classes" and therefore too weak (politically and in every other way) or so closely associated with offenders as to be viewed as self-interested. Those who were aligned with the poor and black were companion targets of the symbolic campaign, along with the Supreme Court—called "effete snobs" by Agnew and "the criminals' lobby" by Edwin Meese a decade later. In any case, they were all despised liberals in the new demonology. The dynamic was summed up by an anonymous U.S. Senator commenting on his Southern colleagues' efforts to pass a bill nullifying the *Miranda* decision and limiting Supreme Court jurisdiction in criminal cases. "They really *hate* the Supreme Court. It's easy for them to use it as a scapegoat to blame all the crime on, because where they come from the Court is already bitterly resented for its civil rights decisions, and any attack on it is popular."[88]

The liberals didn't have much of a program to offer as an alternative to the get-tough direction. In the face of an attack on rehabilitation (to be discussed later) they had given way, forfeiting the "soft" seat in the debate over how state authority should be exercised. They were left with either the radical view that crime policy would remain repressive as long as society was (surely a "counsel of despair," as law professor Francis Allen has commented) or a modified version of get-tough that could not compete in legislative corridors or on the nightly news with the zeal of the original.[89]

Shifting Punishment Rationales.   Although rehabilitation was always more an ideal than a reality, by the 1970s it had been the dominant punishment rationale among criminologists and reform-minded correctional administrators for a full century.[90] It justified the indeterminate sentence on what now appears to be a quaint faith that the moral authority of judges and correctional administrators was synonymous with the ability to predict human behavior. To judges fell the task of divining the theoretically appropriate period of prison treatment by balancing the personal characteristics and psychosocial history of a wrongdoer with the seriousness of the current crime and history of prior offenses. Closer than the judge to the inmate's postconviction behavior, the parole board was to identify the magic moment when rehabilitation had occurred and the inmate was ready to rejoin society.[91] (The parole board also served other political and administrative purposes of the sort that were to become more important in the next twenty years. It maintained the fiction that judges were pulling out the stops against dangerous criminals by taking on the task of mitigating those harsh sentences, and helped to control the size of the prison population as well.[92])

Cracks in the professional consensus supporting rehabilitation as the proper rationale for punishment emerged in the late 1960s and widened by the mid-1970s.[93] Doubts about theory became concrete proposals for policy change when it became apparent that opposition to the indeterminate sentence could be shared by liberals and conservatives. Liberals rejected the assumptions of indeterminacy that prison could be a rehabilitative environment and that judges and parole board members could determine when a prisoner had reformed. In fact, research seemed to suggest that no effective techniques for rehabilitation existed, in or out of prison, and that mere mortals could not make the predictions of human behavior implicit in a parole release decision.[94] Liberals were also concerned with what Francis Allen calls the "debasement" of the rehabilitative ideal in the prison; the tendency to justify brutal disciplinary techniques, solitary confinement, and prison expansion with the vague and ambiguous rubric of rehabilitation.[95] Some critiques focused not on the corruption of the ideal, but on rehabilitation as an embodiment of the worst features of an individualistic society in which discretion is exercised by the powerful over the vulnerable "to condition the subjects [of rehabilitation programs] to an unthinking conformity to inflexible, externally imposed rules."[96] They pointed out that a "rehabilitative" sentence, with its uncertainties about time to be served and its coerced therapies, could be more punishing than a flat term that ended on a specific day.[97] Furthermore, even without debasement, indeterminacy threatened cherished personal liberties; it required that a prisoner involuntarily exchange basic due process rights for correctional treatment of dubious value.[98]

The political right had always been skeptical of crime control strategies aimed at reforming the criminal, preferring a view of criminal punishment more explicitly announcing the state's power to maintain order and moral balance in society. Conservatives stressed the threat to the public of judicial discretion exercised to grant probation and suspend sentences and parole board release of offenders on parole long before they had served their maximum sentence.[99]

Left and right were (temporarily) unified in the repudiation of rehabilitation and indeterminacy by the emergence of interest in justifying criminal punishment with a modern form of retribution. In 1975, a privately-sponsored group of liberal academics and former government officials, many of them trained as lawyers, concluded that rehabilitation had furthered unequal treatment and exploitation of prisoners. Alternatively, they embraced just deserts—retribution limited by considerations of mercy and proportionality—as the basis for criminal punishment. Grounded on moral rather than utilitarian principles, this rationale would restore the balance in society that is disturbed by the offender's behavior and express society's disapproval of the act.[100] The members of that group would not have quarreled with the analysis of conservative scholar Ernest van den Haag, published the year that they were meeting, that "Unless the future behavior of individual offenders can be objectively predicted, individualized treatment easily becomes capricious and unhelpful—as it has become in our system."[101]

Superficially, liberals and conservatives were in accord on the failure of social intervention by the state and the desirability of a moral basis for punishment.[102] But this agreement did not preclude deep divisions when it came to policy formulation. For liberals, the deficiencies of rehabilitation suggested shorter, definite sentences for serious offenses, less restrictive sanctions for lesser crimes. Politicians and conservative scholars, however, supported harsher penalties with fixed terms and greater certainty of incarceration.[103] The liberals' concern for equity led them to support the ceiling on prison penalties that determinacy would provide, while the conservatives' desire for order fueled their call for mandatory sentences, or rather a floor on the duration of punishment.

Conservatives embraced deterrence as well as the just deserts rationale preferred by liberals. They could, after all, draw on a deep vein of classical tradition that saw man as a rational being who chooses the conduct that gives him the most pleasure and the least pain. The popularity of deterrence also reflected the vogue of neoclassical economics as the neatest analytic model for understanding criminal behavior. University of Chicago economist Gary Becker's 1968 cost-benefit analysis of law enforcement argued that "optimal policies to combat illegal behavior are part of an optimal allocation of resources." Both academics and politicians increasingly embraced the goal of raising the costs of crime in order to reduce it.[104] James Q. Wilson's widely-read and influential 1975 book summed up the conservative approach perfectly: "What the government can do is to change the risks of robbery and the rewards of alternative sources of income for those who, at the margin, are neither hopelessly addicted to thievery nor morally vaccinated against it, and to incapacitate, by prison or some other form of close supervision, those who rob despite the threats and alternatives society provides."[105]

The debate over penal paradigms was not the parochial squabble of the minor discipline of criminology, isolated from larger social and intellectual currents. As public support for law and order reflected the challenges and turmoils of the 1960s, abandonment of the rehabilitative ideal by scholars and professionals reflected the ascendance of darker views of humankind and its modern institutions. Here, too, symbol dominated substance; the rehabilitation ideal could not have generated so many, often contradictory, criticisms on the basis of the rational case against it.

In analyzing the decline of the rehabilitative ideal, Francis Allen has hypothesized that its emergence and survival depend on two key cultural conditions: "widespread belief in the malleability of human character and behavior" and "a sufficient consensus of values to make possible a working agreement on what it means to be rehabilitated."[106] Allen contrasted the United States of the 1970s with two societies in which the ideal flourished—nineteenth century antebellum America and modern China. He concluded that the United States of the 1970s was skeptical about what its institutions—the family and the schools, as well as the criminal law—could do to affect human behavior and was divided as to the ends and means of whatever change could be effected.[107] Starting in the mid-1960s there was—and still is—a broad, popular loss of confidence in the general efficacy of many of society's institutions—business and labor as well as government.[108] A society experiencing a general crisis of authority is likely to be hostile to programs that assume that offenders are amenable to changes dictated by official instruments of social control.

The Exploitation Phase

In the early 1980s street crime seemed to ease slightly. FBI statistics for the years between 1981 and 1984 showed significant decreases in rates of reported murder (23%), robbery (18%), burglary (25%), larceny (12%), and motor vehicle theft (13%).[109] Victimization studies recorded similar declines; in 1984 burglary was 30 percent lower than in 1973, the first year of the surveys.[110] While many reasons were advanced for the trend, it is worth noting that the percentage of 15 to 24-year-olds—the age group most likely to commit common crimes—was 11 percent lower in 1985 than it was in 1980.[111]

Public perceptions matched the trend. Street crime was still a problem to be reckoned with, to be sure. Particular problems in particular cities—like the growth of violent gangs in Los Angeles and the serial murders of children in Atlanta—were genuinely threatening, either directly to potential victims in the affected areas or vicariously to those who heard or read about them.[112] But in general, crime was probably a less salient concern in the early 1980s than it had been in the immediately preceding decades. In a 1968 Gallup poll asking adults what they thought was the most important problem facing the country, crime was mentioned more often than any other except the Vietnam war. By March 1975 crime was the sixth most frequently cited problem, and by June 1982, it had dropped to tenth.[113] A Harris poll taken in 1983 also suggested that for the first time since the 1960s fewer people thought crime was increasing in their area than thought that it was either decreasing or had remained the same.[114]

Despite this glimmer of progress, penal legislation became still harsher during the 1980s. As with some of the policy areas discussed by Edsall, Hodgson, and Kuttner, the consolidation of conservative approaches had become a semi-autonomous force; active grievances were no longer needed to fuel policy activity. For instance, sanctions increased sharply in the 1980s for alcohol-related driving offenses; by 1986 forty-two states imposed mandatory imprisonment for driving while intoxicated.[115] Investment in criminal justice continued to escalate. Overall, direct expenditures for justice activities rose by more than a third in real dollars between 1979–1985.[116] Because of the boom in prison construction, state expenditures grew the most, but costs far outstripped inflation at other governmental levels too—even though many local governments were feeling fiscally pinched and the federal government was reducing domestic spending across the board.

Policymakers generally justify the continuing push to capture and confine in terms of public punitiveness.[117] Certainly support for the get-tough trend in the early 1980s remained high—in some respects even stronger than it had been in more turbulent times. In 1985 76 percent of Americans polled supported the death penalty, as opposed to 60 percent who favored it a decade earlier, and most said they would do so even if it were proven not to deter.[118] A huge 84 percent said they thought the courts were not harsh enough with criminals, compared to 79 percent who felt that way in 1975.[119] The punitive attitude is not limited to violent offenses; in a recent national survey, interviewees favored an average 10 1/2 year sentence for a cocaine sale.[120]

However, the picture that policymakers sketch of consensus support for tough measures is highly oversimplified. Polls show that more people still believe rehabilitation should be the main emphasis of prison than support punishment or incapacitation; and, while they want more prisons, many also say they support nonprison programs that include restitution.[121] The interest in victim compensation also shows up as a chink in the apparently solid wall of support for the death penalty. In two recent polls at least half of those who favored capital punishment said they would support alternative punishments—life sentences without parole or with parole eligibility only after twenty-five years—if they were accompanied by restitution to the victim's family.[122] But these threads of subtlety in the public view are seldom credited or encouraged by politicians, who can win elections and, once in office, retain public confidence more easily with an undiluted law and order message.

Political scientist Stuart Scheingold believes that there is a "powerful current of suggestibility within the public when it comes to crime;" that even passive concern about crime can be politicized and transformed into support for get-tough policies.[123] When people are asked in polls to choose among alternatives presented to them—for example, to decide whether the right amounts of government money are being spent on specified public problems, or to choose the most important national problems from among a list—the results will reflect a far more heightened concern about crime than the responses they give when asked the open-ended question of the Gallup polls, "What do you think is the most important problem facing this country today?" Scheingold concludes that a sense of vicarious victimization can thus be easily aroused and manipulated for political ends.

This suggestibility is, of course, based in part on actual, painful experiences of crime victims and their families. But it is also the expression of persisting structural discontents quite similar to those discussed earlier in this chapter. It would be wrong to assume that the overall improvement of the economy during the early 1980s removed the tensions in working people's lives that shaped their law and order impulses in the late 1960s and 1970s.

Many millions were not touched by the boom. In 1982 and 1983 unemployment hovered just below 10 percent, a postwar high.[124] Edelman has commented that "where people's jobs or church activities underline their alienation rather than promoting satisfying ties to others, the need for symbolic reassurance through politics becomes all the greater."[125] In this light, it is interesting to look at how workers fared during different postwar periods. Between 1948 and 1966 real hourly earnings rose, on the average, 3.2 percent annually. Between 1966 and 1973 they slowed to 2.1 percent and then, during the 1973–1979 business cycle, to .4 percent. During the 1980s real hourly earnings were virtually stagnant—with an average increase of only .1 percent between 1980 and 1987; for construction and retail jobs, which employ almost 20 million workers, they actually decreased significantly.[126] For most working people the Reagan era, with its much-vaunted "expansion," did not bring that sense of movement that defined the prosperity of, for example, the Eisenhower years. Not that workers were objectively much worse off in the 1980s; but their failure to be better off reinforced the cascade of anxieties that made them punitive in earlier times. Edelman's analysis suggests that the crime politics of the 1980s would be as intensely symbolic as those of the 1970s.

It is important to note that the developments that fuel the get-tough program in the 1980s also affect other areas of social policy. The punitive approach has been nicely congruent with two, more general forces. As the U.S. has lost its international economic dominance and national political leaders have more aggressively pursued market-oriented policies, both elites and the public have embraced the traditional American faith in individual responsibility with new fervor. In addition, backlash against feminism and the decline of the civil rights movement have blended into national self-castigation for "family breakdown" and "moral decline," which has led to a new puritanism, what James Q. Wilson calls "a concern for character, propriety and duty."[127] These cultural and political developments have helped to legitimate budget-slashing in student aid programs and food stamps, as well as the trend to make welfare payments conditional on employment. In the pinched 1980s conservatives—the intellectually influential neoconservatives, the New Rightists in the White House, the moderate Republicans who appeal to working people considering a defection from the Democratic party—and the liberals—New Deal and Atari Democrats alike—sounded these themes, and voters responded. The essence of the politics of crime in the 1980s was symbolic exchange in which the politicians promised "character, propriety, and duty" in exchange for public support for a restructuring of what remained of the U.S. welfare state. The real debate going on at the end of the decade was less about what decision makers would do to reduce urban muggings and burglary than about the legitimacy of affirmative government and the shaping of the national character.

From all points on the political spectrum comes acknowledgement that alienation and frustration lead some people to strike out against others. Surely this commonplace observation has as much utility as a partial explanation for the politics of crime as for crime itself. Like the taxpayers' revolt and the English-only movement, the get-tough program has been a lightning rod for broader discontents than are identified by the stated policy target. In a way, the campaign is heir to the recourse to demagoguery that characterized populist movements and McCarthyism. The parallel is clear in W. J. Cash's description of Cole L. Blease, an early twentieth-century governor of South Carolina and the first of the Southern demagogues to appeal to the cotton mill workers whose opportunities for higher pay and advancement were declining.

The man was a sort of *antenna*, as it were, fit to vibrate in perfect unison with [the mill workers'] exact sentiment—in his every word and deed precisely to render what, given all the forces to play upon them, they most secretly wanted: the making vocal and manifest of their slowly gathering melancholy for and resentment against their economic and social lot, without ever losing sight of the paramount question of race.[128]

8

•

UNDERSTANDING THE DRIVE
TO OBSERVE

For better or worse, get-tough promises may not actually be kept.
● Stuart Scheingold, *The Politics of Law and Order*

INTRODUCTION

MANY SCHOLARS HAVE NOTED the modern U.S. clash between, on
the one hand, demands that the state do more and more to address social problems, and, on the other, the dwindling supply of
resources—funds, effective techniques, credible theories—to
meet those demands. Political scientists Malcolm Feeley and
Austin Sarat call it "the policy dilemma" and point to "the politics of promise" that feeds it.[1]

Criminal justice policies effectively illustrate this paradox.
Public frustration with thievery, drugs, and random street violence leads to demands for relief that government cannot satisfy. Faced with failure on the instrumental level, policymakers
increasingly resort to symbolic responses that reflect their individual political needs and cynicism about the prospects of
addressing the substantive demand. These responses can transform policy as surely as the instrumental aim of reducing social
harm from predatory behavior. Symbolic exchanges, in fact,
often serve to hide policy behavior that adapts and transforms
the original demand. An intensely expressed plea for relief in-
cites a dramatic pledge of action, but the most far-reaching policy activity operates on another level, on which a range of ideas
and options can be nurtured in an atmosphere largely obscured
from public view. What emerges may bear little resemblance to
what was promised.

Certainly with the get-tough movement, this tendency was
very pronounced. Despite their promises, the policymakers who
supported greater police protection and expanded prisons did

not have either the funds or the ideas to reduce street crime significantly, or even to demonstrate efficiency at the intermediate goal of capturing and containing criminals. So they turned to increased reliance on human and data surveillance for both investigation and punishment, an approach that was cheaper and more manageable than what had been promised. They counted on criminal justice officials (and, for a time, the federal support for local justice system programs) to develop the new emphasis.

In exploring the sources of spreading observation programs in criminal justice, this chapter examines both the ideas that propelled them and the justice system activity that brought them into being. The next two sections describe the dialectical relationship between the more obviously punitive capture and confinement policies and the newer observation programs, and the appeal of the particular routes chosen. The third section will examine the generating force of LEAA, with its influence on the organizational development of criminal justice as well as its programmatic support for records systems and "alternatives" programs. The final section analyzes the adaptive and transforming behavior of the policy actors who breathed life into the observation thrust of the get-tough trend. It argues that the development of active policy networks on the state and federal levels has made criminal justice practitioners players in the game of distributive politics.

THE DIALECTICS OF GETTING TOUGH

Policy implementation involves more than carrying out the directives of policymakers; policy-making *includes* implementation. "Most, perhaps all, administrative acts make or change policy in the process of trying to implement it."[2] Implementers make policy by adapting or resisting the formal dictates of political leaders, or by honest interpretation that differs from the goals and actions contemplated by those who made the policy. Carrying out the policy that is assigned to them may simply be impossible.[3]

Implementation thus converts the ideal into the possible. The demands of politics are met with the responses of organizations. The creation of implementers is government activity that is manageable; that does not constitute a major departure from routine, introduce too much uncertainty, require the acquisition of too much new information, or generate pervasive conflict.[4] This activity, in turn, informs subsequent policy formulation. The pattern can be seen in the execution of trends as well as in the implementation of individual policies.

Criminal justice is like other policy arenas in this regard, perhaps even more so. Because so many get-tough measures are the result of political opportunism—conceived under pressure, enacted in haste—their execution is often simply administratively or politically infeasible.[5] New resources and procedures may actually reinforce old directions and worsen existing problems, especially if they clog already overburdened courts and jails.[6] Organizational imperatives dominate in courtroom workgroups, where police, lawyers, judges and probation personnel interact to accomplish shared goals. They can easily take precedence over the policy messages of political leaders and the general public.[7]

To find adaptive behavior among policymakers does not explain why particular adaptations were chosen. Observation programs like computerized criminal records systems and intermediate punishments are not the only money-saving and face-saving alternatives to the "hang 'em and flog 'em" approach. Law enforcement might have applied more relaxed standards for arrests (as was done in a few cities), producing a greater show of force at the cost of lower indictment and conviction rates. Sentencing policy might have shortened sentences for some to make room in prison for a wider range of offenders. But these approaches did not fit with institutional pressures on police and corrections.

Although law enforcement representatives often maintain that officers could do their jobs better if they were not constrained by Supreme Court decisions limiting their discretion, the organizational and professional logic of an apparently more moderate stance is apparent. Since the 1950s police have been embarked on a campaign for increased "professionalism," a goal which suggests, among other, more practical things like higher salaries and better training, a more refined image.[8] The aggressive behavior required to increase the ratio of arrests to known offenses would be consonant with the call for law and order but not with the modern police ideal. Besides, beneath the grumbling over court-imposed constraints, many police personnel acknowledge the practical limitations on further increasing the likelihood of apprehension in this country.[9]

The logic of consistent adherence to a punitive trend is equally weak for corrections officials. By the early 1970s prison and jail administrators were feeling the pinch of the first wave of law and order politics and had their hands full with the increasing demands placed on their institutions. Unrelievedly punitive policies would have increased their crowding problems and made it more difficult to maintain institutions that were clean and safe enough to be perceived as legitimate. For parole and especially probation officers, the revived emphasis on just deserts and deterrence as punishment rationales is inconsistent with the century-old traditions of rehabilitation and service by which they have defined themselves professionally. In addition, the consistent application of the new ideologies would appear on the surface to threaten the survival of their jobs.

Given these potential sources of resistance to intensifying the capture and confinement measures, why were observation programs a more likely policy choice than simply retreating from the overtly punitive trend? First, as a recourse for fiscally pressed states and cities, they are almost certainly less expensive than the labor needed for the added processing of more arrestees and more prisoners doing shorter terms. Even more important, the political and organizational costs of modifying traditional approaches would be enormous. To arrest more law violators but do less with them once they have been brought into the system would bring chaos and conflict to the courtroom workgroup, and it would fuel the charge that justice is a "revolving door." (Actually, some of this is now happening despite the increased investment in both types of programs.[10]) Altering sentencing policy to accommodate shorter terms for most offenders in order to impose sanctions on many new ones would expose the politicians who supported the change to the charge of being "soft on crime." In other words, to adapt the punitive policy by mitigating it—even if the outcome were not greater lenience but merely a different form of toughness—risks political challenge in a way that a qualitatively different approach does not.

Elevating the familiar technique of observation—after all, recordkeeping and community supervision are hardly new to criminal justice—to preferred status is relatively safe. Computerized recordkeeping can be seen merely as an efficiency measure, not as a substitute for the human surveillance law enforcement provides. While intermediate punishments jeopardize slightly the claim that get-tough policies are dominant, supervision has the advantage of being somewhat indeterminate. It may reduce penalties for some but can be (and often is) viewed as riding herd on others—minor offenders who would otherwise go unpunished or be subjected to the minimal custody of regular probation.

The method of policy adoption for observation programs also protects them from close public scrutiny. They can generally be put in place under the protective cover of subgovernmental activity. Record systems rarely require legislative approval and, when they do, do not usually generate controversy. Intermediate punishments can be developed as extensions of probation, in which case they appear as a toughening up of that institution. They can be sold to the voters with a get-tough label like "house arrest," as was done in Florida. Finally, observation programs supplement capture and confinement, rather than supplanting it; the policy actors who are creating "persons of interest" files and intensive supervision programs are also still investing in police helicopters and prisons.

It may be somewhat more formally useful to view this interaction between capture and confinement imperatives and the move toward observation programs as manifesting a dialectical contradiction within the criminal justice system.[11] The get-tough program (the "thesis") promises movement toward more punitive and segregative policies. However, this push encounters other priorities of the state—primarily the demand to keep taxes low but also concern for orderly administration of justice and some public distaste for purely repressive measures against minor deviance or morally ambiguous acts. Punitive demands thus overload the policy delivery system and consequently give rise to what superficially appear as their "antithesis"—the apparently more lenient and integrative policies introduced by the observation programs described in Chapters 4 and 5. This contradictory development at least partially destroys the promise of punitiveness as the general public understands it; the push for greater controls in fact produces lesser ones.

But the contradiction may also tend to legitimize a get-tough approach. The public can see widespread application of observation programs as evidence of the existence of legions of lawbreakers who must be dealt with, by whatever method. The contradictory dynamic may thus reproduce itself as a policy spiral: symbolically-determined demands for punitive policies, confronting limits within the policy delivery system, generate movements toward more "lenient" observation programs, which, in turn, confirm impressions of pervasive lawlessness, which feed punitive demands and also justify broadening the reach of criminal justice. Round and up goes the policy spiral.

THE GROWING APPEAL OF OBSERVATION PROGRAMS

The observation programs of the 1980s are creatures of networks of criminal justice administrators, state legislators, and interest groups, some of which represent professionals in law enforcement and corrections and some of which are public interest organizations. Included in Chapters 4 and 5 were historical particulars of subgovernmental activity in the creation of computerized criminal record systems and intermediate punishments. What follows is an historical look at the generation of the aforementioned criminal justice networks and their policy activities. Between police and corrections the timing and pace were different; computerized criminal record systems were being developed in the late 1960s, while intensive probation supervision was only an occasional experiment until the 1980s. But some patterns of policy development are similar.

For each of the areas examined in this book some important limitations on traditional criminal justice approaches had either been reached before law and order demands reached their fever pitch (police) or revealed themselves almost immediately as a result of those demands (prisons). Each program area held the potential for expanding the sphere of power of the institution of criminal justice that sponsored it; both could garner resources and respectability from the increased emphasis on national responses to street crime, primarily through the Safe Streets Act of 1968.

To a great extent the limitations on a consistently hard line program predated the law and order politics of the last twenty years. Pollock and Maitland, in their classic history of English law, explained that in the thirteenth and fourteenth centuries defendants were seldom detained before trial because "imprisonment was costly and troublesome."[12] While prison has consistently been perceived by most of the public as the appropriate punishment for serious offenders, its legitimacy as well as its effectiveness has been questioned almost since it became the predominant sanction in the mid-nineteenth century.[13] After serving on a committee investigating the condition of

English prisons, George Bernard Shaw wrote in the early 1920s that "imprisonment as it exists today is a worse crime than any of those committed by its victims."[14] In law enforcement, too, there were preexisting constraints on intensification. Popular suspicion of police, in part a product of their role as strike-breakers between the 1890s and the 1930s, was a U.S. tradition long predating accusations of brutality during the 1960s protests.[15] Big city conflicts over police budgets have been common throughout the post-World War II period.[16]

Equivalent conflict in corrections between vastly expanded incarceration and resistance to high taxes emerged as a major policy influence only in the mid-1970s. Long-simmering economic problems were manifesting themselves in the fiscal crises of American cities.[17] National tax rebellion was in the air. These pressures effectively put a ceiling on political leaders' willingness to deliver on their promises of throwing the book at every street criminal who could be caught.

In addition, evidence was mounting that more police patrol and increased reliance on prisons was of doubtful crime control efficacy. Increased demands on the justice system create opportunities for evasion; police may hesitate to arrest people for newly enacted gun crimes or enforce drunk driving laws that they think are too harsh.[18] And tougher penalties add to organizational pressures to keep cases moving through the process. The 1973 "Rockefeller drug law" in New York imposed long mandatory minimum sentences but actually reduced the likelihood of indictments and convictions as courts struggled to cope with the increase in the number of defendants who insisted on trials rather than agreeing to a plea bargain.[19]

For defendants who are finally convicted the research is divided on whether harsher penalties are more likely than lesser ones to suppress crime, but for criminal justice professionals this uncertainty is a mere academic quibble.[20] The doubts they acquire from first-hand experience with offenders who return to crime are buttressed by the concern that they will be held responsible for the failures of untested policies. Like the rest of us, criminal justice employees cannot easily cast aside standards and values that have defined their working life. Particularly for those working in corrections, the shift from a reliance on rehabilitation to the harder punishment rationales of retribution and deterrence created professional insecurity and confusion; they could not embrace the new ideologies quickly and consistently. In 1976 Norman Carlson, Director of the

Federal Bureau of Prisons from 1970–1987, perfectly expressed the indeterminacy of corrections in a period of ideological transition. "We forget that most inmates are not sick, that we do not know the cause of crime, and that we have developed no sure cures," he told a Florida law enforcement audience. "This new sense of realism has led to a more balanced philosophy of corrections, one that recognizes that retribution, deterrence, incapacitation, and rehabilitation are all legitimate objectives of incarceration."[21]

THE INFLUENCE OF LEAA

These basic constraints on a consistent, comprehensive program of repression do not impel innovation but constitute what John Kingdon calls the "fertile soil" for new agenda items for public policy in criminal justice.[22] Perhaps the most important of the seeds that fell on that soil were planted by the movement for increased national involvement in "the crime problem." Spurred by Lyndon Johnson's President's Commission on Law Enforcement and Administration of Justice and embodied in the structure and programs of LEAA, the ten-year federal war on crime (1969–1980) was judged by many to be an $8 billion debacle.[23] A decade after its expiration, with crime rates rising and the justice system as beleaguered as ever by charges of inefficiency and injustice, LEAA appears to have warranted the scorn of the contemporaneous critics who charged that it "threw money at the problem" without sense or strategy.[24] But that is not our concern here. Although it cannot be said to have reduced crime or made the operations of criminal justice more rational or fair, LEAA played an important role in changing the nature of U.S. crime control.

The initial, and perhaps most important, political leadership in nationalizing crime policy came not from a control-oriented Republican, but from Lyndon Johnson. Only a few months after he was elected President in 1964, he called on Congress for a "war on crime" and pushed for legislation that created a modest program of federal grants to state and local private and public agencies. The Office of Law Enforcement Assistance dispensed about $7 million a year in grants for experimental projects and for education and training, two-thirds of it to police organizations. More important for shaping a national role for crime policy, Johnson announced, in the same message to Congress, that he would appoint a prestigious commission to investigate the causes of street crime and propose remedies "not only to reduce crime but to banish it."[25] In February 1967 the President's Commission on Law Enforcement and the Administration of Justice, headed by former Attorney General Nicholas DeB. Katzenbach, produced its report, *The Challenge of Crime in a Free Society*, and launched the offensive to meet the President's challenge.

From the outset, the policy thrust of the national program was ambiguous. Although Johnson's early attention to the crime issue can be seen as political response to Goldwater's law and order message, it was also conceived in a social reform context during the development of the Great Society programs. The Commission report gave high priority to strengthening law enforcement, but also stressed the importance of "assuring all Americans a stake in the benefits and responsibilities of American life" as a means of preventing crime.[26] The Omnibus Crime Control and Safe Streets Act, as it was passed in 1968, looked very different from the version initially proposed by the Administration. The original proposal had envisioned grants to cities that would give as much attention to rehabilitation programs and crime prevention education in the schools as to law enforcement. The final bill, transformed by Republicans and conservative southern Democrats, was a grab-bag of hard-line provisions; millions of dollars were earmarked for riot control in the first year, expanded authorization was provided for wiretapping, and legislation was proposed to defeat the Supreme Court's position on confessions.[27] In its early years LEAA always gave at least 50 percent of its action grants to police, often for hardware like helicopters and tanks (even an armored personnel carrier for Louisiana).[28] In later years, however, LEAA gave increased emphasis to community corrections, "diversion" programs intended to remove those accused of less serious offenses from justice processing, and the criminal defense bar.

The dawning of the era of observation can be seen in the patterns of LEAA assistance. Technocratic approaches that made available new ways to track people added luster to police management and to the controls of corrections. One critic of LEAA notes:

Another ubiquitous assumption [behind the Safe Streets Act] was that high technology promised exciting and quick new breakthroughs in crime control. The president's crime commission, police chiefs, Ramsey Clark, academic authorities—all agreed that computers, walkie talkies, surveillance technology, and the like, were about to conquer crime as they had conquered space. Liberals were as enthusiastic as "law and order" conservatives.[29]

LEAA was proud of its role in providing "the leadership, funds, and coordination needed to create" state computerized criminal justice information systems.[30] Reflecting the President's Crime Commission endorsement of a national effort of this kind, the agency funded twenty-five state computerized information systems in its first two years; by 1973 it had spent $50 million on these projects. In the agency's annual report for 1979, the last year of substantial federal funding, nearly every state reported using some of its LEAA grant for either computerized information systems or communications systems, many of which allowed the state-wide exchange of warrants and criminal histories.[31] LEAA also funded the National Law Enforcement Telecommunications System for the interstate exchange of criminal records and made many large grants (totaling $12 million by the end of fiscal year 1973 alone) to Project SEARCH, a consortium of states (now a non-profit corporation), for its contributions to the development of a national criminal history system.[32]

Less of a priority for LEAA was the use of observation technology for controlling offenders in the community. The President's Commission, while endorsing closed-circuit TVs and electric eyes for improving security in prisons, was not so enthusiastic about technological innovations for supervision of offenders. Rejecting the notion of imprinting the hands of check forgers with invisible ink as not rehabilitative, the Commission's Task Force on Science and Technology also noted that the availability of such techniques "raises grave questions about their social value, and there is doubt whether any of them would be acceptable in a free society."[33] Nonetheless, the hardware (cellular telephones, beeper systems, and electronic surveillance devices) funded in the initial police bonanza priovded by LEAA was adaptable for later use in intensive probation supervision programs.

LEAA's major legacy to the later intermediate punishments movement is not, however, a technological one. It is, rather, the dissemination of ideas about diversion and decarceration, in the course of which those ideas were converted and stripped of their challenges to law enforcement and corrections. Previously the province of outsiders to criminal justice—innovators and dissidents who hoped to reduce state power over individuals— programs that sought to reduce justice system intervention at the stages of prosecution and incarceration became incorporated instead into the crime control apparatus.[34]

Research on diversion and decarceration programs has continually found that, where they are staffed with police and corrections employees, control over program participants is maintained despite the declared aims of the projects—sometimes even more control than if the programs had not existed. Furthermore, the programs often reach only minor offenders who, without the "diversion" mechanism, would simply have been sent home or placed on probation.[35] LEAA, in funding thousands of these kinds of programs, extracted their essence— separation from coercive state control—and legitimated a whole new sphere of power for criminal justice.[36] The step from LEAA-funded local and state "alternatives" programs—their original theory debased and their salient features coopted—to the intermediate punishments that were the subject of Chapter 5 was a conceptually and organizationally logical one.

It should not be assumed that LEAA was solely responsible for adding the dimension of observation to the traditional programs of criminal justice. At the time of the President's Commission report computer-based information systems existed in a few large cities and states, including New York, Califiornia, and Pennsylvania.[37] Tests of varying levels of probation supervision and community corrections programs, like the California Youth Authority's Community Treatment Project, were not uncommon.[38] And the approach was not consistently or uncritically endorsed by LEAA; the agency's evaluation of its own special intensive probation projects was essentially negative.[39] But the catalytic effect of LEAA attention was to turn fragmented experiments into nationwide conventional wisdom, a qualitative change that ensured continuing development of the policy direction.

In this and other respects LEAA's influence was organizational as well as programmatic. The existence of a central grant-making presence in Washington increased the flow of information among jurisdictions and fostered a sense of common participation in a national effort. LEAA funded newsletters and conferences, training sessions and educational programs. (One of its largest grant programs, the Law Enforcement Education

Program, provided almost $300 million in loans and grants for college criminal justice courses; during the academic year of 1973–1974 alone it helped students at 95 schools in California to obtain what one report called "shallow, conceptually narrow" professional education.[40]) In bolstering the treasuries of national criminal justice associations like the International Association of Chiefs of Police, the American Correctional Association, and the National Sheriffs Association, LEAA enhanced the professional image that corrections and police had been trying to foster for many years. The national "war on crime" may not have taken much territory, but it provided strong troop support.

The other organizational effect of LEAA was even more important in developing the capacity of the criminal justice system to change (or add) direction from within.[41] A key revision of Johnson's original Safe Streets Act was to change the method of dispensing federal funds for fighting crime. The Administration bill had provided for grants-in-aid to local governments, the principal method used for Great Society programs in the past and one that had helped Johnson build solid electoral majorities in the nation's cities. However, Republicans and southern Democrats in Congress rebelled, arguing that law enforcement was a fundamentally local function and should not be controlled from Washington. In the interests of state's rights (and blocking the political momentum of the Great Society), they pushed through a program of block grants to the states. A State Planning Agency (SPA), created in each state by the governor, would submit a plan to LEAA for the expenditure of its funds; when the plan was approved, the grant would be made, and the SPA would in turn make grants within the state (sometimes to grant-making organizations for regions or cities within the state). Of the action grants 85 percent would be distributed by the SPA according to population. The remainder were discretionary grants made directly by LEAA, which also administered research, demonstration, and training activities.

State involvement in the distribution of federal money may solve some of the problems of remoteness and centralization that attend categorical grants made directly by federal agencies. But it creates new problems, too, especially where the substance and beneficiaries of the federal legislation are not clearly articulated and state capability has not been developed.[42] As an experiment in the New Federalism—a theory not yet articulated in the late 1960s but certainly underlying the conservatives' support of building a state structure to make grants for local law enforcement—the Safe Streets Act demonstrated some of its greatest weaknesses.

Rather than building responsibility in state governments and expanding the range of worthy program participants, the grant-making method for the Safe Streets Act merely ensured that a constituency of grant-getting entrepreneurs for a newly nationalized policy concern would be immediately developed. The SPAs were often staffed and directed by representatives of the justice agencies, and they gave out the money to each other, often to supplement or streamline existing activities rather than to branch out into new approaches to reducing crime. With decision making effectively delegated to a narrow slice of the executive branch in state governments—not a likely locus for much popular policy review—the processes of program planning, grant-giving, and evaluation were so parochial as to be publicly invisible. An unsuccessful grant applicant described the structure and process of SPA grant-giving in New York:

> The law enforcement agencies make grants to themselves by having their boards represented on state and local planning boards. The preponderance of public agencies as grantees also demonstrates the cooptation in fact if not in spirit of outside groups. In New York at least a private group cannot get a grant from CJCC or DCJS [the city funding agency and the SPA] without endorsement of the relevant public agencies. And in fact the agency often submits the proposal and then subcontracts to the private group. This guarantees pretty effective control over the way the private group goes about its work after it gets the grants and what it puts in its work plan before the proposal is negotiated. It inhibits both innovation in and challenge to the sponsoring agencies.[43]

THE SURVIVAL AND SIGNIFICANCE
OF POLICY NETWORKS

The patterns noted above conform to what political scientists expect of distributive policy, policy that provides a subsidy for some activity determined to be desirable by policymakers.[44] The decisionmaking locus in distributive policy—who gets what—rests within a relatively closed circle of middle-level government bureaucrats, legislative subcommittees, and the interest groups that stand to profit from the allocation of public resources. The relationship among policy actors remains fairly stable over time and is characterized by cooperation and compromise. Decisions are relatively invisible to the general public or the media—even sometimes to the larger arenas of government decision making—and are noncontroversial.[45] These conditions obviously provide for the beneficiaries of the policy the greatest leeway for shaping its effects.

The operation of the block grant program of the Safe Streets Act does not perfectly fit the dynamics of distributive policymaking. Legislative units had little role in the politics of distributing LEAA grants. But aberrations in the mechanics of distribution do not alter its basic character. The color of money—for giving and receiving, both of which were sources of power—brought the criminal justice agencies together as interest groups, and their cooperative efforts in sharing it promoted the diverse priorities of all, quite independent of the original intent, however ambiguous, of the legislation to reduce crime and improve the criminal justice system. The ease with which the pie could be divided was furthered by the scatter-shot approach allowed by the legislation and the vast and unfocused guidelines for state plans that were drawn up pursuant to it. The essence of distributive policymaking—allocating power "by the maxim of each according to his claim"—was preserved.[46]

This situation had two consequences relevant for our understanding of the growth of the observation emphasis in criminal justice: it enabled relatively invisible subgovernments to use the LEAA money for the needs they thought most pressing (or that best served their organizational needs), and it gave them practice in policy entrepreneurship. The latter stood them in good stead once the LEAA stream ran dry and they had to search for fresh springs in state governments or other federal agencies. This is not to say that before federal involvement in crime control, law enforcement and corrections administrators never shaped policy, but rather that as a result of nationalization a new and broader range of opportunities presented itself.

Criminal justice officials now act as political players on a state, and sometimes federal, scale. Gone is the purely local identification that has characterized police (and, to a lesser extent, corrections) practice in the past. Of course part of the change can be attributed to the continuing emphasis on professionalism in criminal justice jobs and to the general mobility and fluidity of modern life. But the nationalization of crime control policy through the Safe Streets Act has been important, too. Over and over in the course of my research for this book, criminal justice officials explained how they had obtained resources or garnered support for a progam change by saying something like, "Well, I know this guy from the days when we worked on LEAA business together. . . .".

At the end of the 1980s neither the personae nor the stakes of the policy networks created by LEAA largesse are the same as they were a decade earlier. Once the federal action grant money dried up, many of the SPAs became little more than centers for the state collection and dissemination of justice statistics, removing an important nerve center for the networks.[47] But criminal justice officials now find other avenues for promoting their interests, using techniques of influence and communication that have survived the near-demise of federal support. (Although LEAA has expired, a few of its programs live on, notably youth programs and the support of regional intelligence-gathering programs.[48]) Subgovernmental activity has been particularly important to the intermediate punishments movement of the 1980s. When prison crowding reaches a crisis level, typically governors form task forces to figure out what to do.[49] It is almost inevitably the state and local corrections officials who initiate proposals for addressing the problem and who then, playing the interest group role in the game of distributive politics, bargain with executive office aides, state legislators, and judges.[50] The intensive supervision and house arrest programs that emerge represent the conversion of symbolic politics into organizational opportunity.

9

•

JUST AS MUCH CRIME, MUCH MORE CONTROL

In Los Angeles there are too many signs of approaching helter-skelter: everywhere in the inner city, even in the forgotten white bluecollar boondocks, gangs are multiplying at a terrifying speed, becoming meaner and more life-threatening, a generation being shunted towards some impossible Armegeddon.

● Mike Davis, *City of Quartz*

SUPPOSE THAT THE GET-TOUGH program as we know it at the end of the 1980s was significantly reducing the likelihood that an urban resident would be mugged on the street, or that a wife would be brutally beaten by her husband, or that a store owner would be robbed and shot. Then a willingness to relinquish a limited portion of individual liberties and social justice might conceivably seem appropriate. We could then argue that, while the tradeoff was painful and did not mute the underlying conflicts that make this such a turbulent nation, it served important collective interests.

But the policy trend of the past twenty years has not produced this outcome. One could of course argue that street crime might have been even worse in the 1970s and 1980s if we had not increased police resources and incarceration rates. But apart from such counterfactuals, few can identify victories in the "war on crime" that have moved us closer toward being a society with only modest amounts—at the level, say, of Canada—of such crimes as rape and robbery.[1] While the U.S. population increased by 20 percent between 1970 and 1987, reported FBI Index crime—murder, rape, robbery, assault, burglary, larceny, and auto theft—rose 143 percent.[2]

This chapter tries to explain why the get-tough program hasn't "worked" and to show how drastic—truly repugnant, if we are to live by the values of a liberal democracy—would be the criminal justice measures required to repress a substantial measure of the conduct we fear most. It then assesses, by standards other than crime control effectiveness, the policy directions we have taken. I argue that the significant impacts of the get-tough program are effects on political ideals and social structure. What I see as principally negative consequences fall into two general categories. First is the damage we are doing to individual rights; not just those of offenders but, more broadly, of all of us who might ever be the subject of a record or the friend of a drug dealer or the parent of a probationer. Second, and just as disturbing in my view, is the contribution made by an increasingly refined and pervasive criminal justice system to the segmentation and marginalization of sizable population groups in this society. The get-tough program is interacting with trends in wider arenas of social and economic policy to erode basic economic security and stifle democratic participation for millions of people who are not the criminals who should concern us.

Some of the effects I will discuss may be regarded by many as too speculative to be taken seriously. But in doing research for this book I have repeatedly noted how frequently people touched by the justice system (including those with minor charges or offenses in the distant past, as well as hard-core recidivists) consider themselves branded by it. Even where their lives are full of other problems, the imposition of a sentence or the sense that their record follows them serves as an important emblem of exclusion and objectification, consignment to an outer ring of society where the rewards and responsibilities of participation are negligible. Criminal justice is becoming an increasingly significant contributor to the creation of a large class of "expendable" people.

JUST AS MUCH CRIME

As we have seen in previous chapters, the barriers to an effective get-tough program (in crime control terms) are not theoretical, but fiscal, political, and organizational. It would be absurd to say that no amount of state coercion would reduce street crime. A no-holds-barred effort at repression would presumably cut down on such crimes as robbery, burglary, drug offenses and some kinds of assaults. Pursuing the logic of the law and order view, I have constructed here a hypothetical program of rather terrifying proportions to show how far we would have to go to make a real difference in street crime rates.[3]

A Scenario of Getting Tougher

Picture a "get-tougher" program including vastly increased and more targeted police presence: officers stationed round-the-clock at high-crime locations, provided with detailed information on local robbers and pushers, as well as visible foot patrols on every city block many times a day with expanded license to stop and frisk suspicious-looking passers-by.[4] Patrol would include private spaces as well as public places; the search and seizure provision of the Fourth Amendment would be repealed or reinterpreted to allow the school, home, and workplace to be subject to continual surveillance, supplementing private security. Citizen informers would be paid to provide law enforcement with intelligence on the activities of any neighbor with an arrest record. With such an approach, surely the likelihood would increase that an offense reported to the police would lead to arrest; the odds are now only about one in five, slightly lower for the largest cities.[5] (The total volume of reported crime might not drop because, even though criminal incidents were fewer, the likelihood that they would be reported would probably increase, particularly if penalties were imposed for failing to report crimes.)

The get-tougher approach would also involve major changes in prosecution and adjudication. Career criminal programs would be expanded, and the definition of who is a major offender would be broadened to include everyone with more than one felony arrest. (By contrast, the San Diego Major Violator Unit, as of 1980, focused on robbery and homicide cases in which the defendant had three prior robbery-related charges or one prior conviction for a serious crime within the preceding ten years.[6]) The ancient standard of proving guilt beyond a reasonable doubt would be abandoned in order to reduce the share of felony arrests—roughly one-third in one study of the District of Columbia—that are not prosecuted because the evidence is too weak.[7] The exclusionary rule would no longer impede drug prosecutions, even slightly, because searches would be unrestricted; and confessions extracted from reluctant and poorly informed defendants would be admissible in court. Bail would be denied for more serious offenders (especially robbers and drug offenders, who most often get in trouble while out on bail) and plea bargaining would be eliminated. The numbers of courtrooms and courtroom personnel—from judges and lawyers to clerks—would be multiplied many times over to take on the greater volume of business that would be generated. Presumably, increased resources would mitigate somewhat the organizational imperatives of judges, prosecutors, and police that put the need to expedite the flow of cases ahead of the formal requirements that serious charges lead to indictments and indictments lead to trials.[8]

The "reforms" described thus far would increase our pool of convicted offenders, but to translate that into actual crime reductions would further require much stiffer penalties, since a large percentage of imprisoned criminals are repeaters. One approach might be to incarcerate every felony offender (first-timer or recidivist) until he or she turned thirty—probably a more efficient and less financially costly strategy than, say, requiring twenty-year sentences for all felonies, since many criminologists believe that the rate of offending drops sharply after the teenage years.[9] If the get-tougher program were to expand the use of the death penalty, it would have to do so without much empirical evidence for its effectiveness. Most recent research has not found a deterrent effect for capital punishment.[10] That may be, however, because it is now carried out so rarely; only about 2 percent of murderers convicted in state courts in 1986 were sentenced to death, and few capital sentences actually lead to execution.[11]

While this program would probably lower the odds of getting robbed or shot, it would fall short of eliminating them, for a number of reasons. First, far greater use of incarceration would not improve our ability to apprehend all the bad apples; in fact, it might lower clearance rates for police, since offenders might become cleverer at evading capture. Second, the process of deciding how long and with what devices to incapacitate those we do catch runs up against fundamental limitations in our understanding of uncommon human behavior; we cannot predict with more than modest accuracy which offenders are merely flirting with serious crime and which are entering a long-term relationship.[12] In addition, where crime is an organized business enterprise, as with drug trafficking, it would still be able to recruit workers growing into late adolescence to replace those who are removed from the ranks by the justice process. (This assumes, of course, that there is still a pool of young, low-skilled, underemployed males for whom the lure of the hustle is more appealing than the dead-end secondary labor market jobs that are the principal alternative.) Finally, history provides few examples of the successful repression of consensual criminal activity—prostitution, drug transactions—in which large numbers of people wish to engage.[13] Those activities in turn generate supplementary crime that may cause harm to nonparticipants—drug shootouts, robberies, assaults—and prove almost impossible to deter.

Is it even remotely plausible that such a get-tougher program might be pursued? Weighing the crime control effect of the scenario sketched above is idle speculation because we are not likely to undertake it, given its economic, political, and social costs. One way of looking at the purely fiscal difficulties of moving in that direction is to look at the costs of measures we have taken in recent years and what it would cost to further increase the likelihood that a criminal would be caught, convicted, and incarcerated.

The odds that a serious offense (murder, rape, robbery, aggravated assault, burglary) would result in a prison term rose 72 percent between 1980 and 1986, from 25 to 43 out of every 1,000 known offenses.[14] Between 1979 and 1985 direct expenditures for justice system activities for all levels of government rose 34 percent (adjusted for inflation).[15] To triple the likelihood of sending those offenders to prison would be horrendously expensive. Assuming the same incremental return to increased criminal-justice-system dollar expenditures (for police and courts, as well as corrections) as prevailed during the early 1980s, this prospective accomplishment of the get-tougher program would cost approximately $69.5 billion (in 1988 dollars) above the $45.6 billion expended in 1985 for justice system activities at all levels of government, an increase of almost 150 percent in total system costs.[16] This figure represents an amount equal to roughly half the total size of the federal government budget deficit in 1988.[17] Even such an increased outlay could only, at best, increase the ratio of prison admissions for serious offenses to 129 out of 1,000.[18] And we would have no guarantee of having included the most dangerous or unregenerate offenders in our wider sweep or of having deterred the potentially most serious crimes.

The Ineffectiveness of Present Policies

These calculations are highly speculative and therefore subject to a wide range of error. But they serve to illustrate the general point that it is hardly surprising that the get-tough program of the last twenty years, despite its departures from the more lenient policies of the previous decade, has been marginal at best in controlling crime. By the end of 1985 one out of every thirty-three adult males was under some form of correctional custody (60 percent of them on probation), one of nine if they were black.[19] The financial burden of, say, tripling those proportions and increasing our investment in prisons ten-fold is unimaginable. With a federal deficit that threatens our basic economic well-being and public antagonism against taxes as salient as the outrage over street crime, it is hard to imagine a financial commitment large enough to deliver punitive outcome that matches punitive intent. Nor can we expect that a get-tough program at current levels, if continued long enough, will solve our problems. Despite the current get-tough effort, street crime continues at depressingly high levels. (Herbert Jacob's conclusion that the post-War expansion of resources and capacities in criminal justice constitutes "considerable motion but little progress" probably captures a rough consensus of the criminological community.[20])

Most concerned citizens and justice professionals look at officially reported crime rates as the "bottom line" for any crime control innovation. The official FBI data on reported crimes, based on reports of "crimes known to police" forwarded by law enforcement agencies, are notoriously unreliable. Many crimes go unreported to police, and the local departments apply varying (and sometimes very political) standards to the collection of data.[21] When several crimes are committed on the same occasion, only the most serious one is recorded. Technological developments that have made it easier for both citizens and police to report crime may mean that apparently huge increases in crime are in reality as much reporting wave as crime wave.

However, with all these problems in gathering accurate information, it is nonetheless safe to observe that the official data do not show significant crime reductions that can easily be attributed to the tougher penalties and increased investment in crime control of the past two decades. While the early 1980s saw a dip in the reported incidence of such property and personal crimes as burglary and murder, it has been attributed, at least in part, to a short-term decline in the portion of the population in late adolescence, the most crime-prone years.[22] That respite was enough (or was well enough reported) to reduce to one-third the number of respondents to a 1985 Harris survey who said they felt more uneasy on the streets of their neighborhood than they did a year ago, as compared with 55 percent in 1975; but 40 percent were still worried about crime going up in their area.[23]

Furthermore, that brief respite has apparently ended. The FBI Crime Index rate, having dipped for the years 1980–1984, had risen again by 1987 to the 1979 level.[24] The Index rate of reported burglary, which had dropped by 25 percent between 1980 and 1984, rose again by 6.4 percent in 1985 and 1986 and remained essentially stable in 1987.[25] The National Crime Survey, an alternative source of crime data based on citizen interviews, had previously shown a continuing decline (from 1975–1986) in victimizations for such crimes as robbery and burglary; it showed no statistically significant changes in these crimes between 1984 and 1987.[26] Reports from that data source for 1986 suggest that about 1 percent of U.S. households are now touched by robbery and 5 percent by burglary each year.[27]

Have we conceded defeat in the war on crime too soon? Can we turn this dismal record around if we just persist in our present criminal justice strategies? Probably not. Getting tough has not made our justice system better at catching criminals. Despite equipping more police with better technological resources, the rate of crimes cleared by arrests has actually decreased during the last twenty years.[28] (The ratio of police to the general population has remained more or less constant since 1970, and in some cities police personnel were cut in the fiscal crises of the mid-1970s.[29]) Arrests for serious crimes that will stand up in court are hard to get, and the get-tough emphasis doesn't make them much less elusive. Special efforts to concentrate police resources on the alleged career criminal have been disappointing—expensive arrests that produce relatively few additional convictions and detract from other police functions.[30]

There are also built-in limitations to what the courts can do. Malcolm Feeley writes, "Courts cannot solve the problem of crime or even make a significant dent in it. Thus, in a very real sense, the courts—charged with handling society's failures—will always fail. What the family, the church, the workplace and the school cannot do, neither can the courts."[31] Consider the effect of new, tougher standards and procedures on the work of the courts. Felony prosecutions are no less hindered by weak evidence and reluctant witnesses because there are more of them. Trial delays may get worse when penalties are increased, even when new judges and prosecutors are hired, because fewer defendants are willing to plead guilty. Case load pressures may cause court officers to adopt short-cuts that filter some offenders out of the system, frustrating the get-tough intent.

These impediments to a law-and-order approach for police and courts are unlikely to change. They have at least as much to do with human ingenuity (of the accused) and ambivalence (of the accusers) as with criminal justice system ineptitude. Furthermore, it is hard to escape the conclusion that, for any level of intensity our society could approve and afford, the effect of justice system punishment on future crime is likely to be only marginal. After almost twenty years of intense scholarly interest in the relationship between levels of crime and levels of imprisonment, great doubt still exists about whether the severity of criminal sanctions has a widespread and consistent deterrent effect with respect to serious street crimes.[32] Perhaps the majority view is most simply expressed by criminologist Lee Bowker, who, after finding inconsistent correlations between U.S. crime and imprisonment rates between 1941 and 1978, concluded that the evidence of a substantial relationship is "weak and contradictory" and not to be relied on in policymaking.[33]

Where the threat of punishment does deter crime, it can, by definition, do so only when wrongdoing is perceived to lead with some certainty to apprehension. In general, modern Western justice systems in democratic societies cannot provide that certainty. Certainly ours cannot, as my earlier discussion of clearance rates and the limitations of police patrol suggests.

Incapacitation, which seeks to reduce crime by putting offenders thought likely to be potential recidivists out of commission, is also a crime control strategy of questionable utility. Because of our inability to predict high rates of offending, a little increase in incapacitation does not go a long way; much more drastic increases than have been effected or contemplated in today's get-tough program would be necessary.[34] Even if we were able to achieve a significant decrease in crime rates through expanded incapacitation, public anxiety might not decline correspondingly, given that the level of offending would still be higher than in other eras and countries. And reducing the crime rate marginally does not, by itself, address either the symbolic qualities of the fear of crime or media tendencies to report the terrifying details of the most heinous crimes, no matter how idiosyncratic.

Beyond all these immediate explanations for the instrumental failure of the current policy trend, however, lies a more fundamental one. Interestingly, the conservatives who now promote the get-tough program and the liberals who urged alternatives to incarceration in the late 1960s and early 1970s have erred in the same way in their assumptions about the effect of criminal justice strategies on human behavior. Although espousing very different approaches, both mistakenly assume that law enforcement can, for the citizens it is trying to reach, fundamentally alter the relationship between the state and the economy. The conservatives think that law-abiding behavior can be induced by the credible threat of criminal punishment, while liberals placed their faith in deinstitutionalization, counseling, and "services" (generally nonmaterial assistance, sometimes more). The get-tough perspective ignores the influence of other drives to achieve, acquire, prevail and conquer, the raw material of the struggle for whatever power appears attainable to the targets of the justice system's messages and programs. And the liberal approach confuses modest and isolated justice reforms with changing the structure of opportunities for those most likely to commit street crime. As Francis Allen comments, "The system of criminal justice provides a very narrow base from which to launch movements of fundamental social reconstruction."[35]

MUCH MORE CONTROL

If law and order politics and the policies that flow from it are not protecting us from street crime, what effects are they having? Public opinion data do not suggest that we feel more protected because criminal justice efforts have become more aggressive; attitudes toward both crime and the criminal justice system were strikingly similar in the late 1980s (with the exception of the new importance given to drugs) to what they were in the early 1970s. Franklin Zimring and Gordon Hawkins, in synthesizing death penalty research, have noted that neither rational evaluation nor ethical judgment seems to be as important as instinctive mental states in shaping support for and opposition to capital punishment, which suggests the symbolic nature of its appeal.[36] It may be that public anxiety about crime and desire for tougher approaches has not waned because the problem has not receded; more likely is that nothing—not a healthier economy, not racial peace, not political leadership, not less sensational media messages—has dislodged the symbolic sources of support for the hard line.

If the get-tough program has neither improved public order nor relieved public anxieties, it is diminishing political and social life. These consequences of the get-tough program are as significant as its financial costs or its inability to control street crime. In the course of working on this book I have observed individual and societal outcomes of the policy directions we have taken that impede social progress. The remainder of this chapter will discuss those effects.

Liberal Democracy and the Juggernaut

It has become unfashionable to defend individual rights in the context of crime policy; the liberal flank that used to counter conservative positions on crime has vanished into the social underbrush. But punitive crime policy has implications for the most basic aspects of the relationship between the state and the individual, and they should not be ignored. Similarly, the economic and social disabilities of poor and working people have received scant sympathy from policymakers (Democrats as well as Republicans) during the last decade. But neglecting the ways in which punitive crime policy widens social cleavage invites charges that policies of coercive control, within and outside of the criminal justice system, have aims that go beyond social protection to division and discipline.

As the Warren Court knew when it gave birth to the "due process revolution," U.S. crime policy should testify to and respect the highest ideals of constitutional democracy. The beneficiaries of defendants' rights are not just the guilty, but all of us, since anyone may be subject to police action. Chapter 2 discussed recent shifts in the standards of "fundamental fairness" that we apply to criminal defendants. Some protections extended to the accused during the 1960s have weakened in the 1980s; constitutional scholar Yale Komisar says we are currently living with "a battered exclusionary rule and a shrunken Fourth Amendment." Retreat may become retrenchment as new conservative Supreme Court justices are appointed by President Bush.[37]

Equally important, other erosions of the accomplishments of liberal democracy have accompanied this narrowing of defendants' rights. Two among the panoply of U.S. political values that seem challenged are procedural democracy and the right to contract. The get-tough policy trend—in its dual character, the intensified traditional system and the new surveillance programs—diminishes both and, in doing so, supports concentrated and unaccountable state power. This is a matter that should concern Americans of most political persuasions, not just the liberals who support greater defendants' rights and the radicals whose critique of class-based justice would apply in lenient as well as punitive eras.

Widespread political participation is generally held to be an important feature of democracy.[38] Formal protections of the right to vote and freedom of political communication have been extended throughout U.S. history, on occasion even during the conservative 1980s.[39] But the get-tough program sharply restricts political participation. The effect is direct in that convicted felons—the half-million in prison and the larger number in custody in the community—may not vote, although the vast majority have not committed serious violent crimes and will continue to assume other rights and duties of citizenship. It is indirect (and probably unmeasurable) in subjecting so many lives to the chilling effects of omnipresent surveillance. In the era of computers, someone with even a minor or outdated criminal record may easily surmise that voting or demonstrating or participating in civic activities risks exposure to new and unwanted scrutiny by the state.

This tendency appears particularly significant in light of the truism that in twentieth century United States the poor and near-poor vote less frequently than the middle-class. Census data for 1980 show that people with less than $10,000 in family income comprised 22.5 percent of the population but only 16.9 percent of the voters, while those with family incomes of $25,000 or over were 29 percent of the population but 35.1 percent of the voters. In other words, the poor were 25 percent underrepresented while the affluent were 21 percent overrepresented.[40] The poor are, of course, also overrepresented as subjects of the attention of the criminal justice system. Their deviant behavior is more likely to be defined as criminal, their poverty puts them at a disadvantage during court processing, and they account for a disproportionately large percentage of incarcerated prisoners.[41] The justice system's curb on political participation, therefore, inhibits more than the expression of the views of troublesome and occasionally violent deviants. It deflects challenges to the basic distribution of resources within the society from those most negatively affected. And it reinforces the skew of the political system toward disproportionate representation of the well-off.

This is not to suggest, of course, that thoroughgoing political equality would prevail without a get-tough program. Many law-abiding people who do not live in the shadow of law enforcement surveillance or justice system control do not vote or take part in other forms of political participation. And there are many reasons for not voting. Institutional forces like the legal constraints of voter registration requirements and the political impact of the collapse of party competition appear to be important.[42] But psychosocial factors like apathy and ignorance may also be seen as deriving from institutional influences, one of which is overt or muted control of the justice system. It becomes part of "the suppression of the options and alternatives that reflect the needs of the nonparticipants," encompassing all the various immediate reasons for nonvoting.[43] From this perspective, intermediate punishments and data surveillance become forms of disenfranchisement. While this argument may appear to be solely a plea for the voting rights of those who are imprisoned and surveilled in the community, it extends beyond the concern with minority interests on which libertarian theory is based. At issue here is the basic requirement that modern democracies embrace universal suffrage in order to be fully legitimate.

Similar concerns flow from attention to the justice juggernaut's impact on an adult's capacity to enter into binding agreements. One need not endorse the dynamics of unbridled capitalism to prize the right of individuals to contract, a cornerstone of liberal democracy. The U.S. ideal of individual rights encompasses wide latitude on matters of personal choice, particularly where the use of property—including one's own labor power—is at issue. Here, too, the expansion of justice controls has effects not supportable for their utility at controlling crime. In Chapter 4 I noted the the ever-growing ability of employers and licensing agencies to examine criminal records and the increasingly large range of jobs unavailable to people with criminal records, even where an arrest did not result in conviction or where the offenses are trivial or occurred long ago. This exclusion deprives otherwise employable people of the chance to make a living and consigns others to perpetual underemployment. The restriction on an employee's right to quit an unpalatable job if under community supervision stifles the spirit of initiative revered by U.S. individualism and regulates labor market transactions as surely (if not as frequently) as laws protecting the right of workers to organize.

The get-tough program tampers with other matters of individual choice beyond the control that is necessary and reasonable to repress criminal behavior. The universal availability of criminal histories in "open record" states, law enforcement abuse of the use of computerized records virtually everywhere, and supervision programs that, in effect, monitor family and community life expose small and not-so-small secrets to friends and employers as well as to the state. The lack of a legal theory of privacy to constrain such surveillance robs its subjects of even the dignity of the formal challenge to these exercises of power, no matter how remotely they are related to the control of serious crime.

Economic Democracy and the Juggernaut

The get-tough program impinges on substantive as well as formal equality. For those who believe that democracy should include economic opportunity—the right to a decent job, to progress in realizing an enhanced standard of living, to participation in production and investment decisions—the crime control policy directions of the past twenty years have a clearly regressive impact. They reinforce class divisions in general and isolate the urban underclass in particular. The remainder of this chapter briefly elaborates on these concerns.

The justice juggernaut gets its legitimacy from a very basic moral imperative: it is wrong to steal, defraud, and inflict bodily harm. The concentration on individual deviance that follows from the dominance of that moral premise is easy for politicians and citizens alike, at whatever point on the political spectrum, to understand and support. But adopting it without regard to its social-structural context ensures that policymakers will ignore important implications of the persistence of a great deal of street crime.[44]

The moral failings of individuals are, in part, products of class relationships, cultural values, and material forces. In effectively denying that truism, government is evading a major aspect of its responsibility for maintaining public safety: paying attention to the contexts in which people resort to street crime. In this respect, it is acting like a state with plenty of hospitals but no nutrition, sanitation, or environmental protection programs aimed at keeping the population healthy.[45] Its behavior resembles an anti-cancer program that concentrates entirely on surgery, radioactive treatment, and chemotherapy but entirely ignores the contributions to cancer of social practices like smoking or dumping of toxic wastes.

The state should, of course, have other motivations besides the reduction of street crime for addressing the social dysfunctions that contribute to it. State intervention to mitigate some of the harsher effects of market relations ought to be undertaken primarily for its potential contribution to the general welfare. But a high volume of street crime evidences systemic ills that are effectively ignored by get-tough policies. Law and order politics as the dominant perspective that informs efforts to reduce crime can obscure such criminogenic conditions as what Elliott Currie calls the "disruptive development" of the U.S. economy since World War II (discussed in Chapter 7) and the excessive association between consumption and worth that characterizes this society.

These comments are not meant to suggest that the only societal effects of the criminal justice policy trends of the last twenty years are very general. The get-tough approach also justifies bankrupt policies in specific areas. The increasingly harsh sentences for drug possession as well as sale, coupled with inadequate resources for treatment of addicts, further marginalize urban minority males without touching the problem of serious abuse.[46] In those instances where drug offenders are assigned to intermediate punishment programs—and my experience suggests that such programs are filling up with small-time dealers—they must accept the imposition of conformity that goes beyond the negative prohibition of social harm to the regimentation of participants to be compliant workers and coerced respecters of state authority. Add to that the likelihood that the electronic panopticon reduces its subjects to little more than the sum of the events captured by their criminal records, and it is clear that our society has truly written off some of its young, strong members as potential contributors to our general social welfare.

In the end, however, the most troubling effects of the justice juggernaut on economic democracy are their most general and most pervasive. They tend to reinforce other policy failures that combine to generate increasing class stratification and polarization in the United States.[47] They make it increasingly difficult for the young, the black and Hispanic, and the poor to overcome other obstacles to economic security and independence. They label, tar, and stigmatize. They isolate and confine. They are not the source of inequality and class divisions in the United States, but they feed our failure to live up to the splendid rhetoric of "liberty and justice for all."

PART IV

•

WHAT'S AHEAD

10

•

BROADER AND DEEPER

A good prison system, properly funded, is a natural component of a free democratic society that is needed to protect the American way of life, a life that allows people to strive for a place in the sun.

● Anthony P. Travisono, Executive Director,
American Correctional Association

We're a border city with Kansas, so consequently, being the largest city in the area, our computer is used by some of these other agencies for a multitude of purposes. But we all share criminal information, and now we think that we'll be able to share mug shots, hopefully, over this same network, and eventually fingerprints for AFIS [Automated Fingerprint Identification System] and that sort of thing.

● Larry L. Joiner, Police Chief, Kansas City, Mo.

PREDICTING FUTURE CRIME control policy is almost as problematic as predicting individual human behavior. This is partly because the relationship between the level of crime and the choice of policies to address it is so tenuous. It is tempting to think that whether or not the justice juggernaut prevails throughout the 1990s will hinge principally on fluctuations in the prevalence of crimes that people most fear. Our common-sense expectation would be that if reported street crime rose by 50 percent, the public demand for a get-tougher program would increase, and that correspondingly a drop of 50 percent in the burglary and robbery rates would reduce the public demand for stiffer penalties against those crimes. But, as we have seen elsewhere in this book, where crime and public opinion are concerned, trends are often counterintuitive.

Other forecasting difficulties abound. Forces that shape crime control policy—economic discontents, cultural predispositions, organizational imperatives—are various and interlocking, themselves often determined by external events that are hard to foresee. Furthermore, our particular task of understanding the shape of things to come is complicated by the need to address the two principal policy directions analyzed in preceding chapters—one that deepens or intensifies coercive control and one that broadens it. While the two policy trends are presently complementary and interdependent, they could theoretically become conflicting and independent; their dynamics are different and must be analyzed with different assumptions. We must ask two questions: whether the get-tough program will continue to intensify capture and confinement, and, within that framework or independent of it, whether the role of observation will expand.

In the pages that follow I examine several possible directions future policy might take. Each direction represents a different balance of such forces as major changes in the political or economic climate, crime increases or decreases, the relative influence of the organizational imperatives of criminal justice professionals, and attitudes—public or elite—toward particular social problems like illegal drugs. I conclude that the 1990s are most likely to feature more of the same, that the general get-tough perspective will continue and that it will be accompanied by strong support for surveillance of all kinds. My analysis is finally supported by the view that we have only just entered a period in which, in the larger arena of social policy, individual regimentation is increasingly legitimate, meeting with little resistance from those to be regimented or their representatives.

ALTERNATIVE SCENARIOS

In examining the course of future policy, we might consider four scenarios. They range across the political spectrum from a trend that would intensify the get-tough program with decreased emphasis on observation to a retreat from both the deepening and broadening reach of criminal justice.

The Policy Thaw

Perhaps least likely is what might be called the policy thaw, a rejection of the law and order approach that undergirds both the get-tough program and programs of observation. Theoretically, such a development could occur either by explicit repudiation through such legislative and judicial modifications as sentence reductions and expanded defendants' rights, or by implicit subversion through the exercise of discretion by those who implement criminal justice policies—police, judges, prosecutors, or probation officers.[1] But one of the striking features of the get-tough era has been to shift much primary decision making authority away from criminal justice administrators, parole boards, most notably, to legislative bodies, where policymakers have usually (but not always) found it a political boon that they are not likely to quickly relinquish. A legislative about-face on street crime would require a shift in the political wind of almost unimaginable proportions. The warming trend would have to combine a number of currents.

A simple decrease in crime incidence would probably be a prerequisite for thaw but would almost certainly be insufficient; it would not touch the deeply-rooted symbolic sources of get-tough support. (It is also worth noting that the apparent dip in burglary and robbery crime in the early 1980s did not occasion any calls for a kinder, gentler crime policy; Americans polled on the subject continued to believe overwhelmingly that their local courts were too soft on offenders.[2]) A stronger economy, with benefits broadly distributed across income classes, might make people marginally less fearful and more forgiving, although the evidence admits of varying interpretations and has not been scientifically studied.[3]

Another force, which would probably have an effect only in combination with reduced crime and broadly-distributed economic gains, would be renewed concern with the inequalities in U.S. society—refusal to tolerate the remaining, substantial income gap between blacks and whites; acknowledgement by opinion-makers that poor people are unfairly overrepresented among the chronically ill, the retarded, the illiterate, and the delinquent. A new progressive spirit would not necessarily reduce police protection or return to discredited theories of rehabilitation through criminal punishment. It might, however, apply libertarian principles to the greater depth and breadth of criminal justice. It might, for instance, refuse to tolerate double- and triple-celling and thereby be forced to shorten sentences to give every prisoner a cell. It might prune computerized criminal history files that can be exchanged interstate and grant the subject of a criminal record a right to keep that record private with respect to most employers and others outside criminal justice, especially where the record included arrests without dispositions and old or minor offenses. It might develop a privacy theory that would structure the discretion that judges and probation officers have over "outmates" in intermediate punishment programs. Most basic, in endorsing government intervention in market relations that generate disability and discrimination, the new progressivism might insist on a pattern of crime definitions and sanction levels that more accurately reflects the relative social harms of different offenses. Drug crimes with a low risk of violence would probably be less harshly punished, and environmental and workplace offenses that threaten health and safety would be criminalized and more aggressively enforced. The imposition of longer sentences for crimes committed disproportionately by disadvantaged groups would be subjected to close scrutiny, with a presumption against government participation in any form—including legislative definitions of crimes and determination of sanctions—of differential treatment of racial and income groups.

The Deep-freeze Scenario

At the other end of the political spectrum (and at a different point on the weather map) would be the possibility that in the 1990s the traditional capture and confinement measures would continue to be strengthened but observation programs would shrivel. This would require that the public be willing to spend whatever it takes to raise arrest rates and put many more people away, and that well-publicized opposition arise to the substitution of observation techniques for patrol and imprisonment.

Americans currently appear willing to bear greater cost burdens for criminal justice. Sixty-eight percent of respondents to a 1987 national survey said too little money was spent on "halting the rising crime rate," a higher percentage than those who thought too little was spent on education.[4] And people have put their money where their opinions are; most (but not all) prison and jail bond issues passed during the 1980s, including $3 billion worth in California.[5] On the other hand, community opposition to locating prisons in their areas, except in poor rural communities desperate for any source of economic development, continues unabated. Expensive and time-consuming lawsuits against state prison building plans have become common.[6]

As for the other term in the equation, opposition to intermediate punishments may indeed arise once the public becomes truly aware of them. In a 1987 telephone survey by researchers at Bowling Green State University of a representative sample of almost 2,000 American adults, the majority favored incarceration over probation even for offenses like burglary that yielded property worth less than $10 and assault without any weapon or injury. Furthermore, "respondents who chose imprisonment as a punishment for an offense were asked how long the prison sentence should be. Sentences given ranged from a few days to 'life,' with sentences tending to be much longer than sentences actually served currently."[7] Some politicians encourage this perspective, pushing the public panic button even as they work on developing nonprison programs. Shortly before the voters of California were to be asked to approve a 1988 bond issue for $1.3 billion to be spent on prison and jail construction, Governor George Deukmejian told an audience of police officers at a widely-publicized law enforcement conference, "Some are talking again about finding alternatives to incarceration. Society tried that before, and it didn't work. We will not consider additional alternatives to prison until dangerous criminals consider alternatives to crime. . . . Our motto is that we will release no prisoner before his time."[8]

Despite the strong support for policies even tougher than those we currently have, this second scenario seems almost as unlikely as the first, given the much greater costs of a get-tougher program suggested in the last chapter. The willingness to bear those costs is most likely to pertain in a healthy economy, although one might argue that class conflict has been strong in prior periods of economic stagnation—militant strikes were common in the latter half of the 1930s, for example—and that the juggernaut constitutes a form of class war. In any event, general economic prosperity in the United States seems unlikely in the near future, given continual stagnation in investment and productivity growth and the current mountain of U.S. debt.[9] And an upturn might have the opposite effect; in a strong economy, with benefits distributed across the income spectrum, there would be fewer of the economic insecurities that fuel symbolic demands for the hard-line approach. Also, the political costs seem too high. Although a majority of Americans—not, however, a majority of blacks—consistently view state and local police in a positive light, there is no indication that they would be willing to give them the unbridled discretionary authority that would be necessary to increase arrest and indictment, as described in the get-tougher scenario in Chapter 9.[10]

The prospect of opposition to observation programs raises different issues for the different types of measures. The data surveillance of law enforcement agencies is publicly invisible and likely to remain so. Even if most citizens understood the functions and operations of computerized recordkeeping, they would probably see it not as an impediment to more aggressive policing but as an efficiency measure that modernizes investigation and supplements physical patrol in the way that fingerprint technology, radio cars, and police helicopters have done. Intermediate punishments may well pose more of a public relations challenge as they become a more visible part of the correctional landscape. But the opposition they will generate does not seem likely to outweigh the momentum they have acquired or the organizational needs they satisfy, even if they turn out to be less cost-saving than they now appear to be.

The amount of public resistance to intermediate punishments cannot really be gauged from the limited support for probation suggested by national surveys. For one thing, judges and probation officers in jurisdictions with sizable programs have taken pains to promote them as very restrictive, more protective of the public than traditional probation. Florida's Community Control Program is described by the press as "house arrest," a label that conjures up prison-like confinement. The Bowling Green telephone polls cannot give respondents enough information to enable them to evaluate the use of particular programs for particular defendants. Opposition to intensive probation is likely to wane when people observe at closer range that it is used primarily for offenders with nonviolent offenses. We also cannot tell from public opinion surveys how salient opposition to non-prison penalties may be; the opposition of citizens who have doubts about them may die down as they become an even more standard feature of the correctional landscape.

The True Alternatives Approach

A third possibility for the future is that, rather than supplementing the capture and confinement approach, observation programs would begin to diminish it. A more-or-less conscious decision might be made that certain categories of offenders previously sent to prison—burglars with drug habits, say—could be handled at lower cost and with a minimum of risk to public safety under community supervision. The spread of computerized investigation and intelligence files and the availability of increasingly sophisticated identifiers (like DNA testing) could mean that fewer police investigators were needed to accomplish the same volume of tasks. This scenario might pertain if a massive tax revolt focused public attention on the high costs of prisons and law enforcement personnel or if the country were plunged into long and severe recession. Major economic upheaval—or, for that matter, a crisis of another sort like epidemic or war—could also simply displace crime as a policy issue of great salience for voters. (In 1982, at the depths of the recession of the early 1980s, public opinion polls showed that concern with crime as a national issue plummeted, relative to unemployment and inflation.[11] However, it had become more salient again by 1986.) Observation would be likely to flourish under these circumstances—or if, for some reason, public confidence in criminal justice effectiveness increased—because public quiescence as to crime policy would allow greater latitude for the organizational preferences of justice professionals. The primary locus of decisions about policy would shift again, giving more authority to police officials and "street-level bureaucrats" like judges and probation officers. This scenario could exist within a continuing get-tough framework, or might represent a partial retreat from the overall get-tough trend.

Reducing reliance on what, for most people, are the primary images of law enforcement and punishment seems, however, somewhat unlikely. Sudden social and economic cataclysms that would alter patterns of the policymaking process are improbable. And while the furor over drug abuse continues, quiescence on crime is nearly unimaginable. The Anti-Drug Abuse Act of 1988 clearly testifies to a continuing reliance on both law enforcement personnel and prison sentences. The Act authorized $10.7 million for fiscal year 1989, for example, "to increase the number of Armed Career Criminal Apprehension enforcement personnel . . . by no fewer than 244 full-time equivalent positions over such personnel levels on-board at the Bureau as of September 30, 1988, and for related equipment."[12] It also provides stiff new mandatory prison sentences for federal drug crimes, such as a life term for a third offense of cocaine possession, if the amount is more than 50 grams.[13]

More of the Same

The new drug law is not uniformly committed, however, to the capture and confinement measures described above. It also includes important provisions that rely on data surveillance, and in doing so illustrates the fourth, and most probable, scenario: a policy trend in which the two directions will proceed in tandem, sometimes clashing but generally coexisting. Under the law civil penalties, like the loss of a student loan guarantee or a federally insured mortgage, may supplement criminal convictions; the determination of the drug offenders who have federal benefits that can be withdrawn will certainly be made by computer matching. The law authorizes the director of the Bureau of Justice Assistance to make grants and enter into contracts with state and local law enforcement agencies "for maintaining and operating information sharing systems that are responsive to the needs of participating enforcement agencies in addressing multijurisdictional offenses and conspiracies. . . ." and "establishing and maintaining a telecommunication of the information sharing and analytical programs. . . ."[14] This section elevates the policy status of a hitherto "experimental" program of Regional Information Sharing (RIS) grants that conduct intelligence operations on suspected conspiracies of various kinds.

In conclusion, the immediate future will bring more of what we have been experiencing in both areas. Continuing reliance on police and prisons will be fueled by public frustrations over the intractibility of the drug problem and the widespread perception that it represents a threat by the forces of darkness—blacks and hispanics—to the health, morality, and prosperity of middle-class youth. As for the trend toward greater reliance on observation by both police and corrections, its core appeal will not be the satisfaction of public demands, but the fulfillment of the organizational needs of criminal justice.

INFLUENCES ON THE FUTURE JUGGERNAUT

The glass ball into which I peer to discern the future looks less like the clear crystal used by soothsayers and more like the child's toy full of falling snow that partially obscures the shapes within. To the extent that the contours of crime policy leading up to the year 2000 reveal themselves, however, they do so in the context of three dominant influences that, in combination, support a deeper and broader system of coercive control. This section describes the likely influences of continuing social division and economic instability, support for observation programs from the criminal justice policy networks, and reinforcement of both perspectives of the juggernaut from wider social policy trends.

Continuing Division and Instability

The last twenty-five years have been full of turbulent movements and events: the civil rights movement, the Vietnam War, Watergate, inflation, the recessions of the mid-1970s and early 1980s, the growth of illegal drugs as a major industry. Political and social crisis and economic decline have buffeted the American people and brought about real and perceived instability in many realms of life. While the Great Depression and World War II might seem as likely to have produced social instability, it can be argued that the more recent upheavals have been divisive in a way that those crises were not, pitting black and white, poor and affluent, young and middle-aged against one another. The public effects have been definitive. Confidence in a wide range of public and private institutions—business, the press, and professionals, as well as government and the military—fell from a 1965 high (since scientific polling began in the 1930s) to unprecedented lows in the late 1970s.[15] As one major pollster put it in 1977, "The change is simply massive. Within a ten- to fifteen-year period, trust in institutions has plunged down and down. . . ."[16]

Some of the disillusionment expressed in the polls of the late 1970s and early 1980s turned around in the late 1980s; Congress and the Supreme Court, for instance, seem to have rebounded somewhat from the low levels of public confidence they had in the late 1970s.[17] And the Gallup Poll's "satisfaction index," in which respondents are asked to state whether they are "satisfied or dissatisfied with the way things are going in the United States at this time," went from a low of 12 percent in August 1979, when the measure was first taken, to a high of 66 percent in March of 1986.[18]

But there are new sources of unease among Americans. While fear of unemployment and recession dropped sharply after 1983, drug abuse became very salient, and concern about war and international tensions rose.[19] Furthermore, it seems likely that many workers will experience growing dissatisfaction with the decline in real average hourly earnings for production and nonsupervisory employees that has prevailed since the last business cycle peak in 1978.[20] The federal and trade deficits and third-world debt have also become major economic concerns for many Americans.[21]

As this book goes to press, in the honeymoon period of the Bush Administration, there is no sign of policy developments that would address the structural discontents that contribute to support for get-tough criminal justice programs. The new drug legislation contains neither a coherent strategy nor adequate funding to address either addiction to or casual use of illegal drugs. The Bush Administration seems unlikely to generate significant new economic policies that would address the structural sources of stagnation in the U.S. economy.[22] Furthermore, with continued corporate and government pressures on workers and unions, stagnation in workers' earnings and mounting income inequality are also likely to persist.[23] And with corporate, household, and third-world debt continuing to rise, the risks of U.S. and global financial collapse remain. It seems reasonable to project further U.S. economic stasis and decline relative to major competing economies, a trend that not only empties pockets but bruises collective pride.

For here too, in a larger arena, the expressive as well as the instrumental consequences of political and economic events bolster trends in public attitudes about crime and how to deal with it. Although people do want to feel safe in their homes and on the streets at night, they also want to know that the institutions in which they have invested their trust and their hard-earned dollars are "working;" that they are operating with the efficiency and energy that are hallowed American attributes. Short on evidence that these qualities prevail in the family, the school, the workplace, and the world market, Americans are still insisting, against all reason, that the justice system "work" by indicting, convicting, and incarcerating every serious offender who is arrested. (People seem to be more forgiving of the failure to catch every wrongdoer known to the police. The large numbers of victims who do not report crimes because they think they are "not important enough," combined with the evidence that most people think police are doing a good job, attest to that.[24]) The fundamental limits on the extent to which the criminal justice system can deliver on those demands is not a lesson in tolerance, merely a source of frustration like the deficit or the unemployment rate, only closer at hand and therefore subject to more intense criticism. As long as personal experience, friends' anecdotes, and media reports confirm the inability of justice to be truly comprehensive—and no countervailing education exists to clarify why it is inevitable—the public in general will keep demanding that the holes be plugged.

Its demands are not, of course, entirely displaced fury over larger forces. Crime rates (or perceptions of them, as purveyed by the media) will also fuel law and order attitudes. Street crime is unlikely to fall in the 1990s. The proportion of people in the crime-prone years (14–24) is starting to rise, the loss of good jobs for low-skilled workers shows no sign of abating, the failure of welfare benefits and the minimum wage to keep up with inflation is putting more people in desperate material need— the list of worsening criminogenic conditions is very long. The same problems that stimulate symbolic demands for the control of behavior drive the behavior itself.

Then there's the lure of illegal drugs: the escape their use provides and the material gains to be had from going into the industry. It is impossible to predict either the course of drug use or policy trends with respect to drug crimes. What can be said is that public concern about drugs—and the willingness of politicians to capitalize on that anxiety—has infused new energy into the effort to expand and tighten the grip of criminal justice. The public sense of crisis has been fed by visible, dramatic incidents involving national heroes—the death of University of Maryland basketball star Len Bias and positive tests for cocaine use by New York Mets pitcher Dwight Gooden—and by statistical evidence that the crack plague is worsening the quality of life in large American cities. The National Institute on Drug Abuse, for example, reported huge increases for 1987 in cocaine-related deaths and emergency room visits in many U.S. cities.[25]

Catchy phrases like "just say no," "zero tolerance," and "user accountability" were adopted in the late 1980s by President and Mrs. Reagan and federal law enforcement officials to convey a sense of the drug threat as universal. The new "demand" approach, through which law enforcement seeks to deter consumption rather than cut off the supply of drugs, blurs distinctions between occasional users and addicts and implicates all of both in the escalating (but still rare in most places) violence that accompanies the drug trade. Foreign policy has been affected too, with U.S. military personnel raiding cocaine laboratories in Bolivia, military patrol under consideration for the Mexican border, and then-Vice President Bush decrying, in 1986, "a very real link between drugs and terrorism."[26] In a period of about five years a serious, complex social problem has been turned into a national bugaboo rivaling communism in the 1950s, at least as likely to strengthen the juggernaut as fears of rebellion and decline were destined to generate and sustain it.[27]

Elite and System Support for Observation

During the 1990s all but the diehard liberals among policymakers, for reasons touched on throughout this book, are likely to express strong public support for aggressive police practice and increased incarceration. This will not stand in the way of simultaneous, less visible support for the more lenient—if more pervasive—programs of observation.[28] There are several reasons for a likely continuation and expansion of policymakers' commitment to data surveillance by police and intermediate punishments.

State legislators and governors are better equipped than anyone to assess the delicate balance between being perceived as soft on crime because they're not supporting harsh prison terms and bankrupting the state by running up debt service or angering the voters by raising taxes. They know what the bill for a consistent get-tougher program would be, and they are worried about it. In California there are likely to be 100,000 prisoners by the early 1990s; a conservative projection of the construction costs for prisons either underway or being planned in 1987 was $5 billion.[29] In Delaware it has been estimated that, based on late 1980s incarceration expenditures, a "lifer" admitted between 1984 and 1994 who lives to be 73 will cost the state almost $1.3 million at an inflation rate of 4 percent.[30] The incarceration rhetoric is strong, but it will continue to mask the expansion of other methods of punishment alongside the lengthening of some sentences and the construction of more prisons.

Besides, the observation programs can often legitimately be sold as additional control, not as a substitute for it. Putting an index of investigative files on line for state-wide use brings a new resource to even small-town police departments. (Whether it actually increases clearance rates is irrelevant for this discussion; what is important here is that the scope of control through additional access to information has been potentially widened.) Nonprison sanctions can be promoted as punitive if they are to be instituted in a situation in which there is a strong public perception (accurate or otherwise) that at present many offenders get off scot-free. In 1987 the Commission on the Year 2000 for New York City, appointed by Mayor Ed Koch to make recommendations on future policies for the municipal government, proposed that "house arrest and other alternatives to prison should be used more widely to assure that more people are actually punished for their crimes."[31]

The disciplinary features of the corrections programs also make good selling points. Intermediate punishments hold out the promise of making offenders immediately employable and getting their families off the welfare rolls. Curfews, characteristic of most programs and now proposed around the country for probationers of all kinds, provide another way of managing unruly populations. These features may help policymakers with the political dilemma they face in supporting apparently lenient approaches when the public mood is perceived as punitive.

In the privacy of their offices, policymakers support observation programs—and will continue to do so—for programmatic reasons that they cannot proclaim publicly. Many police officials now believe that unfocused, preventive patrol is simply inefficient, no matter how reassuring it may be to citizens for police to be a visible presence on the streets. As a result some cities, including Denver, now use hitherto random patrol time to go back to the precinct house and check criminal history records on the computer.[32] Support for intermediate punishments rests, in part, on the widely held view of many legislators and judges that prison is ineffective at reducing recidivism. A study by sociologists Richard Berk and Peter Rossi of elite decision makers with influence on prison policy (governors, state legislators, judges) found that most opposed a "punitive future," and that weighting their views by the degree of influence they were likely to have produced an even stronger opposition; that is, the more powerful people were more likely to be in opposition than the less powerful ones.[33] Although this study was done in the mid-1970s, and the climate among elites, as well as among the public, is probably somewhat more punitive now than it was then, the results were unequivocal enough to suggest that the general trend, if not its magnitude, could probably be confirmed in 1989.

The attitudes described above apply to criminal justice administrators and judges as well as to elected officials. Their role is vital in many ways to the balancing act performed by politicians. It is often they who, through their policy ideas and ability to translate them into working programs, have most influenced the views of the legislators. They develop and implement proposals; their information is based on first-hand observation, their stake in the programs deeply personal and professional. They are crucial in winning acceptance among other professionals of a tradeoff, where one seems inevitable, between more traditional justice measures and the new programs. Their endorsements trickle down to the street-level bureaucrats who must actually deliver on the shift in policy. An illustration at the highest level is the speech given in September 1988 by FBI Director William Sessions to the National Law Enforcement Council, a coalition of law enforcement associations. Sessions' principal thrust was that training for local and state law enforcement at the FBI's Training Academy in Quantico, Virginia, was, for budgetary reasons, likely to be curtailed. He sweetened this message, however, with the news that the Automated Fingerprint Identification System, which provides local law enforcement with mail access to criminal histories around the country, would become fully operational within a few months, and that the Bureau would soon be able to conduct DNA matching for a limited number of cases, a technique that Sessions promised would become "the most significant step in law-enforcement forensic capability during the past 100 years."[34]

New federal assistance for local and state observation programs is developing that, though smaller in scale, resembles the pattern of LEAA support during the 1970s: formula grants to states that will be subject to an application process that can largely be controlled by the interest groups of justice professionals. Starting with the Justice Assistance Act of 1984 and continuing with the Anti-Drug Abuse Acts of 1986 and 1988, block grants are once again flowing to state and local law enforcement, and what has been a $10 million grant-in-aid program for the exchange of intelligence information will surely expand.[35] The distributive emphasis is also increasing in the juvenile justice area, where observation programs are flourishing in some states; the bill reauthorizing expenditures for the federal Office of Juvenile Justice and Delinquency Prevention in fiscal year 1989 provided for 70 percent of its funds to be distributed in block grants to the states, as opposed to about 61 percent in prior years.[36] The drug problem and concern about youthful gangs seem to be generating enough pork barrel support for both strands of the get-tough program.

Reinforcement from the Wider Policy Arena

Law and order politics in the late 1960s and early 1970s may have been a kind of stalking-horse for the subsequent attack on the welfare state that dominated domestic policy throughout the 1980s. Street crime was the first of the "social issues" (others were abortion, busing, and school prayer) in the right-wing populism that has greased the skids for a New Right ideology repudiating much of the economic protection that fifty years of social spending and regulation brought to working people.

The link between getting tough on crime and reversing the mildly restributive policies of the New Deal and the Great Society was the "permissiveness" of modern society, which embraced a range of manifestations from vandalism and drug-taking to homosexuality and simple laziness.[37] Variously attributed to the decline of the nuclear family, dependence on social welfare programs, and government interference with the dynamism of the market, the so-called moral decline of the country was presented to the public by neoconservative intellectuals, conservative legislators, and the Reagan Administration as a cancer that would destroy the nation and curb the mobility of hard-working Americans. Proposed solutions included both the shrinkage of the welfare state and the imposition of more vigorous private and public enforcement of social order.[38] These nostrums conveniently coincided with worrisome trade and budget deficits (which suggested the necessity for cuts in government spending) and public opinion polls showing increased fear of war (which targeted the cuts on domestic programs).

The conservative project of shaping a more regimented social order has become, in recent years, as evident in private and civil realms as in the criminal justice system. Perhaps most notable outside the justice system are the conditioning of welfare grants on work and the institution of routine and random screening of both private and public-sector workers for drug and alcohol use. These developments primarily control poor and working people. (When Reagan announced he would ask his cabinet to undergo urine testing, Secretary of State Schultz threatened to resign.) They cast a shadow of stigma over large segments of the population which, among other things, further legitimizes the retrenchment of affirmative government.

Broader trends of social policy thus reinforce the directions of justice policy within it and underly both the intensification of capture and confinement and the spread of observation programs. It seems unlikely that the influence from this wider political sphere will soon diminish. National legislation mandating workfare was passed in late 1988 (to be implemented in 1992), and the idea apparently enjoys wide public support. Even if court challenges of drug testing programs limit the conditions that can justify their application, they are likely to survive in some reduced form, and they are used in a spreading range of occupations. A 1987 survey of 1,019 employers from business, industry, government, and education found that 27 percent tested new employees for drugs, up from 20 percent the previous year.[39] Getting tough is now popular outside the sphere of the criminal law.

11

●

CONCLUSION

If we continue to tolerate the conditions that have made us the most violent of industrial societies, it is not because the problem is overwhelmingly mysterious or because we do not know what to do, but because we have decided that the benefits of changing those conditions aren't worth the costs.

● Elliott Currie, *Confronting Crime*

When Plato tried to define justice, he found he could not stop short of building a commonwealth.

● Learned Hand, "The Speech of Justice"

THIS BOOK IS ABOUT criminal justice policy, not about crime. It provides an analysis of the sources and effects of the trends of the last two decades, not a prescription for reducing crime. But it is impossible to evade completely the bottom line question about crime in this society. I have argued that recent approaches to street crime have amounted to uncontrolled growth in state coercion without a corresponding reduction in violence and thievery. Readers will still want to ask: What else can be done? Are we doomed to present levels of criminality for the foreseeable future?

My short answers to these questions are "very little" and "probably." To make major inroads into the crime problem in the United States would require changes in both general ideology and political economy that run counter to current trends.

This does not mean that some marginal relief may not be achieved. Future demographic shifts may help, for example; the proportion of the male population in the crime-prone 18–24-year-old age range is continuing to drop, so that the Census Bureau predicts that by the year 2000 it will be only 63 percent of what it was in 1980.[1] But that dip will be more pronounced among whites than among blacks or hispanics, where the rates of offending are higher.[2] And the conditions that breed crime among the young may continue to worsen, making a larger share of them vulnerable to the behavior we dread. The selective incapacitation strategy could also yield modest benefits in reducing burglary and robbery if researchers improve, and officials apply, predictive tools to identify more members of the group of "career criminals" who each account for a large number of crimes.[3] This approach will be limited, however, by the availability of other young candidates growing up to take the places of those whose careers are curtailed by confinement. Even if both these possibilities come to pass, they will not make the difference that we all long for. We must expect, I fear, continuing high levels of property and personal offenses, particularly as long as illegal drugs remain readily available.

Does this mean that I (and others who may be inclined to agree with my prediction) am insensitive to the damage done by criminals to their victims and, more broadly, to public order and community? Conservatives sometimes say we do not take crime seriously in this country. They tend to mean that we pay too little heed to crime as a sign of social sickness that proceeds from the "breakdown of the family," the "decline of religion," or some other change that threatens us. For these ills they inevitably prescribe, in addition to get-tough measures discussed in this book, remedies that impose their burdens on the less fortunate among us.

I too think we don't take crime seriously enough, but at another level. As a nation we regard crime as an indicator of the decline in individual morality, or to a lesser extent as a sign of alienation and frustration over individual problems of joblessness and poverty. We don't, however, see it as evidence of flaws in our basic economic and social structure. As long as we don't go behind the "breakdown of values" to acknowledge that the sources of that breakdown are deeply embedded in U.S. economic and social structure, we will indeed not be taking crime seriously.

Conservatives become impatient with those who see individual criminality as a product of the social order, and liberals condemn as simplistic the view of crime as the sum of individual moral choices. One wishes—probably futilely—that the left and right could come together in a larger, more layered view of what generates street crime in late twentieth-century America. Criminal offenders are not only individuals whose particular actions have produced social harm to suffering or inconvenienced victims, requiring individualized redress or repression. They are also classes of people with similar problems and resources that flow from institutional arrangements made at levels far removed from their control. Most have, as conservatives allege, at the individual level, chosen their conduct; but the economic and social arrangements that structured their volition were products of choice, too, made not by the criminals or their forebears but by those who hold political and economic power in this society. Our exclusive focus on crime as the product of the individual offender's choice enables us to suppress the evidence provided by street crime that our general ideology and political economy are defective in creating and sustaining a peaceful, protective society.

In fact, I cannot help suspecting that conservatives as well as progressives know that macro-level forces have a profound effect on crime levels, though they are usually unwilling to say so. James Q. Wilson, while he attributes rising crime rates principally to "the triumph of self-expression," pays "subordinate attention" to such factors as "the corrosive effects of racism" and "urban out-migration."[4] But he, like other conservatives, sees the tail wagging the dog. He maintains, for example, that the consumerist society that encourages crime is the product of a national ethos of immediate gratification rather than a victory for business leaders (with government assistance) in their perpetual search for new and refined markets.

It is not criminal justice policies that have generated our criminal society, and it will not be criminal justice policies that alter it. Justice policy simply cannot alter the contest over the distribution of power that determines the nature and extent of crime in the contemporary United States.[5] Determining interest rates, allocating tax burdens, and setting the minimum wage, together, certainly have more long-term effect on crime rates than adjusting sentence lengths and putting more police on the street. Policies that would have more than marginal effects on street crime would have to acknowledge and adjust the extent to which aggressively market-oriented policies have perpetuated a class society, with the lower rungs relegated to desperate and criminogenic conditions and the middle rungs consigned to resentment and frustration that breeds punitive approaches.

Of course, macroeconomic policies do not directly produce social pathology. Influences like advertising and the media bring information about the divisions created by our system to the poor as well as messages about the importance of consumption as the ultimate measure of worth. And our liberal ideology (liberal in the classic nineteenth century sense, with economic and social freedom for the individual as the ultimate goal of society) contributes, too.[6] The appeal of doing business in illegal drugs is strikingly American: the individual can make a quick killing, the field is open to those at the bottom, symbols of success—fancy cars, gold chains—are like those found in legal endeavors.

The problem is too basic to be addressed by what are usually called "social programs"—job training, parenting workshops, remedial education. The social reform effort of the 1960s is often criticized as being too little, too late. But the more trenchant rebuke is that it relied on a modest investment in after-the-fact and individually-rooted correctives for poverty and inequality. Building "human capital"—often for jobs that did not exist or led nowhere—was easier than stemming capital flight, adopting an "industrial policy" that would improve the kinds and quality of available jobs, or conditioning government benefits to the affluent on socially useful behavior, as we are now doing with the poor.

If those approaches were not undertaken twenty years ago, they surely won't be undertaken now. Our commitment to a planned society is weaker on the cusp of the 1990s than it was going into the 1970s. One of the many reasons for this is that street crime—and the juggernaut that highlights it—has legitimized inequality by suggesting that the principal beneficiaries of a set of more progressive economic and social welfare policies are, at bottom, undeserving and would not contribute to a more productive society. The urban minority male has been socially constructed as a "universal threat," a symbol of disorder likely to induce rigidity in public response.[7] The disproportionate involvement of young blacks in street crime, rather than underscoring their exclusion from the rhythms and rewards of mainstream U.S. society, ultimately deflects attention from it. As candidates for the generosity of welfare capitalism, young black and Hispanic street toughs lose more by their undeniable individual culpability than they gain by their obvious need. This is not likely to change until we abandon our virtually exclusive emphasis on individual guilt as the analytic perspective for understanding crime.

Consider the prospect of a significant future labor shortage, as some predict for the early twenty-first century. In such an eventuality, if America is to provide opportunities for all citizens and remain economically competitive in the world market, fundamental choices will have to be made about whether to make a major public investment in the labor force to prepare people for the demanding jobs of an information society. The alternative is to bear the burden of maintaining and controlling a large, partially employed underclass, since the private sector is not likely to make an investment sufficient to meet the need. We may have already effectively made our choice by first subjecting many people to brutalizing conditions and then labelling them as criminal. To many voters and policymakers alike, support for public investment in a group so threatening and stigmatized will not seem very appealing.

NOTES

1. Capture, Confine, and Observe

1. News stories on the candidates' charges and countercharges began in June 1988 and were almost continuous until the November 8 election. See, e.g., *New York Times*, July 5 and August 26. Polls and interviews that suggested the salience of this and other "social issues" in the campaign can be found in *New York Times*, September 14 and September 20. The brouhaha over Dukakis' membership in the ACLU and the organization's response to it is described in *New York Times*, September 27; the earlier attack on the ACLU by Edwin Meese occurred in a speech to the California Peace Officers Association in 1982. Frank Carrington, *Crime and Justice: A Conservative Strategy* (Washington, D.C.: The Heritage Foundation, 1983), 8.

2. *New York Times*, September 23, 1988.

3. P.L. 100–690.

4. *Corrections Compendium* 13, September-October 1988:11–20.

5. George B. Vold and Thomas J. Bernard, *Theoretical Criminology* (New York: Oxford University Press, 1986), 349.

6. James Q. Wilson, *Thinking About Crime*, rev. ed. (New York: Vintage Books, 1985), 237.

7. In the interest of not cluttering up the reader's introduction to the themes of this book with frequent footnotes, authority for the general statements made in this chapter will be found in more detailed discussion of the policy trends presented in chapters 2 and 3.

8. Fred P. Graham, *The Due Process Revolution: The Warren Court's Impact on Criminal Law* (New York: Hayden Book Company, 1970).

9. Herbert Jacob, *The Frustration of Policy: Responses to Crime by American Cities* (Boston: Little, Brown, 1984).

10. A classic work on symbolic politics is Murray Edelman, *The Symbolic Uses of Politics* (Urbana, Ill.: University of Illinois, 1964).

11. The literature on subsystem politics is vast. See J. Leiper Freeman, *The Political Process* (New York: Random House, 1965) for a theoretical discussion; Arnold J. Meltsner and Christopher Bellavita, *The Policy Organization* (Beverly Hills, Calif.: Sage, 1983) describes the policy subgovernments in education; A. Lee Fritscher, *Smoking and Politics: Policymaking and the Federal Bureaucracy*, 4th ed. (Englewood Cliffs, N.J.: Prentice-Hall, 1989) is a study of the tobacco subsystem.

12. U.S. Department of Justice, Bureau of Justice Statistics, *Report to the Nation on Crime and Justice*, 2nd ed., 1988, 12.

13. Federal Bureau of Investigation, *Uniform Crime Reports, Crime in the United States 1987* (Washington, D.C.: U.S. Government Printing Office, 1988), 7; Federal Bureau of Investigation, *Uniform Crime Reports, Crime in the United States 1968* (Washington, D.C.: U.S. Government Printing Office, 1969), 5; Carol B. Kalish, "International Crime Rates," *Special Report* (U.S. Department of Justice, Bureau of Justice Statistics, 1988). The FBI's *Crime in the United States, Uniform Crime Reports* is a standard, multi-year source to which I shall refer frequently in this book. All subsequent citations will refer to it as *Uniform Crime Reports* with the appropriate year.

14. Notable in this area is the Victim Services Agency of New York City.

15. Robert Elias, *The Politics of Victimization: Victims, Victimology and Human Rights* (New York: Oxford University Press, 1986), 160–163.

16. Herbert L. Packer, *The Limits of the Criminal Sanction* (Stanford, Calif.: Stanford University Press, 1968), 365.

17. See Samuel Bowles and Herbert Gintis, *Schooling in Capitalist America: Educational Reform and the Contradictions of Economic Life* (New York: Basic Books, 1976); and Herman Schwendinger and Julia R. Schwendinger, "The Standards of Living in Penal Institutions" in David F. Greenberg, ed., *Crime and Capitalism: Readings in Marxist Criminology* (Palo Alto, Calif.: Mayfield, 1981), 401–402.

18. The divergence between the actual extent and range of crime and "the crime problem" that engenders popular concern is discussed in Raymond J. Michalowski, *Order, Law and Crime* (New York: Random House, 1985), 3–6.

2. The "Get-tough" Approach

1. For criminalization patterns through 1977 (which also suggest that the volume of legislation creating crimes began well before the late 1960s), see Anne M. Heinz, *Governmental Responses to Crime. Legislative Responses to Crime: The Changing Content of Criminal Law* (Washington, D.C.: National Institute of Justice, 1982). Documentation of the gigantic increases in per capita and general expenditures for police and corrections from 1962–1982 can be found in U.S. Department of Commerce, Bureau of the Census, *Compendium of Government Finances,* (Washington, D.C.: U.S. Government Printing Office, 1962, 1967, 1972, 1977, 1982.) Those reports indicate, however, no significant change in a third area, the proportion of state and local expenditures represented by criminal justice—police and corrections only, since courts reports include civil as well as criminal expenditures. (The apparent discrepancy between the lack of growth by this measure and the huge increases in per capita and general expenditures is explained by the fact that government expenses in general, and at the state and local level in particular, have expanded hugely since World War II.) Later figures, still unavailable at this writing, will surely reflect substantial increases in this measure as well, caused by the prison construction boom.

2. U.S. Department of Justice, Bureau of Justice Statistics, press release, September 11, 1988; U.S. Department of Justice, Bureau of Justice Statistics, "State and Federal Prisoners, 1925–85," *Bulletin*, October 1986, table 1.

3. U.S. Department of Justice, Bureau of Justice Statistics, "Correctional Populations in the United States 1985," 1987, table 1.1.

4. Timothy J. Flanagan and Katherine M. Jamieson, *Sourcebook of Criminal Justice Statistics 1987* (U.S. Department of Justice, Bureau of Justice Statistics, 1988), table 6.18; U.S. Department of Justice, Bureau of Justice Statistics, "Prisoners in 1987," *Bulletin*, April 1988, table 2. *Sourcebook of Criminal Justice Statistics* is a standard, multi-year source to which I shall refer frequently in this book. All subsequent citations will refer to it as *Sourcebook* with the appropriate year.

5. "Prisoners in 1987," 2.

6. U.S. Department of Justice, Bureau of Justice Statistics, "Jail Inmates 1984," *Bulletin*, May 1986, table 1.

7. The figures for 1971 come from *Sourcebook 1987*, table 6.18. The Delaware increase from a rate of 32 in 1971 to 327 in 1987 should be viewed in light of an administrative reform by which the state combined its prison and jail systems, so that the high rate includes inmates who would, in most states, be counted in the jail rate. The 1987 figures come from "Prisoners in 1987," table 2.

8. Patrick A. Langan, John V. Fundis, Lawrence A. Greenfeld, and Victoria W. Schneider, "Historical Statistics on Prisoners in State and Federal Institutions, Yearend 1925–86," U.S. Department of Justice, Bureau of Justice Statistics, 1988, table 2.

9. *Sourcebook 1985*, table 6.13.

10. U.S. Department of Justice, Bureau of Justice Statistics, "Jail Inmates 1987," *Bulletin*, December 1987, table 4; *Sourcebook 1985*, table 6.16.

11. Barry Krisberg, Ira M. Schwartz, Paul Litsky, and James Austin, "The Watershed of Juvenile Justice Reform," *Crime and Delinquency* 32 (1) (1986):5–38.

12. Ibid., 24.

13. This conclusion is based on data for the rate of change in the incarceration rate between 1971–1987 and for the rate of change for reported FBI Index crime rates (all crimes, violent crimes, and robbery) between 1970–1986. (The one-year lag is to allow for the effect of a change in crime on incarceration. While it takes much longer than a year to build prisons in response to more punitive policies, the "in-out" decisions of judges are often independent of the availability of prison space.) Correlations were as follows: for the entire period 1971–1987, -0.16 (total crime), -0.04 (violent crime), -0.14 (robbery); for the earlier period 1971–1980, 0.06 (total crime), 0.18 (violent crime), 0.04 (robbery); for the later period 1980–1987, -0.08 (total crime), -0.04 (violent crime), -0.17 (robbery). None of these correlations was significantly different from zero. Incarceration rates for 1971 and 1980 came from *Sourcebook 1987*, table 6.18; and for 1987 from "Prisoners in 1987," table 2. Crime rates are from *Uniform Crime Reports 1970*, table 3; *Uniform Crime Reports 1979*, table 4; and *Uniform Crime Reports 1986*, table 5.

14. *Uniform Crime Reports 1986*, table 1.

15. *Uniform Crime Reports 1969*, chart 17; *Uniform Crime Reports 1987*, table 20.

16. *Uniform Crime Reports 1970*, table 23; *Uniform Crime Reports 1987*, table 25.

17. For a summary of research on reasons why prosecutors do not get convictions, see Brian Forst; Judith Lucianovic, and Sarah J. Cox, *What Happens After Arrest?* (Washington, D.C.: INSLAW, 1977), ch. 5.

18. One study of a career criminal unit in San Diego found that the conviction rate for career criminals was high before the program was introduced (89.5%) and that the increase was therefore marginal (to 91.5%). U.S. Department of Justice, *An Exemplary Project: Major Violator Unit—San Diego, California* (Washington, D.C.: U.S. Government Printing Office, 1980). A 1986 study of the Repeat Offender Project of Washington, D.C., found a slight increase in convictions but also found that as the share of convictions increased for career criminals, it dropped for others charged with serious offenses. Susan E. Martin, "Policing Career Criminals: An Examination of an Innovative Career Criminal Program," *Journal of Criminal Law and Criminology* 77 (1986):1159–1182.

19. "Prisoners in 1987," table 10.

20. It is important to note that the definition of sentencing, as used in this discussion, includes not only judges' decisions but those of others—prosecutors, prison and parole officials—who determine whether offenders will go to prison and how much time they serve. This broader view was adopted by the Panel on Sentencing Research established by the National Research Council of the National Academy of Sciences to review sentencing research conducted in the 1970s. See Alfred Blumstein, Jacqueline Cohen, Susan E. Martin, and Michael H. Tonry, eds., *Research on Sentencing: The Search for Reform* (Washington, D.C.: National Academy Press, 1983), 5–6.

21. Charles A. Moore and Terance D. Miethe, "Regulated and Unregulated Sentencing Decisions: An Analysis of First-year Practices Under Minnesota's Felony Sentencing Guidelines," *Law and Society Review* 20 (1986):253–277.

22. John H. Kramer and Robin L. Lubitz, "Pennsylvania's Sentencing Reform: The Impact of Commission-Established Guidelines," *Crime and Delinquency* 31 (1985):498.

23. Kevin Krajick, "Abolishing Parole: An Idea Whose Time Has Passed," *Corrections Magazine* 9 (1983):36. For a synthesis of research that suggests that legislative reforms have made only modest contributions to the increasing incarceration rates, see Blumstein et al, *Research on Sentencing*.

24. U.S. Department of Justice, Bureau of Justice Statistics, "Sentencing and Time Served," *Special Report*, June 1987, 2.

25. Sentencing "reforms" have also included the restriction or abolition of plea bargaining and the development of sentencing guidelines. Because they seem to be less significant determinants of the rush to confinement, I am not discussing their effects. Plea bargaining bans—which have not been widely adopted—have not been found to increase substantially the proportion of convicted offenders who receive prison terms, though they apparently increase sentence severity, particularly

for lesser offenders. Sentencing guidelines appear to have little effect on the likelihood of a prison term or the severity of a sentence, principally because their adoption by judges is generally voluntary and because they generally describe past sentencing practices as a standard for judges attempting to be currently consistent. Guidelines adopted in Minnesota are an important exception; they are mandated by the legislature, and they represent an explicit policy choice to increase the use of prison for serious violent offenses and decrease it for property offenders. For a fuller discussion of the impacts of these trends, see Blumstein et al, *Research on Sentencing*, ch. 4.

26. Andrew von Hirsch, *Doing Justice* (New York: Hill and Wang, 1976), 133.

27. Donald F. Anspach, Peter M. Lehman, and John H. Kramer, "Maine Rejects Indeterminacy: A Case Study of Flat Sentencing and Parole Abolition," University of Southern Maine, 1983.

28. David Brewer, Gerald E. Beckett, and Norman Holt, "Determinate Sentencing in California: The First Year's Experience," *Journal of Research in Crime and Delinquency* 18 (1981):200–231.

29. Lynne Goodstein, John H. Kramer, and Laura Nuss, "Defining Determinacy: Components of the Sentencing Process Ensuring Equity and Release Certainty," *Justice Quarterly* 1 (1984):62.

30. Kramer and Lubitz, "Pennsylvania's Sentencing Reform," 482.

31. Allen J. Beck and Thomas Hester, "Prison Admissions and Releases," *Special Report* (U.S. Department of Justice, Bureau of Justice Statistics, 1986), 4.

32. Stevens Clarke, "Felony Sentencing in North Carolina, 1976–1986: Effects of Presumptive Sentencing Legislation," Institute of Government, University of North Carolina (1987).

33. Lynne Goodstein and John Hepburn, "Determinate Sentencing in Illinois: An Assessment of Its Develpment and Implementation," *Criminal Justice Policy Review* 1 (1986):305–328.

34. U.S. Department of Justice, Bureau of Justice Statistics, "Setting Prison Terms," *Bulletin*, August 1983, figure 2.

35. Colin Loftin and David McDowall, "'One with a Gun Gets You Two': Mandatory Sentencing and Firearms Violence in Detroit," *The Annals* 455 (1981):155.

36. Ibid., 156.

37. Milton Heumann and Colin Loftin, "Mandatory Sentencing and the Abolition of Plea Bargaining: The Michigan Felony Firearm Statute," *Law and Society Review* 13 (1979):393–430, table 3.

38. Other studies have shown similar adaptive patterns. See, e.g., Joint Committee on New York Drug Law Evaluation, *The Nation's Toughest Drug Law: Evaluating the New York Experience* (New York: The Association of the Bar of the City of New York, 1977) and Michael L. Rubenstein and Teresa J. White, "Alaska's Ban on Plea Bargaining," *Law and Society Review* 13 (1979):367–383.

39. Statistical Analysis Center, Delaware, "Lifers in Delaware: Future Costs and Populations through 1994" (1985).

40. *Sourcebook 1981*, table 6.24.

41. American Bar Association press release, July 22, 1987.

42. *New York Times*, November 1, 1987; "Prisoners in 1987," table 8. In 1989 the Supreme Court ruled that the guidelines, despite challenge in many federal courts, did not violate the constitutional separation of powers. See *Criminal Justice Newsletter*, June 1, 1988, 5.

43. *Sourcebook 1987*, table 2.36.

44. U.S. Department of Justice, Bureau of Justice Statistics, "Capital Punishment 1987," *Bulletin*, July 1988, 4.

45. P.L. 100–690.

46. "Capital Punishment 1987," table 4; NAACP Legal Defense and Education Fund, Inc., "Death Row, U.S.A.," March 1, 1988.

47. "Capital Punishment 1987," 8.

48. Ibid.; William J. Bowers, *Legal Homicide: Death as Punishment in America, 1864–1982* (Boston: Northeastern University Press, 1984), table 1–4.

49. *Lockhart v. McCree*, 476 U.S. 162 (1986); *McCleskey v. Kemp*, 481 U.S. 279 (1987). For a review of recent Supreme Court rulings on the death penalty, see Michael Meltsner, "On Death Row, the Wait Continues," in Herman Schwartz, ed. *The Burger Years: Rights and Wrongs in the Supreme Court, 1969–1986* (New York: Viking Penguin, 1987), 169–176.

50. Henry Schwarzschild, "Foreword," in Bowers, *Legal Homicide*, xx.

51. A more extensive discussion of American ambivalence about execution can be found in Franklin Zimring and Gordon Hawkins, *Capital Punishment and the American Agenda* (New York: Cambridge University Press, 1986).

52. "Capital Punishment 1987," 7.

53. Ibid., table 8.

54. Bowers, *Legal Homicide*, 51–52.

55. Zimring and Hawkins, *Capital Punishment*, 28–30.

56. For an absorbing account of this strategy, see Michael Meltsner, *Cruel and Unusual: The Supreme Court and Capital Punishment* (New York: Random House, 1973).

57. *Furman v. Georgia*, 408 U.S. 238 (1972).

58. *Sourcebook 1986*, table 2.23.

59. Zimring and Hawkins, *Capital Punishment*, 41.

60. Ibid., 67, 99.

61. U.S. Department of Justice, Bureau of Justice Statistics, "Criminal Victimization 1987," *Bulletin*, October 1988, table 6.

62. U.S. Department of Justice, Bureau of Justice Statistics, "Criminal Victimization in the United States, 1985," table 98.

63. Samuel Walker, *Popular Justice* (New York: Oxford University Press, 1980), 27.

64. *Sourcebook 1987*, table 4.17.

65. Herbert Jacob, *The Frustration of Policy: Responses to Crime by American Cities* (Boston: Little, Brown, 1984), 101–111; James P. Levine, "The Ineffectiveness of Adding Police to Prevent Crime," *Public Policy* 23 (1975):523–545; George L. Kelling, Tony Pate, Duane Dickman, and Charles E. Brown, *The Kansas City Preventive Patrol Experiment: A Technical Report* (Washington, D.C.: Police Foundation, 1974), ch. V. For a review of econometric studies of the effectiveness of

police expeditures, see David J. Pyle, *The Economics of Crime and Law Enforcement* (New York: St. Martin's Press, 1983), Ch. 9.

66. Albert J. Reiss, *The Police and the Public* (New Haven: Yale University Press, 1971), 8.

67. 384 U.S. 436 (1966).

68. American Bar Association Criminal Justice Section, "Criminal Justice in Crisis," November 1988, ch. 2.

69. In a 1986 decision, *Moran v. Burbine*, 475 U.S. 412, a majority of Justices including O'Connor (who wrote the opinion), Burger, White, Blackmun, Powell, and Rehnquist held that police who incorrectly told a defense attorney they were "through" questioning a suspect and failed to inform the suspect that the attorney had phoned for him did not invalidate a confession obtained after the suspect waived his *Miranda* rights. The opinion, however, endorsed *Miranda*, at 419, as "strik[ing] the proper balance between society's legitimate law-enforcement interests and the protection of the defendant's Fifth Amendment rights. . . ."

70. This discussion relies heavily on Yale Kamisar, "The 'Police Practice' Phases of the Criminal Process and the Three Phases of the Burger Court," in Herman Schwartz, ed., *The Burger Years: Rights and Wrongs in the Supreme Court 1969–1986* (New York: Viking Penguin, 1987), 143–168.

71. *Michigan v. Tucker*, 417 U.S. 433 (1974).

72. 467 U.S. 649 (1984), at 659.

73. Ibid., at 657.

74. 470 U.S. 298 (1985), at 314.

75. Kamisar,"Police Practice' Phases of the Criminal Process," 157.

76. U.S. Department of Justice, *Attorney General's Task Force on Violent Crime: Final Report* (Washington, D.C.: U.S. Government Printing Office, 1981), 55; "President's Task Force on Victims of Crime: Final Report," 1982, 14.

77. *United States v. Leon*, 468 U.S. 897 (1984); *Massachusetts v. Sheppard*, 468 U.S. 981 (1984).

78. Craig D. Uchida; Timothy S. Bynum; Dennis Rogan; and Donna Murasky, "The Effects of *United States v. Leon* on Police Search Warrant Policies and Practices," Police Executive Research Forum, 1986:36–37.

79. Edwin Meese 3d, "A Rule Excluding Justice," *New York Times*, April 15, 1983.

80. *Criminal Justice Newsletter*, November 1, 1988.

81. *Criminal Justice Newsletter*, June 21, 1982.

82. Wayne R. LaFave, "Fourth Amendment Vagaries (Of Improbable Cause, Imperceptible Plain View, Notorious Privacy and Balancing Askew)," *Journal of Criminal Law and Criminology* 74 (1983):1222.

83. Edwin Butterfoss, "As Time Goes By: The Elimination of Contemporaneity and Brevity as Factors in Search and Seizure Cases," *Harvard Civil Rights/Civil Liberties Law Review* 21(2) (1986):603–650.

84. George Fletcher, *Rethinking Criminal Law* (Boston: Little, Brown and Co., 1978), 836–839.

85. Lisa Callahan, Connie Mayer, and Henry J. Steadman, "Insanity Defense Reform in the United States—Post-Hinckley," *Mental and*

Physical Disability Law Reporter 11 (1987): table 1. About half of U.S. states use the M'Naghten rule, which holds that insanity is a defense to a criminal act only when the court finds that a defendant "was laboring under such a defect of reason, from disease of the mind" that he did not understand the wrongness of his act or at least did not know that what he was doing was wrong. *M'Naghten's Case*, 8 Eng. Rep. 718 (1843), at 722. Many others have adopted the American Law Institute's *Model Penal Code* test, which applies the somewhat broader and more modern standard that the defendant must prove that, "as a result of mental disease or defect he lacks substantial capacity either to appreciate the criminality of his conduct or to conform his conduct to the requirements of law." American Law Institute, *Model Penal Code and Commentaries* (Philadelphia: American Law Institute, 1985), Section 4.01.

86. Callahan et al, "Insanity Defense Reform," 54. Basic works on the insanity defense include Donald H. J. Hermann, *The Insanity Defense: Philosophical, Historical and Legal Perspectives* (Springfield, Ill.: Charles C. Thomas, 1983) and Abraham S. Goldstein, *The Insanity Defense* (New Haven: Yale University Press, 1967).

87. Montana Code Annotated Section 46–14–102 (1979).

88. Callahan et al, "Insanity Defense Reform," 55.

89. Ibid., table 2.

90. *Stack v. Boyle*, 342 U.S. 1 (1951).

91. John S. Goldkamp, "Danger and Detention: A Second Generation of Bail Reform," *Journal of Criminal Law and Criminology* 76 (1985):1–75.

92. Federal Bail Reform Act of 1966, 18 U.S.C. Section 3146 (1966) (now repealed); Federal Bail Reform Act of 1984, 18 U.S.C. Section 1342 (Supp. 1985).

93. *U.S. v. Williams*, 753 F. 2d 329 (1985).

94. *United States v. Salerno*, 107 S. Ct. 2095, 2102. (1987).

95. 23 D.C. Code Ann. Sec. 1322 (Supp. 1985.)

96. Goldkamp, "Danger and Detention," tables 7 and 8, n.62.

97. Marvin Wolfgang, Robert M. Figlio and Thorsten Sellin, *Delinquency in a Birth Cohort* (Chicago: University of Chicago Press, 1972), especially Chapter 6.

98. Jan M. Chaiken and Marcia R. Chaiken, *Varieties of Criminal Behavior* (Santa Monica, Calif.: RAND Corporation, 1982).

99. Peter W. Greenwood and A. Abrahamse, *Selective Incapacitation* (Santa Monica, Calif.: RAND Corporation, 1982), viii.

100. See, for example, its endorsement by a U.S. Department of Justice economist as a way to save money, Edwin W. Zedlewski, "Making Confinement Decisions," *Research in Brief*, U.S. Department of Justice, National Institute of Justice, July 1987. Zedlewski's analysis has been challenged in David F. Greenberg, "The Cost-Benefit Analysis of Imprisonment," unpublished paper, 1988.

101. Holcomb B. Noble, "The Major Offense Bureau: Concentrated Justice," *Police Magazine* 1 (1978):60.

102. Daniel McGillis, *Major Offense Bureau: Bronx District Attorney's Office, New York* (Washington, D.C.: U.S. Government Printing Office, 1977), 4–5.

103. Eleanor Chelimsky and Judith Dahmann, *Career Criminal*

Program National Evaluation: Final Report (U.S. Department of Justice, National Institute of Justice, 1981), 1.

104. Cornelius J. Behan, "Repeat Offender Experiment," *Police Chief* 53(3) (1986):90–96.

105. U.S. Department of Justice, Office of Juvenile Justice and Delinquency Prevention, "Habitual Juvenile Offenders: Guidelines for Citizen Action and Public Response," n.d.

106. Quoted in Mark Thompson, "Born to Burgle," *Student Lawyer* 15 (1986):13–18.

107. Chelimsky and Dahmann, *Career Criminal Evaluation*, 127.

108. Ibid., 128.

109. *Brinegar v. U.S.*, 338 U.S. 160, 180 (1949).

110. John Klofas and Ralph Weisheit, "Guilty but Mentally Ill: Reform of the Insanity Defense in Illinois," *Justice Quarterly* 4 (March 1987):42–43.

111. U.S. General Accounting Office, "Impact of the Exclusionary Rule on Federal Criminal Prosecutions," Report #GGD-79–45, April 19, 1979, 11.

112. U.S. Department of Justice, National Institute of Justice, "The Effects of the Exclusionary Rule: A Study in California," 1982, 10.

113. James J. Fyfe, "The NIJ Study of the Exclusionary Rule," *Criminal Law Bulletin* 19 (1983):256.

114. Richard van Duizend, L. Paul Sutton, and Charlotte A. Carter, *The Search Warrant Process: Preconceptions, Perceptions, Practices* (Williamsburg, Va.: National Center for State Courts, 1984), 91.

115. For a discussion of the loosening of the warrant requirement, see Butterfoss, "As Time Goes By'.

116. *New York Times*, May 27, 1987.

117. U.S. General Accounting Office, "Criminal Bail: How Bail Reform is Working in Selected District Courts," Report #GGD-88–6 (October, 1987), 32.

118. Ibid., 18.

119. National Institute of Justice, "The Effects of the Exclusionary Rule," 12.

120. Sheldon Krantz, Bernard Gilman, Charles G. Benda, Carol Rogoff Hallstrom, and Gail J. Nadworny, *Police Policymaking* (Lexington, Mass.: Lexington Books, 1979), 189–192.

121. U.S. General Accounting Office, "Criminal Bail," 30. The figure of 93 percent is derived from table 2.5.

122. Noble, "The Major Offense Bureau."

123. See McGillis, *Major Offense Bureau, Bronx District Attorney's Office*. This evaluation found that 94 percent of the convictions obtained by the career criminal unit in the Bronx led to prison terms as opposed to 79 percent in a group of cases given routine processing. The difference in outcome is probably overstated, however, because the comparison group was made up of cases that had been screened and rejected for the career criminal program, "presumably due to limits in the nature of the offense, the offender, or the available evidence" (p. 72).

124. Vera Institute of Justice, *Felony Arrests: their Prosecution and Disposition in New York City's Courts* (New York: Longman, 1981); see

also Charles Silberman, *Criminal Violence, Criminal Justice* (New York: Random House, 1978), 257–261.

125. President's Commission on Law Enforcement and the Administration of Justice, *Task Force Report: Science and Technology* (Washington, D.C.: U.S. Government Printing Office, 1967), 61.

126. See, for example, Ernest Van den Haag, *Punishing Criminals: Concerning a Very Old and Painful Question* (New York: Basic Books, 1975).

127. Samuel Walker, *Sense and Nonsense about Crime*, 2d edition (Monterey, C.A.: Brooks/Cole, 1988), 37–43.

128. Malcolm M. Feeley, *The Process Is the Punishment: Handling Cases in a Lower Criminal Court* (New York: Russell Sage Foundation, 1979), ch. 7.

129. Patrick A. Langan and Lawrence A. Greenfeld, "The Prevalence of Imprisonment," *Special Report*, U.S. Department of Justice, Bureau of Justice Statistics, July 1985.

130. "Prisoners in 1987," table 2.

131. U.S. Department of Justice, Bureau of Justice Statistics, "Imprisonment in Four Countries," *Special Report*, 1987, table 2.

132. "Prisoners in 1987," 3. One man in every 225 (.445%) for the country as a whole was in state prison on the last day of 1987, but only one woman in every 4,725 (.021%). Notice that these figures do not include jails or juvenile institutions, which could increase the prevalence of *confinement* (as opposed to *imprisonment*) by 50 percent in some states. See James Austin and Robert Tillman, "Ranking the Nation's Most Punitive States," *Focus*, entire issue, n.d.

133. Ibid.

134. "Correctional Populations 1985," tables 5.6 and 5.9; U.S. Department of Commerce, Bureau of the Census, *Statistical Abstract of the United States 1988*, tables 17 and 19.

135. U.S. Department of Justice, Bureau of Justice Statistics, "Probation and Parole 1987," *Bulletin*, November 1988, tables 1 and 2.

136. Ibid., 2.

137. "Correctional Populations 1985," table 1.1.

138. The figure for black males was obtained by subtracting from the total of blacks under custody the proportion of women in the population in custody (15%) and by subtracting from the total black population the proportion of women (52.6%) in 1985, and then dividing the former by the latter.

139. "Correctional Populations 1985," table 1.1.

140. "The Prevalence of Imprisonment," 5.

141. Alfred Blumstein and Elizabeth Graddy, "Prevalence and Recidivism in Index Arrests: A Feedback Model," *Law and Society Review* 16(2) (1981–1982):265–290.

3. The "Check 'Em Out" Approach

1. Intelligence Authorization Act for FY 1986, 5 U.S.C. Section 9101.

2. For a review of the availability of criminal history records to noncriminal justice users, as of 1988, see SEARCH Group, *Public Ac-*

cess to Criminal History Record Information (U. S. Department of Justice, Bureau of Justice Statistics, 1988).

3. SEARCH Group, *Compendium of State Privacy and Security Legislation, 1987 Overview—Privacy and Security of Criminal History Information* (U.S. Department of Justice, Bureau of Justice Statistics, 1988), 7.

4. U.S. Department of Justice, Bureau of Justice Statistics, "State Criminal Records Repositories," *Technical Report*, 1985, 1.

5. James J. Hornung, Peter G. Neumann, David D. Redell, Janlori Goldman, and Diana R. Gordon, "A Review of NCIC 2000: The Proposed Design for the National Crime Information Center," unpublished study submitted to the Subcommittee on Civil and Constitutional Rights of the House Judiciary Committee, February 1989, 12.

6. FBI public information office, December 1988.

7. "Statement of FBI Assistant Director Lawrence K. York Before the House Subcommittee on Civil and Constitutional Rights" (Mar. 24, 1986), 2.

8. Basic data on FBI files come from information prepared by the FBI public information office in November 1988. The states that participated in Triple-I as of August 1987 were California, Colorado, Connecticut, Delaware, Florida, Georgia, Idaho, Michigan, Minnesota, Missouri, New Jersey, New York, North Carolina, Ohio, Oklahoma, Oregon, Pennsylvania, South Carolina, Texas, Virginia, and Wyoming.

9. Belinda R. McCarthy, "Introduction," in Belinda R. McCarthy, ed., *Intermediate Punishments: Intensive Supervision, Home Confinement, and Electronic Surveillance* (Monsey, N.Y.: Criminal Justice Press, 1987), 1.

10. Joan Petersilia, *Expanding Options for Criminal Sentencing* (Santa Monica, Calif.: Rand, 1987), vii.

11. Billie S. Erwin, "Evaluation of Intensive Probation Supervision in Georgia: Final Report," Georgia Department of Corrections, 1987, 7–8.

12. Todd R. Clear, Suzanne Flynn, and Carol Shapiro, "Intensive Supervision in Probation: A Comparison of Three Projects," in McCarthy, *Intermediate Punishments*, 31.

13. Joan Petersilia, "Georgia's Intensive Probation: Will the Model Work Elsewhere?" in McCarthy, *Intermediate Punishments*, 21–29.

14. Petersilia, *Expanding Options*, 36–39.

15. Charles M. Friel and Joseph B. Vaughn, "A Consumer's Guide to the Electronic Monitoring of Probationers," *Federal Probation* 50(3) (1986):3–14.

16. Annesley K. Schmidt, "Electronic Monitoring of Offenders Increases," in U.S. Department of Justice, National Institute of Justice, *NIJ Reports*, January-February 1989, 2–5.

17. Petersilia, *Expanding Options*, 57.

18. Michel Foucault, *Discipline and Punish* (New York: Pantheon, 1977), 220–221.

19. Neal Miller, "A Study of the Number of Persons with Records of Arrest or Conviction in the Labor Force," U.S. Department of Labor, Technical Analysis Paper no. 63, 1979.

20. NCIC figures came from the FBI public infomation office. The

New York estimate was obtained in a December 1984 interview with an official of the New York State Division of Criminal Justice Services.

21. Erwin, "Intensive Probation Supervision in Georgia", table 6; U.S. Department of Justice, Bureau of Justice Statistics, "Probation and Parole 1985," *Bulletin*, January 1987, table 1.

22. Frank S. Pearson and Daniel B. Bibel, "New Jersey's Intensive Supervision Program: What is It Like? How is It Working?" *Federal Probation* 50(2) (1986):25.

23. Athan Theoharis and John Stuart Cox, *The Boss: J. Edgar Hoover and the Great American Inquisition* (Philadelphia: Temple University Press, 1988), 313.

4. The Electronic Panopticon

1. *New York Times*, May 12, 1984.

2. *New York Times*, August 3, 1984.

3. *New York Times*, January 5, 1985.

4. This is a New York City example that I have heard cited several times. A recent study of police innovations in large U.S. cities notes, of Houston police with computer terminals in their cars, "Officers cruising down the street often idly type in the license plate numbers of cars driving ahead or parked at sleazy motels or private clubs in the faint hope that something interesting will turn up, like hitting a jackpot in a slot machine." Jerome H. Skolnick and David H. Bayley, *The New Blue Line: Police Innovation in Six American Cities* (New York: The Free Press, 1986), 101.

5. SEARCH Group, Inc., *Intelligence and Investigative Records* (Washington, D.C.: U.S. Government Printing Office, 1985), 10.

6. An example of the relaxed standards for intelligence is the revision of the U.S. Attorney General's guidelines governing FBI domestic security/terrorism investigations, which went into effect in March 1983. See U.S. Congress, Senate, *Hearing Before the Subcommittee on Terrorism of the Senate Committee of the Judiciary on Attorney General's Guidelines for Domestic Security (Smith Guidelines)*, 98th Congress, March 25, 1983, and "Domestic Security Investigation and Individual Rights under the Justice Department's New Guidelines," Section on Individual Rights and Responsibilities, American Bar Association, January 14, 1985. Perhaps the most widely publicized, unopposed use of computerized intelligence files for street crime purposes in the 1980s is the Los Angeles Police Department's gang file, in which juveniles hanging out on ghetto street corners are said to be routinely included. See Mike Davis, "Los Angeles: Civil Liberties between the Hammer and the Rock," *New Left Review* 170 (1988): 37–60.

7. Michel Foucault, *Discipline and Punish: The Birth of the Prison* (New York: Pantheon, 1977).

8. Donald A. Marchand and Eva G. Bogan, *A History and Background Assessment of the National Crime Information Center and Computerized Criminal History Program* (University of South Carolina, Bureau of Governmental Research and Service, 1979), 2–4.

9. Samuel Walker, *A Critical History of Police Reform* (Lexington, Mass.: Lexington Books, 1977), 43–47.

10. Marchand and Bogan, *Assessment of NCIC*, 14–25; see also Richard Gid Powers, *Secrecy and Power: The Life of J. Edgar Hoover* (New York: Free Press, 1987), 156.

11. Marchand and Bogan, *Assessment of NCIC*, 29.

12. David M. Gordon, Richard Edwards, and Michael Reich, *Segmented Work, Divided Workers* (Cambridge: Cambridge University Press, 1982), ch. 5.

13. Samuel Walker, *Sense and Nonsense About Crime: A Policy Guide*, 2d ed. (Monterey, Calif.: Brooks-Cole, 1988), table 14.1.

14. Elliott Currie, *Confronting Crime: An American Challenge* (New York: Pantheon, 1985), 117.

15. A notable exception to this statement is the work of political scientist Alan F. Westin, whose classic book, *Privacy and Freedom*, warned, in 1967, of the dangers of widespread data surveillance. See Alan F. Westin, *Privacy and Freedom* (New York: Atheneum, 1967), esp. ch. 7.

16. *New York Times*, June 12, 1962.

17. President's Commission on Law Enforcement and the Administration of Justice, *The Challenge of Crime in a Free Society* (Washington, D.C.: U.S. Government Printing Office, 1967), 204.

18. Ibid., 267. See also President's Commission on Law Enforcement and Administration of Justice, *Task Force Report: Science and Technology* (Washington, D.C.: U.S. Government Printing Office, 1967), 69.

19. Safe Streets Act, 42 U.S.C.A. 3701 *et seq;* U.S. Department of Justice, *LEAA Eleventh Annual Report, Fiscal Year 1979* (Washington, D.C.: U.S. Government Printing Office, 1979), 97.

20. U.S. Department of Justice, Law Enforcement Assistance Administration, *Directory of Automated Criminal Justice Information Systems* (Washington, D.C.: U.S. Government Printing Office, 1976).

21. U.S. Congress, House of Representatives, *Hearings Before a Subcommittee of the Committee on Governmental Operations, On Multistate Regional Intelligence Projects*, 97th Congress, May 27 and 28, 1981, 15–21.

22. The following account of the struggle over control of computerized criminal records relies heavily on an unpublished history of LEAA, Mae Churchill and Harold Brackman, "The Hidden Agenda: LEAA and the Tools of Repression," 1980. Also useful is Gordon Karl Zenk, *Project SEARCH: The Struggle for Control of Criminal Information in America* (Westport, Conn.: Greenwood, 1979).

23. June 15, 1971, 31.

24. Letter from Jerome J. Daunt to O.J. Hawkins (SEARCH Chairman), dated May 8, 1970, from a collection of materials obtained by Churchill and Brackman under the Freedom of Information Act.

25. *Menard v. Mitchell*, 328 F. Supp. 718 (1971).

26. Lawyer's Committee for Civil Rights Under Law, *Law and Disorder III: State and Federal Performance under Title I of the Omnibus Crime Control and Safe Streets Act of 1968* (Washington, DC: Lawyer's Committee for Civil Rights Under Law, 1973), 46.

27. U.S. General Accounting Office, "Overview of Activities Funded by the Law Enforcement Assistance Administration," Report No. GGD-78-21, November 29, 1977.

28. "Comments of the FBI on the Report on Inspection and Briefing at the National Crime Information Center, Prepared by the Task Force on Science and Technology and the Criminal Justice System of the Scientists' Institute for Public Information," in U.S. Congress, House of Representatives, *Hearings Before the House Subcommittee on Civil and Constitutional Rights, Committee on the Judiciary, on the National Crime Information Center*, 95th Congress, August 3, 1977, 94–95.

29. The role of SEARCH as a vehicle for LEAA influence over the states during this period is evident in the SEARCH newsletters of 1971–1973 and is discussed in Churchill and Brackman, ch. 4, 75–86.

30. U.S. General Accounting Office, "Development of a Nationwide Criminal Data Exchange System," B-171019, January 16, 1973.

31. See "Cointelpro: The FBI's Covert Action Programs Against American Citizens," in U.S. Congress, Senate, Select Committee to Study Governmental Operations with Respect to Intelligence Activities, *Supplementary Detailed Staff Reports of Intelligence Activities and the Rights of Americans*, final report, 94th Congress, April 14, 1976; Burnham, David, *The Rise of the Computer State* (New York: Random House, 1983), 84–85.

32. Burnham, *The Rise of the Computer State*, 69.

33. Quoted in Richard S. Allinson, "LEAA's Impact on Criminal Justice: A Review of the Literature," *Criminal Justice Abstracts* 11 (1979), 608.

34. Ibid., 621.

35. U.S. General Accounting Office, "Federal Crime Control Assistance: A Discussion of the Program and Possible Alternatives," Report No. GGD-78-28, January 27, 1978, 1.

36. Department of Justice, *LEAA Eleventh Annual Report*.

37. The 1971 figure comes from a statement by J. Edgar Hoover in U.S. Congress, Senate, *Hearings Before the Subcommittee on Constitutional Rights, Senate Committee on the Judiciary, on Federal Data Banks, Computers and the Bill of Rights*, 92d Congress, March 15, 1971, 914. Current data on NCIC files are taken from a presentation made by William A. Bayse, Assistant Director, FBI Technical Services Division, at the annual meeting of Computer Professionals for Social Responsibility, Palo Alto, Calif., November 19, 1988.

38. U.S. Congress, House of Representatives, *Hearings Before the Subcommittee on Civil and Constitutional Rights, Committee on the Judiciary, on FBI Authorization Request for Fiscal Year 1987*, 99th Congress, March 24, 1986, 55. There is considerable overlap between records held in these two repositories.

39. U.S. Department of Justice, Bureau of Justice Statistics, "State Criminal Records Repositories," *Technical Report*, October 1985, 1.

40. Ibid., 2. All ten of the most populous states, as determined by the 1980 census, have automated a portion of their records. All of those states that have no plans for automating records, except Massachusetts and Indiana, are among the twenty least populous states. U.S. Department of Commerce, Bureau of the Census, *Statistical Abstract of the United States 1986*, table 11.

41. See Kenneth C. Laudon, *The Dossier Society: Value Choices in the Design of National Information Systems* (New York: Columbia Univ. Press, 1986), chs. 5 and 9.

42. SEARCH Group, Inc., *Compendium of State Privacy and Security Legislation—Privacy and Security of Criminal History Information* (U.S. Department of Justice, Bureau of Justice Statistics, 1988), 6.

43. SEARCH Group, Inc., *Public Access to Criminal History Record Information* (U.S. Department of Justice, Bureau of Justice Statistics, 1988), 19–21.

44. Unless otherwise noted, the material that follows in this chapter comes either from original research conducted between mid-1984 and late 1988 or from a previously published article on this subject, Diana R. Gordon, "The Electronic Panopticon: A Case Study of the Development of the National Criminal Records System," *Politics and Society* 15(4) (1986–1987):483–511. Research consisted of approximately fifty interviews with state and local law enforcement officials and investigators; examination of criminal justice records system program materials from a dozen states; analysis of congressional testimony on criminal records information systems at hearings held during the 1970s and 1980s by the House of Representatives Committee on the Judiciary and its Subcommittee on Civil and Constitutional Rights; and observation of record entry and inquiry procedures in Albany, New York; Aurora, Colorado; and San Jose and Sacramento, California.

45. Arizona Criminal Code, art. 13, sec. 3821 (1988).

46. *New York Times*, February 14 and March 3, 1989.

47. SEARCH Group, Inc., *Intelligence and Investigative Records*, 9. The report goes on (at 10–11) to stress the anticipatory quality of intelligence records: "While intelligence and investigative data share common characteristics, there is also an important difference between these types of information—the purpose for which the information is created and maintained. Investigative data are compiled for the relatively narrow purpose of identifying the person who committed a particular crime or otherwise solving the crime. Intelligence information, by contrast, is compiled for the rather broad purpose of identifying a particular individual, or, more often, a group of individuals thought likely to commit crimes in the future."

48. "Criminal Intelligence File Guidelines," State of California Department of Justice, Division of Law Enforcement, n.d., 1.

49. Davis, "Los Angeles," 57.

50. My conclusions are based on observations and interviews in only six cities. More systematic research is needed to confirm the range of use patterns and to explain the variation in them.

51. Intelligence Authorization Act for FY 1986, P.L. No. 99–169, codified in part at 5 U.S.C. Sec. 9101.

52. P.L. 98–473.

53. Exchange between David Nemecek, NCIC Section Chief, and James Dempsey, Assistant Counsel, in U.S. Congress, House of Representatives, *Hearing Before the Subcommittee on Civil and Constitutional Rights, Committee on the Judiciary, on FBI Authorization Request for FY 1986*, 99th Congress, April 25, 1985, 165–66.

54. *New York Times*, March 6, 1988; *Rogan v. City of Los Angeles*, U.S. Dist. Ct. Central California, no. CV 85–0989.

55. This comment came from an interview with the author, November 1984. For a full cite for *The Dossier Society*, see note 41.

56. See, for example, anecdotes provided in the National Crime

Information Center booklet, "The Investigative Tool: A Guide to the Use and Benefits of NCIC," Washington, D.C.: Federal Bureau of Investigation, undated.

57. "HRA/ACD Day Care/Head Start Program Fingerprinting and Criminal Record Review Report for the Month of October, 1985," Human Resources Administration, City of New York, unpaginated.

58. See David Flaherty, "Protecting Privacy in Police Information Systems," *University of Toronto Law Journal* 36 (1986):116–148.

59. *Menard v. Mitchell*, at 726.

60. U.S. Congress, Senate, *Hearings Before the Subcommittee on Constitutional Rights, Senate Committee on the Judiciary, on Federal Data Banks, Computers and the Bill of Rights*, 92d Congress, March 10, 1971, 649.

61. This provision, originally the Crime Control Act of 1973, P.L. No. 93–83, is now Sec. 812(b) of the Justice Assistance Act of 1984, P.L. 98–473. See SEARCH Group, *Public Access to Criminal History Record Information*, 6–7.

62. U.S. Congress, Senate, Committee on Government Operations, *Protecting Individual Privacy in Federal Gathering, Use and Disclosure of Information: Report to Accompany S.3418*, 93d Congress, September 26, 1974, 23. The cite for the Privacy Act is 5 U.S.C. sec. 552a.

63. See, for example, U.S. Congress, House of Representatives, *Hearings Before House Subcommittee No. 4 of the Committee on the Judiciary, on H.R. 13315*, 92d Congress, March 16, 22, and 23, 1972, April 13 and 26, 1972; U.S. Congress, House of Representatives, *Hearings Before the House Subcomittee on Civil and Constitutional Rights, Committee on the Judiciary, on H.R. 188, H.R. 9783, H.R. 12574 and H.R. 12575*, 93d Congress, July 26, August 2, September 26, October 11, 1973, February 26, 28, March 5, 28, and April 3, 1974; U.S. Congress, House of Representatives, *Hearings Before the House Subcommittee on Civil and Constitutional Rights, Committee on the Judiciary, on H.R. 8227*, 94th Congress, July 14 and 17 and September 5, 1975.

64. 28 Code of Federal Regulations, sec. 20.

65. MITRE Corporation, "Implementing the Federal Privacy and Security Regulations," McLean, Va.: MITRE Corporation, 1977.

66. SEARCH Group, *Compendium of State Privacy and Security Legislation*, 4–5.

67. U.S. Department of Justice, Bureau of Justice Statistics, *Report to the Nation on Crime and Justice*, 2nd ed., 1988, 60.

68. U.S. Department of Justice, Bureau of Justice Statistics, "Tracking Offenders 1984," *Bulletin*, January 1988, table 1.

69. U.S. Office of Technology Assessment, *An Assessment of Alternatives for a National Computerized Criminal History System* (Washington, D.C.: Government Printing Office, 1982), 91–102.

70. Herbert S. Miller, "The Closed Door: The Effect of a Criminal Record on Employment with State and Local Public Agencies." U.S. Department of Labor, Manpower Administration Office of Research and Development, Report no. 81–09–70–02, 1972.

71. *Central Valley v. Younger*, Sup. Ct. California, Co. of Alameda. Case nos. 497394–6 and 524298–6 (1984).

72. Joan Petersilia, *Racial Disparities in the Criminal Justice System* (Santa Monica, Calif.: Rand Corporation, 1983).

73. See, for example, *Jones v. New Orleans*, U.S. Dist. Ct., Eastern Dist. La., Civil Action no. 83–703 (1985); *Smith v. Gates*, Sup. Ct. Calif., Co. of Los Angeles, Case no. CA 000619 (1984); *Emma v. Boston*, U.S. Dist. Ct., Civil Action no. 85-3232-Y (1985).

74. *New York Times*, August 25, 1985.

75. U.S. Congress, House of Representatives, *Hearings Before the Subcommittee on Civil and Constitutional Rights, House Committee on the Judiciary, on FBI Oversight and Authorization for FY 1989*, 100th Congress, March 10, 1988, 63.

76. *Jones v. New Orleans.*

77. "20-20" (ABC news program), September 13, 1984.

78. *Jones v. New Orleans.* This was a class action brought on behalf of several hundred people alleged to have been wrongfully detained because of "problems in the law enforcement computer systems used by the New Orleans Police Department and Jefferson Parish Sheriff's Office." A 1985 settlement included an agreement for improved police training and an overhaul of procedures for entry and inquiry into the system.

79. See news reports in late 1984 and early 1985 of police spying in Los Angeles, for example, "California Agencies Got Spy Dossiers on Non-Criminal Groups from Chicago Police," *Los Angeles Times*, December 6, 1984, and "Has Daryl Gates Won Again?" *Los Angeles Herald Tribune*, January 13, 1985. The most prominent and acknowledged case of political surveillance by the FBI in the 1980s was the investigation, conducted out of fifty-nine FBI offices from 1981–1985, of the Committee in Solidarity with the People of El Salvador and hundreds of its affiliates. See *New York Times*, September 15, 1988.

80. For a similar analysis from a governmental source, see U.S. Department of Health, Education and Welfare, *Report of the Secretary's Advisory Committee on Automated Personal Data Systems, Records Computers and the Rights of Citizens* (Washington, D.C.: U.S. Government Printing Office, 1973), 19.

81. Letter from then–FBI Director William H. Webster to Representative Don Edwards (D., CA), Chairman, Subcommittee on Civil and Constitutional Rights, Committee on the Judiciary, April 12, 1985.

82. "Minutes, National Crime Information Center Advisory Policy Board, October 5–6, 1983," unpublished FBI document.

83. *New York Times*, January 1, 1984.

84. Testimony of D. Lowell Jensen, U.S. Congress, House of Representatives, *Hearing Before the Subcommittee on Civil and Constitutional Rights, House Committee on the Judiciary, on FBI Authorization Request for FY 1986*, 99th Congress, April 25, 1985, 104.

85. "Economic Crime Index Proposal," included in *Hearings on Oversight and Authorization 1989*, 99–100.

86. "Agreements and Recommendations of the Attorney General's Bank Fraud Working Group," U.S. Department of Justice photocopied report, April 2, 1985.

87. "Summary of the Rationale for Certain of the Matters Set Forth in the Attached Agreements and Recommendations of the Justice Department-Supervisory Agencies Working Group," U.S. Department of Justice photocopied report, April 2, 1985, 3.

88. U.S. Congress, House of Representatives, Committee on Govern-

ment Operations, *Federal Response to Criminal Misconduct and Insider Abuse in the Nation's Financial Associations*, 98th Congress, 1984, House Rept. 1137, 2.

89. Yehezkel Dror, *Public Policymaking Reexamined* (San Francisco: Chandler Publishing Company, 1968), ch. 2.

90. See chapter 7.

91. Laudon, *Dossier Society*, 105.

92. V. O. Key, *Public Opinion and American Democracy* (New York: Alfred A. Knopf, 1961), 32.

93. See chapter 7.

94. See Alan F. Westin, "Public and Group Attitudes Toward Information Policies and Boundaries for Criminal Justice," in SEARCH Group, Inc., *Information Policy and Crime Control Strategies* (U.S. Department of Justice, Bureau of Justice Statistics, 1984), 37.

95. Seymour Martin Lipset and William Schneider, *The Confidence Gap: Business, Labor and Government in the Public Mind* (New York: The Free Press, 1983).

96. Samuel Walker, *Popular Justice: A History of American Criminal Justice* (New York: Oxford University Press, 1980), 127–238.

97. *Criminal Justice Newsletter*, November 1, 1984.

98. For a review of research on this and related questions, see Erika S. Fairchild, "Interest Groups in the Criminal Justice Process," *Journal of Criminal Justice* 9(2) (1981). She concludes, among other things, that "Criminal justice legislation is generally conceived by small numbers of influential legislators, administrators, and interest group representatives and enacted on a consensual basis by state legislatures".

99. President's Commission, *The Challenge of Crime*.

100. James N. Danziger, William H. Dutton, Rob Kling and Kenneth L. Kraemer, *Computers and Politics* (New York: Columbia University Press, 1982).

101. *Sourcebook 1987*, table 1.1.

102. Graham T. Allison, *The Essence of Decision* (Boston: Little, Brown and Co., 1971), 85.

103. Murray Edelman, *The Symbolic Uses of Politics* (Urbana, Ill.: University of Chicago Press, 1964).

104. Ibid., 19.

105. Albert J. Reiss, *The Police and the Public* (New Haven: Yale University Press, 1971).

106. Laudon, *Dossier Society*, 233.

107. Ibid., 97.

108. *Burns v. Ohio*, 360 U.S. 258 (1959); *Douglas v. California*, 372 U.S. 353 (1963); *Gideon v. Wainwright*, 372 U.S. 335 (1963).

109. *In re Oliver*, 333 U.S. 257 (1948).

110. A few federal cases have, however, acknowledged that the FBI, in maintaining and disseminating criminal history information sent to it by local law enforcement, "energizes" the record and gives it a different character. *Menard v. Mitchell* (II), 498 F.2d 1017 (1974), at 1026; *Tarlton v. Saxbe*, 507 F.2d 1116 (1974), at 1126.

111. *Paul v. Davis*, 424 U.S. 693 (1976), at 713.

112. *Reporters Committee for Freedom of the Press v. U.S. Department of Justice*, 57 U.S. Law Week 4373 (March 21, 1989).

113. Ibid., at 4379.

114. Roberto Mangabeira Unger, *Law and Modern Society* (New York: The Free Press, 1976), 54.

115. 28 U.S.C. sec. 534.

116. *Menard v. Mitchell*, 328 F. Supp. 718 (1971).

117. Ibid., at 720.

118. In 1974 the record subject sued to have his record expunged on the basis that the arrest had been downgraded to a detention, and won. *Menard v. Saxbe*, 498 F. 2d 1017 (1974). The other outcome of the 1971 case was that Congress immediately authorized the FBI to release arrest information for employment purposes where allowed by state law.

119. *Paul v. Davis*, at 735, n. 18 (Brennan, J., dissenting).

120. Laudon, *Dossier Society*, 309–313.

121. *New York Times*, November 21, 1985.

5. Community as Prison

1. David J. Rothman, *Discovery of the Asylum: Social Order and Disorder in the New Republic* (Boston: Little, Brown and Company, 1971), 51–52. Rothman found that before the American Revolution 20 percent of the penalties handed out by the New York Supreme Court were capital sentences.

2. Ibid., 48.

3. Alice Morse Earle, *Curious Punishments of Bygone Days* (Montclair, N.J.: Patterson Smith, 1969), 101.

4. Charles Lionel Chute and Marjorie Bell, *Crime, Courts and Probation* (New York: Macmillan and Co., 1956), 33–36.

5. See, for example, *Gehrmann v. Osborne*, 79 N.J. Eq. 430 (1912), in which the court states, at 443, "An indefinite suspension of sentencing has been the custom in this jurisdiction beyond the memory of those connected with the administration or practice of the criminal law in this state."

6. John Augustus, *John Augustus, First Probation Officer* (Montclair, N.J.: Patterson Smith, 1972), 9.

7. David J. Rothman, *Conscience and Convenience: The Asylum and Its Alternatives in Progressive America* (Boston: Little, Brown and Co., 1980), 44.

8. *Sourcebook 1980*, tables 6.1. and 6.2.

9. Chute and Bell, *Crime, Courts and Probation*, ix.

10. Augustus, *John Augustus*, 100–101.

11. See, for example, Andrew von Hirsch, *Doing Justice* (New York: Hill and Wang, 1976) and Richard Singer, *Just Deserts: Sentencing Based on Equality and Desert* (Cambridge, Mass.: Bollinger, 1979).

12. David Fogel, ". . . *We Are the Living Proof* . . ." *The Justice Model for Corrections* (Cincinnati: W. H. Anderson, 1975), 250. See also Patrick D. McAnany, "Mission and Justice: Clarifying Probation's Legal Context," in Patrick D. McAnany, Doug Thomson, and David Fogel, eds., *Probation and Justice: Reconsideration of Mission* (Cambridge, Mass.: Oelgeschlager, Gunn, and Hain, 1984), 52–63.

13. Douglas R. Thomson, "The Changing Face of Probation in the USA," in John Harding, ed., *Probation and the Community: A Practice and Policy Reader* (London: Tavistock Publications, 1987), 109.

14. Peter Greenwood, with Allan Abrahamse, *Selective Incapacitation* (Santa Monica, Calif.: RAND Corporation, 1982).

15. Walter L. Barkdull, "Probation: Call It Control and Mean It," in Lawrence F. Travis III, Martin D. Schwartz, and Todd R. Clear, *Corrections: An Issues Approach*, 2nd ed. (Cincinnati: Anderson, 1983).

16. Todd R. Clear and Vincent O'Leary, *Controlling the Offender in the Community* (Lexington, Mass.: Lexington Books, 1983), chs. 2 and 3.

17. See, e.g., American Bar Association, *Standards for Criminal Justice: Sentencing Alternatives and Procedures* (Boston: Little, Brown, 1980), Standard 18–2.3.

18. See American Friends Service Committee Working Party, *Struggle for Justice* (New York: Hill and Wang, 1971.) This little volume was a rallying cry for the movement of the 1970s that based its program of determinate sentencing and penal reform on the concern that the rehabilitation rationale for punishment cloaked the arbitrary and hypocritical exercise of state power. It still influences those who argue that voluntary organizations should replace or supplement criminal punishment with service to offenders.

19. Extremely influential in this regard was the study of studies compiled in Alfred Blumstein, Jacqueline Cohen, and Daniel Nagin, eds., *Deterrence and Incapacitation: Estimating the Effects of Criminal Sanctions on Crime Rates* (Washington, D.C.: National Academy of Sciences, 1978). See also Jacqueline Cohen, "Incapacitation as a Strategy for Crime Control: Possibilities and Pitfalls," in Norval Morris and Michael Tonry, eds., *Crime and Justice: Annual Review of Research*, 5 (Chicago: University of Chicago, 1983), 1.

20. See Vernon Fox, *Community-Based Corrections* (Englewood Cliffs, N.J.: Prentice-Hall, 1977), for an approving account of the possibilities for "community-based corrections."

21. See PACT Institute of Justice, " The VORP Book," Valparaiso, Ind., 1983.

22. Todd R. Clear, Susan Flynn and Carol Shapiro, "Intensive Supervision in Probation: A Comparison of Three Projects," in Belinda R. McCarthy, *Intermediate Punishments: Intensive Supervision, Home Confinement and Electronic Surveillance* (Monsey, N.Y.: Criminal Justice Press, 1987), 31. The most fundamental operational features of these programs—increased officer contacts with probationers and lower caseloads for supervision—are hardly new. They were tried in the 1960s and 1970s with high hopes for outcomes of reduced recidivism, never realized. See J. Banks, A. L. Porter, R. L. Rardin, T. R. Silver, and V. E. Unger, *Evaluation of Intensive Special Probation Projects* (U.S. Department of Justice, National Institute of Law Enforcement and Criminal Justice, 1977).

23. *The Corrections Yearbook 1981* (South Salem, N.Y.: Criminal Justice Institute, 1981), 30–31; *The Corrections Yearbook 1987* (South Salem, N.Y.: Criminal Justice Institute, 1987), 34–35.

24. Kevin Krajick, "'Not on My Block': Local Opposition Impedes the Search for Alternatives," *Corrections Magazine* VI (1980):15–27.

25. Joan Petersilia, *Expanding Options for Criminal Sentencing* (Santa Monica, Calif.: RAND Corporation, 1987), vii.

26. Ronald P. Corbett, Jr., Donald Cochran, and James M. Byrne, "Making Change in Probation: Principles and Practice in the Implementation of an Intensive Probation Supevision Program," in McCarthy, *Intermediate Punishments*, 51–65.

27. David C. Anderson, *Crimes of Justice: Improving the Police, the Courts, the Prisons* (New York: Times Books, 1988), 225.

28. President's Commission on Law Enforcement and Administration of Justice, *The Challenge of Crime in a Free Society* (Washington, D.C.: U.S. Government Printing Office, 1967), 171.

29. See Billie S. Erwin, "Turning Up the Heat on Probationers in Georgia," *Federal Probation* 50 (June 1986):17–24; and U.S. Department of Justice, Office of Justice Programs, "Intensive Supervision Probation and Parole (ISP)," *Program Brief*, 1987 (Washington, D.C.: U.S. Government Printing Office, 1987).

30. U.S. Department of Justice, Bureau of Justice Statistics, "State and Federal Prisoners, 1925–85," *Bulletin*, October 1986, table 1.

31. Frank T. Judge III, "Relief for Prison Overcrowding: Evaluating Michigan's Accelerated Parole Statute," in *University of Michigan Journal of Law Reform* 15 (1982), 548, at n. 5.

32. "Prisoners in 1982," (U.S. Department of Justice, Bureau of Justice Statistics, 1983), 3.

33. Twenty-one state corrections agencies reported having emergency release programs—some created by legislation—as of 1986. *Corrections Yearbook 1987*, 22.

34. "Prisoners in 1982," 3.

35. National Conference of State Legislatures, *Recent Trends in State Corrections Spending*, Legislative Finance Papers Series, Denver, Colo., 1985, as cited in Petersilia, "Expanding Options," 2.

36. Erwin, "Turning Up the Heat," 17.

37. *New York Times*, December 18, 1985.

38. Richard A. Berk and Peter H. Rossi, *Prison Reform and State Elites* (Cambridge, Mass.: Barringer, 1977), 93. See also Barbara Ann Stolz, "Interest Groups and Criminal Law: The Case of Federal Criminal Code Revision," *Crime and Delinquency* 30 (1984):91–106. For a discussion of the influence of criminal justice agencies on policy implementation, see Malcolm M. Feeley and Austin D. Sarat, *The Policy Dilemma: Federal Crime Policy and the LEAA, 1968–1978* (Minneapolis: University of Minnesota Press, 1980), chapters 3 and 4. See also Erika S. Fairchild, "Interest Groups in the Criminal Justice Process," *Journal of Criminal Justice* 9 (1981):181–194.

39. Sheldon Glueck and Eleanor T. Glueck, *500 Criminal Careers* (New York: Knopf, 1930), 332.

40. Chute and Bell, *Crime, Courts and Probation*, 231.

41. Douglas Lipton, Robert Martinson, and Judith Wilks, *The Effectiveness of Correctional Treatment: A Survey of Treatment Evaluation Studies* (New York: Praeger, 1975).

42. U.S. Comptroller General, *State and County Probation: Systems in Crisis* (Washington, D.C.: Government Printing Office, 1976).

43. President's Crime Commission on Law Enforcement and the Administration of Justice, *The Challenge of Crime in a Free Society* (Washington, D.C.: President's Crime Commission, 1967), 161, table 2;

"Correctional Populations in the United States 1985" (U.S. Department of Justice, Bureau of Justice Statistics, 1987), table 1.2.

44. *Sourcebook 1986*, tables 6.2 and 6.22.

45. *Corrections Yearbook 1987*:81–83.

46. Personal communication from Ben Jones, APPA Secretary, April 1988.

47. Byrne, James, "What Does Intensive Probation Supervision *Really* Mean?" Center for Criminal Justice Research, University of Lowell, Lowell, Massachusetts, 1986, 1.

48. Personal interview, August 1987.

49. Over a nine-month period I talked with at least a dozen evaluators of nonprison programs of the new variety, many of them working for state corrections departments or under contract to them. In addition, I discussed my observations with Todd Clear of Rutgers University and Joan Petersilia of the RAND Corporation, prominent researchers on probation who are now studying intermediate punishments.

50. *Sourcebook 1973*, table 6.26; *Sourcebook 1985*, tables 6.30 and 6.32.

51. *Statistical Abstract 1986*, table 11.

52. *Corrections Yearbook 1982* (South Salem, N.Y.: Criminal Justice Institute, 1982), 17–18; *Corrections Yearbook 1983* (South Salem, N.Y.: Criminal Justice Institute, 1983), 24.

53. *Bergen County Record*, April 4, 1982; U.S. Department of Justice, Bureau of Justice Statistics, "Prisoners in 1982," *Bulletin*, September 1983, table 4.

54. *Uniform Crime Reports 1980*, table 4; *Uniform Crime Reports 1970*, table 3.

55. U.S. Department of Justice, Bureau of Justice Statistics, "Setting Prison Terms," *Bulletin*, August 1983, figure 2.

56. U.S. Department of Justice, Bureau of Justice Statistics, "Probation and Parole 1981," *Bulletin*, August 1982, 2–3; "Probation and Parole 1982," 3–4.

57. Personal interview, April 1988.

58. Fla. Stat., ch. 83–131, as quoted in Joseph H. Evans, Linda Smith, and Joan K. Hall, "A Study of the Impact of Community Control as an Alternative to Incarceration," Florida Mental Health Institute, University of South Florida, 1986, 7.

59. Ibid., 5.

60. Ibid., 40.

61. For a description of this local program, see Petersilia, *Expanding Options*, 41–45.

62. Annesley K. Schmidt, "Electronic Monitoring of Offenders Increases," in U.S. Department of Justice, National Institute of Justice, *NIJ Reports*, January-February 1989, 2.

63. Among a sample of ISP participants who joined the program before 1986, the median time served before entering was 3.6 months, the mean 4.2 months. Frank S. Pearson, "Research on New Jersey's Intensive Supervision Program," Institute for Criminological Research, Sociology Department, Rutgers University, 1987, 90.

64. "Intensive Supervision Program, Progress Report," State of New Jersey, Administrative Office of the Courts, 1988, 4.

65. Pearson, "Research," 33.

66. Frank S. Pearson and Daniel B. Bibel, "New Jersey's Intensive Supervision Program: What is It Like? How is It Working?" *Federal Probation* 50 (June 1986), 26.

67. Pearson and Bibel, "New Jersey's ISP," 27; Evans, Smith, and Hall, "Study," 103.

68. Ibid., 102.

69. Ibid., 86.

70. Ethan A. Nadelmann, "U.S. Drug Policy: A Bad Export," *Foreign Policy* (Spring 1988), 93.

71. Pearson, "Research," 35.

72. Ibid., 106.

73. Ibid., 107.

74. Evans, Smith, and Hall, "Study," 104–107.

75. *Statistical Abstract 1986*, table 32; U.S. Department of Justice, Bureau of Justice Statistics, "Correctional Populations in the United States 1985," 1987, table 5.6.

76. Pearson, "Research," 119; Evans, Smith, and Hall, "Study," 102.

77. For a discussion of the Weberian distinction between domination and legitimacy as applied to the acceptance of norms, see Joseph Gusfield, *Symbolic Crusade* (Urbana, Ill.: University of Illinois, 1963), 63–65.

78. Quoted in Rothman, *Conscience and Convenience*, 64.

79. David T. Stanley, *Prisoners Among Us: The Problem of Parole* (Washington, D.C.: Brookings, 1976), 97.

80. For a discussion of changing perspectives on the policy implementation process, see Robert K. Nakamura and Frank Smallwood, *The Politics of Policy Implementation* (New York: St. Martin's Press, 1980), ch. 1.

81. Michael Lipsky, *Street-level Bureaucracy: Dilemmas of the Individual in Public Services* (New York: Russell Sage, 1980), 140–145.

82. Francis A. Allen, *The Decline of the Rehabilitative Ideal: Penal Policy and Social Purpose* (New Haven: Yale University Press, 1981), 49–59.

83. This view accords with those expressed in a 1984 survey of the officers in the Alabama Supervised Intensive Restitution Program. John T. Whitehead and Charles A. Lindquist, "Intensive Supervision: Officer Perspectives," in McCarthy, *Intermediate Punishments*, 76.

84. For an evaluation of intensive supervision that concludes that it may improve "social adjustment" without reducing recidivism, see Lawrence A. Bennett, "A Reassessment of Intensive Service Probation," in McCarthy, *Intermediate Punishments*, 113–132.

85. "Intensive Supervision Program Progress Report," New Jersey Administrative Office of the Courts, January 1988, 6.

86. Frank S. Pearson, "Taking Quality Into Account: Assessing the Benefits and Costs of New Jersey's Intensive Supervision Program," in McCarthy, *Intermediate Punishments*, 87.

87. Rothman, *The Discovery of the Asylum*, 84.

88. Subsequent references to the evaluation of the New Jersey and Florida programs, unless otherwise noted, come from Frank S. Pearson, "Research on New Jersey's Intensive Supervision Program: Final

Report," Institute for Criminological Research, Rutgers University, New Brunswick, N.J., 1987; and Joseph H. Evans, Linda Smith, and Joan K. Hall, "A Study of the Impact of Community Control as an Alternative to Incarceration," Florida Mental Health Institute, University of South Florida, 1986. The quasi-experimental New Jersey study uses sophisticated statistical techniques not discussed here to measure the effects of the program as compared with traditional correctional programs of prison and parole. The Florida study describes itself as "formative," that is, less concerned with measuring impact and more focused on the performance of the probation system in implementing the enabling legislation and administrative procedures of the community control program; in calculating effects no experimental design is attempted. The goals summarized in the text are stated explicitly in the New Jersey evaluation. While they are only implied in the Florida study, their importance is clear from interviews with administrators and officers.

89. Billie Erwin, "Evaluation of Intensive Probation Supervision in Georgia," Georgia Department of Corrections, 1987, 64–65.

90. "Probation and Parole 1987," table 1.

91. Erwin, "Evaluation," 65.

92. The average annual cost is taken from *The Corrections Yearbook 1987*, 83. This figure may be too high, since it incorporates the higher costs of intensive supervision where it exists. It is unlikely, however, that the number of intensively supervised offenders is large enough yet to distort the national figure significantly.

93. Petersilia, *Expanding Options*, 2.

94. "Community Control II (Electronic Anklets) Preliminary Field Assessment of Tampa Pilot Project," draft report, Florida Department of Corrections, Probation and Parole Services, 1988.

95. Pearson and Bibel, "New Jersey's ISP," 27–28.

96. Edward J. Latessa, "The Effectiveness of Intensive Supervision with High Risk Probationers," in McCarthy, *Intermediate Punishments*, 110.

97. John F. Wallerstedt, "Returning to Prison," *Special Report*, U.S. Department of Justice, Bureau of Justice Statistics, November 1984, table 1.

98. Joan Petersilia, *Granting Felons Probation: Public Risks and Alternatives* (Santa Monica, Calif.: RAND Corporation, 1985).

99. A discussion of public attitudes toward punishment in the 1980s is included in chapter 7.

100. See Max Weber's discussion of legal domination and "the triumph of formalist juristic rationalism," e.g., "The Social Psychology of the World Religions," in H. H. Gerth and C. Wright Mills, *From Max Weber: Essays in Sociology* (New York: Oxford University Press, 1946).

101. Frances Fox Piven and Richard A. Cloward, *Why Americans Don't Vote* (New York: Pantheon, 1988), 3.

102. Michelle Sviridoff and James W. Thompson, "Links between Employment and Crime: A Qualitative Study of Riker's Island Releasees," *Crime and Delinquency* 29 (1983):201–203.

103. *New York Times*, May 23, 1988.

104. U.S. Department of Justice, Bureau of Justice Statistics, "Correctional Populations in the United States 1986," 1989, cover table.

105. *Annual Report, 1986–87*, Department of Corrections, State of Florida, 51.

106. Personal communication from Harvey Goldstein, assistant director for probation, New Jersey Administrative Office of the Courts, January 1988.

107. Personal communication from Don Van Nostrand, administrator, Policy Analysis and Planning, New Jersey Department of Corrections, June 1988.

108. *Annual Report*, 30.

109. See Carol Warren, "New Forms of Social Control," *American Behavioral Scientist* 24 (1981):724–40.

110. Evans, Smith, and Hall, "Study," 140.

111. See Augustus, *John Augustus*.

112. Georgette Bennett, *CrimeWarps: The Future of Crime in America* (New York: Anchor Press, 1987), 271.

113. *United States v. United States District Court*, 407 U.S. 297 (1972), at 313.

114. Ronald P. Corbett, Jr. and Gary T. Marx, "When a Man's Castle Is His Prison," unpublished paper, 1987.

115. Lisa Callahan, Connie Mayer, and Henry J. Steadman, "Insanity Defense Reform in the United States—Post-Hinkley," *Mental and Physical Disability Law Reporter* 11 (Jan.-Feb. 1987):54–59.

116. Donna Hamparian et al., "Youth in Adult Courts: Between Two Worlds" (U.S. Department of Justice, National Institute for Juvenile Justice and Delinquency Prevention, 1982), 5.

117. *Bell v. Wolfish*, 441 U.S. 520 (1979), at 540.

118. See *Hudson v. Palmer*, 468 U.S. 517 (1984), for a Supreme Court determination that it has not been able to find any prisoner expectations of privacy that are "reasonable." The Court said, at 547, "Prison administrators therefore should be accorded wide-ranging deference in the adoption and execution of policies and practices that in their judgment are needed to preserve internal discipline and to maintain institutional security."

119. 107 S. Ct. 3164 (1987).

120. Ibid., at 3168.

121. For a discussion of consent issues as they pertain to electronic devices, see the exchange of views in Bonnie Berry, "Electronic Jails: A New Criminal Justice Concern," *Justice Quarterly* 2 (1985):1–22.

122. *Schneckloth v. Bustamonte*, 412 U.S. 218 (1973).

123. Samuel Warren and Louis Brandeis, "The Right to Privacy," *Harvard Law Review* 4 (1890):193–220.

124. *Bell v. Wolfish*, at 547.

125. See *Smith v. Maryland*, 442 U.S. 735 (1979) and *United States v. Karo*, 468 U.S. 705 (1984).

126. Rolando V. del Carmen and Joseph B. Vaughn, "Issues in the Use of Electronic Surveillance," *Federal Probation* 50 (June 1986), 65.

127. *Minnesota v. Murphy*, 465 U.S. 420 (1984).

128. del Carmen and Vaughn, "Electronic Surveillance," 67–69.

129. *Beardon v. Georgia*, 461 U.S. 660 (1983)

130. For a recent study, see Bennett, "A Reassessment." For earlier research, see Douglas Lipton, Robert Martinson, and Judith Wilks,

The Effectiveness of Correctional Treatment: A Survey of Treatment Evaluation Studies (New York: Praeger, 1975).

131. Charles M. Friel, "Critical Issues in the Future of Community Corrections," address delivered at the annual meeting of the American Probation and Parole Association, August 25, 1987.

132. *Criminal Justice Newsletter*, December 1, 1988.

133. Sunil B. Nath, "Intensive Supervision Project: Final Report," Florida Probation and Parole Commission, 1974.

134. "The Intensive Supervision Program: A Process Evaluation," New York State Division of Probation, 1982, 52.

135. Emile Durkheim, *Selected Writings*, Anthony Giddens, ed. (Cambridge, U.K.: Cambridge University Press, 1972), 127–128.

136. Emile Durkheim, *The Rules of Sociological Method* (New York: Free Press, 1982), 129.

137. John Conrad, "News of the Future: The Intensive Revolution," *Federal Probation* 50 (June 1986), 84.

138. Samuel Walker, *Sense and Nonsense about Crime: A Policy Guide*, 2nd ed. (Monterey, Calif.: Brooks-Cole, 1988), 43.

139. For a study of tougher sentencing laws that resulted in greater minimums for lesser offenses, but not for the more serious crimes, see Colin Loftin and David McDowall, "'One with a Gun Gets You Two': Mandatory Sentencing and Firearms Violence in Detroit," *The Annals* 455 (1981):150–167.

140. As the numbers of people with prison and probation sentences have soared in recent years, so have revocations from community supervision programs. Prison admissions from parole and other conditional release violations increased as a percentage of new court commitments by 47 percent between 1979 and 1984, the latest year for which data are available. *Sourcebook 1981*, table 6.27; *Sourcebook 1986*, table 6.24.

141. "Probation and Parole 1981," 2; U.S. Department of Justice, Bureau of Justice Statistics, "Probation and Parole 1986," *Bulletin*, December 1987, table 1.

142. James M. Byrne, "Probation," *Crime Study File* (U.S. Department of Justice, National Institute of Justice, 1988).

143. Florida Stat. Ch. 948.01(5).

144. Michel Foucault, *Discipline and Punish* (New York: Pantheon, 1977), 297. Foucault's image conjures forth multiple and pervasive sites of punishment outside the officially designated sphere of the criminal law and yet mediated by it and by disciplinary activites in basic institutions such as schools, hospitals, and families.

145. For a discussion of the ways in which contemporary community supervision programs blur the boundaries of penal control and disperse its powers in the larger society, see Stanley Cohen, *Visions of Social Control* (Cambridge, U.K.: Polity Press, 1985), ch. 2.

146. For a discussion of this dynamic in inner-city ghettoes, see William Julius Wilson, *The Truly Disadvantaged: The Inner City, the Underclass, and Public Policy* (Chicago: University of Chicago Press, 1987). That it is not confined to black communities is made clear in Fred Block, Richard A. Cloward, Barbara Ehrenreich, and Frances Fox Piven, *The Mean Season: The Attack on the Welfare State* (New York: Pantheon, 1987), 37.

147. Joseph E. Jacoby and Christopher S. Dunn, "National Survey on Punishment for Criminal Offenses: Executive Summary," Bowling Green State University, 1987; Russ Immarigeon, "Surveys Reveal Broad Support for Alternative Sentencing," *National Prison Project Journal* (9) (Fall 1986):1–4.

148. Tom R. Tyler and Renee Weber, "Support for the Death Penalty: Instrumental Response to Crime or Symbolic Attitude?" *Law and Society Review* 17 (1982):21–45.

6. Contexts of the Juggernaut

1. U.S. Department of Justice, Bureau of Justice Statistics, "Criminal Victimization in the United States, 1986," August 1988, table 1.

2. Ibid., 3.

3. Ibid., table 17.

4. There is an extensive literature on the symbolic functions of politics. A classic theoretical work is Murray Edelman, *The Symbolic Uses of Politics* (Urbana, Ill.: University of Illinois, 1964); more recent and more focused on the dynamics of symbolic politics is Charles Elder and Roger Cobb, *The Political Uses of Symbols* (New York: Longman, 1983).

5. Norbert Elias, *The Civilizing Process: The History of Manners*, vol. 1 (New York: Urizen Books, 1978), 203.

6. Douglas Hay, "Property, Authority and the Criminal Law," in Douglas Hay, Peter Linebaugh, John G. Rule, E. P. Thompson, and Cal Winslow, *Albion's Fatal Tree: Crime and Society in Eighteenth-Century England* (New York: Pantheon, 1975), 21.

7. This example comes from Jeffrey H. Reiman, *The Rich Get Richer and the Poor Get Prison: Ideology, Class, and Criminal Justice* (New York: Wiley, 1979), 45–46.

8. Ted Robert Gurr, "Historical Trends in Violent Crime: A Critical Review of the Evidence," in Norval Morris and Michael Tonry, eds., *Crime and Justice: An Annual Review of Research*, vol. 3 (Chicago: University of Chicago, 1981), 295–353. For long-term trends in punishment, see Michel Foucault, *Discipline and Punish* (New York: Pantheon, 1977.)

9. Hay, "Property, Authority and the Criminal Law."

10. Louis Chevalier, *Laboring Classes and Dangerous Classes* (Princeton, N.J.: Princeton University Press, 1973), 3.

11. Pieter Spierenburg, *The Spectacle of Suffering* (Cambridge, U.K.: Cambridge University Press, 1984), 6.

12. Harold J. Berman and William R. Greiner, *The Nature and Functions of Law*, 4th ed. (Mineola, N.Y.: Foundation Press, 1980), 575.

13. Perry Anderson, *Passages from Antiquity to Feudalism* (London: Verso, 1978), 161.

14. Spierenburg, *The Spectacle of Suffering*, 9. Other sources for criminal justice history before the eighteenth century include J. M. Beattie, *Crime and the Courts in England, 1660–1800* (Princeton, N.J.: Princeton University Press, 1986); John Bellamy, *Crime and Public Order in England in the Late Middle Ages* (London: Routledge and Kegan Paul, 1973); Foucault, *Discipline and Punish*; V. A. C. Gatrell, Bruce Lenman, and Geoffrey Parker, eds., *Crime and the Law: The Social History of Crime in Western Europe since 1500* (London: Europa

Publications, 1980); Barbara A. Hanawalt, *Crime and Conflict in English Communities, 1300–1348* (Cambridge, Mass.: Harvard University Press, 1979); John L. McMullan, *The Canting Crew: London's Criminal Underworld, 1550–1700* (New Brunswick, N.J.: Rutgers University Press, 1984); and L. A. Knafla, ed., *Crime and Criminal Justice in Europe and Canada* (Waterloo, Canada: Wilfred Laurier University Press, 1981).

15. Spierenburg, *The Spectacle of Suffering*, 12.

16. See Hanawalt, *Crime and Conflict;* and Gurr, "Historical Trends."

17. Charles Petit-Dutaille, *Documents Nouveaux sur les Moeurs Populaires et le Droit de Vengeance dans les Pays-Bas au XV Siecle* (Paris, 1908), cited in translation in Norbert Elias, *The Civilizing Process*, 200.

18. Hanawalt, *Crime and Conflict*, 272.

19. *Uniform Crime Reports 1986*, table 6.

20. Gurr, "Historical Trends," 312.

21. Spierenburg, *The Spectacle of Suffering*, 202.

22. Ibid., 179–181.

23. Philip Jenkins, "From Gallows to Prison? The Execution Rate in Early Modern England," in *Criminal Justice History: An International Annual* VII (1986):62.

24. Lawrence Stone, "Interpersonal Violence in English Society," *Past and Present* 101 (1983):25.

25. Jenkins, "From Gallows to Prison?" 54.

26. Ibid., 66. For an extended discussion of the transition in England from reliance on capital punishment and whipping to the punishments of prison and transportation, see J. M. Beattie, *Crime and the Courts in England, 1660–1800*.

27. The classic work that makes the case for the relationship between penal policy and the mode of production is Otto Kirchheimer and Georg Rusche, *Punishment and Social Structure* (New York: Columbia University Press, 1938).

28. Hay, "Property, Authority and the Criminal Law," 18.

29. John Locke, "An Essay Concerning the True Original, Extent, and End of Civil Government," in *Two Treatises of Civil Government* (New York: E. P. Dutton, 1953), 163–64.

30. Hay, "Property, Authority and the Criminal Law," 25.

31. Dario Melossi and Massimo Pavarini, *The Prison and the Factory: Origins of the Penitentiary System* (London: Macmillan, 1981), 130.

32. Ibid., 162.

33. The origins of criminology are presented in many basic texts, including Don C. Gibbons, *Society, Crime and Criminal Behavior* (Englewood Cliffs, N.J.: Prentice-Hall, 1982), ch. 2.

34. Joyce Oldham Appleby, *Economic Thought and Ideology in Seventeenth-Century England* (Princeton, N.J.: Princeton University Press, 1978), 18.

35. Cesare Beccaria, *Essay on Crimes and Punishments*, Edward D. Ingraham, trans. (Stanford, Calif.: Academic Reprints, 1953), 94.

36. For a discussion of the sources and strains of classical criminol-

ogy, see George B. Vold and Thomas J. Bernard, *Theoretical Criminology* (New York: Oxford University Press, 1986), esp. ch. 2.

37. John Herman Randall, Jr., *The Making of the Modern Mind* (Boston: Houghton, Mifflin, 1940), 461.

38. For an intelligent exposition of the treatment approach, see Don C. Gibbons, *Changing the Lawbreaker* (Englewood Cliffs, N.J.: Prentice-Hall, 1965).

39. Quoted in Henry Steele Commager, *The American Mind: An Interpreter of American Thought and Character Since the 1880s* (New Haven, Conn.: Yale University Press, 1950), 207.

40. Sidney Fine, *Laissez Faire and the General-Welfare State: A Study of Conflict in American Thought, 1865–1901* (Ann Arbor: Ann Arbor Paperbacks/University of Michigan Press, 1964), 173.

41. John A. Garraty, *The New Commonwealth, 1877–1890* (New York: Harper Torchbooks, 1968), 331.

42. Ibid., 328.

43. This and subsequent quotations from the 1870 meeting of the American Prison Congress are taken from Arthur Evans Wood and John Barker Waite, *Crime and Its Treatment* (New York: American Book Company, 1941), 532–533.

44. Francis T. Cullen and Karen E. Gilbert, *Reaffirming Rehabilitation* (Cincinnati, Ohio: Anderson, 1982), 79–80.

45. For the historical context of the founding of what is now the American Correctional Association, see David J. Rothman, *Conscience and Convenience: The Asylum and Its Alternatives in Progressive America* (Boston: Little, Brown and Co., 1980), 31–33.

46. For a discussion of the role of "vicarious victimization" in shaping reactions to crime, see Wesley G. Skogan and Michael G. Maxfield, *Coping with Crime: Individual and Neighborhood Reactions* (Beverly Hills, Calif.: Sage, 1981), ch. 9.

47. *The Politics of Law and Order: Street Crime and Public Policy* (New York: Longman, 1984), ch. 2 and 3.

48. Emile Durkheim, *The Division of Labor in Society* (New York: Free Press, 1933), 108.

49. Scheingold, *The Politics of Law and Order*, 39. See also Skogan and Maxfield, *Coping with Crime*.

50. Arthur Stinchcombe, Rebecca Adams, Carol A. Heimer, Kim Lane Scheppele, Tom W. Smith, and D. Garth Taylor, *Crime and Punishment—Changing Attitudes in America* (San Francisco: Jossey-Bass, 1980), ch. 3.

51. For an interesting discussion of the power of these perspectives on child abuse, see Barbara J. Nelson, *Making an Issue of Child Abuse: Political Agenda Setting for Social Problems* (Chicago: University of Chicago Press, 1984).

52. Scheingold, *The Politics of Law and Order*, 57. Scheingold contrasts his approach with those of the conservative political scientist James Q. Wilson and the Marxist criminologist Richard Quinney. Representative works are James Q. Wilson, *Thinking About Crime* (New York: Random House, 1975) and Richard Quinney, *Class, State and Crime*, 2nd ed., (New York: Longman, 1980).

53. Scheingold, *The Politics of Law and Order*, 54.

54. The literature on subsystem politics is vast. See J. Leiper Freeman, *The Political Process* (New York: Random House, 1965) for a theoretical discussion; Arnold J. Meltsner and Christopher Bellavita, *The Policy Organization* (Beverly Hills, Calif.: Sage, 1983) describes the policy subgovernments in education; A. Lee Fritscher, *Smoking and Politics: Policymaking and the Federal Bureaucracy*, 4th ed. (Englewood Cliffs, N.J.: Prentice-Hall, 1989) is a study of the tobacco subsystem.

55. H. L. A. Hart, *The Concept of Law* (Oxford: Clarendon Press, 1961).

56. John Hagan, "The Symbolic Politics of Criminal Sanctions," in Stuart Nagel, Erika Fairchild, and Anthony Champagne, eds., *The Political Science of Criminal Justice* (Springfield, Ill.: Charles C. Thomas, 1983), 30.

57. Edelman, *The Symbolic Uses of Politics*, 41–55.

58. See, for example, Kirk R. Williams, "Economic Sources of Homicide: Reestimating the Effects of Poverty and Inequality," *American Sociological Review* 49 (1984):283–289; and William McCord and Jose Sanchez, "The Treatment of Deviant Children: A Twenty-Five Year Follow-Up Study," *Crime and Delinquency* 29 (1983):238–253.

59. See, for example, the works cited in note 14 of this chapter.

60. For a synthesis of the "paradigm revolution" in criminology, see William J. Chambliss, "Toward A Radical Criminology," in David Kairys, ed., *The Politics of Law: A Progressive Critique* (New York: Pantheon Books, 1982), 230.

61. The classic work on this tension is Herbert L. Packer, *The Limits of the Criminal Sanction* (Stanford, Calif.: Stanford University Press, 1968).

62. For a definition of the politics of promise in criminal justice, and a discussion of its dynamics in the context of federal involvement in the control of street crime, see Malcolm Feeley and Austin D. Sarat, *The Policy Dilemma: Federal Crime Policy and the LEAA, 1968–1978* (Minneapolis: University of Minnesota Press, 1980).

63. These two models are specified in detail in Packer, *The Limits of the Criminal Sanction*.

64. John W. Kingdon, *Agendas, Alternatives, and Public Policies* (Boston: Little, Brown, 1984), 78–82.

7. Understanding the Push to Capture and Confine

1. Thomas Byrne Edsall, *The New Politics of Inequality* (New York: W. W. Norton, 1984).

2. Godfrey Hodgson, *America in Our Time* (New York: Vintage Books, 1976).

3. Robert Kuttner, *The Revolt of the Haves* (New York: Simon and Schuster, 1980).

4. The following paragraphs represent my effort at synthetic reconstruction of the writers' analyses, which I find useful; the phases I describe are not explicitly conceptualized in any of these works.

5. While Republicans found in this trend an ideological windfall, Democrats tried to reap its benefits too. Kuttner points out that after

the passage of Proposition 13, the 1978 California initiative cutting property taxes by more than $6 billion, Democratic Governor Jerry Brown became a convert, and Jimmy Carter's White House staff cast it in terms of a manifestation of the fiscal conservatism the President had predicted long ago. Kuttner, *The Revolt of the Haves,* 81–82, 93.

6. See Congressional Budget Office, "The Changing Distribution of Federal Taxes: 1975–1990" (Congress of the United States, Congressional Budget Office, 1987), table 11.

7. For a discussion of mainstream, Marxist, and cultural explanations of the politicization of crime, see Stuart A. Scheingold, *The Politics of Law and Order: Street Crime and Public Policy,* (New York: Longman, 1984), esp. ch. 2.

8. *Statistical Abstract 1988,* table 626.

9. Richard M. Scammon and Ben J. Wattenberg, *The Real Majority* (New York: Coward-McCann, Inc., 1970), 60.

10. A summary of concerns expressed in Gallup polls through the 1960s is presented in Scammon and Wattenberg, *The Real Majority,* 38–39.

11. Cited in Herbert L. Packer, "Nixon's Crime Program and What It Means," *The New York Review of Books,* October 22, 1970, 30.

12. "Introduction," Richard Harris, *The Fear of Crime* (New York: Praeger, 1969), 2.

13. Garry Wills, *Nixon Agonistes: The Crisis of the Self-Made Man* (Boston: Houghton Mifflin, 1969), 51–52.

14. *Uniform Crime Reports 1969,* 3.

15. President's Commission on Law Enforcement and the Administration of Justice, *The Challenge of Crime in A Free Society* (Washington, D.C.: U.S. Government Printing Office, 1967), 25–27.

16. Don C. Gibbons, *Society, Crime, and Criminal Behavior,* 106.

17. President's Commission, *Challenge of Crime,* figures 3 and 4.

18. Allan Silver, "The Demand for Order in Civil Society: A Review of Some Themes in the History of Urban Crime, Police and Riot," in David Bordua, *The Police: Six Sociological Essays* (New York: John Wiley and Sons, 1967), 20–22.

19. President's Commission, *Challenge of Crime,* 211.

20. *Statistical Abstract 1961,* table 10; *Statistical Abstract 1971,* table 17.

21. *Uniform Crime Reports 1969,* charts 9 and 11.

22. President's Commission, *Challenge of Crime,* 55–56.

23. U.S. Department of Commerce, Bureau of the Census, *Census of Governments 1962,* vol. 4, "Compendium of Government Finances," table 37; U.S. Department of Commerce, Bureau of the Census, *Census of Governments 1967,* vol. 4, "Compendium of Government Finances," table 36; inflation rate calculated from *Economic Report of the President* (Washington, D.C.: U.S. Government Printing Ofiice, 1988), table B-3.

24. The population of youth aged 15–19 increased 26.7 percent between 1960–1965, while arrests of persons under 18 in that same period jumped 52 percent for the FBI Index offenses of murder, rape, robbery, assault, larceny, burglary, and auto theft. U.S. Bureau of the Census, *Current Population Reports,* Series P-25; President's Commission, *Challenge of Crime,* 56.

25. Stanley Cohen, "Breaking Out, Smashing Up and the Social Context of Aspiration," in Barry Krisberg and James Austin, *Children of Ishmael: Critical Perspectives on Juvenile Justice* (Palo Alto, Calif.: Mayfield, 1978), 257–279.

26. For a structural analysis of delinquency, see David F. Greenberg, "Delinquency and the Age Structure of Society," in David F. Greenberg, ed., *Crime and Capitalism: Readings in Marxist Criminology* (Palo Alto, Calif.: Mayfield, 1981), 118–139.

27. U.S. Department of Labor, *Employment and Training Report of the President* (Washington, D.C.: Government Printing Office, 1981), table A-30.

28. *Uniform Crime Reports 1964*, table 30.

29. Murray Edelman, *The Symbolic Uses of Politics* (Urbana, Ill.: University of Illinois, 1964), 172–174.

30. *New York Times*, July 17, 1964.

31. *New York Times*, July 19, 1964.

32. *New York Times*, August 15, 1964.

33. *New York Times*, August 30, 1964.

34. George C. Wallace, *"Hear Me Out"* (Anderson, S.C.: Droke House, 1968), 43. For other examples of Wallace's campaign use of the crime issue, see Jody Carlson, *George C. Wallace and the Politics of Powerlessness: The Wallace Campaigns for the Presidency, 1964–1976* (New Brunswick, N.J.: Transaction Books, 1981), 129.

35. J. Anthony Lukas, *Common Ground: A Turbulent Decade in the Lives of Three American Families* (New York: Knopf, 1985), 134.

36. See the discussions of Wallace's shifting stands on civil rights in Carlson, *George C. Wallace and the Politics of Powerlessness*, ch. 3, and Marshall Frady, *Wallace* (New York: Meridian Books, 1968), 123–127; the political development of Louise Day Hicks is described in Lukas, *Common Ground*, ch. 9.

37. Agnew, Spiro T., *The Wisdom of Spiro T. Agnew* (New York: Ballantine, 1969), 40.

38. Harris, *The Fear of Crime*, 21–30.

39. *New York Times*, August 9, 1968.

40. Lewis Chester, Godfrey Hodgson, and Bruce Page, *An American Melodrama: The Presidential Campaign of 1968* (New York: Dell, 1969), 405–406.

41. Richard Hofstadter, *The Paranoid Style in American Politics* (New York: Knopf, 1965), 3.

42. *New York Times*, September 18, 1968. Gallup figures were somewhat different. 56 percent approved, 31 percent disapproved, and 13 percent had no opinion. George H. Gallup, *The Gallup Poll: Public Opinion, 1935–1971*, vol. 3 (New York: Random House, 1972), 2160.

43. *New York Times*, March 19, 1964.

44. Carlson, *George C. Wallace and the Politics of Powerlessness*, 65.

45. Louis Harris, *The Public Looks at Crime and Corrections* (Washington, DC: Joint Commission on Correctional Manpower and Training, 1968), 2.

46. Ibid., 11–12.

47. Ibid., 14.

48. Scammon and Wattenberg, *The Real Majority*, 331–332.

49. Carlson, *George C. Wallace and the Politics of Powerlessness*, 129.

50. Chester, Hodgson, and Page, *An American Melodrama*, 309.

51. The following data come from Carlson, *George C. Wallace and the Politics of Powerlessness*, ch. 8, which synthesizes many factors that distinguish Wallace supporters from those who voted for Nixon or Humphrey.

52. Ibid., 99.

53. Carlson's data (table 8.8) show Wallace voters as being 44.7 percent at middle or upper levels in socioeconomic status, as compared with 26.2 percent for Humphrey voters and 58.4 percent for Nixon voters. But many Wallace voters apparently retained working-class sympathies. Scammon and Wattenberg present data from the University of Michigan Survey Research Center that show 64 percent of Wallace voters identifying with the working class and 80 percent coming from a working class family, as opposed to 55 percent and 68 percent for Humphrey voters and 44 percent and 57 percent for Nixon voters. Scammon and Wattenberg, *The Real Majority*, 195.

54. Scammon and Wattenberg, *The Real Majority*, 197.

55. Quoted in Hodgson, *America in Our Time*, 174.

56. Wills, *Nixon Agonistes*, 54.

57. Elliott Currie, *Confronting Crime: An American Challenge* (New York: Pantheon, 1985), 175–177.

58. See Herbert Gans, *The Levittowners* (New York: Vintage Books, 1967); B. M. Berger, *Working-Class Suburb: A Study of Auto Workers in Suburbia* (Berkeley, Calif.: University of California Press, 1960).

59. U.S. Department of Commerce, Bureau of the Census, *Historical Satistics*, Series C-54, C-62, C-67, C-68, C-73.

60. Peter A. Lupsha and William J. Siembieda, "The Poverty of Public Services in the Land of Plenty: An Analysis and Interpretation," in David C. Perry and Alfred J. Watkins, *The Rise of the Sunbelt Cities* (Beverly Hills, Calif.: Sage, 1977), table 2.

61. U.S. Department of Commerce, Bureau of the Census, *Current Population Reports*, series P-60.

62. A discussion of the tension between the liberal consensus of the 1950s and early 1960s and the growing restiveness of blacks can be found in Hodgson, *America in Our Time*, esp. chs 4 and 8.

63. For a discussion of racial attitudes of whites in the 1960s, see Jerome Skolnick, *The Politics of Protest* (New York: Simon and Schuster, 1969), ch. 5.

64. Samuel Bowles, David M.Gordon, and Thomas E. Weisskopf, *Beyond the Wasteland: A Democratic Alternative to Economic Decline* (Garden City, N.Y.: Anchor Press/Doubleday, 1983), 24–26.

65. Evocative examples abound in Studs Terkel, *Working* (New York: Avon Books, 1975).

66. Quoted in Chester, Hodgson, and Page, *An American Melodrama*, 761.

67. Wills, *Nixon Agonistes*, 272–273.

68. Hodgson, *America in Our Time*, 333.

69. *Economic Report of the President 1988* (Washington, D.C.: U.S. Government Printing Office, 1988), tables B-3 and B-30.

70. See Edsall, *The New Politics of Inequality*, 209–212, for an expla-

nation of how the redistributive effects of the income tax shifted from the wealthy to the working and middle class.

71. Bowles, Gordon, and Weisskopf, *Beyond the Wasteland*, 25.

72. Of course, there were other outlets for the discontents of working people. As Patricia Cayo Sexton and Brendan Sexton note, in their general study of the conditions and views of workers at the beginning of the 1970s, "The symptoms of the alienation are found in voting behavior, work habits, absenteeism on the job, strikes, hard-hat disturbances, backlash, antagonism to students, and feelings of distrust and impotence." *Blue Collars and Hard Hats: The Working Class and the Future of American Politics* (New York: Vintage, 1971), 196.

73. Edsall, *The New Politics of Inequality*, 39.

74. Kevin Phillips, *The Emerging Republican Majority* (New Rochelle, New York: Arlington House, 1969), 470.

75. Hodgson, *America in Our Time*, 421–422.

76. Wallace, *"Hear Me Out"*, 16–17.

77. Quoted in Chester, Hodgson, and Page, *An American Melodrama*, 762. These writers pungently sum up the differences in approach of these two political manipulators: "If, especially in his stressing of the issue of law and order, Wallace was angling for the same fish as Nixon, it has to be said that where Nixon used a dry fly, Wallace baited his hook with good old Southern country blood-red crawlers" (p. 313).

78. *Uniform Crime Reports 1980*, table 2.

79. U.S. Department of Justice, Bureau of Justice Statistics, "Criminal Victimization in the United States," 1983.

80. "The Harris Survey," May 24, 1982.

81. Peter Steinfels, *The Neoconservatives* (New York: Simon and Schuster, 1979), 55.

82. Ibid., 8.

83. Irving Kristol, *Reflections of A Neoconservative* (New York: Basic Books, 1983), xiii.

84. James Q. Wilson, *Thinking About Crime* (New York: Vintage, 1975), 222–223.

85. Steinfels, *The Neoconservatives*, 58–59; Edward Banfield, *The Unheavenly City: The Nature and the Future of Our Urban Crisis* (Boston: Little, Brown, 1970), 171–172.

86. *Sourcebook 1986*, table 6.22.

87. Quoted in Francis T. Cullen and Karen E. Gilbert, *Reaffirming Rehabilitation* (Cincinnati: Anderson, 1982), 97.

88. Quoted in Harris, *The Fear of Crime*, 61.

89. Francis A. Allen, *The Decline of the Rehabilitative Ideal: Penal Policy and Social Purpose* (New Haven: Yale University Press, 1981), 64.

90. The rehabilitation rationale had come to prevail in other western countries as well. Typical of the perspective is this comment from an English penal history published in 1914, "It is idle to argue that no one should gain advantage from having been in prison—the hardship is so crushing that we must have a counterpoise to neutralize it. A man *should* be benefited by prison, in the sense that a patient should be benefited by a necessary operation." George Ives, *A History of Penal*

Methods: Criminals, Witches, Lunatics (London: Stanley Paul and Co., 1914), 374.

91. As the warden of a federal prison wrote in the 1960s, "It is the function of parole boards, with the assistance of institutional staff, to make a social prognosis and act on it. Where board members are experienced persons out of the correctional field, as is often the case, astute decisions can often be made even in the absence of much clinical data." Quoted in Karl Menninger, *The Crime of Punishment* (New York: Viking Press, 1969), 82–83.

92. Cullen and Gilbert, *Reaffirming Rehabilitation*, 7–9.

93. The general public still supported rehabilitation, however. In a national Harris poll taken in November 1967, 72 percent of respondents thought the primary purpose of prison should be rehabilitation, as opposed to 7 percent in favor of punishment, 12 percent supporting "protecting society"—presumably another lable for incapacitation—and 9 percent "not sure." *Sourcebook 1974*, 218.

94. Seé Norval Morris, *The Future of Imprisonment* (Chicago: University of Chicago, 1974), 34–36 and David F. Greenberg, "The Incapacitative Effect of Imprisonment: Some Estimates," *Law and Society Review* 9 (1975):541–580.

95. Allen, *The Decline of the Rehabilitative Ideal*, 49–57.

96. American Friends Service Committee Working Party, *Struggle for Justice* (New York: Hill and Wang, 1971), 45.

97. David F. Greenberg, "Rehabilitation Is Still Punishment," *The Humanist* 32 (1972).

98. The liberal critique was articulated forcefully and early in American Friends Service Committee, *Struggle for Justice*. The emphasis on the loss of rights that accompanies the indeterminate sentence is strong in Andrew von Hirsch, *Doing Justice* (New York: Hill and Wang, 1976).

99. See the report of 1976 Congressional testimony to this effect by Arizona Congressman Sam Steiger, in Cullen and Gilbert, *Reaffirming Rehabilitation*, 96–97.

100. von Hirsch, *Doing Justice*.

101. Ernest van den Haag, *Punishing Criminals: Concerning a Very Old and Painful Question* (New York: Basic Books, 1975), 61.

102. The brevity of this account of a complex and involving policy debate blurs what was a somewhat confusing philosophical overlap of the various camps in the 1970s debate over punishment rationales. Those who shared general areas of the political spectrum—the American Friends Service Committee and the Committee for the Study of Incarceration on the liberal side, for instance—did not necessarily agree on all important perspectives. In fact, the latter group shared with the solidly conservative scholar Ernest van den Haag support for "justice"— that is, what is deserved sanction for the offense committed—as a legitimate rationale for incarceration, although it differed strongly on what was deserved and was not willing also to endorse the utilitarian rationale of deterrence, as van den Haag was. Van den Haag acknowledged, however, as the Committee for the Study of Incarceration did not, that "retributive justice cannot be ultimately just unless destributive justice is." van den Haag, *Punishing Criminals*, 32. In this he was

much closer to the American Friends Service Committee, which believed that "the construction of a just system of criminal justice in an unjust society is a contradiction in terms." American Friends Service Committee, *Struggle for Justice*, 16. The important difference between them is, of course, that van den Haag was willing to settle for a lawful society, given that he did not support redistribution necessary to the creation of a fully just one.

103. One of the most influential conservative scholars did not, in fact, support longer sentences (arguing a sort of "law of diminishing returns" theory), but argued for the deterrent and incapacitative effects of short sentences more widely imposed. See Wilson, *Thinking About Crime*, 193–203.

104. Gary S. Becker, *The Economic Approach to Human Behavior* (Chicago: University of Chicago Press, 1976), 79, reprinted from "Crime and Punishment: An Economic Approach," *Journal of Political Economy* 72 (1968):169–217.

105. Wilson, *Thinking About Crime*, 199.

106. Allen, *Decline of the Rehabilitative Ideal*, 11.

107. Ibid., 16–29.

108. Seymour Martin Lipset and William Schneider, *The Confidence Gap: Business, Labor and Government in the Public Mind* (New York: The Free Press, 1983). See also, for more recent indicators, Louis Harris, "Confidence in Institutions Down, Led by Sharp Decline in Trust in White House," The Harris Survey, May 8, 1988.

109. *Uniform Crime Reports 1984*, 7–34.

110. U.S. Department of Justice, Bureau of Justice Statistics, "Criminal Victimization 1984," *Bulletin*, October 1985, table 3.

111. *Statistical Abstract 1987*, table 20.

112. For research that suggests that "vicarious victimization" is an important dimension in the fear of crime, see Wesley G. Skogan and Michael G. Maxfield, *Coping with Crime: Individual and Neighborhood Reactions* (Beverly Hills, Calif.: Sage, 1981).

113. Gallup, *The Gallup Poll: Public Opinion, 1935–1971*, 2107; George H. Gallup, *The Gallup Poll: Public Opinion, 1972–1977* (Wilmington, Del.: Scholarly Resources, 1978), 443; *The Gallup Poll: Public Opinion, 1982* (Wilmington, Del.: Scholarly Resources, 1983), 136.

114. *Sourcebook 1986*, figure 2.1.

115. U.S. Department of Justice, Bureau of Justice Statistics, *Report to the Nation on Crime and Justice*, 2nd ed., 1988, 94.

116. *Sourcebook 1986*, table 1.6; *Economic Report of the President 1988*, table B-3.

117. Criminal justice officials and political leaders often see their policy orientation as significantly less punitive than that of the general public. See Richard A. Berk and Peter H. Rossi, *Prison Reform and State Elites* (Cambridge, Mass.: Ballinger, 1977) and Francis T. Cullen, Timothy S. Bynum, Kim Montgomery Garrett, and Jack R. Greene, "Legislator Ideology and Criminal Justice Policy: Implications from Illinois," in Erika S. Fairchild and Vincent J. Webb, eds., *The Politics of Crime and Criminal Justice* (Beverly Hills, Calif.: Sage, 1985.)

118. *Sourcebook 1986*, tables 2.23 and 2.25.

119. Ibid., table 2.11.

120. Joseph E. Jacoby and Christopher S. Dunn, "National Survey on Punishment for Criminal Offenses: Executive Summary," Bowling Green State University, 1987. See also *Sourcebook 1987*, table 2.28.

121. For a review of public opinion surveys on prison policy, see Timothy J. Flanagan and Susan L. Caulfield, "Public Opinion and Prison Policy: A Review" *Prison Journal* 64 (1984):31–46.

122. Russ Immarigeon, "Public Supports Alternatives to Executions," in *Jericho* (43) (Spring 1987), 11. See also Philip W. Harris, "Oversimplification and Error in Public Opinion Surveys on Capital Punishment," *Justice Quarterly* (1986):429–455.

123. Scheingold, *The Politics of Law and Order*, 44.

124. *Statistical Abstract 1987*, tables 637, 638.

125. Edelman, *The Symbolic Uses of Politics*, 191.

126. *Economic Report of the President 1988*, table B-46; *Statistical Abstract 1987*, tables 676, 661.

127. James Q. Wilson, *Thinking About Crime*, rev. ed. (New York: Vintage Books, 1985), 238.

128. W. J. Cash, *The Mind of the South* (New York: Vintage Books 1941), 258–259.

8. Understanding the Drive to Observe

1. James O'Connor, *The Fiscal Crisis of the State* (New York: St. Martin's Press, 1973), ch. 6; Malcolm Feeley and Austin D. Sarat, *The Policy Dilemma: Federal Crime Policy and the LEAA, 1968–1978* (Minneapolis: University of Minnesota Press, 1980).

2. Charles E. Lindblom, *The Policy-Making Process* (Englewood Cliffs, N.J.: Prentice-Hall, 1980), 64.

3. Erwin Hargrove, *The Missing Link: The Study of the Implementation of Social Policy* (Washington, D.C.: The Urban Institute, 1976).

4. Eugene Bardach, *The Implementation Game* (Cambridge, Mass: M.I.T. Press, 1977).

5. The 1973 New York law imposing mandatory minimum sentences on drug offenders—proposed by Governor Nelson Rockefeller, who was preparing to run for reelection the following year—allowed, for instance, for plea bargaining for the most serious charges but not for lesser felonies, which meant that defendants in all categories might receive the same penalties, a clearly inequitable outcome, and surely one that was not intended by the legislators. See Malcolm Feeley, *Court Reform on Trial: Why Simple Solutions Fail* (New York: Basic Books, 1983), 123–127.

6. Jack Hausner and Michael Seidel, *An Analysis of Case Processing Time in the District of Columbia Superior Court* (Washington, D.C.: INSLAW, 1981).

7. James Eisenstein and Herbert Jacob, *Felony Justice: An Organizational Analysis of Criminal Courts* (Boston: Little, Brown, 1977), ch. 2.

8. Charles Saunders, *Upgrading the American Police: Education and Training for Better Law Enforcement* (Washington, D.C.: Brookings, 1970).

9. Research conducted in ten U.S. cities has shown that between 1948–1978 the ratio of arrests to offenses known to urban police either remained about the same or declined, despite rising crime and increased police personnel. Herbert Jacob and Robert L. Lineberry, (with Anne M. Heinz, Michael J. Rich, and Duane H. Swank) *Governmental Responses to Crime: Crime and Governmental Responses in American Cities* (Washington, D.C.: National Institute of Justice, 1982), 67.

10. In two separate articles within three days at the end of 1988 (December 30 and January 2, 1989) the *New York Times* noted that the shortage of prison space was forcing early release of inmates in Connecticut and New York, primarily drug offenders. This is not uncommon elsewhere in the country.

11. For a review of dialectics in Marx and elsewhere, see Roy Bhaskar, "Dialectics," in Tom Bottomore, ed., *A Dictionary of Marxist Thought* (Cambridge, Mass.: Harvard University Press, 1983), 122–29.

12. Sir Frederick Pollock and Frederic William Maitland, *A History of English Law* (Cambridge: Cambridge University Press, 1898), 58–90.

13. David J. Rothman, *The Discovery of the Asylum: Social Order and Disorder in the New Republic* (Boston: Little, Brown, 1971), 242–245.

14. George Bernard Shaw, *The Crime of Imprisonment* (New York: Philosophical Library, 1946), 13.

15. See Sidney L. Harring, *Policing a Class Society: The Experience of American Cities* (New Brunswick, N.J.: Rutgers, 1983), ch. 6 and Samuel Walker, *A Critical History of Police Reform* (Lexington, Mass.: D.C. Heath and Co., 1977), 14.

16. Herbert Jacob, *The Frustration of Policy: Responses to Crime by American Cities* (Boston: Little, Brown, 1984), ch. 4.

17. John Mollenkopf, "The Crisis of the Public Sector in America's Cities," in Roger E. Alcaly and David Marmelstein, *The Fiscal Crisis of American Cities* (New York: Vintage, 1976), 113–131.

18. See, e.g., Donald T. Campbell and H. Laurence Ross, "The Connecticut Crackdown on Speeding: Time-Series Data in Quasi-Experimental Analysis," *Law and Society Review 3* (1968):33–53.

19. U.S. Department of Justice, *The Nation's Toughest Drug Law: Evaluating the New York Experience* (Washington, D.C.: U.S. Government Printing Office, 1978).

20. For a range of studies comparing the outcomes of greater and lesser penalties, see Joan Petersilia and Susan Turner, with Joyce Peterson, *Prison versus Probation in California: Implications for Crime and Offender Recidivism* (Santa Monica, Calif.: Rand Corporation, 1986); Michael R. Gottfredson, Susan D. Mitchell-Herzfeld, and Timothy J. Flanagan, "Another Look at the Effectiveness of Parole Supervision," *Journal of Research in Crime and Delinquency* 19 (1982):277–298; and Charles A. Murray and Louis A. Cox, Jr., *Beyond Probation* (Beverly Hills, Calif.: Sage, 1979.)

21. "LEAA Newsletter" 6 (July-August 1976), 7.

22. John W. Kingdon, *Agendas, Alternatives, and Public Policies* (Boston: Little, Brown, 1984), 78–82.

23. The literature on the problems of LEAA is vast. See Twentieth

Century Fund Task Force on the Law Enforcement Assistance Administration, *Law Enforcement: The Federal Role* (New York: McGraw-Hill, 1976); Richard S. Allinson, "LEAA's Impact on Criminal Justice: A Review of the Literature," *Criminal Justice Abstracts* 11 (1979); and Feeley and Sarat, *The Policy Dilemma*.

24. Feeley and Sarat, *The Policy Dilemma*, 10.

25. Allinson, "LEAA's Impact on Criminal Justice," 611.

26. President's Crime Commission on Law Enforcement and Administration of Justice, *The Challenge of Crime in a Free Society* (Washington, D.C.: U.S. Government Printing Office, 1967), vi.

27. Omnibus Crime Control and Safe Streets Act of 1968, P.L. 90–35.

28. Twentieth Century Fund, *Law Enforcement*, 27 and 139, n. 14.

29. Allinson, "LEAA's Impact on Criminal Justice," 616–617.

30. U.S. Department of Justice, Law Enforcement Assistance Administration, "LEAA Sixth Annual Report, Fiscal Year 1974," 73.

31. Twentieth Century Fund, *Law Enforcement*, 76–77; U.S. Department of Justice, Law Enforcement Assistance Administration, "LEAA Eleventh Annual Report, Fiscal Year 1979."

32. Gordon Karl Zenk, *Project SEARCH: The Struggle for Control of Criminal Information in America* (Westport, Conn.: Greenwood, 1979).

33. President's Commission on Law Enforcement and Administration of Justice, *Task Force Report: Science and Technology* (Washington, D.C.: President's Crime Commission, 1967), 45.

34. For a review of research that documents this process, see James Austin and Barry Krisberg, "Wider, Stronger and Different Nets: The Dialectics of Criminal Justice Reform," *Journal of Research in Crime and Delinquency* 18 (1981):165–196.

35. See, e.g., Sally Hillsman-Baker, *Court Employment Program Evaluation: Final Report*, New York: Vera Institute of Justice, 1979, Ch. IV.

36. It is impossible to know exactly how many pretrial diversion and community corrections programs were funded by LEAA. Austin and Krisberg note that agency officials' report of 1,200 diversion programs is a very conservative estimate, since records of programs funded not directly by the agency but out of state block grants are incomplete. Austin and Krisberg, "Wider, Stronger and Different Nets," 170. Feeley comments that "LEAA all but turned diversion into a household word." Feeley, *Court Reform on Trial*, 83. We do not have even approximate figures for community corrections programs.

37. President's Commission on Law Enforcement and Administration of Justice, *Task Force Report: The Police* (Washington, D.C.: U.S. Government Printing Office, 1967).

38. President's Commission on Law Enforcement and Administration of Justice, *Task Force Report: Corrections* (Washington, D.C.: U.S. Government Printing Office, 1967), 29.

39. J. Banks, A. L. Porter, R. L. Rardin, T. R. Silver, and V. E. Unger, *Evaluation of Intensive Special Probation Projects* (U.S. Department of Justice, National Institute of Law Enforcement and Criminal Justice, 1977).

40. California Department of Justice, "1975 California Comprehen-

sive Plan for Criminal Justice," 1974, 7–8; National Commission on Higher Education for Police Officers, *The Quality of Police Education* (San Francisco: Jossey-Bass, 1978), as quoted in Allinson, "LEAA's Impact on Criminal Justice," 639.

41. The best description of this aspect of the legislative history of the Safe Streets Act and its implications can be found in Feeley and Sarat, *The Policy Dilemma*, ch. 2. For the full picture of the politics of the Act's passage, see Richard Harris, *The Fear of Crime* (New York: Praeger, 1969).

42. For a critique of the SPAs' contributions to criminal justice federalism, see Feeley and Sarat, *The Policy Dilemma*.

43. Twentieth Century Fund, *Law Enforcement*, 98.

44. The classic work on policy typology is Theodore J. Lowi, "American Business, Public Policy, Case Studies, and Political Theory," *World Politics:* 16 (1964):677–715.

45. Randall B. Ripley, *Policy Analysis in Political Science* (Chicago: Nelson-Hall, 1985), ch. 3.

46. Theodore J. Lowi, *The End of Liberalism: The Second Republic of the United States* (New York, Norton, 1979), 297.

47. See *Directory of Criminal Justice Issues in the States* (Washington, D.C.: Criminal Justice Statistics Association, 1986), appendix 1.

48. *Sourcebook 1986*, table 1.13.

49. See, for example, Frank T. Judge III, "Relief for Prison Overcrowding: Evaluating Michigan's Accelerated Parole Statute," *University of Michigan Journal of Law Reform* 15 (1982):547–576.

50. For a number of examples of the dynamics of distributive policy on the federal level, see Randall B. Ripley and Grace A. Franklin, *Congress, The Bureaucracy and Public Policy* (Chicago: Dorsey, 1987), ch. 4.

9. Just as Much Crime, Much More Control

1. Excluding property offenses from this aim is deliberate. International data suggest—though comparisons are tricky because of differences among countries in definitions of crimes and methods of reporting—that some property crime rates for some industrialized countries, especially for burglary, are higher than in the U.S.. Canada, according to Interpol figures for 1984, had a homicide rate one-third of ours and a robbery rate of less than half, but its burglary rate was 12 percent higher. U.S. Department of Justice, Bureau of Justice Statistics, "International Crime Rates," *Special Report*, May 1988, table 4.

2. *Uniform Crime Reports 1970*, table 3; *Uniform Crime Reports 1987*, table 4.

3. I feel the need to state explicitly that in sketching the forthcoming hypothetical I am in no way advocating such a program. I agree, in fact, with Mike Davis, when he says, of the Los Angeles war on gangs, "More repression only sows dragon's teeth" and suggests that "only extermination will ultimately conquer." "Los Angeles: Civil Liberties Between the Hammer and the Rock," *New Left Review* 170 (July/August 1988):59.

4. For a summary of evaluations of police innovations that appear to have some crime control effect, see James Q. Wilson, *Thinking About Crime*, rev. ed. (New York: Vintage Books, 1985), 68–74. My description exaggerates the techniques tried in these experiments, for the purpose of exploring their logical consequences.

5. *Sourcebook 1987*, table 4.17.

6. Debra Whitcomb, *An Exemplary Project: Major Violator Unit—San Diego, California*, U.S. Department of Justice, National Institute of Justice (Washington, D.C.: U.S. Government Printing Office, 1980), 2–3.

7. Brian Forst, Judith Lucianovic, and Sarah J. Cox, *What Happens After Arrest* (Washington, D.C.: INSLAW, 1977), exhibit 5.1.

8. James Eisenstein and Herbert Jacob, *Felony Justice: An Organizational Analysis of Criminal Courts* (Boston: Little-Brown, 1977).

9. A debate has been raging in the criminological community about whether the age-specific arrest rates reflect changes in the number of offenders or changes in the rate at which active criminals commit crimes. See Alfred Blumstein, Jacqueline Cohen, and David P. Farrington, "Career Criminal Research: Its Value for Criminology," *Criminology* 26 (1988):1–35; and Michael R. Gottfredson and Travis Hirschi, "The True Value of Lambda Would Appear to Be Zero: An Essay on Career Criminals, Criminal Careers, Selective Incapacitation, Cohort Studies, and Related Topics," *Criminology* 24 (1986):213–233. For a synthesis of studies on the duration of criminal careers, see Alfred Blumstein, Jacqueline Cohen, Jeffrey A. Roth, and Christy A. Visher, eds., *Criminal Careers and "Career Criminals"* (Washington, D.C.: National Academy Press, 1986), 85–95.

10. See Theodore Black and Thomas Orsagh, "New Evidence on the Efficacy of Sanctions as a Deterrent to Homicide," *Social Science Quarterly* 58 (1978):616–631 and Scott H. Decker and Carol H. Kohfeld, "An Empirical Analysis of the Effect of the Death Penalty in Missouri," *Journal of Crime and Justice* 10 (1987):23–46.

11. U.S. Department of Justice, Bureau of Justice Statistics, "Felony Sentences in State Courts, 1986," *Bulletin*, February 1989, 1.

12. John Monahan, "The Prediction of Violent Criminal Behavior: A Methodological Critique and Prospectus," in Alfred Blumstein, Jacqueline Cohen, and Daniel Nagin, eds., *Deterrence and Incapacitation: Estimating the Effects of Criminal Sanctions on Crime Rates* (Washington, D.C.: National Academy of Sciences, 1978), 244–269.

13. Norval Morris and Gordon Hawkins, *The Honest Politician's Guide to Crime Control* (Chicago: University of Chicago Press, 1969), 5–6. A word of caution is due here. Perhaps the intractibility of crimes of "vice" could also be overcome with a get-tougher program relying heavily on incapaciation. The People's Republic of China supposedly solved its drug problem by shooting large numbers of users, and it has been suggested that a massive incarceration increase would be cost-effective for drug crimes as well as for FBI Index offenses. Edwin W. Zedlewski, "Making Confinement Decisions," *Research in Brief*, U.S. Department of Justice, National Institute of Justice, July 1987. But see, in response, David F. Greenberg, "The Cost Benefit Analysis of Imprisonment," unpublished paper, 1988.

14. U.S. Department of Justice, Bureau of Justice Statistics, "Prisoners in 1987," table 11.

15. *Sourcebook 1987*, table 1.4. The measure of inflation used was the rate of change in the GNP price deflator. *Economic Report of the President* (Washington, D.C.: U.S. Government Printing Office, 1988), table B-3.

16. The figure for total justice system expenditures comes from *Sourcebook 1987*, table 1.1.

17. The amount of the budget deficit is taken from *Economic Report of the President 1988*, table B-76.

18. There are two problems with this set of calculations. It is, of course, quite improbable that the unit cost of increasing the odds that offenses will lead to incarceration would not increase as the system aimed to be more comprehensive. The uniform rate is assumed for lack of a basis for any other and in the interests of a conservative cost projection. The choice of a conservative approach is appropriate not solely to avert a charge of alarmism, but also because it helps to mitigate the other major problem with the hypothetical. It can be assumed that some offenders have committed more than one of the offenses that make up the denominator of the ratio of prison admissions to offenses committed, so that one admission may increase the ratio by more than 0.001.

19. See chapter 2.

20. Herbert Jacob, *The Frustration of Policy: Responses to Crime by American Cities* (Boston: Little, Brown, 1984), 165.

21. Michael Milakovich, "Politics and Measure of Success in the War on Crime," *Crime and Delinquency* 21 (1975):1–18.

22. After having risen during the 1970s from 11.7 percent to 13.3 percent, the share of the male population in the 18–24 age range dropped back to 11.9 percent in 1986. While the drop was projected to continue into the 1990s, its pace was expected to slow. *Statistical Abstract 1988*, tables 16 and 20.

23. Louis Harris, "The Harris Survey," March 21, 1985.

24. *Uniform Crime Reports 1987*, table 1.

25. *Uniform Crime Reports 1984*, 25; *Uniform Crime Reports 1985*, 24; *Uniform Crime Reports 1986*, 24; *Uniform Crime Reports 1987*, 24.

26. U.S. Department of Justice, Bureau of Justice Statistics, "Criminal Victimization 1987," *Bulletin*, October 1988, table 4.

27. U.S. Department of Justice, Bureau of Justice Statistics, "Households Touched by Crime, 1986," *Bulletin*, June 1987, table 2.

28. In 1969, 86 percent of murders, 27 percent of robberies, and 19 percent of burglaries were cleared by arrest, as compared with 1986 figures of 70 percent, 25 percent and 14 percent. *Uniform Crime Reports 1969*, chart 17; *Uniform Crime Reports 1986*, 155.

29. Dennis C. Smith, "Police," in Charles Brecher and Raymond D. Horton, eds., *Setting Municipal Priorities 1982* (New York: Russell Sage Foundation, 1981), 229–263.

30. Tony Pate, Robert A. Bowers, and Ron Parks, *Three Approaches to Criminal Apprehension in Kansas City: An Evaluation Report* (Washington, D.C.: Police Foundation, 1976); Susan E. Martin, "Policing Career Criminals: An Examination of an Innovative Career Crimi-

nal Program," *Journal of Criminal Law and Criminology* 77 (1986):1159–1182.

31. Malcolm Feeley, *Court Reform on Trial: Why Simple Solutions Fail* (New York: Basic Books, 1983), 19.

32. Note that this statement is much more specific than simply saying that the deterrence hypothesis is invalid. Informal sanctions may deter more effectively than criminal sentences; criminal punishments may deter some people—say, first-time offenders—and not others. A recent empirical test of the deterrent affect of criminal sanctions is Irving Piliavin, Rosemary Gartner, Craig Thornton, and Ross L. Matsueda, "Crime, Deterrence and Rational Choice," *American Sociological Review* 51 (1986):101–119. A straightforward discussion of the problems in determining whether punishment deters crime can be found in Elliott Currie, *Confronting Crime: An American Challenge* (New York: Pantheon, 1985), 53–67.

33. Lee Bowker, "Crime and the Use of Prisons in the United States: A Time Series Analysis," *Crime and Delinquency* 27 (1981), 212. For other deterrence research, see Blumstein, Cohen, and Nagin, *Deterrence and Incapacitation.*

34. We really do not know how much greater those increases would have to be. A 1979 study by Van Dine, Conrad, and Dinitz estimated that increasing the prison population by 523 percent would reduce violent crime in Ohio by less than 30 percent, but they assumed that the only crime prevented was the one for which the 342 felons in their study had been caught, surely an understatement. Stephen Van Dine, John Conrad, and Siman Dinitz, *Restraining the Wicked* (Lexington, Mass.: Lexington Books, 1979), 123.

35. Francis A. Allen, *The Decline of the Rehabilitative Ideal: Penal Policy and Social Purpose.* (New Haven: Yale University Press, 1981), 65.

36. Franklin E. Zimring and Gordon Hawkins, *Capital Punishment and the American Agenda* (New York: Cambridge University Press, 1986), 17–19.

37. Yale Komisar, "The 'Police Practice' Phases of the Criminal Process and the Three Phases of the Burger Court," in Herman Schwartz, ed., *The Burger Years: Rights and Wrongs in the Supreme Court 1969–1986* (New York: Viking Penguin, 1987), 167.

38. Some scholars have, however, held that nonvoting indicates satisfaction with government and has no effect on policy. Robert W. Jackman, "Political Institutions and Voter Turnout in the Industrial Democracies," *American Political Science Review* 81 (1987):405–423.

39. See, for instance, the Voting Rights Act renewal in 1982 and the Supreme Court's 1980 ruling in *PruneYard Shopping Center v. Robins,* 447 U.S. 74, that a state may favor free-speech rights over property rights in allowing political groups access to a private shopping center to circulate petitions.

40. Thomas Byrne Edsall, *The New Politics of Inequality* (New York: Norton, 1984), table 5.1.

41. Robert T. Sigler and Melody Horn, "Race, Income and Penetration of the Justice System," *Criminal Justice Review* 11 (1986):1–7; Jeffrey H. Reiman, *The Rich Get Richer and the Poor Get Prison: Ideol-*

ogy, Class, and Criminal Justice, 2nd ed. (New York: John Wiley and Sons, 1984).

42. For a recent survey of the various explanations of nonvoting, and a strong argument for the effect of voter registration requirements, see Frances Fox Piven and Richard A. Cloward, *Why Americans Don't Vote* (New York: Pantheon, 1988).

43. E. E. Schattschneider, *The Semisovereign People* (Hinsdale, Ill.: The Dryden Press, 1975), 102.

44. For a similar analysis, applied to policy on child abuse, see Barbara J. Nelson, *Making an Issue of Child Abuse: Political Agenda Setting for Social Problems* (Chicago: University of Chicago Press, 1984).

45. I am indebted to Elliott Currie for this analogy. *Confronting Crime*, 30.

46. Alarming increases in health-related consequences of drug use, especially for cocaine, are reported in Community Epidemiology Work Group, "Epidemiology of Drug Abuse in the United States and Europe," U.S. Department of Health and Human Services, June 1988.

47. For a recent treatment of these more general economic trends, see Barry Bluestone and Bennett Harrison, *The Great U-Turn: Corporate Restructuring and the Polarization of America*. (New York: Basic Books, 1988).

10. Broader and Deeper

1. See Michael Lipsky, *Street-level Bureaucracy: Dilemmas of the Individual in Public Services* (New York: Russell Sage, 1980), for an analysis of policy implementers as policymakers.

2. *Sourcebook 1987*, table 2.20.

3. Fear of walking in one's own neighborhood at night increased by fifty percent between 1967, a time of widespread prosperity, and 1981, when incomes of most working people had stagnated. They decreased significantly by 1987 (despite an apparent increase in crime), with a widely-shared perception of economic growth. See *Sourcebook 1981*, table 2.4, and *Sourcebook 1987*, tables 2.18 and 2.19. A somewhat different pattern appears to characterize attitudes toward punishment. Sixty-six percent of respondents to a national poll reported in 1972, before the economic slump of the mid-1970s, that they thought local courts did not deal harshly enough with criminals, a percentage that increased rapidly to 81 percent by 1976. There has been no significant change since then, despite economic growth from the mid-1980s on. See *Sourcebook 1981*, table 2.33, and *Sourcebook 1987*, table 2.20. These apparent anomalies suggest the presence of other, noneconomic influences on the trend in public attitudes toward crime and punishment—media and other reports of the prevalence and seriousness of crime, general perspectives on the performance of public institutions, shifting perspectives on the relative importance of drug offenses.

4. *Sourcebook 1987*, tables 2.4 and 2.6.

5. *Los Angeles Times*, Oct. 26, 1988.

6. *New York Times*, January 2, 1989.

7. Joseph E. Jacoby and Christopher S. Dunn, "National Survey on

Punishment for Criminal Offenses: Executive Summary," Bowling Green State University, 1987, 2. See also *Sourcebook 1987*, table 2.27.

8. *Los Angeles Times*, Oct. 26, 1988.

9. For a current prediction that the U.S. economy is likely to be weak during the next decade, see Benjamin Friedman, *Day of Reckoning* (New York: Random House, 1988).

10. For a summary of public views on police between 1967–1982, see "The Harris Survey," May 24, 1982.

11. George H. Gallup, *The Gallup Poll: Public Opinion 1982* (Wilmington, Del.: Scholarly Resources, Inc., 1983), 136.

12. H.R. 5210, *Congressional Record*, October 21, 1988:H11158.

13. 21 U.S.C. Section 841(b)(1)(A).

14. *Congressional Record*, October 21, 1988:H11157.

15. Seymour Martin Lipset and William Schneider, *The Confidence Gap: Business, Labor and Government in the Public Mind* (New York: The Free Press, 1983). For a picture of the positive attitudes of Americans toward their society in the early 1960s, see Robert E. Lane, "The Politics of Consensus in the Age of Affluence," *American Political Science Review* 59 (December 1965):874–895.

16. Daniel Yankelovich, "Emerging Norms in Public and Private Life," unpublished manuscript quoted in Lipset and Schneider, *The Confidence Gap*, 15.

17. *Sourcebook 1987*, tables 2.7, 2.8, and 2.10.

18. George Gallup, Jr., *The Gallup Poll: Public Opinion 1986* (Wilmington, Del.: Scholarly Resources, Inc., 1987), 208.

19. *Sourcebook 1987*, table 2.1.

20. *Economic Report of the President*, 1988, table B-46; U.S. Department of Labor, Bureau of Labor Statistics, *Employment and Earnings*, various years, tables C-1, C-2, C-4.

21. George Gallup, Jr., *The Gallup Poll: Public Opinion 1987* (Wilmington, Del.: Scholarly Resources, Inc., 1988), 89.

22. On the relationship between conservative economics and economic stagnation, see Samuel Bowles, David M. Gordon, and Thomas E. Weisskopf, "Business Ascendancy and Economic Impasse: A Structural Retrospective on Conservative Economics, 1979–87," *Journal of Economic Perspectives* 3 (1989):107–134.

23. For one recent treatment of these trends and probabilities, see Barry Bluestone and Bennett Harrison, *The Great U-Turn: Corporate Restructuring and the Polarization of America* (New York: Basic Books, 1988).

24. According to the National Crime Survey, 34 percent of victimizations for personal crimes were reported to the police in 1985, and 39 percent of household crimes. (Motor vehicle theft, with the highest rate of reporting, since insurance claims require a police report, is counted as a household crime.) U.S. Department of Justice, Bureau of Justice Statistics, "Criminal Victimization 1987," *Bulletin*, October 1988, table 6. The largest share of those who did not report crimes committed against them (26.4 percent for personal crimes, 28.6 percent for household crimes) did not do so because they thought the offense was "not important enough."

25. Community Epidemiology Work Group, "Epidemiology of Drug

Abuse in the United States and Europe," U.S. Department of Health and Human Services, June 1988.

26. *New York Times*, June 8, 1986.

27. This is not the first such political use of drug taking. For an analysis of drug crackdowns as reflections of race and class antagonisms, see John Helmer, *Drugs and Minority Oppression* (New York: Seabury, 1975).

28. It should be noted that on occasion even consistently conservative legislators abandon the hard-line stance when faced with its implications for civil liberties or social justice, as long as they don't have to be held accountable by the voters. New Hampshire Republican Senator Warren Rudman is said by Congressional staffers to have been very effectual—because of his background as a former state attorney general and his simon-pure conservative reputation—in removing a "good-faith exception" to the exclusionary rule from the Anti-Drug Abuse Act of 1988. He did it in conference committee, where he was unlikely to be taken to task by culturally right-wing New Hampshire voters.

29. *The Corrections Yearbook 1987*, 24.

30. Statistical Analysis Center, State of Delaware, "Lifers in Delaware: Future Costs and Populations through 1994," iii.

31. *New York Times*, July 1, 1987.

32. Jerome H. Skolnick and David H. Bayley, *The New Blue Line: Police Innovation in Six American Cities* (New York: The Free Press, 1986), 129.

33. Richard A. Berk and Peter H. Rossi, *Prison Reform and State Elites* (Cambridge, Mass.: Ballinger, 1977), Chapters 3 and 5.

34. *Law Enforcement News*, October 31, 1988.

35. An incomplete though revealing picture of expenditure trends in federal moneys for local justice programs can be found in *Sourcebook 1987*, table 1.11.

36. *Criminal Justice Newsletter*, November 15, 1988.

37. The perspective on permissiveness is well illustrated by Charles Murray, *Losing Ground: American Social Policy: 1950–1980* (New York: Basic Books, 1984); application of the perspective to delinquency can be found in Travis Hirschi, "Crime and Family Policy," *Journal of Contemporary Studies* 6 (1983):3–16.

38. Perhaps the most explicit scholarly embrace of government's responsibility to coerce social obligation is Lawrence M. Mead, *Beyond Entitlement* (New York: Free Press, 1986).

39. "Recruiting Trends," Collegiate Employment Research Institute, Michigan State University, 1987, 46.

11. Conclusion

1. *Statistical Abstract 1988*, tables 13 and 16.

2. Ibid., tables 15 and 16.

3. The development of improved predictors is an area of intense scholarly interest at this time. Two prominent researchers involved in it are Alfred Blumstein and Jacqueline Cohen of Carnegie-Mellon University.

4. James Q. Wilson, *Thinking About Crime*, rev. ed. (New York: Vintage Books, 1985), 240.

5. Many would be skeptical of my argument that economic factors strongly influence crime levels by pointing out that street crime began to escalate in the 1960s during a very prosperous period and was relatively low during the Depression. But these arguments overlook other features of those periods, the increasing youth unemployment in the 1960s and the strong family and government supports of the latter 1930s. Some will argue alternatively, with Wilson, that "the nature of man," corrupted by post-World War II permissiveness, is the principal determinant of criminality; but how then to explain the lower incidence of violence in European countries that are more permissive than we are with respect to sexual behavior and the disciplining of children? See Elliott Currie's discussion of all these issues in *Confronting Crime* (New York: Pantheon, 1985), esp. chs. 2 and 4.

6. For a cogent modern statement of classic liberalism, see Milton Friedman, *Capitalism and Freedom* (Chicago: University of Chicago Press, 1962).

7. Murray Edelman, *The Symbolic Uses of Politics* (Urbana, Ill.: University of Illinois, 1964), 14–15.

BIBLIOGRAPHY

Abel, Richard, ed., *The Politics of Informal Justice: The American Experience*. New York: Academic Press, 1982.

Agnew, Spiro T., *The Wisdom of Spiro T. Agnew*. New York: Ballantine, 1969.

"Agreements and Recommendations of the Attorney General's Bank Fraud Working Group," U.S. Department of Justice, April 2, 1985.

Allen, Francis A. *The Decline of the Rehabilitative Ideal: Penal Policy and Social Purpose*. New Haven: Yale University Press, 1981.

Allinson, Richard S., "LEAA's Impact on Criminal Justice: A Review of the Literature," *Criminal Justice Abstracts* 11 (1979).

Allison, Graham T., *The Essence of Decision*. Boston: Little, Brown and Co., 1971.

American Bar Association Criminal Justice Section, "Criminal Justice in Crisis," November 1988.

American Bar Association, *Standards for Criminal Justice: Sentencing Alternatives and Procedures*. Boston: Little, Brown, 1980.

American Friends Service Committee Working Party, *Struggle for Justice*. New York: Hill and Wang, 1971.

American Law Institute, *Model Penal Code and Commentaries*. Philadelphia: American Law Institute, 1985.

Anderson, David C., *Crimes of Justice: Improving the Police, the Courts, the Prisons*. New York: Times Books, 1988.

Anderson, Perry, *Passages from Antiquity to Feudalism*. London: Verso, 1978.

Anspach, Donald F; Peter M. Lehman; John H. Kramer, "Maine Rejects Indeterminacy: A Case Study of Flat Sentencing and Parole Abolition," University of Southern Maine, 1983.

Annual Report, 1986–87, Department of Corrections, State of Florida.

Appleby, Joyce Oldham, *Economic Thought and Ideology in Seventeenth-Century England*. Princeton. N.J.: Princeton University Press, 1978.

Augustus, John, *John Augustus, First Probation Officer*. Montclair, N.J.: Patterson Smith, 1972.

Austin, James and Barry Krisberg, "Wider, Stronger and Different Nets: The Dialectics of Criminal Justice Reform," *Journal of Research in Crime and Delinquency* 18 (1981).

Austin, James and Robert Tillman, "Ranking the Nation's Most Punitive States," *Focus*, entire issue, n.d.

Balbus, Isaac D., *The Dialectics of Legal Repression: Black Rebels Before the American Criminal Court*. New Brunswick, N.J.: Transaction, 1977.

Banfield, Edward, *The Unheavenly City: The Nature and the Future of Our Urban Crisis*. Boston: Little, Brown, 1970.

Banks, J.; A.L. Porter; R.L. Rardin; T.R. Silver; and V. E. Unger, *Evaluation of Intensive Special Probation Projects*. U.S. Department of Justice, National Institute of Law Enforcement and Criminal Justice, 1977.

Bardach, Eugene, *The Implementation Game*. Cambridge, Mass: M.I.T. Press, 1977.

Barkdull, Walter L., "Probation: Call It Control and Mean It," in Travis, Lawrence F., III; Martin D. Schwartz; and Todd R. Clear, *Corrections: An Issues Approach*, 2d edition. Cincinnati: Anderson, 1983.

Beattie, J.M., *Crime and the Courts in England, 1660–1800*. Princeton: Princeton University Press, 1986.

———, "The Pattern of Crime in England, 1660–1800," *Past and Present* 62 (1974).

Beccaria, Cesare, *On Crimes and Punishments*. (trans. Edward D. Ingraham). Stanford, Calif.: Academic Reprints, 1953.

Beck, Allen J. and Thomas Hester, "Prison Admissions and Releases," *Special Report*. U.S. Department of Justice, Bureau of Justice Statistics, 1986.

Becker, Gary S., *The Economic Approach to Human Behavior*. Chicago: University of Chicago Press, 1976.

Beecher, Janice A.; Robert L. Lineberry; and Michael J. Rich, "The Politics of Police Responses to Urban Crime," in Lewis, Dan A., *Reactions to Crime*. Beverly Hills, Calif.: Sage, 1981.

Behan, Cornelius J., "Repeat Offender Experiment," *Police Chief* 53 (1986).

Bellamy, John, *Crime and Public Order in England in the Late Middle Ages*. London: Routledge and Kegan Paul, 1973.

Bennett, Georgette, *CrimeWarps: The Future of Crime in America*. New York: Anchor Press, 1987.

Bennett, Lawrence A., "A Reassessment of Intensive Service Probation," in McCarthy, Belinda R., *Intermediate Punishments: Intensive Supervision, Home Confinement and Electronic Surveillance*. Monsey, N.Y.: Willow Tree Press, 1987.

Berger, B.M., *Working-Class Suburb: A Study of Auto Workers in Suburbia*. Berkeley: University of California Press, 1960.

Berk, Richard A. and Peter H. Rossi, *Prison Reform and State Elites*. Cambridge, Mass.: Ballinger, 1977.

Berman, Harold J. and Greiner, William R., *The Nature and Functions of Law*. 4th edition. Mineola, N.Y.: Foundation Press, 1980.

Berry, Bonnie, "Electronic Jails: A New Criminal Justice Concern," *Justice Quarterly* 2 (1985).

Bhaskar, Roy, "Dialectics," in Tom Bottomore, ed., *A Dictionary of Marxist Thought*. Cambridge, Mass.: Harvard University Press, 1983.

Black, Theodore and Orsagh, Thomas, "New Evidence on the Efficacy of Sanctions as a Deterrent to Homicide," *Social Science Quarterly* 58 (1978).

Block, Fred; Richard A. Cloward; Barbara Ehrenreich; and Frances Fox Piven, *The Mean Season: The Attack on the Welfare State*. New York: Pantheon Books, 1987.

Blomberg, Thomas G.; Gordon P. Waldo; and Lisa C. Burcroff, "Home Confinement and Electronic Surveillance," in McCarthy, Belinda R., *Intermediate Punishments: Intensive Supervision, Home Confinement and Electronic Surveillance*. Monsey, N.Y.: Willow Tree Press, 1987.

Bluestone, Barry and Bennett Harrison, *The Great U-Turn: Corporate Restructuring and the Polarization of America*. New York: Basic Books, 1988.

Blumberg, Abraham S., *Criminal Justice: Issues and Ironies*. 2d edition. New York: New Viewpoints, 1979.

Blumstein, Alfred, Jacqueline Cohen, and David P. Farrington, "Career Criminal Research: Its Value for Criminology." *Criminology* 26 (1988).

Blumstein, Alfred; Jacqueline Cohen; S.E. Martin; and Michael H. Tonry, eds., *Research on Sentencing: The Search for Reform*. Washington, D.C.: National Academy Press, 1983.

Blumstein, Alfred; Jacqueline Cohen; and Daniel Nagin, eds., *Deterrence and Incapacitation: Estimating the Effects of Criminal Sanctions on Crime Rates*. Washington, D.C.: National Academy Press, 1978.

Blumstein, Alfred; Jacqueline Cohen; Jeffrey A. Roth, and Christy A. Visher, eds., *Criminal Careers and "Career Criminals."* Washington, D.C.: National Academy Press, 1986.

Blumstein, Alfred and Elizabeth Graddy, "Prevalence and Recidivism in Index Arrests: A Feedback Model," *Law and Society Review* 16 (1981–82).

Bordua, David, *The Police: Six Sociological Essays*. New York: John Wiley and Sons, 1967.

Bowers, William J., *Legal Homicide: Death as Punishment in America, 1864–1982*. Boston: Northeastern University Press, 1984.

Bowker, Lee, "Crime and the Use of Prisons in the United States: A Time Series Analysis," *Crime and Delinquency* 27 (1981).

Bowles, Samuel and Herbert Gintis, *Schooling in Capitalist America: Educational Reform and the Contradictions of Economic Life*. New York: Basic Books, 1976.

Bowles, Samuel; David M. Gordon; and Thomas E. Weisskopf, *Beyond the Wasteland: A Democratic Alternative to Economic Decline*. Garden City, N.Y.: Anchor Press/Doubleday, 1983.

Bowles, Samuel; David M. Gordon; and Thomas E. Weisskopf, "Business Ascendancy and Economic Impasse: A Structural Retrospective on Conservative Economics, 1979–87," *Journal of Economic Perspectives* 3 (1989).

Braithwaite, John, *Inequality, Crime and Public Policy*. London: Routledge & Kegan Paul, 1978.

Brewer, David; Gerald E. Beckett ; and Norman Holt, "Determinate Sentencing in California: The First Year's Experience," *Journal of Research in Crime and Delinquency* 18 (1981).

Burnham, David, *The Rise of the Computer State*. New York: Random House, 1983.

Butterfoss, Edwin, "As Time Goes By: The Elimination of Contemporaniety and Brevity as Factors in Search and Seizure Cases," *Harvard Civil Rights/Civil Liberties Law Review* 21 (1986).

Bynum, Timothy S., "Prosecutorial Discretion and the Implementation of a Legislative Mandate," in Morash, Merry, *Implementing Criminal Justice Policies*. Beverly Hills, Calif.: Sage, 1982.

Byrne, James M., "The Control Controversy: A Preliminary Examination of Intensive Probation Supervision Programs in the United States," *Federal Probation* 50 (June 1986).

———, "Probation," *Crime Study File*. U.S. Department of Justice, National Institute of Justice, 1988.

Caldeira, Gregory A., "Elections and the Politics of Crime: Budgetary Choices and Priorities in America," in Nagel, Stuart; Erika Fairchild; and Anthony Champagne, eds., *The Political Science of Criminal Justice*. Springfield, Ill.: Charles C. Thomas, 1983.

California Department of Justice, "1975 California Comprehensive Plan for Criminal Justice," 1974.

Callahan, Lisa, Connie Mayer, and Henry J. Steadman, "Insanity Defense Reform in the United States—Post-Hinckley," *Mental and Physical Disability Law Reporter* 11 (1987).

Campbell, Donald and H. Lawrence Ross, "The Connecticut Crackdown on Speeding," *Law and Society Review* 3 (1968).

Carey, Sarah C., *Law and Disorder*, vol. 4. Washington, D.C.: Lawyer's Committee for Civil Rights Under Law, 1973.

Carlson, Jody, *George C. Wallace and the Politics of Powerlessness: The Wallace Campaigns for the Presidency, 1964–1976*. New Brunswick, N.J.: Transaction Books, 1981.

Carlson, Kenneth, *Mandatory Sentencing: The Experience of Two States*. Washington, D.C.: National Institute of Justice, 1982.

Carrington, Frank, *Crime and Justice: A Conservative Strategy*. Washington, D.C.: Heritage Foundation, 1983.

Cash, W.J., *The Mind of the South*. New York: Vintage Books, 1941.

Chaiken, Jan and Marcia Chaiken, *Varieties of Criminal Behavior*. Santa Monica, Calif.: RAND Corporation, 1982.

Chambliss, William, J. "The State, the Law and the Definition of Behavior as Criminal or Delinquent," in Glaser, Daniel (ed.), *Handbook of Criminology*. Indianapolis: Bobbs-Merrill, 1974.

———, "Toward A Radical Criminology," in David Kairys, ed., *The Politics of Law: A Progressive Critique*. New York: Pantheon Books, 1982.

Chelimsky, Eleanor and Judith Dahmann, *Career Criminal Program National Evaluation, Final Report*. Washington, D.C.: National Institute of Justice, 1981.

Chester, Lewis; Hodgson, Godfrey; and Page, Bruce, *An American Melodrama: The Presidential Campaign of 1968*. New York: Dell, 1969.

Chevalier, Louis, *Laboring Classes and Dangerous Classes*. Princeton, N.J.: Princeton University Press, 1973.

Christie, Nils, "Conflicts as Property," *British Journal of Criminology* 17 (1977).

———, *Limits to Pain*. Oslo: Universitetsforlaget, 1981.

Churchill, Mae and Harold Brackman, "The Hidden Agenda: LEAA and the Tools of Repression," 1980.

Chute, Charles Lionel and Marjorie Bell, *Crime, Courts and Probation*. New York: Macmillan and Co., 1956.

Clarke, Stevens, "Felony Sentencing in North Carolina, 1976–1986: Effects of Presumptive Sentencing Legislation," Institute of Government, University of North Carolina (1987).

Clear, Todd R.; Suzanne Flynn; and Carol Shapiro, "Intensive Supervision in Probation: A Comparison of Three Projects," in McCarthy, Belinda R. *Intermediate Punishments: Intensive Supervision, Home Confinement and Electronic Surveillance*. Monsey, N.Y.: Criminal Justice Press, 1987.

Clear, Todd R. and Vincent O'Leary, *Controlling the Offender in the Community*. Lexington, Mass.: Lexington Books, 1983.

Cohen, Jacqueline, "Incapacitation as a Strategy for Crime Control: Possibilities and Pitfalls," in Morris, Norval and Michael Tonry, eds., *Crime and Justice: Annual Review of Research*, Vol. 5. Chicago: University of Chicago, 1983.

Cohen, Stanley, "Breaking Out, Smashing Up and the Social Context of Aspiration," in Krisberg, Barry and James Austin, eds., *The Children of Ishmael*. Palo Alto, Calif.: Mayfield, 1978.

———, *Visions of Social Control*. Cambridge, U.K.: Polity Press, 1985.

———, ed., *Social Control and the State*. New York: St.Martin's, 1983.

Commager, Henry Steele, *The American Mind: An Interpreter of American Thought and Character Since the 1880s*. New Haven, Conn.: Yale University Press, 1950.

"Community Control II (Electronic Anklets) Preliminary Field Assessment of Tampa Pilot Project," draft report, Florida Department of Corrections, Probation and Parole Services, 1988.

Community Epidemiology Work Group, "Epidemiology of Drug Abuse in the United States and Europe," U. S. Department of Health and Human Services, June 1988.

Congressional Budget Office, "The Changing Distribution of Federal Taxes: 1975–1990." Congress of the United States, Congressional Budget Office, 1987.

Conrad, John P., "News of the Future: The Intensive Revolution," *Federal Probation* 50 (June 1986).

Cook, Fay Lomax, "Crime and the Elderly: The Emergence of a Policy Issue," in Lewis, Dan A., *Reactions to Crime*. Beverly Hills, Calif.: Sage, 1981.

Corbett, Ronald P., Jr.; Donald Cochran; and James M. Byrne, "Making Change in Probation: Principles and Practice in the Implementation of an Intensive Probation Supevision Program," in McCarthy, Belinda R., *Intermediate Punishments: Intensive Supervision, Home Confinement and Electronic Surveillance*. Monsey, N.Y.: Criminal Justice Press, 1987.

Corbett, Ronald P. Jr., and Gary T. Marx, "When A Man's Castle Is His Prison," unpublished paper, 1987.

Corrections Yearbook 1981. South Salem, N.Y.: Criminal Justice Institute, 1981.

Corrections Yearbook 1987. South Salem, N.Y.: Criminal Justice Institute, 1987.

"Criminal Intelligence File Guidelines," State of California Department of Justice, Division of Law Enforcement, n.d.

Cullen, Francis T.; Timothy S. Bynum; Kim Montgomery Garrett; Lynn A. Curtis, ed., *American Violence and Public Policy*. New Haven, Conn.: Yale University Press, 1985.

Cullen, Francis T.; Timothy S. Bynum; Kim Montgomery Garrett; and Jack R. Greene, "Legislator Ideology and Criminal Justice Policy: Implications from Illinois," in Fairchild, Erika S., and Vincent J. Webb, eds., *The Politics of Crime and Criminal Justice*. Beverly Hills, Calif.: Sage, 1985.

Cullen, Francis T. and Karen E. Gilbert, *Reaffirming Rehabilitation*. Cincinnati, Ohio: Anderson, 1982.

Currie, Elliott, *Confronting Crime: An American Challenge*. New York: Pantheon, 1985.

Dahl, Robert A., *Dilemmas of Pluralist Democracy: Autonomy vs. Control*. New Haven, Conn.: Yale University Press, 1982.

Danziger, James N.; William H. Dutton; Rob Kling; and Kenneth L. Kraemer, *Computers and Politics*. New York: Columbia University Press, 1982.

Davies, Thomas Y., "A Hard Look at What We Know (and Still Need to Learn) About the 'Costs' of the Exclusionary Rule," *American Bar Foundation Research Journal* (Summer 1983).

Davis, Mike, "Los Angeles: Civil Liberties between the Hammer and the Rock," *New Left Review* #170 (July/August 1988).

Decker, Scott H. and Kohfeld, Carol H., "An Empirical Analysis of the Effect of the Death Penalty in Missouri," *Journal of Crime and Justice* 10 (1987).

del Carmen, Rolando V. and Vaughn, Joseph B., "Issues in the Use of Electronic Surveillance," *Federal Probation* 50 (June 1986).

Department of Corrections, Florida, "Community Control II(Electronic Anklets) Preliminary Field Asessment of Tampa Pilot Project" (draft), Feb. 1, 1988.

Directory of Criminal Justice Issues in the States. Washington, D.C.: Criminal Justice Statistics Association, 1986.

"Domestic Security Investigation and Individual Rights under the Justice Department's New Guidelines," Section on Individual Rights and Responsibilities, American Bar Association, January 14, 1985.

Donzelot, Jacques, *Policing of Families*. New York: Pantheon, 1979.

Dror, Yehezkel, *Public Policymaking Reexamined*. San Francisco: Chandler Publishing Company, 1968.

Durkheim, Emile, *The Rules of Sociological Method*. New York: Free Press, 1982.

———, *Selected Writings*. (ed., Anthony Giddens). Cambridge, U.K.: Cambridge University Press, 1972.

Earle, Alice Morse, *Curious Punishments of Bygone Days*. Montclair, N.J.: Patterson Smith, 1969.

Economic Report of the President. Washington, DC: U.S. Government Printing Office, 1988.

Edelman, Murray, *The Symbolic Uses of Politics*. Urbana, Ill.: University of Illinois, 1964.

Edsall, Thomas Byrne, *The New Politics of Inequality*. New York: Norton, 1984.

Eisenstein, James and Jacob, Herbert, *Felony Justice: An Organizational Analysis of Criminal Courts*. Boston: Little, Brown, 1977.

Elder, Charles and Roger Cobb, *The Political Uses of Symbols*. New York: Longman, 1983.

Elias, Norbert, *The Civilizing Process: The History of Manners* (Vol. I). New York: Urizen Books, 1978.

Elias, Robert, *The Politics of Victimization: Victims, Victimology and Human Rights*. New York: Oxford University Press, 1986.

Erwin, Billie S., "Evaluation of Intensive Probation Supervision in Georgia," Georgia Department of Corrections, 1987.

———, "Turning Up the Heat on Probationers in Georgia," *Federal Probation* 50 (June 1986).

Evans, Joseph H.; Linda Smith; and Joan K. Hall, "A Study of the Impact of Community Control as an Alternative to Incarceration," Florida Mental Health Institute, University of South Florida, 1986.

Fairchild, Erika S., "Interest Groups in the Criminal Justice Process," *Journal of Criminal Justice* 9 (1981).

Fairchild, Erika S., and Vincent J. Webb, eds., *The Politics of Crime and Criminal Justice*. Beverly Hills, Calif.: Sage, 1985.

Federal Bureau of Investigation, *Uniform Crime Reports, Crime in the United States*, various years. Washington, D.C.: U.S. Government Printing Office.

Feeley, Malcolm, *Court Reform on Trial: Why Simple Solutions Fail*. New York: Basic Books, 1983.

———, *The Process Is the Punishment: Handling Cases in a Lower Criminal Court*. New York: Russell Sage Foundation, 1979.

Feeley, Malcolm and Austin D. Sarat, *The Policy Dilemma: Federal Crime Policy and the LEAA, 1968–1978*. Minneapolis: University of Minnesota Press, 1980.

Finckenauer, James O., "Crime as a National Political Issue, 1964–76—from Law and Order to Domestic Tranquility," *Crime and Delinquency* 24 (1978).

Fine, Sidney, *Laissez Faire and the General-Welfare State: A Study of Conflict in American Thought, 1865–1901*. Ann Arbor: Ann Arbor Paperbacks/University of Michigan Press, 1964.

Fishman, Mark, "Crimes Waves as Ideology," *Social Problems* 25 (1978).

Flaherty, David, "Protecting Privacy in Police Information Systems," *University of Toronto Law Journal* 36 (1986).

Flanagan, Timothy J. and Susan L. Caulfield, "Public Opinion and Prison Policy: A Review," *Prison Journal* 64 (1984).

Fletcher, George, *Rethinking Criminal Law*. Boston: Little, Brown and Co., 1978.

Florida Department of Corrections, Probation and Parole Services, "Community Control Orientation Booklet," no date.

Florida Department of Corrections, Probation and Parole Services, "Community Control II (Electronic Anklets): Preliminary Field Assessment of Tampa Pilot Project," February 1, 1988.

Fogel, David, *"...We Are the Living Proof..." The Justice Model for Corrections*. Cincinnati: W.H. Anderson, 1975.

Forst, Brian; Judith Lucianovic, and Sarah J. Cox, *What Happens After Arrest?* Washington, D.C.: INSLAW, 1977.

Foucault, Michel, *Discipline and Punish.* New York: Pantheon, 1977.

Fox, Vernon, *Community Based Corrections.* Englewood Cliffs, N.J.: Prentice-Hall, 1977.

Frady, Marshall, *Wallace.* New York: Meridian Books, 1968.

Freeman, J. Leiper, *The Political Process.* New York: Random House, 1965.

Friedman, Benjamin, *Day of Reckoning.* New York: Random House, 1988.

Friedman, Milton, *Capitalism and Freedom.* Chicago: University of Chicago Press, 1962.

Friel, Charles M., "Critical Issues in the Future of Community Corrections," address delivered at the annual meeting of the American Probation and Parole Association, August 25, 1987.

Friel, Charles M. and Joseph B. Vaughn, "A Consumer's Guide to the Electronic Monitoring of Probationers," *Federal Probation* 50 (June 1986).

Friel, Charles M.; Joseph B. Vaughn; and Rolando del Carmen, "Electronic Monitoring and Correctional Policy: The Technology and Its Application," U.S. Department of Justice, National Institute of Justice, June 1987.

Fritscher, A. Lee, *Smoking and Politics: Policymaking and the Federal Bureaucracy,* 4th edition. Englewood Cliffs, N.J.: Prentice-Hall, 1989.

Fyfe, James J., "The NIJ Study of the Exclusionary Rule," *Criminal Law Bulletin* 19 (1983).

Gallup, George, *The Gallup Poll: Public Opinion, 1935–1971.* New York: Random House, 1972.

Gallup Organization, *The Gallup Poll: Public Opinion, 1972–1977.* Wilmington, Del.: Scholarly Resources, 1978.

Gallup Organization, *The Gallup Poll: Public Opinion 1982.* Wilmington, Del.: Scholarly Resources, Inc., 1982.

Gans, Herbert, *The Levittowners.* New York: Vintage Books, 1967.

Garland, David and Peter Young, "Towards a Social Analysis of Penality," in Garland, David and Peter Young, eds., *The Power to Punish: Contemporary Penality and Social Analysis.* London: Heinemann, 1983.

Garraty, John A., *The New Commonwealth 1877–1890.* New York: Harper Torchbooks, 1968.

Gatrell, V.A.C.; Bruce Lenman; and Geoffrey Parker (eds.), *Crime and the Law: The Social History of Crime in Western Europe since 1500.* London: Europa Publications, 1980.

General Accounting Office, *State and County Probation: Systems in Crisis.* Washington, D.C.: Government Printing Office, 1976.

Gerth, H.H. and C. Wright Mills, *From Max Weber: Essays in Sociology.* New York: Oxford University Press, 1946.

Gettinger, Stephen, "Intensive Supervision: Can It Rehabilitate Probation?" *Corrections Magazine* IX (1983).

Gibbons, Don C., *Changing the Lawbreaker.* Englewood Cliffs, N.J.: Prentice-Hall, 1965.

————, "The Limits of Punishment as Social Policy," National Council on Crime and Delinquency, 1988.

————, *Society, Crime, and Criminal Behavior*. Englewood Cliffs, N.J.: Prentice-Hall, 1982.

Goldkamp, John S., "Danger and Detention: A Second Generation of Bail Reform," *Journal of Criminal Law and Criminology* 76 (1985).

Goldstein, Abraham, *The Insanity Defense*. New Haven: Yale University Press, 1967.

Goldstein, Herman, *Policing A Free Society*. Cambridge, Mass.: Ballinger, 1977.

Goodstein, Lynne and John Hepburn, "Determinate Sentencing in Illinois: An Assessment of Its Development and Implementation," *Criminal Justice Policy Review* 1 (1986).

Goodstein, Lynne; John H. Kramer; and Laura Nuss, "Defining Determinacy: Components of the Sentencing Process Ensuring Equity and Release Certainty," *Justice Quarterly* 1 (1984).

Gordon, David M.; Richard Edwards; and Michael Reich, *Segmented Work, Divided Workers*. Cambridge: Cambridge University Press, 1982.

Gordon, Diana R., "The Electronic Panopticon: A Case Study of the Development of the National Criminal Records System," *Politics and Society* 15 (1986–87).

Gottfredson, Michael R. and Travis Hirschi. "The True Value of Lambda Would Appear to Be Zero: An Essay on Career Criminals, Criminal Careers, Selective Incapacitation, Cohort Studies, and Related Topics." *Criminology* 24 (1986).

Gottfredson, Michael R.; Susan D. Mitchell-Herzfeld; and Timothy J. Flanagan, "Another Look at the Effectiveness of Parole Supervision," *Journal of Research in Crime and Delinquency* 19 (1982).

Graham, Fred P., *The Due Process Revolution: The Warren Court's Impact on Criminal Law*. New York: Hayden Book Company, 1970.

Greenberg, David F., "The Cost-Benefit Analysis of Imprisonment," unpublished paper, 1988.

————, "Delinquency and the Age Structure of Society," in Greenberg, David F., ed., *Crime and Capitalism: Readings in Marxist Criminology*. Palo Alto, Calif.: Mayfield, 1981.

————, "Rehabilitation Is Still Punishment," *The Humanist* 32 (1972).

————, "The Incapacitative Effect of Imprisonment: Some Estimates," *Law and Society Review* 9 (1975).

Greenberg, David F. amd Humphries, Drew, "The Cooptation of Fixed Sentencing Reform," *Crime and Delinquency* 26 (1980).

Greenwood, Peter, with Allan Abrahamse, *Selective Incapacitation*. Santa Monica, Calif.: RAND Corporation, 1982.

Gurr, Ted Robert, "Historical Trends in Violent Crime: A Critical Review of the Evidence," in Morris, Norval and Michael Tonry, eds., *Crime and Justice: An Annual Review of Research* 3 (1981).

————, *Rogues, Rebels and Reformers: A Political History of Urban Crime and Conflict*. Beverly Hills, Calif.: Sage, 1976.

Gusfield, Joseph, *Symbolic Crusade*. Urbana, Ill.: University of Illinois, 1963.

Hagan, John, "Symbolic Justice: "The Status Politics of the American Probation Movement," *Sociological Focus* 12 (1979).

_____, "The Symbolic Politics of Criminal Sanctions," in Nagel, Stuart; Erika Fairchild; and Anthony Champagne, eds., *The Political Science of Criminal Justice*. Springfield, Ill.: Charles C. Thomas, 1983.

Hamparian, Donna, et al, "Youth in Adult Courts: Between Two Worlds." U.S. Department of Justice, National Institute for Juvenile Justice and Delinquency Prevention, 1982.

Hanawalt, Barbara A., *Crime and Conflict in English Communities, 1300–1348*. Cambridge, Mass.: Harvard Univerity Press, 1979.

Harding, John, ed., *Probation and the Community: A Practice and Policy Reader*. London: Tavistock Publications, 1987.

Hargrove, Erwin, *The Missing Link: The Study of the Implementation of Social Policy*. Washington, D.C.: The Urban Institute, 1976.

Harring, Sidney L., *Policing a Class Society*. New Brunswick, N.J.: Rutgers University Press, 1983.

Harris, Louis, "The Harris Survey," various dates.

Harris, Louis, *The Public Looks at Crime and Corrections*. Washington, D.C.: Joint Commission on Correctional Manpower and Training, 1968.

Harris, Philip W., "Oversimplification and Error in Public Opinion Surveys on Capital Punishment," *Justice Quarterly* 3 (1986).

Harris, Richard, *The Fear of Crime*. New York: Praeger, 1969.

Hart, H.L.A., *The Concept of Law*. Oxford: Clarendon Press, 1961.

Hausner, Jack and Michael Seidel, *An Analysis of Case Processing Time in the District of Columbia Superior Court*. Washington, D.C.: INSLAW, 1981.

Hay, Douglas, "Property, Authority and the Criminal Law," in Hay, Douglas; Peter Linebaugh; John G. Rule; E.P. Thompson; and Cal Winslow, *Albion's Fatal Tree: Crime and Society in Eighteenth-Century England*. New York: Pantheon, 1975.

Heinz, Anne M., *Governmental Responses to Crime. Legislative Responses to Crime: The Changing Content of Criminal Law*. Washington, D.C.: National Institute of Justice, 1982.

Heinz, Anne; Herbert Jacob; and Robert Lineberry, eds., *Crime in City Politics*. New York: Longman, 1983.

Helmer, John, *Drugs and Minority Oppression*. New York: Seabury, 1975.

Hermann, D.H.J, *The Insanity Defense: Philosophical, Historical and Legal Perspectives*. Springfield, Ill.: Charles C. Thomas, 1983.

Heumann, Milton and Colin Loftin, "Mandatory Sentencing and the Abolition of Plea Bargaining: The Michigan Felony Firearm Statute," *Law and Society Review* 13 (1979).

Heumann, Milton; Colin Loftin; and David McDowall; "Federal Firearms Policy and Mandatory Sentencing," *Journal of Criminal Law and Criminology* 73 (1982).

Hillsman-Baker, Sally, *Court Employment Program Evaluation: A Summary of Findings*. New York: Vera Institute of Justice, 1979.

Hirschi, Travis, "Crime and Family Policy," *Journal of Contemporary Studies* 6 (1983).

Hobsbawm, Eric J., *Primitive Rebels*. New York: Praeger, 1963.

Hodgson, Godfrey, *America in Our Time*. New York: Vintage Books, 1976.

Hofstadter Richard, *The Paranoid Style in American Politics*. New York: Knopf, 1965.

Hopkins, Andrew, "Imprisonment and Recidivism: A Quasi-Experimental Study," *Journal of Research in Crime and Delinquency* 13 (1976).

Hornung, James J.; Peter G. Neumann; David D. Redell; Janlori Goldman; and Diana R. Gordon, "A Review of NCIC 2000: The Proposed Design for the National Crime Information Center," unpublished study submitted to the Subcommittee on Civil and Constitutional Rights of the House Judiciary Committee, February 1989.

"HRA/ACD Day Care/Head Start Program Fingerprinting and Criminal Record Review Report for the Month of October, 1985," Human Resources Administration, City of New York, unpaginated.

Hudzik, John K., *Federal Aid to Criminal Justice*. Washington, D.C.: National Criminal Justice Association, 1984.

Hussey, Frederick A. and Stephen P. Lagoy, "The Determinate Sentence and Its Impact on Parole," *Criminal Law Bulletin* 19 (1983).

Immarigeon, Russ, "Public Supports Alternatives to Executions," *Jericho* #43 (Summer 1987).

―――, "Surveys Reveal Broad Support for Alternative Sentencing," *National Prison Project Journal* #9 (Fall 1986).

Inciardi, James A., *Radical Criminology: The Coming Crisis*. Beverly Hills, Calif.: Sage, 1980.

"Intensive Supervision Program: A Process Evaluation," New York State Division of Probation, 1982.

"Intensive Supervision Program: Progress Report, January 1988," Administrative Office of the Courts, State of New Jersey.

Ives, George. *A History of Penal Methods: Criminals, Witches, Lunatics*. London: Stanley Paul and Co., 1914.

Jacob, Herbert, *The Frustration of Policy: Responses to Crime by American Cities*. Boston: Little, Brown, 1984.

Jacob, Herbert and Robert L. Lineberry; with Anne M. Heinz; Michael J. Rich; and Duane H. Swank, *Governmental Responses to Crime: Crime and Governmental Responses in American Cities*. Washington, D.C.: National Institute of Justice, 1982.

Jacoby, Joseph E. and Christopher S. Dunn, "National Survey on Punishment for Criminal Offenses: Executive Summary," Bowling Green State University, 1987.

Jenkins, Philip, "From Gallows to Prison? The Execution Rate in Early Modern England," in *Criminal Justice History: An International Annual* VII (1986).

John Augustus, First Probation Officer. Montclair, N.J.: Patterson Smith, 1972.

Joint Committee on New York Drug Law Evaluation, *The Nation's Toughest Drug Law: Evaluating the New York Experience*. New York: The Association of the Bar of the City of New York, 1977.

Judge, Frank T. III, "Relief for Prison Overcrowding: Evaluating Michigan's Accelerated Parole Statute," in *University of Michigan Journal of Law Reform* 15 (1982).

Kalish, Carol B., "International Crime Rates," *Special Report*. U.S. Department of Justice, Bureau of Justice Statistics, May 1988.

Kant, Immanuel, *The Metaphysical Elements of Justice*. New York: Bobbs-Merrill, 1965.

Kelling, George L.; Tony Pate; Duane Dickman; and Charles E. Brown, *The Kansas City Preventive Patrol Experiment: A Technical Report*. Washington, D.C.: Police Foundation, 1974.

Key, V.O., *Public Opinion and American Democracy*. New York: Alfred A. Knopf, 1961.

Kingdon, John W., *Agendas, Alternatives, and Public Policies*. Boston: Little, Brown, 1984.

Kirchheimer, Otto and Georg Rusche, *Punishment and Social Structure*. New York: Columbia University Press, 1938.

Klofas, John and Ralph Weisheit, "Guilty but Mentally Ill: Reform of the Insanity Defense in Illinois," *Justice Quarterly* 4 (1987).

Komisar, Yale, "The 'Police Practice' Phases of the Criminal Process and the Three Phases of the Burger Court," in Schwartz, Herman, ed., *The Burger Years: Rights and Wrongs in the Supreme Court 1969–1986*. New York: Viking Penguin, 1987.

Knafla, L.A. (ed.), *Crime and Criminal Justice in Europe and Canada*. Waterloo, Canada: Wilfred Laurier University Press, 1981.

Krajick, Kevin, "Abolishing Parole: An Idea Whose Time Has Passed," *Corrections Magazine* 9 (1983).

Krajick, Kevin, "'Not on My Block:' Local Opposition Impedes the Search for Alternatives," *Corrections Magazine* 6 (1980).

Kramer, John H. and Robin L. Lubitz, "Pennsylvania's Sentencing Reform: The Impact of Commission-Established Guidelines," *Crime and Delinquency* 31 (1985).

Krantz, Sheldon; Bernard Gilman; Charles G. Benda; Carol Rogoff Hallstrom; and Gail J. Nadworny, *Police Policymaking*. Lexington, Mass.: Lexington Books, 1979.

Krisberg, Barry and James Austin, *The Children of Ishmael: Critical Perspectives on Juvenile Justice*. Palo Alto, Calif.: Mayfield, 1978.

Krisberg, Barry; Ira M. Schwartz; Paul Litsky; and James Austin, "The Watershed of Juvenile Justice Reform," *Crime and Delinquency* 32 (1986).

Kristol, Irving, *Reflections of A Neoconservative*. New York: Basic Books, 1983.

Kuttner, Robert, *The Revolt of the Haves*. New York: Simon and Schuster, 1980.

LaFave, Wayne, "Fourth Amendment Vagaries (Of Improbable Cause, Imperceptible Plain View, Notorious Privacy and Balancing Askew)," *Journal of Criminal Law and Criminology* 74 (1983).

Langan, Patrick A.; John V. Fundis; Lawrence A. Greenfeld; and Victoria W. Schneider, "Historical Statistics on Prisoners in State and Federal Institutions, Yearend 1925–86," U.S. Department of Justice, Bureau of Justice Statistics, 1988.

Langan, Patrick A. and Lawrence A. Greenfeld, "The Prevalence of Imprisonment," *Special Report*, U.S. Department of Justice, Bureau of Justice Statistics, July 1985.

Latessa, Edward J., "The Effectiveness of Intensive Supervision with

High Risk Probationers," in McCarthy, Belinda, *Intermediate Punishments: Intensive Supervision, Home Confinement and Electronic Surveillance*. Monsey, N.Y.: Criminal Justice Press, 1987.

Laudon, Kenneth C., *The Dossier Society: Value Choices in the Design of National Information Systems*. New York: Columbia Univ. Press, 1986.

Lawyer's Committee for Civil Rights Under Law, *Law and Disorder III: State and Federal Performance under Title I of the Omnibus Crime Control and Safe Streets Act of 1968*. Washington, D.C.: Lawyer's Committee for Civil Rights Under Law, 1973.

Lea, John and Jock Young, *What Is To Be Done About Law and Order?* Middlesex, U.K.: Penguin, 1984.

LEAA Eleventh Annual Report, Fiscal Year 1979. U.S. Department of Justice, Law Enforcement Assistance Administration, 1980.

Lemert, Edwin M., "Diversion in Juvenile Justice: What Hath Been Wrought?" *Journal of Research in Crime and Delinquency* 18 (1981).

Levine, James P., "The Ineffectiveness of Adding Police to Prevent Crime," *Public Policy* 23 (1975).

———, "Jury Toughness: The Impact of Conservatism on Criminal Court Verdicts," *Crime and Delinquency* 29 (1983).

Lindblom, Charles E., *The Policy-Making Process*. Englewood Cliffs, N.J.: Prentice-Hall, 1980.

Lipchitz, Joseph W., "Back to the Future: An Historical View of Intensive Probation Supervision," *Federal Probation* 50 (June 1986).

Lipset, Seymour Martin and William Schneider, *The Confidence Gap: Business, Labor and Government in the Public Mind*. New York: The Free Press, 1983.

Lipsky, Michael, *Street-level Bureaucracy: Dilemmas of the Individual in Public Services*. New York: Russell Sage, 1980.

Lipton, Douglas; Robert Martinson; and Judith Wilks, *The Effectiveness of Correctional Treatment: A Survey of Treatment Evaluation Studies*. New York: Praeger, 1975.

Locke, John, "An Essay Concerning the True Original, Extent, and End of Civil Government," in *Two Treatises of Civil Government*. New York: E. P. Dutton, 1953.

Loftin, Colin and David McDowall, "'One with a Gun Gets You Two': Mandatory Sentencing and Firearms Violence in Detroit," *The Annals* 455 (1981).

Lowi, Theodore J., "American Business, Public Policy, Case Studies, and Political Theory," *World Politics* 16 (1964).

———, *The End of Liberalism: The Second Republic of the United States*. New York: Norton, 1979.

Lukas, J. Anthony, *Common Ground: A Turbulent Decade in the Lives of Three American Families*. New York: Knopf, 1985.

Lupsha, Peter A. and William J. Siembieda, "The Poverty of Public Services in the Land of Plenty: An Analysis and Interpretation," in Perry, David C. and Alfred J. Watkins, *The Rise of the Sunbelt Cities*. Beverly Hills, Calif.: Sage, 1977.

Marchand, Donald A. and Eva G. Bogan, *A History and Background Assessment of the National Crime Information Center and Computerized Criminal History Program*. University of South Carolina, Bureau of Governmental Research and Service, 1979.

Martin, John Bartlow, *Break Down the Walls: American Prisons— Present, Past and Future*. New York: Ballantine Books, 1954.

Martin, Susan E., "Policing Career Criminals: An Examination of an Innovative Career Criminal Program," *Journal of Criminal Law and Criminology* 77 (1986).

Martinson, Robert, "What Works—Questions and Answers About Prison Reform," *The Public Interest* (Spring 1974).

Mathiesen, Thomas, "The Future of Control Systems—The Case of Norway," in Garland, David and Young, Peter, eds., *The Power to Punish: Contemporary Penality and Social Analysis*. London: Heinemann, 1983.

Matza, David, *Delinquency and Drift*. New York: John Wiley and Sons, 1964.

McAnany, Patrick D.; Doug Thomson; and David Fogel, eds., *Probation and Justice: Reconsideration of Mission*. Cambridge, Mass.: Oelgeschlager, Gunn, and Hain, 1984.

McCarthy, Belinda R., *Intermediate Punishments: Intensive Supervision, Home Confinement and Electronic Surveillance*. Monsey, N.Y.: Criminal Justice Press, 1987.

McCord, William and Jose Sanchez, "The Treatment of Deviant Children: A Twenty-Five Year Follow-Up Study," *Crime and Delinquency* 29 (1983).

McGillis, Daniel, *An Exemplary Project: Major Offense Bureau, Bronx District Attorney's Office, New York*. Washington, D.C.: U.S.Government Printing Office, 1977.

McMullan, John L., *The Canting Crew: London's Criminal Underworld, 1550–1700*. New Brunswick, N.J.: Rutgers University Press, 1984.

Mead, Lawrence M., *Beyond Entitlement*. New York: Free Press, 1986.

Melossi, Dario and Massimo Pavarini, *The Prison and the Factory: Origins of the Penitentiary System*. London: Macmillan, 1981.

Meltsner, Arnold J. and Christopher Bellavita, *The Policy Organization*. Beverly Hills, Calif.: Sage, 1983.

Meltsner, Michael, *Cruel and Unusual: The Supreme Court and Capital Punishment*. New York: Random House, 1973.

———, "On Death Row, the Wait Continues," in Schwartz, Herman, ed. *The Burger Years: Rights and Wrongs in the Supreme Court, 1969– 1986*. New York: Viking Penguin, 1987.

Menninger, Karl, *The Crime of Punishment*. New York: Viking Press, 1969.

Merton, Robert K., *Social Theory and Social Structure*. New York: Free Press, 1968.

Michalowski, Raymond J., *Order, Law, and Crime*. New York: Random House, 1985.

Milakovich, Michael, "Politics and Measure of Success in the War on Crime," *Crime and Delinquency* 21 (1975).

Miller, Arthur, *The Assault on Privacy: Computers, Data Banks, and Dossiers*. Ann Arbor: University of Michigan Press, 1971.

Miller, Herbert S., "The Closed Door: The Effect of a Criminal Record on Employment with State and Local Public Agencies." U.S. Department of Labor, Manpower Administration Office of Research and Development, Report No. 81-09-70-02, 1972.

Miller, Neal, "A Study of the Number of Persons with Records of Arrest or Conviction in the Labor Force," U.S. Department of Labor, Technical Analysis Paper no. 63, 1979.

Mollenkopf, John, "The Crisis of the Public Sector in America's Cities," in Alcaly, Roger E. and Marmelstein, David, *The Fiscal Crisis of American Cities*. New York: Vintage, 1976.

Monahan, John, "The Prediction of Violent Criminal Behavior: A Methodological Critique and Prospectus," in Alfred Blumstein, Jacqueline Cohen, and Daniel Nagin, eds., *Deterrence and Incapacitation: Estimating the Effects of Criminal Sanctions on Crime Rates*. Washington, D.C.: National Academy of Sciences, 1978.

Moore, Charles A. and Terance D. Miethe, "Regulated and Unregulated Sentencing Decisions: An Analysis of First-year Practices Under Minnesota's Felony Sentencing Guidelines," *Law and Society Review* 20 (1986).

Morris, Norval, *The Future of Imprisonment*. Chicago: University of Chicago, 1974.

Morris, Norval and Gordon Hawkins, *The Honest Politician's Guide to Crime Control*. Chicago: University of Chicago Press, 1969.

Morris, Norval and Michael Tonry, eds., *Crime and Justice: An Annual Review of Research*, Vol. 3. Chicago: University of Chicago, 1981.

Morris, Norval and Michael Tonry, eds., *Crime and Justice: An Annual Review of Research*, Vol. 5. Chicago: University of Chicago, 1983.

Murray, Charles A., *Losing Ground: American Social Policy: 1950–1980*. New York: Basic Books, 1984.

Murray, Charles A. and Louis A. Cox, Jr., *Beyond Probation*. Beverly Hills, Calif.: Sage, 1979.

Nakamura, Robert K. and Frank Smallwood, *The Politics of Policy Implementation*. New York: St. Martin's Press, 1980.

Nath, Sunil B., "Intensive Supervision Project: Final Report," Florida Probation and Parole Commission, 1974.

Nelson, Barbara J., *Making an Issue of Child Abuse: Political Agenda Setting for Social Problems*. Chicago: University of Chicago Press, 1984.

Noble, Holcomb B., "The Major Offense Bureau: Concentrated Justice," *Police Magazine* 1 (1978).

O'Connor, James, *The Fiscal Crisis of the State*. New York: St. Martin's Press, 1973.

Packer, Herbert L., *The Limits of the Criminal Sanction*. Stanford, Calif.: Stanford University Press, 1968.

———, "Nixon's Crime Program and What It Means," *The New York Review of Books*, October 22, 1970.

PACT Institute of Justice, "The VORP Book," Valparaiso, Ind., 1983.

Pate, Tony, Robert A. Bowers, and Ron Parks. *Three Approaches to Criminal Apprehension in Kansas City: An Evaluation Report*. Washington, D.C.: Police Foundation, 1976.

Pearson, Frank, "Research on New Jersey's Intensive Supervision Program," Institute for Criminological Research, Sociology Department, Rutgers University, 1987.

Pearson, Frank S. and Daniel B. Bibel, "New Jersey's Intensive Supervision Program: What Is It Like? How Is It Working?" *Federal Probation* 50 (June 1986).

Petersilia, Joan, *Expanding Options for Criminal Sentencing*. Santa Monica, Calif.: RAND, 1987.

_____, "Georgia's Intensive Probation: Will the Model Work Elsewhere?" in McCarthy, Belinda R., *Intermediate Punishments: Intensive Supervision, Home Confinement and Electronic Surveillance*. Monsey, N.Y.: Criminal Justice Press, 1987.

_____, *Granting Felons Probation: Public Risks and Alternatives*. Santa Monica, Calif.: RAND Corporation, 1985.

Petersilia, Joan and Susan Turner, with Joyce Peterson, *Prison versus Probation in California: Implications for Crime and Offender Recidivism*. Santa Monica, Calif.: RAND Corporation, 1986.

Phillips, Kevin, *The Emerging Republican Majority*. New Rochelle, New York: Arlington House, 1969.

Piliavin, Irving; Rosemary Gartner; Craig Thornton; and Ross L. Matsueda, "Crime, Deterrence and Rational Choice," *American Sociological Review* 51 (1986).

Piven, Frances Fox and Richard A. Cloward, *Why Americans Don't Vote*. New York: Pantheon, 1988.

Pollock, Sir Frederick and Frederic William Maitland, *A History of English Law*. Cambridge, U.K.: Cambridge University Press, 1898.

Poulantzas, Nicos, *State, Power, Socialism*. London: Verso, 1980.

President's Commission on Law Enforcement and Administration of Justice, *The Challenge of Crime in A Free Society*. Washington, D.C.: D.C.: U.S. Government Printing Office, 1967.

President's Commission on Law Enforcement and Administration of Justice, *Task Force Report: Corrections*. Washington, D.C.: U.S. Government Printing Office, 1967.

President's Commission on Law Enforcement and Administration of Justice, *Task Force Report: The Police*. Washington, D.C.: U.S. Government Printing Office, 1967.

President's Commission on Law Enforcement and Administration of Justice, *Task Force Report: Science and Technology*. Washington, D.C.: U.S. Government Printing Office, 1967.

Pyle, David J., *The Economics of Crime and Law Enforcement*. New York: St. Martin's Press, 1983.

Quinney, Richard, *Class, State and Crime*, 2d edition. New York: Longman, 1980.

Randall, John Herman, Jr., *The Making of the Modern Mind*. Boston: Houghton, Mifflin, 1940.

"Recruiting Trends," Collegiate Employment Research Institute, Michigan State University, 1987.

Reiman, Jeffrey H., *The Rich Get Richer and the Poor Get Prison: Ideology, Class, and Criminal Justice*. New York: Wiley, 1979.

Reiss, Albert J., *The Police and the Public*. New Haven: Yale University Press, 1971.

Ripley, Randall B. and Grace A. Franklin, *Congress, The Bureaucracy and Public Policy*. Chicago: Dorsey, 1987.

Ripley, Randall B. and Franklin, Grace A., *Congress, The Bureaucracy and Public Policy*. Chicago: Dorsey, 1987.

Rothman, David J., *Conscience and Convenience: The Asylum and Its Alternatives in Progressive America*. Boston: Little, Brown and Co., 1980.

——, *The Discovery of the Asylum: Social Order and Disorder in the New Republic.* Boston: Little, Brown, 1971.

Rubenstein, Michael L. and Teresa J. White, "Alaska's Ban on Plea Bargaining," *Law and Society Review* 13 (1979).

Saunders, Charles, *Upgrading the American Police: Education and Training for Better Law Enforcement.* Washington, D.C.: Brookings, 1970.

Scammon, Richard M. and Ben J. Wattenberg, *The Real Majority.* New York: Coward-McCann, Inc., 1970.

Schattschneider, E.E., *The Semisovereign People.* Hinsdale, Ill.: The Dryden Press, 1975.

Scheingold, Stuart A., *The Politics of Law and Order: Street Crime and Public Policy.* New York: Longman, 1984.

Schmidt, Annesley K., "Electronic Monitoring of Offenders Increases," in U.S. Department of Justice, National Institute of Justice, *NIJ Reports*, January-February 1989.

Schwartz, Herman, ed., *The Burger Years: Rights and Wrongs in the Supreme Court 1969–1986.* New York: Viking Penguin, 1987.

Schwendinger, Herman and Julia R. Schwendinger, "The Standards of Living in Penal Institutions" in David F. Greenberg, ed., *Crime and Capitalism: Readings in Marxist Criminology.* Palo Alto, Calif.: Mayfield, 1981.

Scull, Andrew, *Decarceration: Community Treatment and the Deviant—A Radical View*, 2d edition. New Brunswick, N.J.: Rutgers University Press, 1984.

SEARCH Group, *Compendium of State Privacy and Security Legislation, 1987 Overview—Privacy and Security of Criminal History Information.* U.S. Department of Justice, Bureau of Justice Statistics, 1988.

SEARCH Group, *Intelligence and Investigative Records.* Washington, D.C.: U.S. Government Printing Office, 1985.

SEARCH Group, *Public Access to Criminal History Record Information.* U.S. Department of Justice, Bureau of Justice Statistics, 1988.

Sexton, Patricia Cayo and Brendan Sexton, *Blue Collars and Hard Hats: The Working Class and the Future of American Politics.* New York: Vintage, 1971.

Shaw, George Bernard, *The Crime of Imprisonment.* New York: Philosophical Library, 1946.

Sigler, Robert T. and Melody Horn, "Race, Income and Penetration of the Justice System," *Criminal Justice Review* 11 (1986).

Silberman, Charles, *Criminal Violence, Criminal Justice.* New York: Random House, 1978.

Silver, Allan, "The Demand for Order in Civil Society: A Review of Some Themes in the History of Urban Crime, Police and Riot," in Bordua, David, *The Police: Six Sociological Essays.* New York: John Wiley and Sons, 1967.

Singer, Richard, *Just Deserts: Sentences Based on Equality and Desert.* Cambridge, Mass.: Bollinger, 1979.

Skogan, Wesley G. and Maxfield, Michael G., *Coping with Crime: Individual and Neighborhood Reactions.* Beverly Hills, Calif.: Sage, 1981.

Skolnick, Jerome, *The Politics of Protest*. New York: Simon and Schuster, 1969.

Skolnick, Jerome and David H. Bayley, *The New Blue Line: Police Innovation in Six American Cities*. New York: The Free Press, 1986.

Smith, Dennis C., "Police," in Charles Brecher and Raymond D. Horton, eds., *Setting Municipal Priorities 1982*. New York: Russell Sage Foundation, 1981.

Spierenburg, Pieter, *The Spectacle of Suffering*. Cambridge, U.K.: Cambridge, 1984.

Statistical Analysis Center, Delaware, "Lifers in Delaware: Future Costs and Populations through 1994." (1985)

Stanley, David T., *Prisoners Among Us: The Problem of Parole*. Washington, D.C.: Brookings, 1976.

Steinfels, Peter, *The Neoconservatives*. New York: Simon and Schuster, 1979.

Stinchcombe, Arthur; Rebecca Adams; Carol A. Heimer; Kim Lane Scheppele; Tom W. Smith; and D. Garth Taylor, *Crime and Punishment—Changing Attitudes in America*. San Francisco: Jossey-Bass, 1980.

Stolz, Barbara Ann, "Interest Groups and Criminal Law: The Case of Federal Criminal Code Revision," *Crime and Delinquency* 30 (1984).

Stone, Lawrence, "Interpersonal Violence in English Society," *Past and Present* 101 (1983).

Sviridoff, Michelle and James W. Thompson, "Links between Employment and Crime: A Qualitative Study of Riker's Island Releasees," *Crime and Delinquency* 29 (1983).

Terkel, Studs, *Working*. New York: Avon Books, 1975.

Theoharis, Athan and John Stuart Cox, *The Boss: J. Edgar Hoover and the Great American Inquisition*. Philadelphia: Temple University Press, 1988.

Thompson, Mark, "Born to Burgle," *Student Lawyer* 15 (1986).

Travis III, Lawrence F.; Martin D. Schwartz; and Todd R. Clear, *Corrections: An Issues Approach*, 2d edition. Cincinnati: Anderson, 1983.

Twentieth Century Fund Task Force on the Law Enforcement Assistance Administration, *Law Enforcement: The Federal Role*. New York: McGraw-Hill, 1976.

Tyler, Tom R. and Renee Weber, "Support for the Death Penalty: Instrumental Response to Crime or Symbolic Attitude?" *Law and Society Review* 17 (1982).

Uchida, Craig D.; Timothy S. Bynum; Dennis Rogan; and Donna Murasky, "The Effects of *United States v. Leon* on Police Search Warrant Policies and Practices," Police Executive Research Forum, 1986.

Unger, Roberto Mangabeira, *Law and Modern Society*. New York: The Free Press, 1976.

U.S. Congress, House of Representatives, Committee on Government Operations, *Federal Response to Criminal Misconduct and Insider Abuse in the Nation's Financial Associations*, 98th Congress, 1984, House Rept. 1137.

U. S. Congress, House of Representatives, *Hearings Before a Subcommittee of the Committee on Governmental Operations, On Multistate Regional Intelligence Projects*, 97th Congress, May 27 and 28, 1981.

U. S. Congress, House of Representatives, *Hearing Before the Subcommittee on Civil and Constitutional Rights, Committee on the Judiciary, On FBI Authorization Request for FY 1986*, 99th Congress, April 25, 1985.

U.S. Congress, House of Representatives, *Hearings Before the Subcommittee on Civil and Constitutional Rights, Committee on the Judiciary, on FBI Authorization Request for Fiscal Year 1987*, 99th Congress, March 24, 1986.

U.S. Congress, House of Representatives, *Hearings Before the Subcommittee on Civil and Constitutional Rights, House Committee on the Judiciary, on FBI Oversight and Authorization for Fiscal Year 1989*, 100th Congress, March 10, 1988.

U.S. Congress, House of Representatives, *Hearings Before the House Subcomittee on Civil and Constitutional Rights, Committee on the Judiciary, on H.R. 188, H.R. 9783, H.R. 12574 and H.R. 12575*, 93d Congress, July 26, August 2, September 26, October 11, 1973, February 26, 28, March 5, 28, and April 3, 1974.

U.S. Congress, House of Representatives, *Hearings Before the House Subcommittee on Civil and Constitutional Rights, Committee on the Judiciary, on H.R. 8227*, 94th Congress, July 14 and 17 and September 5, 1975.

U.S. Congress, House of Representatives, *Hearings Before House Subcommittee No. 4 of the Committee on the Judiciary, on H.R. 13315*, 92d Congress, March 16, 22, and 23, 1972, April 13 and 26, 1972.

U.S. Congress, House of Representatives, *Hearings Before the House Subcommittee on Civil and Constitutional Rights, Committee on the Judiciary, on the National Crime Information Center*, 95th Congress, August 3, 1977.

U.S. Congress, Senate, *Committee on Government Operations, Protecting Individual Privacy in Federal Gathering, Use and Disclosure of Information: Report to Accompany S.3418*, 93d Congress, September 26, 1974.

U.S. Congress, Senate, *Hearings Before the Subcommittee on Terrorism, Senate Committee on the Judiciary, On Attorney General's Guidelines for Domestic Security (Smith Guidelines)*, 98th Congress, March 25, 1983.

U.S. Congress, Senate, *Hearings Before the Subcommittee on Constitutional Rights, Committee on the Judiciary, On Federal Data Banks, Computers and the Bill of Rights*, 92d Cong., March 10, 15, 1971.

U.S. Congress, Senate, Select Committee to Study Governmental Operations with Respect to Intelligence Activities, "Cointelpro: The FBI's Covert Action Programs Against American Citizens," in *Supplementary Detailed Staff Reports of Intelligence Activities and the Rights of Americans*, Final Report, 94th Congress, April 14, 1976.

U.S. Department of Commerce, Bureau of the Census, *Census of Governments 1962*, Vol. 4, "Compendium of Government Finances."

U.S. Department of Commerce, Bureau of the Census, *Census of Governments 1967*, Vol. 4, "Compendium of Government Finances."

U.S. Department of Commerce, Bureau of the Census, *Compendium of Government Finances*, 1962, 1967, 1972, 1977, 1982.

U.S. Department of Commerce, Bureau of the Census, *Current Population Reports*, Series P-25, P-60.

U.S. Department of Commerce, Bureau of the Census, *Statistical Abstract of the United States 1988.*

U.S. Department of Commerce, Bureau of the Census, *Statistical Abstract of the United States 1986.*

U.S. Department of Health, Education and Welfare, *Report of the Secretary's Advisory Committee on Automated Personal Data Systems, Records Computers and the Rights of Citizens.* Washington, D.C.: U.S. Government Printing Office, 1973.

U.S. Department of Justice, "Address of the Honorable Edwin Meese III, Attorney General of the United States Before the Congressional Youth Leadership Council, National Young Leaders Conference," March 29, 1988.

U.S. Department of Justice, *An Exemplary Project: Major Violator Unit—San Diego, California.* Washington, D.C.: U.S. Government Printing Office, 1980.

U.S. Department of Justice, *Attorney General's Task Force on Violent Crime: Final Report.* Washington, D.C.: U.S. Government Printing Office, 1981.

U.S. Department of Justice, *The Nation's Toughest Drug Law: Evaluating the New York Experience.* Washington, D.C.: U.S. Government Printing Office, 1978.

U.S. Department of Justice, Bureau of Justice Statistics, "Capital Punishment 1987" *Bulletin,* July 1988.

U.S. Department of Justice, Bureau of Justice Statistics, "Correctional Populations in the United States 1985," 1987.

U.S. Department of Justice, Bureau of Justice Statistics, "Correctional Populations in the United States 1986," 1989.

U.S. Department of Justice, Bureau of Justice Statistics, "Criminal Victimization in the United States, 1986," 1988.

U.S. Department of Justice, Bureau of Justice Statistics, "Criminal Victimization 1984," *Bulletin,* October 1985.

U.S. Department of Justice, Bureau of Justice Statistics, "Criminal Victimization 1987," *Bulletin,* October 1988.

U.S. Department of Justice, Bureau of Justice Statistics, "Households Touched by Crime, 1986," *Bulletin,* June 1987.

U.S. Department of Justice, Bureau of Justice Statistics, "Imprisonment in Four Countries," *Special Report,* 1987.

U.S. Department of Justice, Bureau of Justice Statistics, "International Crime Rates," *Special Report,* May 1988.

U.S. Department of Justice, Bureau of Justice Statistics, "Jail Inmates 1984," *Bulletin,* May 1986.

U.S. Department of Justice, Bureau of Justice Statistics, "Jail Inmates 1986," *Bulletin,* October 1987.

U.S. Department of Justice, Bureau of Justice Statistics, "Jail Inmates 1987," *Bulletin,* December 1988.

U.S. Department of Justice, Bureau of Justice Statistics, "Open vs. Confidential Records: Proceedings of a BJS/SEARCH Conference," NCJ-113560, November 1988.

U.S. Department of Justice, Bureau of Justice Statistics, "Police Employment and Expenditure Trends," *Special Report,* February 1986.

U.S. Department of Justice, Bureau of Justice Statistics, "The Prevalence of Imprisonment," *Special Report,* July 1985.

U.S. Department of Justice, Bureau of Justice Statistics, "Prisoners in 1987," *Bulletin*, April 1988.

U.S. Department of Justice, Bureau of Justice Statistics, "Probation and Parole 1981," *Bulletin*, August 1982.

U.S. Department of Justice, Bureau of Justice Statistics, "Probation and Parole 1982," *Bulletin*, September 1983.

U.S. Department of Justice, Bureau of Justice Statistics, "Probation and Parole 1985," *Bulletin*, January 1987.

U.S. Department of Justice, Bureau of Justice Statistics, "Probation and Parole 1986," *Bulletin*, December 1987.

U.S. Department of Justice, Bureau of Justice Statistics, "Probation and Parole 1987," *Bulletin*, November 1988.

U.S. Department of Justice, Bureau of Justice Statistics, *Report to the Nation on Crime and Justice*, second edition, 1988.

U.S. Department of Justice, Bureau of Justice Statistics, "Sentencing and Time Served," *Special Report*, June 1987.

U.S. Department of Justice, Bureau of Justice Statistics, "Setting Prison Terms," *Bulletin*, August 1983.

U.S. Department of Justice, Bureau of Justice Statistics, *Sourcebook of Criminal Justice Statistics*, various years.

U.S. Department of Justice, Bureau of Justice Statistics, "State and Federal Prisoners, 1925–85," *Bulletin*, October 1986.

U.S. Department of Justice, Bureau of Justice Statistics, "State Criminal Records Repositories," *Technical Report*, October 1985.

U.S. Department of Justice, Bureau of Justice Statistics, "Tracking Offenders 1984," *Bulletin*, January 1988.

U.S. Department of Justice, Federal Bureau of Investigation, *Uniform Crime Reports*, various years.

U.S. Department of Justice, Law Enforcement Assistance Administration, *Directory of Automated Criminal Justice Information Systems*. Washington, D.C.: U.S. Government Printing Office, 1976.

U.S. Department of Justice, Law Enforcement Assistance Administration, "LEAA Eleventh Annual Report, Fiscal Year 1979."

U.S. Department of Justice, Law Enforcement Assistance Administration, "LEAA Sixth Annual Report, Fiscal Year 1974."

U.S. Department of Justice, National Institute of Justice, *The Effects of the Exclusionary Rule: A Study in California*. Washington, D.C.: U.S. Government Printing Office, 1982.

U.S. Department of Justice, *The Nation's Toughest Drug Law: Evaluating the New York Experience*, Washington, D.C.: U.S. Government Printing Office, 1978.

U.S. Department of Justice, Office of Justice Programs, "Intensive Supervision Probation and Parole (ISP)," *Program Brief*. Washington, D.C.: U.S. Government Printing Office, 1987.

U.S. Department of Justice, Office of Juvenile Justice and Delinquency Prevention, "Habitual Juvenile Offenders: Guidelines for Citizen Action and Public Response," n.d.

U.S. Department of Labor, Bureau of Labor Statistics, *Employment and Earnings*, various years.

U.S. Department of Labor, *Employment and Training Report of the President*. Washington, D.C.: Government Printing Office, 1981.

U.S. House of Representatives, Committee on Government Operations,

Federal Response to Criminal Misconduct and Insider Abuse in the Nation's Financial Associations, 98th Congress, 1984, House Rept. 1137.

U.S. General Accounting Office, "Criminal Bail: How Bail Reform is Working in Selected District Courts," Report #GGD-88-6 (October 23, 1987).

U.S. General Accounting Office, "Development of a Nationwide Criminal Justice Data System," Report B-171019, January 16, 1973.

U.S. General Accounting Office, "Federal Crime Control Assistance: A Discussion of the Program and Possible Alternatives," Report # GGD-78-28, January 27, 1978.

U.S. General Accounting Office, "Impact of the Exclusionary Rule on Federal Criminal Prosecutions," Report #GGD-79-45, April 19, 1979.

U.S. General Accounting Office, "Overview of Activities Funded by the Law Enforcement Assistance Administration," Report No. GGD-78-21, November 29, 1977.

U.S. Office of Technology Assessment, *An Assessment of Alternatives for a National Computerized Criminal History System*. Washington, DC: Government PPrinting Office, 1982.

van den Haag, Ernest, *Punishing Criminals: Concerning a Very Old and Painful Question*. New York: Basic Books, 1975).

_____, "Punitive Sentences," *Hofstra Law Review* 7 (1978).

Van Dine, Stephen; John Conrad; and Simon Dinitz, *Restraining the Wicked*. Lexington, Mass.: Lexington Books, 1979.

van Duizend, Richard; L. Paul Sutton; and Charlotte A. Carter, *The Search Warrant Process: Preconceptions, Perceptions, Practices*. Williamsburg, Va.: National Center for State Courts, 1984.

Vera Institute of Justice, *Felony Arrests: Their Prosecution and Disposition in New York City's Courts*. New York: Longman, 1981.

Vold, George B. and Bernard, Thomas J., *Theoretical Criminology*. New York: Oxford University Press, 1986.

von Hirsch, Andrew, *Doing Justice*. New York: Hill and Wang, 1976.

von Hirsch, Andrew and Hanrahan, Kathleen J., *The Question of Parole: Retention, Reform or Abolition*. Cambridge, Mass.: Ballinger Publishing Co., 1979.

Walker, Samuel, *A Critical History of Police Reform*. Lexington, Mass.: Lexington Books, 1977.

_____, *Popular Justice: A History of American Criminal Justice*. New York: Oxford University Press, 1980.

_____, *Sense and Nonsense About Crime*, 2d edition. Monterey, Calif.: Brooks-Cole, 1988.

Wallace, George C., *"Hear Me Out."* Anderson, S.C.: Droke House, 1968.

Wallerstedt, John F., "Returning to Prison," *Special Report*, U.S. Department of Justice, Bureau of Justice Statistics, November 1984.

Warren, Carol, "New Forms of Social Control: The Myth of Deinstitutionalization," *American Behavioral Scientist* 24 (1981).

Warren, Samuel and Brandeis, Louis, "The Right to Privacy," *Harvard Law Review* 6 (1890).

Weber, Max, "The Social Psychology of the World Religions," in Gerth, H.H. and Mills, C. Wright, *From Max Weber: Essays in Sociology*. New York: Oxford University Press, 1946.

Westin, Alan F., *Privacy and Freedom*. New York: Atheneum, 1967.

——, "Public and Group Attitudes Toward Information Policies and Boundaries for Criminal Justice," in SEARCH Group, Inc., *Information Policy and Crime Control Strategies*. U.S. Department of Justice, Bureau of Justice Statistics, 1984.

Whitcomb, Debra, *An Exemplary Project: Major Violator Unit—San Diego, California*, U.S. Department of Justice, National Institute of Justice. Washington, D.C.: U.S. Government Printing Office, 1980.

Whitehead, John T. and Charles A. Lindquist, "Intensive Supervision: Officer Perspectives," in McCarthy, Belinda, *Intermediate Punishments: Intensive Supervision, Home Confinement and Electronic Surveillance*. Monsey, N.Y.: Criminal Justice Press, 1987.

Williams, Kirk R., "Economic Sources of Homicide: Reestimating the Effects of Poverty and Inequality," *American Sociological Review* 49 (1984).

Wills, Garry, *Nixon Agonistes: The Crisis of the Self-Made Man*. Boston: Houghton Mifflin, 1969.

Wilson, Joseph G., *Are Prisons Necessary?* Philadelphia: Dorrance, 1950.

Wilson, James Q., *Thinking About Crime*. New York: Random House, 1975.

Wilson, James Q., *Thinking About Crime*, revised edition. New York: Vintage Books, 1985.

Wilson, James Q., *Varieties of Police Behavior: The Management of Law and Order in Eight Communities*. New York: Atheneum, 1971.

Wilson, William Julius, *The Truly Disadvantaged: The Inner City, the Underclass, and Public Policy*. Chicago: University of Chicago Press, 1987.

Wolfgang, Marvin E.; Robert M. Figlio; and Thorsten Sellin, *Delinquency in a Birth Cohort*. Chicago, Ill.: University of Chicago Press, 1972.

Wood, Arthur Evans and John Barker Waite, *Crime and Its Treatment*. New York: American Book Company, 1941.

Zedlewski, Edwin W., "Making Confinement Decisions," *Research in Brief*, U.S. Department of Justice, National Institute of Justice, July 1987.

Zenk, Gordon Karl, *Project SEARCH: The Struggle for Control of Criminal Information in America*. Westport, Conn.: Greenwood, 1979.

Zimring, Franklin E. and Gordon Hawkins, *Capital Punishment and the American Agenda*. New York: Cambridge University Press, 1986.

Note on Newsletters

THESE DAYS some of the most up-to-date, reliable information on criminal justice can be found in newsletters. Some of these are published by organizations, some by publishing companies; some appear regularly, while others are occasional. Listed below are the newsletters which were most helpful in the preparation of this book:

Corrections Compendium (Contact Center, Lincoln, Nebr.), monthly.

CPSR Newsletter (Computer Professionals for Social Responsibility, Palo Alto, Calif.), quarterly.

Criminal Justice Newsletter (Pace Publications, New York, N.Y.), bi-monthly.

Focus (National Council on Crime and Delinquency, San Francisco, Calif.), occasional.

Interface (SEARCH Group, Inc, Sacramento, Calif.), quarterly.

Jericho (Unitarian Universalist Service Committee, Boston, Mass.), quarterly (discontinued, as of the end of 1987).

Law Enforcement Newsletter (John Jay College of Criminal Justice, New York, N.Y.), bi-monthly.

National Prison Project Journal (American Civil Liberties Union, Washington, D.C.), quarterly.

NIJ Reports (U.S. Department of Justice, National Institute of Justice), bimonthly.

INDEX

acquitted defendants, inclusion in computerized criminal records system, 72

Agnew, Spiro T., 174, 184

Aid to Families with Dependent Children, 181

Allen, Francis, 184, 187

Alvarado, Anthony, 50

Alvarez, Erio, 104

American Civil Liberties Union, Republican attitude toward, 3

American Correctional Association, 138, 159

American National Election Study, 178

American Probation and Parole Association, 101

American values: "breakdown" of, as cause of crime, 240; and movements of 1960s, 172–173; and support for law and order policies, 190–191

Anti-Drug Abuse acts, 3–4, 229–230, 236

Arizona: sentencing laws in, 21; Sex Offender Registration Tracking Database, 63

Armed Career Criminal Apprehension enforcement personnel, 229

arrests: of chronic delinquents, 31–32; leading to convictions, 72; and narrowing of defendants' rights, 26; offenses cleared by, *see* clearance rates; percentage of reported crimes leading to, 26; probability for black males, 41; rates, 18, 38

Attorney General's Task Force on Violent Crime, recommendation on exclusionary rule, 28

Attorney General's Working Group, 77

Augustus, John, 93

authoritarianism. *See* regimentation; state power

background checks, 51–53. *See also* employers, access to computerized criminal records system

bail, denial of: and get-tougher approach, 209; and preventive detention, 30–31, 37

Bail Reform Act of 1966, 31

Bail Reform Act of 1984, 31; use of preventive detention provision of, 37

Banfield, Edward, 183

bank depositers, checks on, 77–78

Beccaria, Cesare, 157–158

Becker, Gary, 186

Bentham, Jeremy, 53, 89

Bias, Len, 233

black males: impact of computerized criminal history records on, 73; incarceration rates, 40–41, 48–49; proportion in intensive probation supervision programs, 112; unemployment, 54–55. *See also* black youth

black youth: and future crime rates, 239–240; unemployment among, compared with